Ararat in America

Armenians in the Modern and Early Modern World

Recent decades have seen the expansion of Armenian Studies from insular history to a broader, more interactive field within an inter-regional and global context. This series, *Armenians in the Modern and Early Modern World*, responds to this growth by promoting innovative and interdisciplinary approaches to Armenian history, politics, and culture in the period between 1500 and 2000. Focusing on the geographies of the Mediterranean, Middle East, and Contemporary Russia [Eastern Armenia], it directs specific attention to imperial and post-imperial frameworks: from the Ottoman Empire to Modern Turkey/Arab Middle East; the Safavid/Qajar Empires to Iran; and the Russian Empire to Soviet Union/Post-Soviet territories.

Series Editor

Bedross Der Matossian, *University of Nebraska, Lincoln, USA*

Advisory Board

Levon Abrahamian, *Yerevan State University, Armenia*
Sylvie Alajaji, *Franklin & Marshal College, USA*
Sebouh Aslanian, *University of California, Los Angeles, USA*
Stephan Astourian, *University of California, Berkley, USA*
Houri Berberian, *University of California, Irvine, USA*
Talar Chahinian, *University of California, Irvine, USA*
Rachel Goshgarian, *Lafayette College, USA*
Ronald Grigor Suny, *University of Michigan, USA*
Sossie Kasbarian, *University of Stirling, UK*
Christina Maranci, *Tufts University, USA*
Tsolin Nalbantian, *Leiden University, the Netherlands*
Anna Ohanyan, *Stonehill College, USA*
Hratch Tchilingirian, *University of Oxford, UK*

Published and Forthcoming Titles

The Politics of Naming the Armenian Genocide: Language, History and "Medz Yeghern," Vartan Matiossian
Picturing the Ottoman Armenian World: Photography in Erzerum, Kharpert, Van and Beyond, David Low

Ararat in America

*Armenian American Culture and Politics
in the Twentieth Century*

Benjamin F. Alexander

I.B. TAURIS
LONDON • NEW YORK • OXFORD • NEW DELHI • SYDNEY

I.B. TAURIS

Bloomsbury Publishing Plc

50 Bedford Square, London, WC1B 3DP, UK

1385 Broadway, New York, NY 10018, USA

29 Earlsfort Terrace, Dublin 2, Ireland

BLOOMSBURY, I.B. TAURIS and the I.B. Tauris logo are
trademarks of Bloomsbury Publishing Plc

First published in Great Britain 2024

Series design by Adriana Brioso

Cover image: 37th annual convention A.G.B.U., 1951, by Flash Foto Co. (© Project SAVE
Armenian Photograph Archives and Digital Commonwealth. Courtesy of Gloria Tashjian.)

A catalogue record for this book is available from the British Library.

Library of Congress Cataloging-in-Publication Data
Names: Alexander, Benjamin F., 1962- author.
Title: Ararat in America : Armenian-American culture and politics in the
twentieth century / Benjamin F. Alexander.
Other titles: Armenian-American culture and politics in the twentieth century
Description: London ; New York : I.B Tauris, 2023. | Series: Armenians in the modern
and early modern world | Includes bibliographical references and index.
Identifiers: LCCN 2023012716 (print) | LCCN 2023012717 (ebook) |
ISBN 9780755648818 (HB) | ISBN 9780755648856 (pbk.) | ISBN 9780755648825 (epdf) |
ISBN 9780755648832 (ebook) | ISBN 9780755648849
Subjects: LCSH: Armenian Americans–History–20th century. | Armenian
Americans–Politics and government–20th century. | Armenian Americans–Religion.
Classification: LCC E184.A7 A54 2023 (print) | LCC E184.A7 (ebook) |
DDC 973/.0491992–dc23/eng/20230420
LC record available at https://lccn.loc.gov/2023012716
LC ebook record available at https://lccn.loc.gov/2023012717

ISBN:	HB:	978-0-7556-4881-8
	ePDF:	978-0-7556-4882-5
	eBook:	978-0-7556-4883-2

Typeset by Integra Software Services Pvt. Ltd.

To find out more about our authors and books visit www.bloomsbury.com
and sign up for our newsletters.

To the memory of my parents,
Arsen Vaharshak Alexander (né Iskenderian)
and
Mabelle Fairchild Alexander

Figures

Contents

Maps

Acknowledgments

First, I want to make a humble apology to all persons who helped me with this book whose names are left out here. I started this project as a doctoral dissertation at the City University of New York (CUNY) Graduate Center back in 1998. From the starting point to the dissertation defense, and then from there to the book contract, I've been through multiple changes in method of note-taking, file storage, and research approach, not to mention different stages of personal development. Along the way, I know I've forgotten some of the encounters and conversations I had, and lost track of where I made record of this or that interaction. I've had a number of people help me translate text and understand certain phenomena that I was seeing, people I fully intended to thank at the time, but only some of whom I've kept track of to name here. So, if you helped me and your name isn't here, please accept both my thanks and my apologies.

As I expanded my original dissertation into a larger-scale book manuscript, individuals who generously read portions of my work and offered me suggestions and factual corrections include Gerard (or Jirair) Libaridian, Aram Arkun, Simon Payaslian, Owen Miller, and Ara Sanjian. Aram has been helpful in many other ways as well, someone I could always talk to for insights and encouragement. Ara Sanjian kindly let me see some of his prepublished writing, when it could fill in some gaps for me. I was also helped greatly by the privilege of consulting with Rouben Adalian, Anahad Ajemian, Edward Alexander (no relation), Haig Asadourian, Sarkis Atamian, Levon Avdoyan, Edward Azadian, George Bashian Jr., Florence Chakerian, Dr. Hagop Martin Deranian, Krikor Der Hovannesian, Marjorie Housepian Dobkin, Rev. Dr. Peter Doghramji, Noubar Dourian, Lionel Galstaun, Arthur Gregorian, George Harutunian, Dikran Kaligian, M. Manoog Kaprielian, Charlotte Kechejian, Diana and Michael Keleshian, Dickran Kouymjian, Gerard (Jirair) Libaridian, Scott Lucas, Fr. Krikor Maksoudian, Sylva Natalie Manoogian, Vartan Matiossian, Lou Ann Matossian, Arpena Mesrobian, Khatchig Mouradian, Dennis Papazian, Souren Papazian, Paul Sagsoorian, Edward Simsarian, Harold Takooshian, James H. Tashjian, Bertha Turnamian, Hagop Vartivarian, Hratch Zadoian, and Chris Zakian, among many others.

A great deal of my research for this project was done at the Krikor and Clara Zohrab Information Center at the Eastern Diocese of the Armenian Apostolic Church in New York. Directors and assistant directors who were very kind and helpful to me there include Fr. Krikor Maksoudian, Aram Arkun, Rachel Goshgarian, Taleen Babayan, Ludmilla Batchelor, Anahid Sahagian, and the current director and assistant, Jesse Arlen and Andrew Kayaian. I also visited a number of other resource centers for this research, as well as the headquarters of both the Armenian Democratic Liberal (ADL) party and the Armenian Revolutionary Federation (ARF), both in Watertown, Massachusetts. The persons I met at the ARF, though not at liberty to make any archives available to me, did give me some published volumes that were very helpful; at the ADL, I wish to thank Mr. Kevork Marashlian as well as the district leadership for allowing me to peruse and photocopy archival materials. At the Armenian Cultural Foundation in Arlington, Massachusetts, I received generous assistance from Bob Mirak and Ara Ghazarians. I was also a frequent visitor at the National Association for Armenian Studies and Research (NAASR) in Belmont, Massachusetts, where gracious hospitality and access to a wealth of materials were afforded by Marc Mamigonian, Sandra Jurigian, Shushan Teager, and Ruby Chorbajian; I want to thank Ruby in particular for the excellent job she did of cataloguing the Avedis Derounian papers, a gold mine of material. My visits to the Armenian Library and Museum of America (ALMA) in Watertown, back in the early stages, brought me enlightening and stimulating conversation with Gary Lind-Sinanian and Jon McCollum (now a professor of music at Washington College in Maryland). For access to church records, I thank Very Rev. Fr. Muron Aznikian and Marina Dilakian at St. Illuminator's Church in New York, and Fr. Vazken Karayan and Noubar Dorian at Holy Cross Armenian Church in Union City, NJ. At the Library of Congress, I thank Levon Avdoyan and his successor as Armenian specialist Khatchig Mouradian for their assistance. Also helpful in obtaining materials were Eric Davidson and Kate Stoutenburgh in the New York Public Library's Map Division, Harout Darakdjian at the Armenian Missionary Association of America Paramus site, and Donna McRae at the University of Montana library. In addition, I very much appreciate Mrs. Arpena Mesrobian for making a copy of her brother's unpublished short play *Marriage by Ballot* available to me.

As noted above, the book started out as a doctoral dissertation at CUNY, so everybody whom I thanked at that stage deserves to be thanked again now. First off, it was a privilege to have Professor Thomas Kessner for an advisor. Advising me took patience, and I heartily thank him for having had it. Beyond that, his knowledge of history and the historical profession, his sense of what the process of scholarship is all about, his adeptness at mentoring, and his professional integrity have all been qualities that made the dissertation adventure a pleasure, which is saying a lot, as anyone who has ever done a dissertation will understand. I also very much appreciate the guidance and the kind encouragement that I received from the other professors on my committee: Martin Burke, Barbara Welter, Mehdi Bozorgmehr, and Gerald Markowitz. At the proposal stage, which also involved a professorial committee, I received very helpful additional guidance from Professors Ervand Abrahamian, Phillip Cannistraro, and Judith Stein. Sadly, only some of the professors named in this paragraph are still with us to hear my thanks (as is also true of the individuals I mention both above and below).

I wish to specially thank Anny Bakalian, author of a fine sociological work on the same subject, who was an invaluable mentor to this project at the dissertation stage and after. It was a stroke of good luck that, after I had gotten to know her book, she took a job at the CUNY Graduate Center, with an office that I could stroll over to for a chat any time. Anny encouraged me with this dissertation to the fullest, sharing very helpful insights of her own with me throughout the process. She also gave the dissertation manuscript a thorough read, rendering detailed and incisive comments, and she further advised me to expand the chronological scope for the book stage.

In the course of the writing process at the dissertation stage, I took part in three seminars where I received valuable suggestions on chapter drafts from fellow students. Professors Kessner, Burke, and David Berger ably facilitated these seminars, and I wish to thank my fellow students Rosalie Bachana, Marcella Bencivenni, Dorothy Browne, Moira Egan, Marcia Gallo, Carol Giardina, Hilary-Anne Hallett, Anne Hayes, Bob Johnson, Steve Levine, Carol Quirke, and Christolyn Williams for the exchange of ideas that I think we mutually enjoyed. A number of times when I traveled to Boston at the early stages to visit research sites, my friend Elizabeth Pallitto, who lived up there at the time, gave me a place to stay, for which I'm grateful. And, through it all, there was Betty Einerman, the empathic, helpful, and supportive assistant program officer the whole time I was at the CUNY Graduate Center.

I very much appreciate Bedross Der Matossian for inviting me to have this book published in his series. I thank the anonymous reviewers for their suggestions, and at the press, I wish to thank Rory Gormley, Yasmin Garcha, Kaveya Saravanan, Paige Harris, Dharanivel Baskar, and Faiza Zakaria for their varied roles in shepherding the book along to completion.

Finally, I want to thank in advance any of you who, after reading this book, will let me know what I got right, what I got wrong, what I could have done a better job of, and so forth. The conversation doesn't end with the publishing of a book; in fact, much of it now begins.

Introduction

More than once, when I have told somebody that my current research project was about Armenian American immigrant experiences or, more briefly, "Armenians," that same person has later introduced me to someone else by saying, "I'd like you to meet Ben Alexander. He's doing research on the Armenian genocide." I suspect, sadly, that the average person, if taking a word-association test and given "Armenian" for a cue, would reflexively say "genocide."[1] Understandably, especially since it attained its hundredth anniversary in 2015, the genocide appears to have been the focus of many of the most recent books that have anything to do with Armenians.

The genocide happened, of course, and its effects have loomed large in the lives of Armenians ever since. It also looms large in this book. Even so, the words *Armenian* and *genocide* are not joined at the hip in the present volume. My main objective with this book is to discuss Armenian identity and Armenian experiences, specifically in the United States. Armenians have a place, not only in the annals of groups that have suffered heinous massacres and extermination programs, but also in the story of American immigrant and ethnic history and of American and world political, diplomatic, and social history. Within that framework, they resemble other ethnic communities in some ways while having their own unique story in others. And if anything is clear from Armenian Americans' own interactions with their host society in the decades after 1915, it is that, while they wanted it to be known that the Young Turk regime of the Ottoman Empire had murdered their parents, siblings, children, and friends in cold blood during the second year of the First World War, it was never the *only* thing they wanted to talk about or be known for.

Nor was the genocide the Armenians' only problem in the twentieth century. A fierce partisan division that predated the First World War dominated many facets of Armenian life through much of the twentieth century, and is not entirely gone even now. Outsiders to the Armenian community heard little about this factor during the World War I years, when Armenian spokesmen lobbying for favorable policies for their homeland took care to keep the conflicts subtle and appear to speak with one voice, but the schism was hard for the larger American population to miss in 1934, when nine members of a nationalist Armenian party stood trial for the assassination of an Armenian archbishop in a New York church. In 1956 the split in the Armenian Apostolic Church became even more formalized at the global level, with the two sides loudly calling upon others to take sides and striving to expose each other's bad faith to all who would listen. Of course, it would be an equally big mistake to imagine that this partisan schism was the only feature of Armenian American life or the only aspect of that life that Americans heard about, but it did persist as a steady undercurrent in the Armenian story.

This book seeks to reconstruct the dynamics of Armenian American community life, with emphasis on how the formal institutions—the churches, the party clubs, the newspapers—interacted with both their Armenian constituencies and the non-Armenian cultural mainstream that surrounded them in America. Robert Mirak's exemplary work *Torn between Two Lands* has already chronicled the world of Armenian immigrants to America up through the eve of the First World War; I pick up the story with the war and carry it forward to the end of the century.

- 1 -

Because so much of the discourse about Armenian identity draws from its history, including that of ancient times, some brief background on who the Armenians were in the larger picture is in order here. Historians differ over exactly how the Armenian, or *Hye*, nationality came into being. They agree that the region now known as historic Armenia, straddling present-day Turkey and Transcaucasia (part of the Soviet Union until 1991), was one of the first to see agriculture and the use of New Stone Age tools and weapons; that between 3000 and 1500 BC various Caucasian and Indo-European tribes inhabited the region; that over time tribes either absorbed or blended with each other; and that in the ninth century BC a kingdom known as Urartu was formed, from which the Armenian nationality emerged. Scholars differ on exactly which groups, and from where, merged or evolved into this nationality, but a distinct Armenian identity and language seem to have existed as far back as 600 BC.

Located in the borderlands between Europe and Asia, Armenia over the years had both the good fortune of being a point of passage for ideas and trade and the bad fortune of being a trampling ground for the marauding armies of rival empires. Through it all, Armenians would seem to have lived in the periphery of the ancient civilizations and their consciousness, judging from how few times one finds them mentioned in works of general world history. Between 600 BC and the early modern era, the whole swath of territory comprising southern Europe and the Near East saw many empires rise and fall, including those of Alexander the Great, the Romans, Persia, Byzantium, and Muslim Arabs. For part of the final century before the birth of Christ, Armenians themselves ruled a regional empire, at its peak in the reign of King Tigranes the Great (95–55 BC), which spanned from the Caucasus Mountains on its northeastern border to the Mediterranean Sea on the southwest side and covered a total of 238,000 square miles.

Throughout the dizzying chronology of wars, conquests, treaties, and rebellions, different parts of historic Armenia maintained varying degrees of autonomy, at times paying tribute and having their political, even religious, leaders coronated or deposed by outside overlords. Common identity did not exactly mean unity: the mountainous topography in much of the region, the behavior of competing empires, and the behavior of rival landed Armenian elites militated against any single seat of power

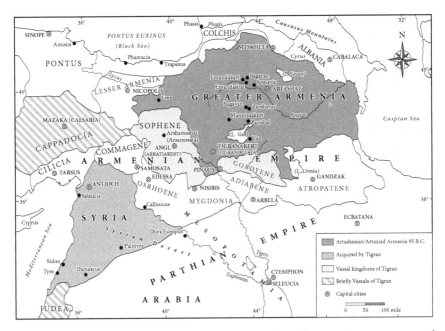

Map I.1 Armenia's short-lived empire, 189–63 BC. Map by Robert H. Hewsen, courtesy of Richard G. Hovannisian.

or common loyalty binding all Armenians together for any great length of time. Even so, in the fourth century AD the adoption of Christianity as the national religion and the creation of a written Armenian alphabet provided the tools with which a national identity could be sustained against adverse odds. From the late fourth century to the mid-seventh century, when Armenia was partitioned between the rival empires of Persia and Byzantium, Armenian Christians at times found themselves fending off demands for religious conformity. Indeed, to this day Armenians celebrate June 2 as the anniversary of the 451 Battle of Avarayr, in which Armenians under the command of Vardan Mamikonian, warrior from a wealthy and aristocratic Armenian family, battled against Persian forces that were attempting to restrict the practice of Christianity and coerce conversions to Zoroastrianism (which Armenians in pre-Christian days had practiced).

Throughout the Near East and Europe, Christian belief took root, as did hierarchical church structures, with bishops over priests and powerful patriarchs over bishops. The Armenian Apostolic Church bore a theology that, while being to all intents and purposes the same religion as that preached by the Roman Catholic and Eastern Orthodox churches, retained just enough distinctiveness not to be absorbed into the neighboring church structures. The governing and preaching elites, it should be remembered, demanded that the Christian faithful not only love God and neighbor, but hue to precisely the right doctrines about how Christ could be both God and man. Accordingly, conflict raged in the fifth century between the Monophysites,

Figure I.1 The Armenian Alphabet at the Melkonian Educational Institute in Nicosia, Cyprus. Photo from Wikimedia Commons, licensed under the Creative Commons Attribution-Share Alike 3.0 Unported license.

who insisted that their savior had a solely divine nature, and the Dyophysites, who argued that Christ had two distinct natures, divine and human. In 451, the same year as the Battle of Avarayr, the Byzantine emperor at Constantinople (the seat of regional power that had risen as Rome declined) called the Council of Chalcedon to reconcile this monumental question (one that to modern-day sensibilities might seem more like abject semantic hair-splitting). The Armenian church, too occupied that year (understandably) to send a delegation to the council, maintained a position that did not conform to either Dyophysitism or Monophysitism, though it was closer to the latter than the compromise resolutions drafted at Chalcedon would allow. Whether intentionally or otherwise, the crafting of their own Christology allowed Armenian theologians to keep their church nationally distinctive as well as spiritually so. Treated as heretical by its brethren in Christ outside, the Armenian church hierarchy also engaged in its share of heresy-hunting amid its own flock.

In 650, Armenians found themselves in the path of an onslaught by the Damascus-based Muslim Arab empire. For a time, Armenians and their Arab rulers coexisted in peace. More than once after 680, however, the Arabs intensified their demands for control, Armenians rebelled, and bloody massacres and forced conversions to Islam followed. Even so, Armenian noble families continued to exist and prosper, though still vulnerable to massacre. Armenia became an independent kingdom again in 886 and enjoyed a two-century golden age in architecture, sculpture, art, and literature, especially evident in its magnificent capital at Ani, but that high watermark of autonomy ended with the Byzantine invasion of 1045. Conquest by the Seljuk Turks followed in 1064, though Cilicia, an Armenian kingdom established in 1198, remained independent for nearly three more centuries. The sixteenth century saw the Ottoman (Turkish) Empire expand into the Armenian highlands. In the seventeenth century, Cilicia and most of the mainland of historic Armenia were incorporated into the

Ottoman Empire; Armenians on the Caucasus, later to be Russian territory, were governed during these years by a newly constituted Persian Empire.[2]

In the political order that lasted with minor changes up through the First World War, the Turks of the Ottoman Empire managed the governance of non-Muslim minorities through the millet system. Under this arrangement, an ethnoreligious group's spiritual leadership held official authority to manage its civil affairs while answering to the greater authority of the Turkish government. The Ottoman Empire at the dawn of the nineteenth century had three major millets: Greek Orthodox, which included not only Greeks but also Serbs, Bulgarians, and various other Balkan nationalities; Armenian Apostolic, which as noted held much in common with the Orthodox faith but maintained its separateness; and Jewish. Armenians in most parts of the Empire, including southern Syria, Lebanon, Cyprus, and Egypt, were subject to the authority of the Armenian Patriarchate of Constantinople, the Catholicosate of Aghtamar, or the Patriarchate of Jerusalem, while those in Cilicia were under the Catholicosate of Sis. Missionary activity later led to the creation of two additional Armenian millets, Protestant and Catholic. Within each millet, the spiritual leaders had vast civil powers over their constituents. As subject minorities, the people of the millets were heavily taxed and given ongoing reminders of their inferior position.[3]

The disadvantages of being Armenian were not shared evenly within the millet. In Constantinople, home of the empire's largest Armenian community—it numbered about 150,000 in 1800 and 225,000 around 1850—a coterie of about two hundred wealthy Armenian men of the *amira* class held office in the empire, received special political immunities, and dominated the life of the Armenian millet throughout the empire. Below the *amira* class, there was a stratum of prosperous Armenian merchants whose work took them to all the modern trading centers of Europe as they dealt in spices, jewelry, and various luxury items of fabric and glass. Far more numerous in Constantinople and other cities was the middle class of tradesmen, organized into ninety-eight guilds (*esnafs*) by mid-century with forty thousand Armenian members throughout the empire. Most Armenians in the urban centers, however, were unskilled laborers and the unemployed or underemployed poor; over 70 percent of Armenians lived in the countryside and farmed, generally raising both livestock and crops. Even those who owned their own land, as many did, bore a heavy tax burden and often fell prey to plundering raids by Kurdish nomads. In addition, the young women and girls lived in constant fear of rape or of abduction, forced conversion, and forced marriage.[4]

There were still Armenians living under Persian rule in the nineteenth century. Until late in the century, Armenians in northern Persia could be beaten for walking on the public streets when it was raining, owing to a superstition of ritual pollution. A combination of internal and external pressures brought a stop to this practice by the 1880s.[5]

The mid-to-late nineteenth century marked the years when the relationship became increasingly volatile between the Armenians—long called "the loyal millet"—and their Turkish overlords. Several concurrent factors influenced this. Pressure was coming to bear on the Sultan from foreign powers, mainly the Russians and the British, to institute reforms in the treatment of the empire's Christian minorities. In a recurring scenario throughout the nineteenth century, the Sultan, either by his own initiative or under duress, announced a slate of reforms that would benefit Armenians. The reforms, while not effective enough to make a lasting difference to Armenians, nonetheless seemed threatening enough to Turks and Kurds to evoke an anti-Armenian backlash. The Armenians, meanwhile, were going through a cultural renaissance of their own, making them progressively more receptive to nationalist ideologies; this would cause them at least to appear as less of a "loyal millet." Successful independence revolts by other nationality groups made Armenian nationalism seem even more threatening to the Turkish government.[6]

Tensions grew more severe in the 1860s and 1870s as repressive imperial measures provoked Armenian uprisings in several provinces. The Russo-Turkish War of 1877–8 made the grievances of the Armenians more of an international issue. The victorious Russians gained possession of three provinces with large Armenian populations—Kars, Ardahan, and Batum—and secured the right in the Treaty of San Stefano to occupy the remaining Armenian territories to force reforms. However, Great Britain intervened and, as a measure to check Russian power, negotiated the Treaty of Berlin. Article 61 of this treaty, superseding Article 16 of the San Stefano accord, maintained the call for reforms but required the immediate evacuation of the Russian troops, thus removing the means of enforcing the reforms. Mkrtich Khrimian, former Armenian patriarch who had toured Europe championing the cause of limited self-rule for the Armenians and acceptance of Article 16 of San Stefano, returned to Turkish Armenia a broken and discouraged man as a result of Article 16's reversal. Soon, he was among the voices of armed struggle. Historian Louise Nalbandian records his metaphor that became famous in Armenians' oral traditions for years to come. As he said in a sermon at Constantinople:

> He had gone to Berlin with a petition for reforms which in itself was merely a piece of paper. There, in the council chamber, where the diplomats of the European Powers, who had placed on the table before them a "Dish of Liberty." One by one the Bulgarians, Serbians, and Montenegrins strode into the chamber, and with their iron spoons, scooped into the delicious dish, taking out a portion for themselves. When his turn came, the Armenian was armed only with the fragile paper on which the petition was written. As he dipped into the dish on the paper, his paper spoon gave way and crumpled, leaving him deprived of any share of the luscious treat.

Iron spoons, of course, meant guns and the respect in the international community that comes of having armed force rather than mere supplication.[7]

The 1880s and after saw the founding of formal political parties, including two that played a major role in twentieth-century life. In 1887 and 1890, respectively, the Hunchag and the Tashnag parties, both secretive organizations that blended socialist ideology and Armenian nationalism, came into existence. The Social Democratic Hunchagian party, organized in Geneva, sported a fairly doctrinaire Marxist bent. In 1890 came the birth in Tiflis, a Russian-ruled eastern Armenian province, of the Armenian Revolutionary Federation (ARF), known by the Armenian word for federation, *Tashnagzutiun*, from which was derived the shorter word *Tashnag* (or *Dashnak*) by which members came to be identified. (The word literally refers to harmony; *tashnag* is also the Armenian word for piano.) During the next twenty-five years the party, based in Russian-ruled Armenia, gained the loyalty of Armenians in a swath of towns and villages on both the Russian and Turkish sides of the border. As the memoirs of ARF leader Rouben Der Minasian, published in English in 1963, show, the ARF made itself the source of law, justice, and retribution for disloyalty in all Armenian communities where it could establish itself as such, while putting arms into the hands of otherwise defenseless Armenians.[8]

After yet another round of Armenian uprisings, European demands for reforms, and disingenuous promises from the Sultan, a wave of mass slaughter known as the Hamidean massacres took place in 1895–6, involving the deaths of between one and two hundred thousand Armenians and the forced conversions of many to Islam (and apostasy from the faith after such conversion was punishable by death). Yet from there, the darkest moment in Armenian history started out with fresh glimmers of new hope. In 1908, after years of clandestine struggle, the reformist Committee of Union and Progress (CUP), or Young Turk faction of the Ottoman Empire, marched on Constantinople and seized the instruments of power. Sultan Abdul-Hamid, associated by Armenians with the Hamidean massacres of 1895–6, though allowed to keep his spiritual title of caliph, was deposed from political leadership. A constitutional government was inaugurated on July 24. Many Armenians believed that a new era had begun for their status in the empire. The Tashnag party worked openly in concert with the Young Turks both before and after the coup, electing six of the twelve Armenian deputies to the newly created parliament. The Hunchags responded warily, neither embracing nor actively opposing the new order. Also in 1908, the Armenian Constitutional Democratic, or Ramgavar, party was founded in Egypt, centering on Armenians who identified with the authority of the church and with the merchant class, and also attracting some defectors from the other partisan groups. A 1909 conservative coup brought Abdul-Hamid back to the sultanate for ten days, during which time at least twenty thousand Armenians in Cilicia perished in what would be known as the Adana massacres. While the Young Turk regime prosecuted and convicted several hundred individuals in a series of courts-martial and sentenced forty-one Muslims (as well as six Armenians) to death, it was observed that some Young Turk officials in Cilicia had supported the killings. The courts-martial also appear to have convicted some innocent scapegoats while allowing those most responsible for the killing to elude justice.[9]

In 1912 and 1913, as the Turks fought the Balkan Wars against Greece, Serbia, Montenegro, Bulgaria, and Romania, tensions heightened between Armenians and the Ottoman government, with attacks on Armenians by Kurdish tribes apparently encouraged by Turkish authorities. At this point the European powers of Russia, Britain, and France were attempting to bring pressure to bear on the government for reforms favorable to the safety and rights of the Armenian population. Armenians, especially in the ARF, welcomed these negotiations while also defending themselves as best they could. By the end of 1913 the Turkish government (the CUP, back in power after some brief interruptions, but not at all trustworthy in its dealing with Armenians) had agreed to allow the European powers to send a team of inspectors to oversee reforms in the empire's Armenian provinces, and the inspectors began arriving

Map I.2 Armenian provinces in the nineteenth-century Ottoman Empire. Map by Robert H. Hewsen, courtesy of Richard G. Hovannisian.

the following spring. The start of the Great War late that summer brought that whole uncertain process to a halt.[10]

Thus, Armenians in the Ottoman Empire on the eve of the First World War lived a precarious existence. Yet it would be misleading to think that this was the whole story. Armenians still had a vibrant culture and were able, at least some of the time, to keep the intrusion of their oppressors at bay as they lived their lives. The majority dwelled in rural towns and villages. An Armenian child typically grew up knowing a wide variety of nuts, berries, and larger fruits that grew bountifully in the region—walnuts, hazelnuts, mulberries, peaches, pears, etc. Standards of living were far from uniform. Some areas were more conducive to private landowning than others, and within a typical town or village there were varying degrees of land and personal property holdings. Differences notwithstanding, surviving memories depict life as closely knit, with families of a village sharing many communal responsibilities and united in suspicion of other villages.

- 2 -

Village economies tended to emphasize both self-sufficiency and diversification. A typical rural Armenian family had both vegetation and livestock under its care. Much depended on the ability to adapt to the variables of geography and topography, and to work cooperatively. If a village lacked a river or stream for washing and bathing, community members would build a canal, then share in the duties of keeping it clean and structurally sound. In towns like Agn, built on a hillside, farmers over the centuries made terrace gardens for themselves by removing rocks and gravel and transporting large amounts of arable soil up to the ledges from the plains below. In the village of Palu, in Kharpert, whole families took part in the intricate steps of growing and harvesting cotton, separating the fibers from the dirt and the other parts of the plant, making the fibers into threads, and weaving cloth out of those threads. *Ghaysee* apricots played a large part in the economy of the hillside town of Agn. Armenians who lived near rivers like the Euphrates knew about many species of fish and about different designs of nets to catch them.[11]

Recorded recollections depict the Armenian population as holding a pervasive faith in education. Vatche Ghazarian, in a compatriotic society's official history of Habousi, writes, "Even the humblest farmer made the necessary sacrifices to insure his children receive an education." Especially after 1908, the number of schools multiplied in villages as well as cities. Educational opportunities for girls increased in the late nineteenth and early twentieth centuries, albeit fitfully. Ethnographer Susie Hoogasian Villa found that girls were more likely to be denied education if the only available school was in a neighboring village to which a long walk was required, or if male elders in her family saw education as corrupting. Hoogasian Villa's own grandmother was reported to have been kept illiterate "because her four brothers feared that she would write love letters if she learned to read and write." Vahé Tachjian notes that when the church-run Vartanian (later Mesrobian) school in the Dersim sanjak in Kharpert opened its doors to girls in 1865, by order of the regional primate, conservatives made their displeasure known. Even so, he finds in his study of Dersim, much of the Armenian educational activity in the pregenocide years was co-ed, and the building of schools throughout the vilayets of Turkey increased dramatically after 1908. As early as the late nineteenth century, villages in the old world could draw upon compatriots who had emigrated to the cities of the United States for money to run schools. Village-based compatriotic societies in the twentieth century, moreover, not infrequently had the words "educational society" in their names and had the support of the education of young persons from their respective villages on both sides of the ocean among their missions.[12]

On the eve of the war, the United States already had a visible and vibrant Armenian immigrant community, old enough to have spawned a second and third generation. Armenians had also, by this time, distinguished themselves as a group with a notably high rate of upward economic mobility, with niches in the Oriental rug and photoengraving trades and, in rural Fresno, California, in the farming of raisins, melons, and vegetables. In most other locales they were not numerous enough to dominate any single residential sections, but there were substantial Armenian neighborhoods in Worcester and Watertown, Massachusetts, and Detroit, Michigan, as well as pockets of Armenian settlement in many of the country's other urban centers.[13]

Armenian migration to the United States in the nineteenth century received its first major stimulus in the 1830s when American Protestant missionaries began journeying to Turkey and setting up shop. After finding it futile to proselytize to Muslims, these clergymen quickly turned their attention to Armenian Apostolic Christians, where they enjoyed substantial success. The presence of these missionaries opened some channels of communication, which in turn inspired a handful of young Armenians, estimated at fewer than one hundred, to travel to America to study. Some received theological degrees and returned to propagate the faith in their homeland; others remained in the United States. In the 1860s and 1870s another string of migrants appeared, these more in pursuit of commercial opportunities. It was during these years that Armenians in America first became associated with the Oriental rug trade. According to historian Robert Mirak, it was generally not the wealthy merchants of Constantinople, the capital of the Ottoman Empire, who migrated at this time, but rather, ambitious young men, many of whom had been educated at the missionary schools and colleges run by the American Board. Some came to the United States in the employ of American missionaries, like Hagop Bogigian, who traveled to Massachusetts as the manservant to one. Bogigian presently became a successful rug merchant in the Boston area, an enterprise he began by renting window space in a shoe store and displaying an inventory of three rugs he had brought with him from Turkey.[14]

It was in the late 1870s that substantial numbers of immigrants, now coming from the artisan and peasant classes, began making the voyage to America. As was true with so many other immigrant groups, particular spots attracted streams of co-ethnics after a handful of individual migrants found employment in specific industries and communicated the news to family and friends in their villages of origin. Sometime between 1878 and 1880, Aaron Yenovkian arrived in Worcester, Massachusetts, and began work at the Washburn & Moen Manufacturing Company, a producer of wire. His letter home to Kharpert Province drew more immigrants, and in the 1880s and 1890s the number of Armenians in Worcester grew, to 250 in 1887 and over 600 in 1891, many coming from Kharpert Province, and many working at the Washburn & Moen factory, alongside Irish, Lithuanian, Polish, and Finnish workers, supervised largely by members of the earlier-settled Swedish community. Similarly, in Providence, Rhode Island, in 1889, by which time the city already had one Armenian rug merchant and two Armenian grocers, one Alexan Bedrosian is reported to have arrived from the Armenian village of Khuyly and taken a job at the very large Nicholson File Company. Several others soon followed. During those same years, Armenians from Diarbekir and Musa Dagh, areas with large concentrations of skilled silkworm cultivators and silkweavers, streamed into the New Jersey locales of Jersey City and West Hoboken (now Union City) and filled jobs in the Gibbernard and Schwantzenbach silk mills, or settled in South Manchester, Connecticut, to work for Cheney Brothers. Around 1900, Armenians from Kghi, later joined by those from the regions of Palu, Van, and Sivas, were drawn to the American Steel and Foundry Company in Granite City, Illinois, dwelling in both Granite City and the neighboring Madison. In Troy, New York, Armenians found a niche in the making of cuffs, collars, and shirts.[15]

As Armenian communities formed in these various industrial cities, it was not long before small but notable numbers of these immigrants left factory employment and became independent proprietors. This was helped, obviously, by the fair though smaller number of Armenian immigrants who arrived with money and commercial backgrounds and began their new-world life as self-employed merchants. Krikor Markarian, it is reported, arrived in Worcester in 1889 at the age of fifteen, worked a few years at Washburn & Moen, and as early as 1895 was able to open a tobacco-importing business in the city. While such speedy mobility was the exception, and exact percentage figures are not available, the Immigration Commission found Armenians to show a notably high incidence of rising from wage work to business ownership. A study of the small city of New Britain, Connecticut, in 1909, found 6 percent of Armenians to be in business at a time when the corresponding figure was 6.6 percent for Jews, 3.4 percent for Italians, and less than 1 percent for Irish, Lithuanians, and Slovaks. Another study of Boston and New York in 1915 found over 46 percent of gainfully employed Armenians to be in the ranks of artisans and shopkeepers.[16]

As noted, California also attracted Armenian immigrants. In 1881 and 1882, a group of brothers named Seropian from Worcester moved to Fresno, in the healthy climate of the San Joaquin Valley, starting when one, Hagop, was advised by his doctor to relocate. Letters from them drew immigrants from the Turkish Armenian region of Marsovan, while even more migrated there from the eastern United States, and a colony was promptly in the making. The Seropian brothers gained both prosperity and attention as a curiosity when they established a mule-driven express service between Fresno and San Francisco, competing with the more expensive railroads. While most Armenian migrants settled in cities, a small number went from farming life in the old country to farming life in America. Most prominent were those of Fresno, California, where by 1913 Armenians had already taken the lead in production of raisins, melons, and vegetables. A small "Armenian village" also formed in the border area between Salem Depot, New Hampshire, and Lawrence, Massachusetts. Spawned at the turn of the twentieth century by a tiny handful of families from the villages of Habousi and Garmer, in the province of Kharpert, they grew into an important dairy and vegetable farming locus worked by three generations, competing with nearby Italian farmers in the marketplace of Lawrence.[17]

Where there were Armenians, there soon were Armenian churches. The community in Worcester was the first to start its own Armenian Apostolic congregation in 1889, using rented space at first but then mounting a wooden church building on Laurel Hill in 1891. Armenian communities in other cities contributed to the Worcester effort and then followed the pattern for themselves. In 1898, the church in America got its first bishop. Protestant congregations, smaller in number but equal in commitment, sprang up in the communities as well. Armenian political conflicts permeated the Armenian churches, especially the Apostolic congregations, from the very start, sometimes turning violent. There were also some turf wars between clergy in those formative years.[18]

There was also a full-fledged Armenian-language press, dominated by the competing political parties, with several papers circulating nationally, in contrast with those of most other groups, which were printed and sold in the confines of individual cities. The Tashnag party began publishing *Hairenik* (Fatherland), first from New York in 1899 before relocating to Boston in 1900, and *Asbarez* (Arena) on the West Coast in 1908. The Constitutional Ramgavars, from their inception in 1908, published *Azk* (Nation) from Boston. The Armenian Evangelical (Protestant) denomination and its missionary association in the United States began publishing *Gotchnag* (Churchbell) in 1900. Though formally nonpartisan, it tended to echo the non-Tashnag point of view on political issues. The Hunchags published *Eridasart Hayastan* (Young Armenia) starting in 1903.[19]

On the eve of the First World War, Armenian men in America substantially outnumbered the women by a ratio greater than six to one. Among the attempts to address this imbalance was a scheme by community leaders in Worcester to pay the travel fare of orphaned Armenian girls in the Ottoman Empire to come and be married off to local bachelors. Some marriages were arranged by overseas correspondence, and in a number of instances money changed hands between eager bachelors and the fathers of prospective brides.[20]

- 3 -

Armenians in America, while they put down roots, established their livelihoods, and made lives with their families and communities, involved themselves in the affairs of their ancestral homeland and made efforts to affect its future. In recent decades, historians of American immigrant experiences have emphasized the phenomenon of diasporic nationalism, whereby members of an immigrant community whose homeland is not a stable and sovereign nation-state feel an attachment to the homeland and a shared sense of identity as members of a dispersed nationality, a sense of common community with persons in other parts of the world who share that nationality and that ancestral homeland. Diasporic nationalists also advocate for the political status of their homeland. (Decades before immigration historians began writing about this phenomenon, mid-twentieth-century political historians addressed it, but they did so in the form of complaining about the influence of those meddling hyphenates over the nation's foreign policy.)[21]

In the case of the Armenians, expressions of diasporic nationalism were tightly enmeshed with a rivalry, mainly between two partisan camps: the Armenian Revolutionary Federation (ARF), or Tashnag party, and a loosely defined non-Tashnag, increasingly *anti*-Tashnag, coalition. The chain of events surrounding the thousand-day republic of 1918–20, their effect on the controversies surrounding the actions of an archbishop in 1933 and his assassination at the end of that year, and the split of the Armenian Apostolic Church from that point onward all centered on that schism. To the sorrow of many, the schism held an important place in the discourse through most of the twentieth century, even when the community appeared to have enough other problems to worry about. And yet, this study seeks to move past the obvious approach of treating the partisan schism merely as a missed opportunity for unity. Unity is good, of course, and it is certainly better if archbishops are not assassinated and factions of church congregations do not lock each other out of the House of the Lord. However, writing history in terms of what might have been runs the risk of losing sight of what happened and why it happened in the actual story.

Among other things, I see the feud as representing not only a turf war between leadership elites (which it indisputably was), but also a debate between contrasting ideas about how to be an ethnic group in America, especially in the 1930s when a new second generation was starting to come of age and integrate into America's mainstream educational and occupational infrastructures. In this vein, I introduce the terms *militant ethnicity* and *celebratory ethnicity*, linking conflicting perceptions of the situation in the homeland with conflicting visions of ethnic identity in the United States—all taking place amid the fact that both camps agreed on the importance of being both good Armenians and good Americans.

Closely related is my notion of a *symbiotic marketing relationship* between leadership elites, including editors, priests, and party field workers, and the general population of Armenian immigrants and their descendants. The word *marketing* should not be construed as implying top-down manipulation. Community leaders did not influence constituents into thinking or acting in a way that they did not wish to think or act. They did, however, powerfully shape the perceptions of their constituents, with the full and informed consent of the constituents whose perceptions they powerfully shaped. Indeed, the use of the word *marketing* is not meant to underplay the active role of community members at large, but rather to analyze the specific framework within which they played that active role.

Newspapers, of course, were a tangible physical product being marketed to buyers, and one of the scholarly discourses to which this book seeks to contribute is the study of the role that the ethnic press plays in an immigrant community. Anna D. Jaroszyńska-Kirchmann, in the introduction to her book about a major Polish press outlet, observes of the larger topic, "The foreign-language press found its leaders among a generation of immigrants, who combined the idea of service to their communities with acute business sense. Immigrant publishers, editors, and journalists built their publishing ventures, proving their entrepreneurial spirit and imagination no less than their American counterparts."[22] At first glance this description might not seem to apply to the Armenian press, as it was operated by political parties, but a key fact still holds up: the publishers, whether partisan institutions or private entrepreneurs, needed members of the immigrant community to buy their papers to stay in operation. Thus, they could reasonably be expected to serve all the same functions and abide by all the same mandates to maintain their marketing relationship with their readers.

Jaroszyńska-Kirchmann, alluding to the earlier work of Jürgen Habermas, further notes that the participatory nature of many immigrant newspapers provided readers with a public sphere—I call it a *virtual village square*—in which issues relevant to an ethnic community could be aired and debated.[23] This held very true with the Armenians during the period under consideration here. Many of the letters to the editor echoed the sentiments of the editors, especially where specific events in the partisan feud were concerned, such as the Tourian affair of 1933. But many other contributions from readers showed debates. Questions of how young people should behave with each other at dances, of whether intermarriage harms the preservation of ethnic identity, of whether the old-world expectations and dictates of immigrant parents hinder the integration of the young into the more modern society they live in, of how to find the right blend of tradition and modernism, of how to be good Armenians and good Americans at the same time—all of these themes appear in the Armenian press, and show dynamic interaction by readers with both each other and the editors on matters of great import to themselves.

Clearly, then, the use of the word *marketing* in this book does not in any way reduce community members to passive receivers. They were absolutely not.

For much of the twentieth century, the rival political parties dominated the newspapers that brought the latest news from the ancestral homeland, the diaspora, and the local community to Armenian immigrants and their descendants. During the life of the thousand-day republic, whose governance the Tashnag party dominated, Armenians who got their news from the Tashnag press understood the situation with their homeland by way of one narrative, and those who got their news from the non-Tashnag press understood it by way of quite another. Throughout the elapsing years, the rival presses kept the memories of those disparate narratives fresh in their readers' minds. As a result, on July 1, 1933, at the Century of Progress Exposition in Chicago, when Archbishop Levon Tourian ordered the removal of the flag of that republic from the stage of the Armenian Pavilion before he would ascend the stage to speak, one set of Armenians felt their sense of national identity deeply wounded, while another set saw no problem with honoring the Primate's wishes. The responses to Archbishop Tourian's assassination that following December divided along the same party lines. In the several decades after that, the division stayed strong, and the press played a major part in rehearsing and reinforcing the contested memories and conflicting narratives.

The parties also ran clubhouses that their members frequented. Starting in the 1930s, the same decade that the leading parties began publishing papers in English as well as Armenian so as to keep the American-born generation included in their outreach, they began—for exactly the same reason—operating youth organizations featuring lectures, athletic tournaments, and dances. Moreover, in a trend that climaxed in the 1930s and was further solidified in the 1950s, the churches became either Tashnag or anti-Tashnag in their orientation. Indeed, partisanism played an integral part in the symbiotic marketing relationship between the ethnic elites and the general Armenian population during the years being explored here.

An important point still needs to be made about the discourse between ethnic community and cultural mainstream, closely related as well to the dynamic between generations and between rival factions: at no time was the conflict one of whether to be more Armenian or more American. Over the past several decades, historians have appropriately revised the model of a dichotomy between assimilation on the one hand and cultural preservation on the other, replacing it with a more nuanced picture of an acculturation, or adaptation process that involved, not only a cultural synthesis of the ethnic and the American, not only the embrace of what sociologist Herbert Gans calls "symbolic ethnicity," but also an assertion by immigrants and their descendants of the right to call themselves American on their own terms rather than on terms dictated to them by the cultural mainstream, and even at times to offer lessons in Americanism and patriotism to the host society. June Granatir Alexander, in her study of Slovak Americans in the interwar years, finds that the immigrant press was able to turn the rhetoric of Americanization on its head by painting immigrant communities as more American in spirit than those whose hyperpatriotism took the form of paranoia and bigotry.[24]

That theme comes up in this study in a number of contexts. There is the irony in the 1920s whereby, while American cultural conservatives saw the morals of the youth as declining and blamed immigrants for having brought in corrupting ideas and values, Armenian and other immigrant elders saw America's own cultural mainstream as bearing the seeds of their American-born sons and daughters' moral destruction, and felt that too much assimilation could mean loss of virtue. But at no time did Armenians quibble among themselves over whether it was their task to be good Americans: they took that as a given. When editors of the competing partisan papers exhorted their readers to show their loyalty to their host country and pursue success in its educational and economic institutions, they were not merely conforming to expectations. Their own efforts at lobbying for policies favorable to the ancestral homeland, and policies favorable to their aspirations for influence in the homeland and the diaspora's future, depended on being able to claim that they spoke for a community of patriotic Americans and that their distinctive qualities of Armenianness made their community, not lesser Americans, but special Americans.

This book traces the development of the Armenians' creation of a life for themselves as an ethnic community in the United States, the efforts of the leading political parties to affect the future of their ancestral homeland, and the dynamic between those two realms. Chapter 1 chronicles the First World War years, showing (among many other things) how the partisan press created two distinct zones of reality between the Tashnags, who identified with the thousand-day republic, and the non-Tashnags, who looked to Boghos Nubar Pasha to light the way for Armenia's future. Chapter 2, on the 1920s, emphasizes more of the cultural aspects, as a rural population accustomed to arranged marriages and hierarchical family relationships came to terms with life in a more liberal and urbanized host society that was itself changing and experiencing culture shock. Chapter 3 highlights the intensification of the partisan schism with December 24, 1933, murder of Archbishop Levon Tourian and the trial and conviction of nine members of the Tashnag party for the crime. The point is made that the partisan press, dating back to the First World War era, played an enormous role in cultivating the division whereby two sets of Armenians would view that murder in completely opposite ways, heavily affected by their memories of events a decade and a half earlier. Chapter 4 drives home the connection between the political and the cultural, showing how the political parties, in efforts to keep themselves in existence in the United States for the long haul, reached out to the youth in the 1930s and after, and took great care to keep them loyal to Armenia—and to each party's particularistic image of Armenia—while at the same time seeking success and acceptance in the American context.

Chapters 5, 6, and 7 deal with the years of the Second World War and the Cold War. Significantly, by this time Armenians no longer had even the fiction of keeping their quarrels in the family: the Tashnag and anti-Tashnag leadership cadres condemned each other for outsiders to hear, something they had taken care not to do during the First World War. Moreover, the rival partisan factions now took every opportunity to call each other bad Americans as well as bad Armenians. Chapter 5 focuses on the world war and its immediate aftermath, with its effects on both social and political life. The Cold War provided the Tashnag party with the perfect opportunity to assert its American credentials, making American patriotism and the struggle to liberate Armenia from the Soviet yoke synonymous. Chapter 6 demonstrates how this dynamic fit in with the larger picture of the US government's Cold War policies and the mainstream American population's enthrallment in the anti-Communist crusade. It also shows how the commemoration of different dates associated with Armenia's history in the First World War years showed the nature of the partisan schism. Chapter 7 chronicles the formalization of the church split and its close connection with international Cold War politics as well as with intra-Armenian community grudges.

In the modern era, Armenian political activism is most associated with the call for the nations of the world to recognize that a genocide took place in 1915 and to hold Turkey accountable. Chapter 8 traces the evolution of that consciousness, which coincided with a tense and tentative diminution of the hostility between the opposing camps in the mid-1970s. This chapter shows how global diasporan leaders, American-based newspaper editors, and Armenian Americans at the ground level all contributed to this shift of focus, with the symbiotic marketing relationship still a point of emphasis. By the 1970s, the Hart-Celler Immigration Act of 1965 had made possible a fresh new influx of Armenian immigrants. (While I introduce those new immigrants into the story and review some key aspects of their impact on the larger community, I leave it to my fellow historians to give these important players' stories their full value.) The chapter also discusses the rise and decline of Armenian terrorist movements and the campaign for presidents and Congress to formally recognize the genocide and to use the actual word. A short epilogue discusses the events of the century's end—the fall of the Soviet Union, the birth of an independent Armenian republic, the conflict with Azerbaijan over Nagorno-Karabagh—and the diasporan responses to them.

This book is a contribution to a field that is comparatively small. (To get a sense of what I mean, go to any university library and survey the amount of shelf space taken up by books dedicated to the many specialized aspects of Italian, Eastern European Jewish, or Chinese immigrant experiences, and compare it to the total scholarly literature on Armenian Americans.) I hope that an increasing number of scholars will write full-length books about Armenian Americans, and about Armenians in the global diaspora. Also, there is room for future works of history about broader topics—that is, books that do not have the word Armenian in their titles—to include Armenian themes in their larger narratives: in works, for example, about the influence of ethnic groups on international policymaking; about the role of global hierarchical churches in world affairs; about the politics of the Cold War in the United States and elsewhere; and about immigrant and ethnic experiences in their own right.

And now, a final note to the reader. The biggest mistake you could possibly make with this book would be to let it be the only book about Armenians in the United States that you read. There is a rich literature of memoirs, including but not limited to those of genocide survivors who made it to the United States (or to other receiving countries), where readers can share the vividness of the experiences recounted. And of course there are other scholarly works, some written and others yet to be, that consider the story from different angles. I commend them to your attention. If this book inspires others to conduct their own studies to see what I've missed, even if their contributions are so good that they leave mine in the dust, I'll feel that my efforts have succeeded and be gratified. Here, in the meantime, is mine.

1

The Contested Homeland

The First World War and the Genocide

For Armenians, Turkey's entry into the Great War came as tragic news. The conflagration had begun in August of 1914, with Britain, France, and Russia aligned against Germany and Austria-Hungary. Now in November the Ottoman Empire, already nicknamed the Sick Man of Europe, launched a campaign against czarist Russia, an empire also in decay. Armenians living in the United States, as well as elsewhere in the diaspora, knew that for their brethren in the historic homeland, which included some provinces of Turkey and others ruled by Russia, nothing good could come of this turn of events. It would force Armenians to fight Armenians. (Armenians were not the only national group in this position: Poles, whose homeland had been under partition and occupation by Austrians, Germans, and Russians since 1795, were pitted against each other in this war.) It would also put Ottoman Armenians in grave danger. Armenians had already endured horrific massacres at the hands of the Turkish sultanic government. It was questionable, now, whether the revolutionary Young Turk regime that had displaced the sultan had any greater regard for Armenian life.

The answer to that question was not long in coming. The invading Turkish forces of Enver Pasha at Sarikanish (Transcaucasia), Khalil Pasha at Tabriz (Persian Azerbaijan), and Jevdey Bey, Enver's fierce brother-in-law, at Khoi (Persia) were effectively driven back in humiliation by czarist troops during the months of January and February of 1915. In the wake of these defeats, Enver and his circle began to blame Armenians in the Turkish ranks. The persecution began in the Ottoman army, where Armenian soldiers were stripped of their guns and put to exhaustive manual labor. Armenian civilians, who had only been allowed to own guns since the Young Turk revolution, were also disarmed.[1]

Persecution quickly turned to killing. On April 23–25, 1915, several hundred leading Armenian intellectual, cultural, and political leaders in the city of Constantinople were taken from their homes and shot, a scenario soon to be replicated throughout the empire. From that month through the end of August, in one village, town, and city after another, the mass extermination campaign that later came to be known as the genocide unfurled. The Turkish government employed local gendarmes, a special force consisting largely of newly released convicts, and some members of the general Turkish and Kurdish population to carry out the killings and deportations. In a typical locale, most of the able-bodied males were taken and killed first. The remaining Armenian inhabitants—women, children, and elderly men—were generally forced to march across the countryside, resulting in death from exhaustion and dehydration for many. Some of the young women and children were sold to Muslims as slaves or concubines; some children had the slightly less onerous fate of being adopted into Turkish families and forced to internalize a new nationality and religion.[2]

Accounts show that Turkish party bosses in the Committee for Union and Progress, men of westernized sophistication, directed the massacres, ordering local Turkish and Kurdish populations, sometimes against their will, to brutalize the Armenians. While explanations involving both military vengeance and religious zealotry were put forth by contemporaries, modern historians have traced it to Pan-Turanism, a hardline Turkish nationalism that could tolerate no internal challenges to Turkish greatness. Armenians, by their sheer presence, by their dominance in all areas of the empire's commerce, and by the presence among them of some revolutionaries, were perceived as a threat to this Turanic nation. It is significant, for understanding the government's motives, that the Armenians' homes throughout the provinces were quickly turned over to Balkan *mujahir* Muslim migrants. One Turkish senator, Ahmed Riza, tried to advocate in the Senate for humanity to the Armenians; after several attempts, he was silenced with the threat that, if he persisted, there would be further acts committed against Armenians to punish him.[3]

While the overwhelming majority of Armenians had no chance to resist expulsion or death, there were a few pockets of localized triumph that would be celebrated in ensuing years for Armenian valor. One such pocket was the defense of the city of Van. When most of the Armenian population of Van province had been killed or marched into exile, the Armenians of the city successfully barricaded themselves in and held the Turks at bay for nearly a month, under the leadership of Aram Manoogian and Armenak Erkanian, before Russian troops arrived and rescued them in mid-May. The Russians defended the new Armenian administration of the city for several weeks, but then withdrew; as many Armenian refugees as could fled with their liberators.[4]

A more famous saga of resistance provided the material for Franz Werfel's 1933 novel *The Forty Days of Musa Dagh*. Six villages in the lowlands of this steep, rugged mountain served as home to a diversified economy that included silk cultivation, beekeeping, and textile goods as well as the standard wheat and barley crops. When the villagers learned of the Turkish evacuation orders, just over four thousand resolved to resist (alongside another two thousand who surrendered from the start). The resisters ascended the mountain and created a temporary governing council led by a young Protestant pastor, Rev. Dikran Andreasian. Despite having much of their food provisions and firepower destroyed at the outset in a drenching rainstorm before they had the chance to build shelter, these villagers not only survived but fought off multiple assaults by Turkish forces, amazingly losing only eighteen of their soldiers. After what was actually more than forty days, on a Sunday in early September when Pastor Andreasian was composing his morning sermon, one of the camp runners showed up with the news that a French battleship had responded to their distress signals. Several ships of France and Britain, one of which thankfully had an Armenian man who could translate, transported the refugees to tent cities in Port Said in Egypt. Many of the men

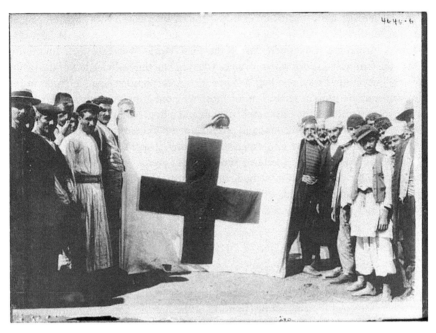

Figure 1.1 Armenians with the flag they used to signal for help after their resistance on Musa Dagh. The photograph was probably taken after their arrival at Port Said, Egypt, in September 1915. LC-B2- 4646-6 [P&P], Library of Congress.

among them subsequently fought as volunteers, alongside others recruited from the immigrant community in America, in the French *Légion d'Orient*.[5]

In the United States, the Armenian community, or *Hayoutiun*, was already well established, though not large compared with other immigrant groups. Through this catastrophe and through subsequent events that unfolded during the course of the war and after, both immigrants and the native-born followed the news and helped their compatriots in various ways. Many did so by donating money. A smaller number of immigrant men joined a volunteer force and went to fight as Armenians. (Others, of course, fought in the war in the uniform of the US military after Congress declared war in April of 1917.) At the start of 1919 many voted in a purely Armenian election held to send delegates to an Armenian congress in Paris. In all events, the Armenian community in the United States felt closely connected to the ways in which the Great War and its ripples were affecting the Armenian ancestral homeland, both in Anatolia, the region under Turkish rule, and on the Caucasus, which at the start of the war still lay under the rule of the Russian czar.

The involvement of Armenian Americans during the war went beyond the general sense of wanting to help their besieged brethren. When members of a global diaspora have an attachment to the ancestral homeland that includes caring about its future political status and having strong beliefs as to who should be in power and how it should be governed, this phenomenon is known as diasporic nationalism. In the case of the Armenians, diasporic nationalism was tightly interwoven with another feature: partisan conflict. In a pattern that most decisively did not hold up in the decades that followed, Armenian spokesmen during the First World War kept their animosity within the family and spoke with one voice when interacting with leaders of the world powers. Put another way, one had to know the Armenian language to listen in on the Armenian partisan quarrels. But for those who did know Armenian, namely the Armenians themselves, the existence of a fierce and bitter feud between two diasporan leadership cadres was conspicuous and prominent: it dominated the discourse in their churches, their social clubs, and especially their newspapers, which were published by the partisan factions. At the same time that the events in the homeland created many traumatic memories for Armenians, the partisan feud ensured that different Armenians would have starkly different versions of these memories and would be at odds with each other over them for decades to come.

- 1 -

From the onset of the crisis the press, the churches, and the local clubs, both partisan and otherwise, kept the community mindful of the need to donate. Fundraising was often incorporated with events designed to satisfy the social and entertainment needs of the givers. It frequently took the form of the *hantess*, which psychiatrist-author Levon Z. Boyajian describes in his New York memoir as "one gigantic get-together, with food, music, dancing, drink and socialization, and in a way a remembrance of what was no longer so—the life in the old country." Picnics, he adds, were the outdoor version of the same idea. Countless local notes in the Armenian American press depicted the scenario wherein some number of Armenians gathered at a local club hall. One or two individuals spoke about the grave conditions in the old country; a procedure such as an auction was employed to raise funds; and then almost invariably some young local talent gave a piano or violin recital. The last part of the evening might well be given over to social dancing.[6]

On homeland-related matters, Armenians were essentially divided between Tashnags and non-Tashnags. Tashnags, that is, members of the Armenian Revolutionary Federation (ARF), were of a more militant-nationalist persuasion on most issues. There were, during these years, three other major parties: the Hunchags, the Reformed Hunchags, and the Constitutional Ramgavars. (Just after the war, the last two parties would merge into the Armenian Democratic Liberal, or Ramgavar, party.) Because the parties controlled the major Armenian press organs, it can fairly be said that most Armenians in America got their news in either Tashnag or non-Tashnag form, a fact that grew more and more significant during the war years.

During the war there were recurring, but unsuccessful, attempts at cooperation between the different partisan factions. In November 1914 when Turkey entered the war, Tashnags and non-Tashnags formed a committee to create a united front for fundraising, but could not agree on where the funds should be sent. Tashnag leaders naturally regarded the Armenian National Bureau in Tiflis, which the party controlled, as the body best suited to receive revenue and channel it where it was needed. The Catholicos at Echmiadzin, spiritual leader of the Armenian Apostolic Church worldwide, declared himself to be the worthy trustee early in 1915, and non-Tashnags on the committee concurred. Both camps agreed that the money should be used for some combination of humanitarian aid and military defense, but the Tashnags appeared to put greater emphasis on the latter. The factions ended up running separate fund drives. The Catholicos, it should be noted, had already dispatched an Armenian National Delegation to Paris. Headed by the wealthy Egyptian Armenian Boghos Boghos Nubar Pasha, who in 1905 had founded the Egypt-based Armenian General Benevolent Union (AGBU), the delegation lobbied the European powers for attention to the needs and interests of Armenians.[7]

Money was not all that Armenians in America, especially first-generation immigrants, found themselves called upon to contribute. As early as May 9, 1915, an approving editorial in the *Boston Sunday Herald* reported the announcement of wealthy immigrant entrepreneur Moses H. Gulesian of Boston that there were already one thousand Armenians in America ready to fight the Turks as volunteers, and that four thousand more could be raised. Gulesian had first written with his proposal to the Canadian minister of militia, and then presented his case to England. While showing due regard for the evils of Great Britain's primary enemy ("The victory of Germany would be a calamity to the world"), Gulesian's letter to the British War Office made clear that the idea of the plan was for the Armenian volunteers to fight in Turkey. It is not altogether clear what became of Gulesian's volunteer force, if indeed it was as big as he claimed, but in August of that year the forty-eight-year-old Gulesian was among those volunteering for officer training at the camp in Plattsburg, New York, under the auspices of the Plattsburg Movement, a venture jointly sponsored by the US War Department and private philanthropy, and spearheaded by the colorful Colonel Leonard Wood.[8] Gulesian would continue to speak of his ability to recruit large numbers of volunteers when testifying before a Senate subcommittee in September 1919.

Gulesian may have played some part in the recruitment of volunteers that took place the following year under Nubar's auspices. Indeed, an important part of the Great War and of the Armenian experience in it was the decision by Great Britain and France in 1916 to undertake a deep surge into the Ottoman Empire's Middle Eastern territory, led by the British general Sir Edmund Allenby. In connection with this, British and French diplomats made promises to a number of ethnic populations and elites of rewards in territory in exchange for providing volunteer forces to assist in the invasion. Two such groups were Arabs and Jews, a key factor sowing the seeds of today's Middle Eastern conflict. The Armenians constituted yet another. In October of that year Sir Mark Sykes of Britain and Georges Picot of France, best known for the notorious secret treaty they made with Russia to carve up the Ottoman territories as spoils of war, asked Boghos Nubar Pasha to recruit Armenian volunteers. They assured him that the recruitment could take place discreetly, that Armenian volunteers would only have to fight against Turks, and that Cilicia, part of the territory they purposed to seize and have the Armenian troops occupy, would become an autonomous Armenian state after the war.[9]

Figure 1.2 Boghos Nubar Pasha, head of the Armenian National Delegation at Paris, regarded by non-Tashnag Armenians as representing the future of Armenia. Photo courtesy of Smbat Minasyan, armenian-history.com.

In accordance with Nubar's agreement with British and French leaders, the Armenian political organizations on American soil went forward with the recruitment of volunteers for the *Legion d'Orient*, originally a combination of Armenians and Syrians, later separated so that recruits from the *Hayoutiun* could call themselves the Armenian Legion. Efforts to recruit 5,000 resulted in an actual figure recorded at 1,172, all immigrants, with large clusters coming from those urban centers known for large Armenian populations, including Boston, New York, and Detroit. Boatloads of these patriots sailed in the spring and summer to France, from there via the Mediterranean to Port Said in Egypt—where they met up with other volunteers including many veterans of the resistance at Musa Dagh—and then to Cyprus, where the actual training occurred.[10]

To facilitate recruitment of the legion, the parties in the United States made yet another attempt at working together by forming the Armenian National Union (ANU), with representatives from the Tashnags, the Hunchags, the Reformed Hunchags, and the Constitutional Ramgavars, joined presently by the Armenian General Benevolent Union (AGBU), the Apostolic Church, and the Evangelical Church. The ANU began its life with a potent internal contradiction: its founding charter designed it as *both* a meeting ground of the different organizations in the United States *and* the American branch of the Armenian National Delegation in Paris. Accordingly, Miran Sevasly, a Boston-based Armenian lawyer originally from the Greek city of Smyrna, served as both the president of the ANU and Nubar's official legate.[11] As one of its founding principles, the ANU claimed the right to be the voice of the Armenian community to the outside world, precluding any independent announcements or actions of import from the component agencies. Given that Tashnags looked to the ARF-dominated Armenian National Bureau at Tiflis, rather than to Nubar, to light the way for Armenia's future, one might reasonably have predicted that, rather than quelling the partisan conflict, the ANU would become a hotspot of it. As will be seen later in this chapter, the creation in May 1918 of the "thousand-day republic" and the divided response to its existence made this scenario for the ANU all the more certain.

- 2 -

The World War I years are commonly associated with intense pressure on immigrant communities from their host society and its government to show their American patriotism and eschew "hyphenism."[12] Former president Theodore Roosevelt told a Columbus Day gathering at Carnegie Hall in 1915 that "the sooner [the hyphenated American] returns to the country of his allegiance the better," and that "those hyphenated Americans who terrorize American politicians by threat of the foreign vote are engaged in treason to the American republic." In a later speech, the same orator compared the immigrant who looked back to the homeland with Lot's wife in the Bible, explicitly adding that he would gladly transform such a malefactor into a pillar of salt. Frances Kellor, head of the National Americanization Committee, wrote with concern in 1918, "There are literally thousands of foreign-language organizations in the United States fighting among themselves for independent and united native countries or to preserve their racial solidarity here. On the other hand, there are but few such organizations whose first interest is Americanization or to help America win the war."[13]

However, as June Granatir Alexander points out in her 2004 book *Ethnic Pride, American Patriotism*, there was an irony here: the government and American civic groups encouraged immigrant communities to demonstrate their American patriotism *as immigrant communities*, such as by marching group by group in patriotic parades and seeking to surpass one another as groups in purchase of war bonds. In so doing, these groups managed to slip in some advertising for their own causes, which in these particular years generally meant independence or autonomy for their historic homelands. What June Alexander finds of the Poles and the Slovaks holds true for the Armenians as well. Indeed, at least fifty Armenians marched in the 1918 Loyalty Day parade, dressed in traditional garb and waving Armenian flags.[14]

Implicit in the rhetoric of Americanization, especially in Teddy Roosevelt's "pillar of salt" remark, was an injunction against putting the cause of one's overseas homeland above the cause of American/Allied victory in the war. However, there seemed to be no ill consequences for championing the two causes together, even as if they were one and the same. The editors of *Azk*, the Constitutional Ramgavar party's organ, did precisely this with an editorial printed just before the Fourth of July in 1918. The main subject was the opportunity for noncitizens serving in the US armed forces to gain citizenship, and the editorial unequivocally urged Armenian soldiers to do so as quickly as possible, partly to receive the added protection of such citizenship if they were taken prisoner abroad, but also to further the cause of Americanization, which the editorial fully endorsed. After approvingly echoing Teddy Roosevelt's disparagement of foreigners who used the country as "a giant boarding house," and also approvingly referring to the efforts by the government and "various patriotic organizations ... to teach immigrants this country's language, and to instill in them an understanding and respect for this country's social and political institutions," the writer depicted service in the war as an opportunity for Americans of different origins to come together with a common purpose and a common language. Toward the end, the editorial instructed readers, "We must come to the realization that the victory of our just national rights is most firmly linked with the victory of the Allies, as well as of America; and the heroic son of Armenia who offers his blood for the star-studded flag, it is for the freedom of Armenia that he makes that sacrifice."[15]

The Armenian press would even, on occasion, presume to point out to the US government what its own national interests were. After it was reported that Turkish troops invading the Persian city of Tabriz had attacked the American consulate and looted an American missionary hospital, the Tashnags' *Hairenik* ran a front-page story asserting that the United States should declare war on Turkey. (Though the United States was allied with Turkey's enemies and at war against Turkey's allies, the two countries never conferred enemy status on each other.) The United States had not hesitated, when forced by events, to declare war on the tyrannical governments of Germany and Austria, *Hairenik* argued. "If ... democracy, liberty, idealism, and justice are not frivolous or meaningless phrases for this great republic ... then America is obligated to draw its sword and make the thunder of its artillery heard by the head of that vampire of the east to which has been given the name 'Turk,' with all the anathema of the ages."[16]

If one might have expected such assertiveness to meet with the disapproval of Hundred Percent Americanizers, it did not come into any conflict with the chief of that camp: Teddy Roosevelt had expressed similar sentiments even before the attacks at Tabriz. In a May 1 speech at Springfield, Massachusetts, the Rough Rider told a crowd, estimated at forty-five hundred, America's failure to include Turkey (and Bulgaria) in its war declarations was "a criminal absurdity." "The Turks have massacred Armenians," he said, but instead of a war declaration "we have appointed days of prayer for the Armenians."[17] He does not appear to have desired to turn those Armenians who agreed with him into pillars of salt.

Armenian spokespersons, adept at using the calls for American loyalty to their advantage as Armenians, also at times incorporated American patriotism into their partisan attacks on each other. Foreshadowing what would become an even more prevalent scenario several decades later in the Cold War era, Armenians of one party occasionally found opportunities to put their partisan rivals on the defensive about their American patriotic credentials. Thus did an editorial in the July 6, 1918, issue of *Azk* refer to the "anti-American and anti-war" stance of the American Socialist party, with its loyalty to the international revolution at the expense of loyalty to American victory in the present European war, and then issued a public interrogation to "our compatriots who profess socialism," a clear reference to the Tashnag party, wanting to know "what position they take toward our country's Socialist party." The editorial, in tones bordering on inquisition, wanted to know whether such Armenians in America desired the election of Wisconsin socialist Victor Berger to Congress and, if so, how they would reconcile that with loyalty to the American and Allied war effort.[18]

Paradoxical to the image of these years as a time when immigrants who spoke for their ethnicities and their homelands received monolithic rebuffs from government officials and civic leaders, Armenians before, during, and for at least a little while after the Great War received much assistance and encouragement from civic notables and political officials. Such an array of names graced the mastheads of both the Friends of Armenia and the American Committee for the Independence of Armenia (ACIA). No less a figure than Supreme Court justice and future secretary of state Charles Evans Hughes, early in 1919, delivered a speech at a New York banquet of the ACIA titled "The Hour of Liberation Has Come," in which he asserted, "We propose tonight to throw such influence as we have into the scale for Armenian independence. It would be unthinkable that Armenia should be left longer under Turkish control, and if it is not under Turkish control, then Armenia should be autonomous." At the same occasion, former secretary of state and presidential candidate William Jennings Bryan gave an oration under the title "Armenia, the Torch-Bearer of American Ideals." Theodore Roosevelt died in his sleep on January 5, having just that evening cabled an impassioned acceptance of the invitation to that gathering. His sister and two daughters attended, as did numerous other luminaries of the time.[19]

- 3 -

From May of 1918 through November of 1920 there existed, on the eastern side of the ancestral homeland, an independent Republic of Armenia whose governance the Tashnag party dominated. Because the political parties published the major newspapers that circulated to America's *Hayoutiun*, Armenians in America experienced the events of the life of the republic through partisan eyes, and thus experienced totally disparate realities, depending on whether they were reading the Tashnag or the non-Tashnag press. Thus, one set of Armenians felt an allegiance to the republic and considered it synonymous with Armenia, while another set barely took notice of the republic's existence and viewed free and independent Armenia as an entity that Boghos Nubar Pasha would bring into existence after the war ended. It was precisely these contested memories that caused those two groups of Armenians in 1933 and 1934 to experience two sharply contrasting realities surrounding the December 1933 murder of Archbishop Levon Tourian in a New York church (as explored in Chapter 3).

To understand all that, it is necessary to consider a series of events that played out while the Great War continued to rage. By the end of 1917, Russia had had its October Revolution and the newly constituted Soviet Communist state had pulled out of the war. This did no favors for the Armenian cause. The extremely punitive Treaty of Brest-Litovsk, signed in March 1918 (though it did not survive the Paris negotiations of 1919), surrendered not only Turkish Armenia but the eastern provinces of Kars, Ardahan, and Batum to Turkey. (Russia had taken these three provinces away from the Ottomans in 1878. On the ground, the Armenians actually managed to regain control of Kars and Ardahan in 1919, though this was undone by the Turkish-Soviet invasions of autumn 1920.) The new Soviet government also made the secret Sykes-Picot treaty public.[20]

Meanwhile, events on the Caucasus had taken on a life of their own. The three nationalities of Transcaucasia—the Armenians, the Georgians, and the Muslim Azeris—staved off absorption into the new Soviet empire through an ever-tense governing coalition. The coalition fell apart by May 1918, largely over differences in how to deal with the Turks, who were after all mortal enemies to the Armenians, close kin to the Azeris, and on neither extreme to the Georgians. When the respective national leaders proclaimed the independent republics of Georgia and Azerbaijan, Armenian governing elites, embodied by the transitory Armenian National Bureau in Tiflis, saw no alternative but to follow suit, ready or not. The Armenian Army Corps and a flood of volunteers fought off the Turks in a series of battlefield engagements, climaxing in the Battle of Sardarabad in late May; here, the Armenians turned back a southbound Turkish invasion headed toward the strategic city of Yerevan, which was soon to become the nation's capital. The Armenian troops pursued the Turks northward toward Alexandropol, aiming to drive them completely out of the eastern, Russian section of historic Armenia. The assault was halted, however, when the Tashnag leadership accepted a truce at Batum at the very end of the month. As quickly

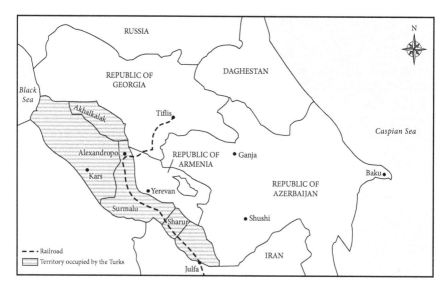

Map 1.1 The Armenian Republic in 1918. From George A. Bournoutian, *History of the Armenian People* (Costa Mesa, CA: Mazda Publishers, 1994), 2:132.

as Sardarabad took its place in the lexicon of place-names associated with Armenian bravery, the truce at Batum joined the annals of bitterly contested memories.[21]

The divided perceptions of reality in the Armenian diaspora between the Tashnag and non-Tashnag camps displayed themselves lavishly in the differing responses of the Armenian American press to the initial announcement of the republic's existence. Before any of the details surfaced, this cryptic blurb ran in the June 29, 1918, issue of the *New York Times*:

> Caucasian Armenia has declared its independence, according to the Berliner Lokal-Anzeiger.
>
> C. R. Katchaznuni has been appointed Premier and A. Shatissian *[sic]* Foreign Minister. The newspaper adds that an Armenian deputation has arrived at Constantinople.[22]

For several days, that was *all* the information to which anybody in the Western Hemisphere, including the Armenian editors in Boston, had access. That did not stop them from knowing exactly what to think of it. *Hairenik* immediately greeted the announcement with a giant-sized front-page headline and a lengthy celebratory article. The corresponding issue of *Azk*, by contrast, ran an unadorned and easy-to-overlook reprint of the *Times* blurb with no further comment. Over the next few days, the editorial page of *Hairenik* expressed total confidence in the actions of Armenia's new rulers, assuming that both the declaration of the republic and the diplomatic mission to Constantinople represented the fruits of hard-won battlefield victory. The editorial page of *Azk*, in contrast, expressed doubt and skepticism, and found the preliminary reports contradictory. If, as earlier reports had indicated, Armenian forces were victorious on the battlefield, one editorial posited, they could not possibly have sent a delegation to Constantinople, the enemy's seat of government.[23] Because these papers and the partisan institutions they represented were where Armenians in America got their news, it is not too much to say that one sector of the *Hayoutiun* understood their nation to have achieved a great milestone, while for another group of Armenians the announcement scarcely merited comment.

When further details arrived, including the fact that the Tashnag military command had negotiated an armistice with the Turks at Batum rather than continuing to fight for control of more Armenian-inhabited territory, contention arose immediately, with non-Tashnags accusing the Tashnag leaders of illegitimately settling for unfavorable terms with the enemy. In late September the non-Tashnag majority in the Armenian National Union issued a resolution, by majority vote, that the delegates who negotiated at Constantinople following the Batum truce "do not represent the Armenian nation's voice and will, and have no right to speak or make arrangements for the Armenian cause." The Tashnag delegates to that body issued their dissenting proclamation, arguing that the Armenians of the Caucasus had fought valiantly against enemies from multiple sides amid conditions of unbelievable suffering, that necessary aid promised from the Allies had not materialized, that the armistice had represented a forcing of the Armenians' enemy to accept their national existence, and that, given the circumstances, the settlement was a step toward, rather than an obstacle to, the fulfillment of the Armenian goal of a unified and independent Armenia. These two positions received even more elaboration on the competing editorial pages.[24]

There were other disputes as well surrounding the declaration of the republic. That fall, the parties within the ANU learned that back in July the delegates attending the Tashnag party's annual convention in Boston had sent a telegram to the new government at Yerevan, congratulating the republic's leaders on the achievement of independence and urging them to keep mindful of Turkish Armenia's needs and interests. From the Tashnag point of view, the telegram made perfect sense: the republic *was* Armenia, and the fight for the rights of Armenians in the western provinces meant a fight for the inclusion of those provinces in that republic which was, again, Armenia. To non-Tashnag groups, however, the sending of this telegram violated the protocol that all official communiqués from Armenian Americans to the outside world must come via the Armenian National Union rather than independently from component organizations. That telegram, moreover, represented a failure to recognize Nubar's delegation at Paris as the bargaining agent for western Armenia. "We hope," an *Azk* editorial declared, "that this error of the Tashnagtsiutiun is not the result of any anti-ANU policy adopted in their latest deputational meeting, but rather came out of reckless and thoughtless enthusiasm."[25]

The next controversy actually spelled the end of the ANU. It began at the start of 1919 when Boghos Nubar Pasha asked the Armenian community in the United States to send four delegates to an Armenian National Congress convening in Paris in tandem with the peace conference. At first the Armenian National Union's Central Committee, in which the Tashnag party was consistently an outnumbered minority, intended to choose the delegates itself—a procedure consistent with what other communities in the diaspora were doing, and seemingly sensible for the short time they had. Vehement protest from the Tashnag and the Hunchags party leaders, however, prompted the ANU's leadership to change course and announce a general election. In the weeks that followed, three tickets of candidates took shape. One, of course, was the Tashnag party. Second was a coalition, or "bloc," of the usual anti-Tashnag groups, namely the Apostolic Church, the Evangelical Church, the AGBU, and the Ramgavar party. The Reformed Hunchags, who opposed the Tashnags but also felt slighted by the "bloc," set up their own ticket, which received little attention. The Hunchags party, also feeling slighted, sat out the elections completely.[26]

The parties and the "bloc" drew up their respective platforms. All agreed that the perpetrators of the 1915 atrocities must be brought to justice and that Armenians living in Turkish orphanages and harems must be released from Turkey. They diverged, however, when it came to territorial priorities. The Tashnag platform called for the recognition of the republic as an independent state, with protection but not control from the League of Nations. The "bloc" platform neither explicitly endorsed nor repudiated the present government of the republic, but it put the emphasis more on securing the territory of the historic Armenian regions of Turkey and called for the creation of an executive committee consisting of Boghos Nubar Pasha and six others. Thus, in the Tashnag platform, "Armenia" was synonymous with the existing republic, expandable but solid, whereas the "bloc" platform conceived of Armenia as a soon-to-be constituted political entity. In the days leading up to the early April elections, the competing presses campaigned vigorously for their respective slates. The Tashnag arguments printed in *Hairenik* made clear that the party regarded "the Armenian people" and the revolutionary struggles of the ARF as interchangeable concepts, and painted elements of the anti-Tashnag bloc as corrupt and disloyal. The editorial page of *Azk* returned the compliment, one *Azk* editorial warning that if Tashnags, with their socialist orientation, dominated the convocation at Paris they would endanger "the likelihood of establishing a government founded on democratic principles," implying of course that Armenia did not currently have such a government.[27]

It would appear, from some rough estimating, that about 44 percent of eligible Armenian voters went to the polls and that their votes were fairly evenly distributed between the Tashnag and bloc candidates, with not all voters voting straight-ticket. After the election, it looked at first as if all four Tashnag candidates had won. However, after the other parties alleged fraud, a commission investigating the returns drew up a revised set of results, sending two Tashnags and two "bloc" members (one Apostolic and one Ramgavar). The Armenian National Union put its seal of approval on the new slate, revoking the credentials of two Tashnag delegates (one of whom had already arrived in Paris). Recriminations flew in all directions, and the ANU crumbled within the year.[28]

And yet, even as Armenians fought fiercely among themselves during these years, they kept their quarrels in the family. During and after the Great War, politicians and the public in both America and Europe generally thought that a united front was addressing them about the Armenian cause. Leaders received a steady flow of letters and telegrams, some signed with recognizably Armenian names, others coming from sympathizers of prominence who were not Armenian. Letterhead names such as the Armenian Press Bureau, the Armenian National Union, the Armenia America Society, and the American Committee for the Independence of Armenia became familiar. The message coming from these and other sources seemed clear, simple, and consistent: the Armenians had suffered much, they represented a bulwark of Christianity and civilization in the Near East, they were contributing to Allied victory in the Great War, and for all these reasons they deserved a free, independent, and well-defended nation-state, comprising historically Armenian lands taken from both the Russian and the Ottoman empires.[29]

One of the more prominent spokesmen for the community—and quite controversial within it—was Vahan Cardashian, founding head of the American Committee for the Independence of Armenia. Born in Caesaria to a family of modest means in 1883, Cardashian migrated to the United States as a young man and received a law degree from Yale in 1908. He then held several positions with the Ottoman government, including High Commissioner for the Turkish exhibitions at the American-sponsored Panama-Pacific Universal Exposition at San Francisco in 1914–15. When he learned of Turkish atrocities against Armenians, including the deportation of his own family, he resigned his commission in a fury, reportedly throwing the decorations he had received from the Turkish government into the Turkish minister's face in Washington. He then began serving in Tashnag institutions in the United States, heading the Armenian Press Bureau prior to ACIA. Working closely with Cardashian at ACIA was his friend, former senator and former ambassador to Turkey James G. Gerard. Though Gerard showed no interest in Armenian partisan allegiances, Cardashian was very much a Tashnag.[30]

Figure 1.3 Vahan Cardashian, vocal lobbyist for the Armenian cause, aligned with the Armenian Revolutionary Federation (ARF). Photo from V. H. Apelian's blog, vhapelian. blogspot.com.

Two different occasions in 1919 when Armenian spokesmen interacted with political leaders whose cooperation they wanted to enlist illustrate both the appearance and the nonreality of a united front: the famous Paris Peace Conference of the winter and spring and the much less noticed Harding hearings that following September. At Paris, two men, each heading a different delegation, spoke for the Armenians: Avedis Aharonian, a Tashnag, representing the republic, and Boghos Nubar Pasha, the decidedly non-Tashnag appointee of the Catholicos who had been in the city with his entourage for several years already. Their audience understood them to represent two parts of historic Armenia, eastern and western; it was not so clear that they also represented two competing partisan factions that claimed to speak for Armenia as a whole. Aharonian, in his speech, called for "reunion of the *republic* with the Armenian provinces of Turkey" (emphasis added); Nubar, in subtle contrast, declared that "independent Armenia" should include all of the Armenian sections of the Ottoman Empire plus "*the territory of* the Armenian Republic of the Caucasus *the population of which* demands union with its brothers in Turkey under one single Armenian state" (emphasis added). Nubar also, in addressing the high rate of success enjoyed by Armenian merchants of the region, presented his data as evidence "that they are quite capable of governing themselves *when the time comes for them to set up an independent state*" (emphasis added). In the concluding portion of his speech, broaching a subject completely absent from the speech of his counterpart, Nubar also noted, "From the first I have also asked that the Great Protecting Powers should give a mandate to one or other of them to administer and organise Armenia."[31] (*Mandate* was the term for the guardianship arrangements over former colonies of defeated powers that came out of the postwar conferences.)[32] The delegates of the world powers hearing Nubar's speech may well not have noticed that his meticulously chosen words betrayed an utter absence of committing himself to recognize the republic's political legitimacy.

Likewise, Armenian notables in the United States appeared to be united, even while being anything but, when they appeared before a Senate subcommittee in session from September 27 to October 19, 1919, chaired by future president Warren G. Harding. Before this committee lay a resolution introduced by Mississippi Democratic senator John Sharp Williams that would essentially guarantee Armenian control of the full swath of its historic homeland. The senators listened to harrowing reports of Armenian suffering as well as assurances from Miran Sevasly that the Armenians could raise between seven and ten thousand from among their own immigrant and American-born population to defend Armenia under this plan. Moses Gulesian mentioned the officer training he had received in 1915 at Plattsburg. Cardashian, along with representatives of the republic, also spoke, not mentioning the idea of a mandate, but asking for recognition and aid for the republic.[33]

On the surface, these men appeared to present a united front. But purportedly, non-Tashnag attorney M. Vartan Malcom opined that Armenia needed the American flag hoisted up on Armenian soil and a capable man put at the head of a temporary government. (The transcript of the hearings does not include this precise remark, though it does show Sevasly as favoring a protective mandate.) In response to Malcom's reported statement, an editorial in *Hairenik* raised the question of how it would seem if a delegation of Americans were to go to Paris and suggest that the French government take over the governance of the United States. "Would it not be the greatest and blackest betrayal of the fatherland?" The editorial proceeded to impugn at length the character and the credentials of Malcom, and of Sevasly and Gulesian, who also testified before the committee.[34]

Indeed, Armenian spokespersons only concealed their differences from those who could not read Armenian. The press of their mother tongue made no attempts to be subtle about the feud. In April and May 1917, as Congress debated the Espionage Act, a clause empowering the president to censor the press in the name of the national interest (which did not make it into the final draft of the bill) evoked a hue and cry of indignation from editors and publishers nationwide. The editorial page of *Azk*, however, had a different reaction. *Azk* used this debate as occasion to reflect and muse over the fact that, while the American government could take punitive action against newspapers that did harm to the American cause, there existed no authority that could discipline the Armenian press organs in America that damaged the Armenian cause and provided aid and comfort to the cause's enemies. The following year, *Hairenik* voiced precisely that same rueful sentiment on its own editorial page. Ultimately, both editorials noted, since no force of law could prevent such misdeeds, Armenian press organs needed to be bound by force of conscience from engaging in disloyalty to their nation's interests. In writing these admonitions, the two papers had very specific transgressors in mind: each other.[35]

The partisan schism continued to doom all efforts at unity in fundraising in the community to failure. Late in 1919, when General Hakob Bagratuni, who represented the republic, and General Antranik Ozanian, formerly of the Tashnag party but now closely aligned with Boghos Nubar Pasha and well-known among Armenians, arrived in the United States to raise funds for the defense of Armenia, it did not take long for their united appeal to split into two competing fund drives, when it became evident to Tashnags that Antranik's "Salvation Fund Drive" would be channeling most of the proceeds through agents other than the republic's own government and military. As with other issues, a war of editorials ensued.[36]

The argument is not being made here that the Armenians lost the chance to control their homeland's future by quarreling over it. That is emphatically *not* what happened. The significance of the partisan conflict lies, not in its effect on the future of Armenia, but rather in the central role that it played in the dynamics of Armenian diasporan life in America and elsewhere. While the parties peddled to their constituents in the diaspora the fiction that their allegiance to the right faction would make a happy future for Armenia, their homeland's actual future lay in the hands of non-Armenians—including the peacemakers at various European cities in 1919 and 1920, and also including Russian and Turkish leaders and American voters.

- 4 -

When the war ended in November 1918, many Armenians and their supporters expected the world's powers to feel, and thus pay, a debt of gratitude to Armenians for their help with the winning of the war. The Armenian newspapers could now finally announce, not only that the Armenian Legion existed, but that it had defeated Turkish troops in a September 1918 engagement, the Battle of Arara, garnering a statement of public praise for their bravery from no less a personage than General Allenby.[37] As the world's leaders, including US president Woodrow Wilson, prepared to converge on Paris, one might have believed that a broad consensus existed among policymakers for giving the needs of Armenia high priority. The United States Inquiry, a presidential advisory commission formed in 1917 to look ahead to the peace process, with up-and-coming journalist Walter Lippmann serving as its secretary, had written on December 22 of that year of the need for "autonomy for Armenia and the protection of Palestine, Syria, Mesopotamia and Arabia by the civilized nations." Wilson himself, a month later in Point 12 of his heralded Fourteen Points speech, had asserted that "the other nationalities which are now under Turkish rule should be assured an undoubted security of life and an absolutely unmolested opportunity of autonomous development." Both Britain and France expressed similar sentiments. The British Foreign Office said in a November 21 memorandum that, in counting the Armenian population for entitlement to land, "the dead and exiles should be taken into account."[38]

That principle would prove hard to sustain when push came to shove, as would all of the other notions on which Armenians set their hopes. For one thing, though the Armenian press touted General Allenby's commendation of the volunteer legion and made its victory at Arara look like a major event in the winning of the war, that battle was actually peripheral and diversionary in the grand scheme of the Anglo-French campaign for the Middle East, and did not give the Armenians any bargaining chips at peace tables. One might also have seen foreshadowings of the gap between ideals and realpolitik in the terms of the Mudros Armistice reached with Turkey by Great Britain and France in October 1918. On a list of garrisons from which the Turks must evacuate, it called for "the withdrawal of troops from Cilicia, except those necessary to maintain order," as if the Turkish government's method of maintaining order in Armenian provinces had already been forgotten. Frustration of the Armenian cause would continue over the next several years.[39]

Paradoxically in light of the years of Turkish denial and self-exoneration that have followed, right after the war one could find strong elements of condemnation of the atrocities against Armenians in the Turkish press, public opinion, and government. Historian Vahakn N. Dadrian, in chronicling this period in Turkey, observes that a population suffering total defeat is in less of a position than otherwise to indulge in defiance and denialism. Talaat Pasha, denying his own decision-making role in the atrocities, decried the "evil deeds" of the empire's authorities at the local level and expressed regret that "we failed to prevent the murder of these Armenians who had no involvement in rebellious activities." General Mustafa Pasha, presiding over the courts martial, described the murders and rapes graphically and said that his fellow Turks had "subjected the Armenians to intolerable conditions, such as no other people had ever experienced throughout history." A flurry of Turkish newspaper editorials called the CUP to task for the mass killings. Animated and heated hearings took place in the Chamber of Deputies in November and December, followed by arrests of ninety persons in late January and early February. Court-martials followed throughout 1919 and 1920. Eighteen persons were sentenced to death, of whom only three were still in the country to execute.[40] Those sentenced in absentia included the CUP leaders, several of whom were assassinated by Armenians within the next few years.

When the peace conference convened at Paris, humanitarian relief work was already underway. It was needed: Armenians were dying by the thousands. Near East Relief, under the directorship of James Levi Barton, intensified its efforts, and Congress appropriated a hundred million dollars and created the temporary American Relief Administration (ARA), which Wilson appointed Herbert Hoover to head. Two different American fact-finding missions visited the provinces of the former Ottoman Empire in the summer of 1919, one dispatched by the peace conference, the other by Wilson. The first, headed by Henry Churchill King, president of Oberlin College, and Charles Richard Crane, a retired industrialist, was originally intended to have inter-Allied representation but ended up being solely American. Touring a large area of the former Ottoman Empire, King and Crane interviewed many Turks, Kurds, Bulgarians, Greeks, and Armenians. Their report, among other points that it made, recommended creation of a separate Armenian state combining territory from both former Turkish and Russian rule, protected by a mandatory power, ideally the United States. In response to the continued horror stories from the region, Wilson sent another commission after his return home from Paris, this one headed by Major-General James G. Harbord, who had led American troops in key battles in France the previous year. The Harbord report confirmed the reports of Armenian misery and danger, though adding that Kurds also had good reason to be terrified of Armenians, and recommended a single, unitary mandate over the combined broad swath of historic Turkey and historic Armenia. That idea, though Armenians could only look on it with horror, was gaining currency in both military and missionary circles.[41]

President Wilson had agreed at Paris to ask Congress to accept an American protective mandate over Armenia, but he ultimately viewed the Versailles Treaty and the League of Nations as most important to the fulfillment of America's duty to the unfortunate Armenians. In his speaking tour in September 1919, where he tried to rally popular support for treaty ratification (which ultimately failed), he mentioned the Armenians several times as a people worthy of solicitude and help, with the implication that his plan would make this a reality. All that his tour achieved, however, was a stroke that left him incapacitated for his remaining years. Meanwhile, it proved impossible to get two-thirds of the Senate to agree on whether to ratify the Versailles Treaty with or without the Lodge Reservations, a set of fourteen stipulations preserving Congress's power to keep the country free from commitment to future foreign entanglements. Thus, the Senate never ratified the treaty, and the United States never joined the League of Nations.[42]

In League circles, there was talk in the early spring of 1920 of possibly creating a nonstate, probably US-based nonprofit organization that could assume the functions of a protective mandate over Armenia, but that idea ultimately came to naught. In May, Wilson sent a message to Congress asking authorization for the US government to accept the mandate. "I believe," he told the lawmakers, "that it would do nothing less than arrest the hopeful processes of civilization if we were to refuse the request to become the helpful friends and advisers of such of these people as we may be authoritatively and formally requested to guide and assist." The Senate not only voted down his proposal but passed a resolution, authored by the president's arch-nemesis Henry Cabot Lodge, chastising him for making it. Senator Lodge, in his capacity as one of the ACIA's executive board members, had cosigned at least one telegram to Wilson in 1919 urging him to remember the Armenians while at Paris. Now, he seemed to suggest that Wilson was remembering them a little too much. Congress did, however, pass an act extending recognition to the Armenian republic—for all the good it did.[43]

On August 10, 1920, the government of Turkey signed the Treaty of Sèvres. The map of Armenia as imagined by the European leaders had shrunk bit by bit during the first half of the year, during gatherings at London and then at San Remo, Italy. Still, the treaty seemed somewhat promising for Armenians, or at least better than nothing. It bound Turkey to recognize Armenia "as a free and independent State," and bound all parties concerned to accept the boundaries of independent Armenia that the delegates at San Remo had asked President Wilson to draw.[44] Wilson, working through an appointed commission (while much debilitated from his stroke), made good on that request: he returned a report in November of that year, producing a map of what came to be called "Wilsonian Armenia," which confirmed a considerable portion of the Armenians' land claims.[45]

As a cruel irony, President Wilson issued his findings at a time when the actual border was moving in the other direction and the republic itself was about to topple. The Turkish nationalist regime of Mustafa Kemal that very same month reached a secret accord with Vladimir Lenin's government of Soviet Russia, wherein the latter ceded back to Turkey the two provinces of Kars and Ardahan that czarist Russia had gained in the Russo-Turkish War of 1877–8 and that, at present, were being governed as part of the Armenian republic. In late September, Turkish troops moved in on that region. At the same time as it was attacked from the west, the government of Armenia was receiving pressure from amassing Soviet troops to the east. The Turks at that time were fighting against the Greeks in Anatolia, and Soviet forces desired passage via the Armenian railway to join the Turkish forces engaged in this campaign. When the government at Yerevan refused to grant this, as well as other concessions involving the repudiation of the provisions of the Sèvres treaty and breaking of relations with the western Allies, the Soviet army invaded. As of mid-October, the Armenian republic was heavily besieged from both sides.[46]

The Armenian government at Yerevan appealed in vain for American and Allied assistance. Far from allowing Armenia membership and affording it protection against enemy attack, the League of Nations, with heavy domination from none other than Great Britain, France, and Italy, denied Armenia membership on the very grounds that its status as a sovereign nation was in jeopardy in the face of the Soviet onslaught.[47] The Tashnag regime desperately capitulated on December 2, 1920, yielding Kars and Ardahan to the Kemalist Turkish government and surrendering its own government to a Soviet-installed junta of five Bolsheviks (the dominant Communist party) and two Tashnags. For the moment, the status of Armenia was that of an "independent Soviet republic" rather than an integral part of the nation-state governed from Moscow, and toleration for Tashnag partisans was assured. Within the week, however, the Revolutionary Committee of the Armenian Bolshevik party arrived at Yerevan, arrested Tashnag leaders, sent General Drastamat "Dro" Ganayan (who had ruled the country for that four-day interim) and other Armenian army officers into exile, and by December 21 had proclaimed Armenia to be subject to all laws of Soviet Russia. Wilson's diplomatic efforts continued into the new year, but on March 12, 1921, the Allied premiers formally repudiated the provisions of the Sèvres treaty as well as the Wilsonian plan for an expanded, independent Armenia.[48]

From late December into January 1921, the Communist regime went on a spree of confiscating and nationalizing property in Armenia, while also failing to allow adequate food supplies to come into the country in these winter months. Turkish troops, meanwhile, were committing more massacres in Kars and Alexandropol. On February 18, those Tashnags who were not in prison staged an all-out insurrection against Soviet rule, briefly gaining control of Yerevan. The Red Army returned to Yerevan on April 2, after putting down a rebellion in Georgia, and routed the Tashnag rebels from the capital city. By summer the entire insurrection had been suppressed. The Soviet government did, however, somewhat slow down in its controlling and transformative demands on Armenia.[49]

At least as devastating to the Armenian cause was the shift in Allied policy toward Turkey. Ironically, the one action taken at Paris that seemed at the time like a move to keep Turkey down and build its enemies up had precisely the opposite effect. In May 1919, British prime minister David Lloyd George and Wilson gave Greece their blessing to land its own occupation troops in the Turkish-controlled, largely Greek- and Armenian-inhabited city of Smyrna. They did so as a preemptive move against Italy, which they knew was poised to invade and had designs on ever-growing portions of Anatolia. They took into consideration, as well, the reports of fresh Turkish atrocities against Christian populations in Anatolia. Greek forces arrived at Smyrna, with British and French naval help, on May 14 and 15. In the fighting that ensued, Turks and Greeks—long-time enemies—committed atrocities against each other. These campaigns, far from making Turkey any weaker, helped accelerate the rise of the Nationalists led by Mustafa Kemal, soon popularly known as Atatürk.[50]

Events of 1920 showed the contradictory nature of allied objectives with Turkey. French diplomats had haggled at Paris for the right to occupy Cilicia as stipulated in the Sykes-Picot accord, and in the fall of 1919 British troops had stepped aside to let the French move in. To the great consternation of the Turks, the occupying force included two Armenian battalions from the Armenian Legion. The Armenians, it should be remembered, understood this as a step toward permanent control of Cilicia for themselves. During this same stretch of time, Turkish governing forces loyal to the Sultan found themselves increasingly challenged by Kemal's Nationalists. Taking advantage of perceived French weakness and wanting to show extreme resistance to the occupation, Kemalists massacred possibly as many as five thousand Armenians, burning several churches where women and children had sought refuge. The French military proved unequal to securing Cilicia from such atrocities, and in fact made a temporary strategic retreat at the worst possible time. The Allies, viewing Kemal's insurgency as a threat to their own control of the defeated Sick Man of Europe, sent troops on March 16 to occupy Constantinople—precisely where the locus of Nationalist hegemony was *not*—and encouraged Greek forces to make still further assaults at Smyrna.[51]

As the war era gave way to the 1920s, Allied determination to treat Turkey as a vanquished enemy gave way to a new set of interests that militated for a shift toward rapprochement. None of this did anything good for the Armenians or, for that matter, the Greeks. The Treaty of Sèvres, though appearing on paper to weaken Turkey, only strengthened it by energizing popular support for the Kemalist regime, which at this point had far more will to fight for territory than the Allies had to restrain it. In October of 1921 France signed a separate accord with the Kemalists at Angora that provided, among other concessions, for French withdrawal from Cilicia—a betrayal of precisely those assurances that the volunteers in the Armenian Legion had counted on as their purpose for serving in that army. The Angora accord, a far cry from what Sykes and Picot had promised Nubar back in 1916, read like an exchange of mutual courtesies between equals. The Greeks, meanwhile, having landed at the city of Smyrna in 1919 with the full blessing of the Allies, were making incursions in other parts of the former Ottoman Empire and threatened to besiege Constantinople, slaughtering Turks in the process. The resulting fury in Turkey significantly boosted the rise of Atatürk to both military and political power. By 1922, the Allies had largely obtained what they needed in the way of territory via the mandate system, and their relations with Greece had also greatly chilled following a regime change in Athens.[52]

Thus, instead of securing their victory over Turkey in the Great War, Britain and France had given Turkey a new war and let her win it. The result was another chapter in the genocide, this time not limited to Armenians. In September 1922, Atatürk's freshly energized troops moved in on Smyrna, massacred several thousand Armenian and Greek civilians, and burned much of the city while American and British officials merely evacuated their own nationals from the city and, with some exceptions, left the rest to their fate, including many refugees who had escaped slaughter in 1915. In November of 1922, the Sultan fled Constantinople on a British destroyer, now making Atatürk's regime at Angora definitively the only government Turkey had.[53]

With the terms of Sèvres clearly null and void, the Powers convened another conference at Lausanne, Switzerland. Occurring in several stages from November 23, 1922, through July 17, 1923, it resulted in a new treaty between Turkey and the European Allies amounting to normalization of relations. Turkey promised to respect the rights of foreigners doing business in Turkey and of religious and ethnic minorities within its borders (the document did not mention Armenians by name), and to protect the rights of foreign schools, missions, and charities operating within its borders. The treaty gave control over the Bosporus and Dardanelles to an International Straits Commission under League of Nations auspices. The United States, though not a party to the treaty negotiations, had a delegation of observers there. The Turkish and Greek delegations also signed an agreement on January 30, 1923, providing for a population swap. Starting May 1 of the following year, Greek nationals living in Turkey (though not including Constantinople) would relocate to Greece, and Turkish nationals in most parts of Greece would cross the same border the other way. Among the side effects of the migration agreement was the displacement of many Armenian refugees in Greece.[54]

While Europeans and Turks deliberated at Lausanne, the Armenian lobby divided again over one of the proposals under discussion: the idea of an Armenian National Home, a quarter for Armenians within Turkish borders with national self-determination and autonomy. George Montgomery, head of the Armenia America Society, proposed the idea in 1921 as an effort at salvaging something for the Armenians on Turkish-controlled soil, in light of the collapse of the Sèvres accord. As Montgomery initially expressed it in a telegram to the State Department, it should "develop into an Armenian Commonwealth and ultimately be reunited with the liberated Caucasian Armenian Republic." Yet another gathering of Armenians and their sympathizers was held in New York, at the Cathedral of St. John the Divine on February 6. At this time France still had some pretense of control in Cilicia, but it was slipping, and as Walter George Smith told the crowd, Armenian lives were in imminent danger. Those in attendance passed resolutions appealing to the delegates who were about to meet in London to make the saving of Armenian lives a priority, either with this plan or with strict enforcement of the Sèvres treaty. Boghos Nubar Pasha, still based in Paris, favored the National Home plan. In a cable to James Gerard on April 16, 1921, he wrote, "The National Delegation wants single independent Armenia such as defined by the Treaty of Sevres with boundaries approximately corresponding to those delimited by President Wilson, and therefore consisting of both Russian and Turkish Armenia." However, he continued, recent developments had created a moral imperative for supporting the National Home proposal even while aspiring for those greater goals in the longer run. "Those who accuse us of wishing to renounce our ideal of a united and independent Armenia, and to create a dualism," he concluded, "are demonstrating if not their bad faith, at least a singular lack of understanding of the realities." The newly reconstituted Armenian Democratic Liberal, or Ramgavar, party campaigned for it through its press organs. The editors at *Hairenik*, along with Gerard and Cardashian, opposed it.[55]

As noted before, one would err to suppose that more agreement among Armenians in the diaspora would have produced a better outcome. The prospect of getting the Turkish delegation to go along with the Armenian Home plan was dead on arrival, and the Allied delegates knew it. They did raise the issue, leading the Turkish delegate at one point to storm out of the room in fury, but an entry that US delegate Joseph C. Grew made in his journal on January 9, 1923, illuminates much. As the delegates were making ready to draft a treaty, he noted, "it has not been determined whether it is wise to present only clauses upon which the Allies intend to insist or to include matters such as the National Armenian Home, upon which they will give way."[56]

After the signing of the European treaty, Grew, who was also the US ambassador to the host country of Switzerland, remained at Lausanne to negotiate a Treaty of Amity and Commerce between Turkey and the United States. This second Lausanne treaty extended many of the provisions of the European accord to American-Turkish relations, especially facilitating trade and travel between the countries on equitable terms, and abrogating the capitulations (the former assurances of immunity from actions in the Turkish courts for Western nationals doing business on Turkish soil, though certain safeguards remained in place). As with the European treaty, this one guaranteed the safety of American philanthropic, religious, and educational institutions in Turkey but made no direct reference to Armenians. As the public knew, American corporate interests, including a father-son team named Chester, anxiously looked forward to normalization of relations so they could get their hands on Turkey's oil, among other resources.[57]

President Calvin Coolidge presented the Lausanne treaty between the United States and Turkey to the Senate for ratification almost a year later, on May 3, 1924. Debate dragged on for three years before the full body acted decisively on it. The division was largely partisan, and the Democratic platform of 1924 contained this explicit plank:

> We condemn the Lausanne treaty. It barters legitimate American rights and betrays Armenia, for the Chester oil concessions.
>   We favor the protection of American rights in Turkey and the fulfillment of President Wilson's arbitral award respecting Armenia.[58]

The issue received much attention and press coverage. Two sets of advocacy groups lobbied in favor of ratification: those who saw normal relations with Turkey as serving the nation's (and/or their own) economic interests, and those connected with missionary work in Turkey who believed it would facilitate their vital work. The latter group included James Barton of Near East Relief. James G. Gerard, still working closely with Vahan Cardashian, made appearances and wrote letters opposing it. At one New York rally, Rabbi Stephen Wise called the Lausanne accord "an abject and humiliating surrender on the part of civilization to Turkey," and further opined, "The fact that we even consider this treaty means that we are losing our ideals. Are two or three Christian colleges in Asia Minor more important than the beatitudes?" A month before Coolidge formally transmitted the treaty to the Senate, on April 5, an audience of about eight hundred packed the Hotel Astor in New York for a debate that almost became physical. In the Senate, William H. King spoke for the opposition when, after a visit to Turkey, he declared, "The treaty which we are asked to ratify ignores the Armenians completely" and characterized the Kemalist movement as pan-Islamist and anti-Christian.[59]

For obvious reasons, Armenian Americans did not like the Lausanne treaty. However, even here, they did not speak with one voice. Cardashian, of course, enjoying Tashnag support, spoke out vehemently against it. In several letters and other statements in the *New York Times*, he sought to remind readers that a large part of the Mosul district of oil fields, affected by the Chester concessions, belonged to Armenia according to the Treaty of Sèvres and the Wilson award, and that Atatürk had presided over a high volume of massacres of Armenians. But the Ramgavar party organ *Baikar*, in an editorial calling Cardashian a charlatan, railed against the anti-Lausanne campaign as bringing contempt and scorn on the Armenian community. "Why," the editorial asked, when foreigners faced hostile critics in America as elsewhere, "do we furnish them with proof that we want the U.S. government to measure and shape its foreign relations according to our needs?"[60]

In a Senate vote taken in executive session in January 1927, the Lausanne accord came six votes short of the two-thirds majority needed to ratify it. However, an exchange of notes at the executive level carried essentially the same effect as the treaty, and in 1927 Joseph Grew took up residence in Istanbul as America's first ambassador to the new regime. Cardashian continued to speak up. In a series of letters to Coolidge, he lectured the president on constitutional law. If the president could override the Senate's rejection of a treaty, he opined in one note, "he would then defeat both the letter and spirit of the Constitution: he would rob the Senate of its concurrent voice in the making of treaties." A later epistle added, "It is most distressing that the President of the United States should be led into doing a thing, which is clearly in violation of the fundamental law of the land."[61]

- 5 -

Besides the personal attributes of Vahan Cardashian, as Armenians entered the 1920s, they disagreed along Tashnag/anti-Tashnag lines on a more fundamental question: how to respond to the absorption of Armenia into the Soviet state. This dominated the discourse of the partisan rivalry for years to come and permeated every aspect of political and social life among the *Hayoutiun*. Moreover, because the Armenian

Apostolic Church had its Holy See with the man known as Catholicos of All Armenians at Echmiadzin, which lay under Soviet rule, the question of the legitimacy of the Soviet state was linked closely with rivalries within the church and with questions of how far the authority of the Catholicos—who so clearly spoke and acted under the tight constraints of the Soviet state—could be honored, especially in matters where the spiritual realm converged with the temporal. That conflict would boil over in 1933, and would continue to boil for the decades that followed.

One thing Armenians shared in the aftermath of the war regardless of party lines was the sense of profound betrayal. They had come out of the war seeing themselves, and reasonably so, as the nationality group that enjoyed the greatest amount of international sympathy, with thoughtful people in the United States, Britain, and other victorious countries regarding them as a brave, virtuous, and long-suffering people who deserved a free, independent, and well-defended homeland for all that they had endured. Many an Armenian coffeehouse displayed the drawing of Woodrow Wilson with his map of Wilsonian Armenia for some years to come. Armenians had soon learned, however, that sympathy and admiration did not give them political capital against the harsh exigencies of global power politics and national self-interest of the countries from which they thought they could expect better. Writing in the June 29, 1921, issue of the *New Republic*, Aghavnie Yeghenian summed up the collective mood. "We cry in anguish and pain. We show our wounds. We call for help. The crowd on the shore throw out some handfuls of pennies which fall leaden into the waters.

Figure 1.4 An illustration of Armenians' wishful thinking after the war. By the time Wilson released this map, Armenia's territory was already shrinking, not expanding. Photo from the program of the World Armenian Congress, New York, 1947, courtesy of National Association for Armenian Studies and Research (NAASR), Belmont, MA.

Our cry has not been understood." Yeghenian recalled a cartoon she had seen in an American magazine, "showing the gaunt figure of Armenia disturbing the peace of a fat congressman who, handkerchief to his eyes, exclaims, 'Get out. You are breaking my heart.'" She found the betrayal by France and Russia, and inaction by the United States, more hurtful than the Turkish massacres. "To be an Armenian in America is to be bitterly disappointed," she lamented. "To this country, this America so beloved, so rich, free, happy, it seems impossible to import the sadness of an Armenian's life."[62]

At the same time that Armenians fought partisan conflicts and smoldered with resentment at the powers over the outcome of the war, they made lives for themselves as immigrants and as descendants of immigrants in the United States, which meant making lives for themselves as Armenians and Americans, navigating what exactly that meant. It is to that theme that this book turns next.

Years of Adjustment

Armenian Americans in the 1920s

The 1920s represented a decade of settling in for Armenian Americans in their lives as an ethnic community in a modern cosmopolitan society. With both the genocide (though the word had not yet come into existence) and the brief moment of an independent republic (for those who had considered it significant) now behind them in memory, Armenians in the United States turned simultaneously to advancing their lives in America and making sense out of their recent history. The Armenian American press continued to report on the latest developments from both Soviet Armenia and the Armenian diaspora. The constant notices about this or that local club having a meeting or a banquet, often for the benefit of some part of the homeland, made clear the collective sense of a vibrant Armenian community in the United States. At the same time, behind the closed doors of individual homes, Armenian parents and children negotiated and navigated the same challenges of cultural change and erosions of tradition that faced other immigrant groups and, for that matter, the American population as a whole.

- 1 -

Some Armenians who lost their families in 1915 needed decades before they could talk about it. Others wanted to do more than talk about it and needed no time to feel ready. Soghomon Tehlirian fell into the latter category. On March 15, 1921, in broad daylight on a busy street in Berlin, Germany, after weeks of careful planning and close observation of his quarry, Tehlirian gunned down Talaat Pasha, one of the principals behind the mass extermination of Armenians. He offered no resistance to his arrest, and made use of his murder trial to remind the world of the great crime of 1915. The jury acquitted him, and Armenians feted him as a hero for decades after.[1]

On July 21, 1922, a trio of Armenians assassinated a second one of the "Three Pashas," Djemal, along with his secretary, in Tbilisi (formerly Tiflis). A month later Enver Pasha met a similar fate. The killings of Talaat and Djemal occurred under the auspices of a Tashnag-orchestrated plan called Operation Nemesis. (Enver was also on the operation's list, but his assassination may have occurred independently.)

Authorized at the Armenian Revolutionary Federation's 1919 World Congress and entrusted largely to the Central Committee of America to plan, Operation Nemesis had several prominent American-based Armenians involved as leaders, including Armen Garo, Shahan Natalie, and Aaron Sachaklian. Not everybody at that 1919 congress had agreed with this method of justice-seeking. Representatives of the government of the republic—Simon Vratsian, Rouben Der Minasian, and Rouben Darbinian—believed that the republic's survival depended on some attempt at friendly relations with Turkey. That persuasion did not prevail, however. Although only a handful of assassinations were actually carried out—eight Turks and three Armenians deemed traitors—the list of possible candidates for execution reached a hundred.[2]

Miles away, at the University of Lvov in Poland, a young Jewish student named Rafel Lemkin had a heated exchange with a professor right after Talaat's assassination over the absence of any legal forum in which Talaat could have stood trial for mass murder. The professor reportedly attempted to explain the supreme importance of a nation's sovereignty with the analogy of a man owning chickens and choosing to kill them. "Why not? It is not your business. If you interfere, it is trespass." Lemkin, to the displeasure of his mentor, replied that "Sovereignty ... cannot be conceived as the right to kill millions of innocent people." Lemkin subsequently attained a law degree, migrated to the United States (changing his first name to Raphael in the process), coined the word *genocide*, and spearheaded a campaign for the United Nations Genocide Convention (see Chapter 8).[3]

The genocide had left an estimated 140,000 Armenian children orphaned. Many had been forcibly adopted by Turkish families and compelled to accept a new nationality and religion as their own.[4] Many thousands more lived in orphanages. Leon Surmelian, living briefly in an orphanage in Constantinople, watched as one day an emissary arrived from Baghdad and announced that the Armenian Women's Club of Baghdad was looking to take two boys with artistic promise and whisk them off to the finest schools of Europe. "The musicians among us," Surmelian recalled years later, "took out their violins, flutes, trumpets and started practicing them vehemently. Others painted furiously." The representative of the benefactors returned, took stock of the various talents, and chose one of the portrait painters along with Surmelian's violin-playing brother. Surmelian himself earned a scholarship in Kansas with his poetry, and commanded sufficient respect from his peers that they took up a collection to buy his discounted steamship ticket. One six-year-old boy in an Adana orphanage who spoke four languages caught the affections of YMCA missionary Reverend B. R. Gabriel of Hamilton, New York, who had lost a son of his own; Reverend Gabriel adopted him and escorted him to America. Helene Pilibosian recalls in her memoir that her grandfather facilitated the entry of two girls, at least one of whom was his niece, by pretending they were his daughters; his real daughters had been killed in the genocide. She describes this practice as common, though at variance with the law.[5]

During these years, a number of Armenian men in America who had wives overseas used their resources to bring them over. For many of the unmarried Armenian girls orphaned or otherwise destitute, the best hope for passage and entry into the United States was arranged marriage. As it happened, with the number of

Figure 2.1 Cousins Elmas Kashmanian (later Sakalian), Serpouhi Derderian, and Musgunaz Kashmanian, survivors of the Armenian Genocide, at an orphanage in Adana, Turkey, 1921. Project SAVE Armenian Photograph Archives, courtesy of Avadis Sakalian.

single young Armenian women in the United States still quite low, such arrangements were also the best hope for many single Armenian men to get wives. Author David Kherdian's father, Melkon "Mike" Kherdian, of Racine, Wisconsin, and his mother Veron Dumehjian, who along with several family members was a refugee in Greece, became betrothed through the mediating efforts of Melkon's mother, who was also in Greece at the time. Melkon's sponsorship made Veron's trip possible, and they were presently married. Karekin Choghajian, who had lost both parents in the genocide and subsequently suffered the death of his intended wife, asked an intermediary to arrange for a young female orphan to be transported to his adoptive city of Syracuse, New York, to have the option of marrying him if she should so choose. Though the intermediary pulled an unscrupulous move in asking for extra money for her passage over, the arrival of a young woman named Louise was a success and led to a 1920 wedding followed by a lasting marriage. In 1930 Khachadoor Pilibosian sailed to France to marry Yeghsa Haboian, whom he had courted by mail. Yeghsa had lost most of her family in the genocide and lived in two orphanages before earning a nursing degree in Beirut and joining her sister in Paris. Yeghsa's brother Mesrob, already in the United States and friends with Khachadoor, arranged the match. "My father was a very friendly, outgoing man and my mother was very much the opposite," their daughter Helene wrote years later, but "the marriage lasted almost 60 years in spite of many disagreements."[6]

Indeed, a number of picture-bride betrothals took place after the First World War. The *New York Times* reported in August of 1922 that the 1,122 passengers on a ship that had just arrived in New York included 200 Greek and Armenian picture brides. "The young women had donned their best frocks in honor of the event," the writer observed. "When the names 'Mary,' 'Helen,' 'Iona,' and others were called out by the waiting men on the piers the girls, most of whom were brunettes, answered and waved their hands with the photograph." Sadly, by day's end, fifteen heartbroken young Greek and Armenian women had gone unclaimed, seemingly by "the hard-to-please men who had apparently looked over the brides that fortune had sent to them and were not satisfied." They would, according to the article, most likely have to sail back. For those picture brides who did start new lives in the United States and elsewhere, the level of happiness in the marriage ran a wide gamut.[7]

Even before the passage of the restriction laws of 1921 and 1924, immigrants to the United States had to satisfy immigration officials that they possessed means of sustenance and also met some fairly rigid criteria of mental and physical fitness. In April of 1905, a decade before the genocide, Donabet Mousekian, who had already judged Turkey an unsafe place in which to be Armenian and had renounced his Turkish citizenship, was refused entry into the United States as "likely to become a public charge" (the promiscuously applied "LPC clause") by virtue of his lacking normally shaped male genitals and being what the Commissioner at Ellis Island called "repulsive in appearance." That he had a host of employable skills and a family including two gainfully employed brothers—one already a US citizen and the other in the process of becoming one—pledging to keep him off public assistance rolls counted for nothing. He was deported. His ultimate fate is unknown, but he anticipated being killed on sight back in Turkey. There was also an episode in 1921 in which a boat with 300 refugees was about to be sent back to Turkey, and four young women committed suicide by jumping ship, despairing at the thought of returning. That particular boatload, it appears, was eventually admitted as donors materialized to post bond for the unfortunate passengers.[8]

Refugees during these years swelled the populations of Armenian communities already in existence. These spots included New York City, of course, as well as the upstate city of Troy; Jersey City, Hoboken, and other nearby municipalities in New Jersey; the Boston/Watertown area; Worcester, also in Massachusetts; and the notable Midwestern city of Detroit, Michigan. Both before and after the genocide, there were migration chains from specific Turkish points of origin to corresponding American destinations: many from Kharpert settled in Worcester; Pawtucket, Rhode Island, attracted migrants from Van, as did Watertown; and Armenians living in Jersey City and West Hoboken (now Union City), New Jersey, tended to hail from Dikranagerd. Migrants from Musa Dagh, whose old-country work in many instances involved silk, either growing the worms that produced it or weaving the finished product, found livelihoods in American silk factories, such as Cheney Brothers in South

Manchester, Connecticut. When Cheney Brothers began to decline in the 1920s, many of its workers relocated to another silk spot, Paterson, New Jersey. In Detroit, the Armenian population rose from 337 in 1910 to 1,692 in 1920, with the $5 day at Henry Ford's automobile plant serving as a magnet for in-migration. California, including what by now was a thriving agricultural enclave in Fresno, also attracted newcomers. Manoug Adoian and his sister Vartoosh, after coming through Ellis Island and then meeting up with their older sister Akabi in Watertown, both took jobs at the Hood Rubber Company. Manoug's refusal to stop going up to the roof to draw chalk sketches on its surface soon got him fired, which gave him more time to visit the Boston Museum of Fine Art and pick up some ideas; he later became the famous painter Arshile Gorky.[9]

By the 1920s, there was an established economic infrastructure that could play a part in receiving the new settlers into both the Armenian community and the American economy. In the mid-1920s, the city of Syracuse, New York, had nearly twenty self-employed Armenian tailors, including at least two sets of brothers who worked together. Several of these family-owned tailor shops were known for their generosity in accepting newcomers as apprentices and assisting them toward opening their own shops later on. In the Boston area, Stephen Mugar, born Papken Der Mugardichian, who migrated with his family from Kharpert in 1906, owned the growing Star Market chain in the 1920s and employed many Armenian immigrants and their children. In West Hoboken, New Jersey, which merged in June 1925 with Union Hill to become Union City, insurance agent and realtor Haig Simsarian helped many Armenian immigrant families settle into the area. Businesses were sources of information as well as jobs. In 1922 Hovhannes Mugrditchian, newly arrived in the Boston area with a wife and a daughter, no knowledge of English, and a debt to his two brothers-in-law for the passage to America, needed a higher-paying job than he had at a local restaurant. He inquired at an Armenian-run barber shop in Watertown where a barber from Kharpert told him about Hood Rubber. In spite of being told on his first day of standing in line to go to hell (which at first he did not even understand), he returned the next day and was hired.[10]

Much of Armenian American life in the 1920s was still localized: recently arrived Armenians, like other first-generation immigrants, cared enormously about what village they hailed from in the construction of their ethnic identities. Genocide survivor Souren Papazian recalls in his memoir that his life choices in Providence, Rhode Island, were held up to scrutiny not only by his family in Providence but by former neighbors from the village of Havav. American circumstances, however, made village identities less air-tight. "Men from Caesarea worked side by side at the Hood Rubber Company in Watertown with men from Bitlis," Isabel Kaprielian-Churchill writes, "just as men from Palu worked at the White Shoe Company in Lynn with villagers from Keghi." In David Kherdian's truth-based novel about the union of his parents, when friends Mike and Jake are in the local coffeehouse in Racine, Wisconsin, telling the waitress Lucy about Mike's bride Veron who is en route, Lucy sympathetically remarks, "I hope there will be someone from her region for her to talk to when she arrives ... or she will feel lost." Writings about these early years refer to the coming together of Armenians from different regions in a way that underscores how novel such mixing felt.[11]

Gathering of Marsovan natives and their friends in Van Cortlandt Park, Bronx, New York, c. 1927.
(Photo courtesy of Paul Sagsoorian)

Figure 2.2 A gathering of Armenians mostly from the Ottoman town of Marsovan (or Merzivan), sometime in the 1920s. Photo from the collection of Paul Sagsoorian, courtesy of Armenian General Benevolent Union (AGBU).

One of the more overt expressions of village identification was the forming of compatriotic societies, associations whose members shared not only a nationality but a regional origin. These organizations, many of whose members knew each other from their villages, got together for periodic dinners and dances, with the food and music reflecting the world they remembered. Immigrants from villages also had specific concerns for their countryfolk back in the old world. In February 1926, Armenians from Horasan, a village in the province of Sivas, held a gala banquet and raised $150 for the poor of that village. One also frequently heard of a compatriotic society raising money to found a new town in Soviet Armenia to commemorate the former village in the Ottoman Empire. In October of 1925, a group of *Habousetzis* (Armenians from the village of Habousi, in Kharpert province) raised $9,500 to transport *Habousetzi* refugees to Soviet Armenia and establish a village. Several months later a compatriotic union called *Havavi Ousoumnasiragan Ungeroutiun* (the latter two words translating literally to "society for the love of education"), made up of Armenians from the village of Havav in the Palu district of Kharpert province, held a soiree in New York, with featured speakers, singers, and a Russian dance troupe, followed by social dancing into the late hours including both the modern American Charleston and some traditional ethnic dances, to fund the building of a town in Soviet Armenia to be called New Havav.[12]

- 2 -

During the 1920s, both mainstream American society and the immigrant communities had their socially conservative traditionalists who perceived the morals of the youth as endangered. A rather curious paradox arose here: many American conservatives viewed every idea and practice that they disliked as foreign, and accordingly blamed immigrants for contaminating their culture. First-generation immigrants, meanwhile, viewed their host society as the source of decadence and rebellion against traditional morality from which they needed to shield their youth. The reality, of course, was that American culture was changing because America was changing: more Americans now lived in towns and cities rather than the countryside, there was a larger middle class whose male and female offspring could finish high school and go to college, the youth of that growing middle class had more time and money to form peer groups and engage in greater pursuits of recreation and amusement, and a larger-than-ever productive sector, combined with the burgeoning advertising industry, was selling that youth culture (and their elders as well) fashions, cosmetics, automobiles, and all manner of recorded and live entertainment. Most alarming of all, to those of the alarmist persuasion, the gender roles and the sexual norms were changing, though not nearly as fast as some commentators imagined. A rise in liberalized ideas of companionate family relations and romantic love ensured that the 1920s would see a high incidence of what two anthropological scholars later termed "domestic revolutions." Thus, as the more recent Armenian immigrants settled into American life and began raising their American-born families, they had the jazz-and-flapper age for a backdrop. The stage was set for domestic revolutions to play themselves out in Armenian households, as they would in many other immigrant and nonimmigrant homes as well.[13]

As noted, there was already an established Armenian community in the United States by the First World War years. Thus, much of the work of community-building and much adapting of culture and navigating of the American environment had already been done. This ensured a degree of continuity between the prewar and postwar years. At the same time, the mass migration triggered by the genocide and by the sense of danger in the years preceding it infused the Armenian American population of the 1920s with many who were now at the start of the adaptation process. Many, though certainly not all, of the first-generation immigrants had come with memories of a small village homestead with livestock to tend, crop-growing rhythms to follow, and children to find marriage partners for. They had transplanted themselves to America's fast-growing, densely populated, culturally heterogeneous cities.

In the towns and villages of the Ottoman Empire that the immigrant generation knew, arranged marriages were common, as was the tightly ritualized betrothal and nuptial sequence. A boy and a girl would sometimes be pledged to each other while they were still suckling infants, if their families were already linked by bonds of friendship. A young boy's uncle might also be searching out potential brides for him in his travels to neighboring villages. If the marriage had been planned early in the girl's childhood, her family might use her first menstruation as the occasion to solemnize the betrothal. In many instances, though, the negotiations between the families began after the boy and the girl had reached marriage age—still very young, especially for the girl—and included a host of ritualistic amenities. During the discovery period, female members of the boy's family might find an opportunity to study the prospective bride's body in the bathhouse for any blemishes that clothing concealed. If the negotiations proceeded satisfactorily, the families performed a rite of betrothal, usually in the house of the girl's family, sometimes in the church. Amazingly, depending on circumstance and locale, the principals to the transaction might or might not be present for this occasion, though ultimately the boy did present the girl with an engagement ring. In some villages, a pact between the two mothers, called a *khoskgab*, set the rituals into motion.[14]

The age of the groom at the time of the wedding ranged from fifteen to twenty. The bride might be as young as twelve, and was frequently not older than fifteen. Ethnographers have found this to have been influenced by two pragmatic factors: the high infant mortality rate, which militated for an early start in bearing children, and young girls' constant fear of rape by Turkish or Kurdish marauders, who were purported to prefer virgins. The rite spanned several days and involved elaborate preparation in both the bride and the groom's entourage, with an air of solemnity among the bride, her family, and friends, in contrast with the revelry found among the groom's party. After the ceremony, friends of the groom might playfully abduct him for the ransom of a festive dinner. At the end of the evening the couple consummated the marriage, and heaven alone might help the bride if the couple could not display a set of bloodied bed sheets, proof of her erstwhile virginity.[15]

Obviously, many practices that worked in the old world were unsustainable in the new. For the immigrant generation, the big question was what types of influence they could retain over their children where marriage practices and other customs were concerned, and what adaptive institutions they could create in America's towns and cities to keep a distinctive sense of Armenianness even while striving to be good Americans. The 1930s would see much more institutionalized forms of intergenerational outreach at the national level, including the launching of youth organizations and English-language weeklies by the parties and a plethora of youth-oriented social events to keep the American-born Armenians mindful of their Armenianness and connected with an Armenian peer group. The efforts and the dialogue vis-à-vis the youth in the 1920s were the more localized, improvisational version of what would crescendo in the 1930s. Like it or not, a front-page 1926 *Hairenik* article advised readers, "at least in this country," the second generation "is the future of our race, and the master of its destiny tomorrow." Alongside such verbal firebells came strategic actions. The forming of Armenian schools was an immediate priority, though almost invariably these were shoestring operations. In a typical community, a handful of either trained teachers or volunteers ran Saturday-morning classes in church basements and wherever else was available, providing a curriculum of Armenian history, language, folktales, and songs. In the beginning, textbooks usually came from the old country, though at least one textbook was offered by the Boston-based Hairenik Press as early as 1917.[16]

Thanks to two doctoral dissertations, those of social psychologist Richard LaPiere (1930) and of anthropologist Harold Nelson (1953), a particularly rich record of Armenian American cultural dynamics in Fresno County, California, has been preserved. The Fresno community, especially in its rural farming towns, held a number of crucial distinctions from other Armenian communities. The combination of rural environment and large concentration of Armenian inhabitants militated for a stronger defense of old-world customs. Fresno was also the locale in which Armenians were most conscious of prejudice against them by the surrounding society. High concentration of fellow ethnics and high degree of prejudice are two factors that Ewa Morawska cites as working against fast, pervasive assimilation. This should not imply that Fresno's Armenian community saw any shortage of ideas and impulses challenging old-world traditions. Rather, the point is that, because this was the environment where traditions would be more strongly fortified, one can surmise that the celebrated drama of intergenerational struggle between old-world traditionalism and new-world cosmopolitanism played itself out even more acutely here than in more urban, cosmopolitan environments.[17]

LaPiere, who concluded his study in 1930, found that many of the immigrants he interviewed expressed a critique of the surrounding American society as being too loose and decadent, often showing exaggerated impressions on the part of these immigrants of how much liberalization had actually taken place. Armenian immigrants knew a social order in which parental, and especially paternal, authority reigned supreme over the children of a family. As the youth of the surrounding American society gained the image of increasing defiance toward their parents, Armenian youth found themselves caught between two conflicting dictates. One second-generation Armenian told LaPiere, "When the Armenian child comes into contact with the idea that parents are something to be tolerated and evaded he may begin to question the validity of his own attitude," that is, of the instilled veneration for the parents' word. One immigrant father lamented to LaPiere with reference to his children, "They get bad ideas from running around too much with children who haven't proper homes," while another remarked, "Children are given too much freedom here. I do not like the dancing in public which goes on, the way they want to go out at night, and the way that they are sent to school together."[18]

Indeed, for Armenian parents, any tolerance of unchaperoned contact between boys and girls represented a challenge to tradition. Because a bride's virginity on her wedding night was so crucial in old-world tradition, interaction between the sexes had been meticulously regulated. LaPiere reported that the sexual mores "are exceptionally strict and have been clung to by the Armenian immigrants here in America with remarkable fidelity considering the pressures operating against such customs." That boys and girls were seated together in the public schools was a novelty to Armenian children and a source of worry to many of their parents. One respected Fresno community member told LaPiere that Armenian parents constantly asked him, "What can we do to keep our children from the evil influences of American life?" A woman, with her son translating, complained to LaPiere, "Americans have no morals, they are always getting divorced."[19]

In a pattern that would hold up, with modifications, in the more urbane youth culture of the following decade, LaPiere found that members of the young generation of the late 1920s wanted their parents to alter their views, but not to extremes. American-born informants tended to concur with their parents' sense of membership in a culture with inherent virtues that too much Americanization could corrupt. Their ideal, therefore, was not to reject tradition, but to update and modify it. A San Francisco professional who had grown up in the Fresno *Hayoutiun* offered this comparison of Armenian family culture in the American context:

> The Armenian home develops finer values, higher ethical codes, and stronger moral qualities, than can the typical American home for people. It is a stronger influence in the life of the people. Yet it has its detrimental qualities considering the accepted standards of American society. The life of the Armenian youth is stunted. He does not have the contacts and experiences which would give him full social development for the life outside the home which he will have to live.[20]

This notion of an ideal blend between traditional virtue and modern sophistication would reign supreme in much of the discourse of the following decade when youth emerged in larger numbers and had their own English-language editorial pages on which to air their perceptions. It should also be noted that, where gender roles and sexual norms were concerned, the youth culture of the American mainstream wanted to challenge tradition in modest increments rather than by the great leaps and bounds that their conservative elders imagined.[21]

In the evolution of gender-role norms, circumstances as well as customs played some crucial roles. To begin with, Armenian men right along had outnumbered the women. Because of the stigma against marriage to an *odar* (literally the Armenian word for "foreigner," commonly used to mean a non-Armenian), many men had remained single; after the Great War, as has been noted, many bachelors sought wives from abroad, some by picture. With the ratio as it was, a young marriageable Armenian woman had a position of advantage, thus leverage, in any marriage she might enter. Also, because complete extended families on this side of the ocean were few, an Armenian bride was less likely to have her in-laws under the same roof. Thus, while Armenian American society was still male-dominant, the status of an Armenian woman in her married life was higher now than it would have been in the old country. Even so, growing Armenian girls continued to endure intense restrictions, with boys swept along by the forces of modernism at a swifter rate. The young Armenian males spent more time in places where they might be exposed to American influences, such as schools and workplaces. Thus, they could at times be heard complaining of how difficult it was to date Armenian girls, dealing with both their less modernized ways and the ever-watchful eyes of their parents. "Because Armenian girls are not allowed to go out with us," one young man reported to LaPiere, "we go out when we can get away from home with the American girls." He appeared, all other things being equal, to prefer Armenian companions, cynically noting of American girls that "they think that they can do anything while they are with us and nobody that counts to them will know about it," and adding that Armenian girls had somewhat more liberty to go on dates to Armenian dances.[22]

Anthropologist Harold Nelson, in his 1953 dissertation, found that, in the 1920s, many elements of the old-world marriage ritual continued to be practiced in the Armenian community, but notably less so where American-born offspring of immigrants were involved. With young Armenians who had lived their formative years in the old country before migrating as older children or teenagers, it was not unusual for the families to be involved in the matchmaking process, though arranged marriage by outright decree appears to have been rare. Frequently, a young man would arrange through an intermediary to get himself invited to the home of the girl who had caught his fancy, and then would either ask for her hand or ask his family to arrange for her to be asked. The two families would still investigate each other, and, if things looked promising, the two families would enjoy a series of visits together during which time the young man might give the object of his affections a *khosgab*, a prebetrothal gift, frequently a wristwatch. Shortly after, a betrothal would be announced, a festive occasion in itself with either a luncheon or a full-course dinner. The wedding retained some traditional customs: the groom, his parents, the best man, and others would form a party to call upon the bride's family. Sometimes the custom would be followed whereby the bride's family locked the groom's party out until the best man promised the bride's family a dinner. The ceremony in this era still did not have a kiss. The wedding reception most often involved traditional Armenian dishes and an Armenian orchestra playing familiar folk dances. In some instances, some revelers would abduct either the bride or the groom, the ransom being either money or a dinner to be provided by the best man or the maid of honor. Someone in the groom's party might also "steal" a vase or a garment from the bride's house during the earlier visit, display it during the reception dancing, and collect the promise of a dinner from the bride's parents for its safe return. The late 1920s and beyond saw a steady evolution of the customs, with the predictable decline and disappearance of many invasive practices alongside the continuance of the more innocuous ones.[23]

The statistics of marriage reflect the trajectory of cultural change. Sifting through the marriage records in Fresno County, LaPiere found the average age of men and women getting married in 1905 to be 25.5 and 19.25, respectively. In 1910, those figures had risen to 27.54 and 21, and in 1915, 32 and 25. He also notes that, prior to 1915, the oldest bride was 28 years old, whereas in 1915, nine brides were older than 28 and six of these (probably widows remarrying) were over 37. By 1920, the male-female ratio was evening out, and the proportion of Armenian adults who were married was now substantially higher than before. Marriage of Fresno Armenians with non-Armenians was virtually nonexistent at this time, as was divorce.[24]

Extant evidence outside of Fresno is more sketchy, particularly when it comes to quantifying any tendencies of behavior. A few general patterns can be gleaned, however. Rural Fresno County differed from most other Armenian-inhabited spots in that its physical environment was more conducive to sustaining tradition. Thus, there is no doubt that the same culture wars and domestic revolutions associated with Fresno County occurred wherever there were Armenians, but on a battlefield more decisively tilted toward more rapid liberalization. Anecdotal evidence can be found of young people's satirical view of the generation gap. Apparently sometime in the 1920s, Harry A. Sachaklian, brother of Syracuse history author Arpena Mesropian, wrote a one-act verse play titled *Marriage by Ballot*, which depicted an extended family of Armenian parents, aunts, and uncles huddled together in savory merriment as they contrived to get their children matched up one by one. Lest there be any mistaking the author's message, a handwritten note on the front cover calls it "a farcical, satirical comedy on a prevalent custom peculiar to Armenians," and he concludes the piece by writing, "The characters in this farce are by no means fictitious. Of course, the names are assumed, but—boy oboy—not the people in it."

Early in the play, family patriarch Boghos Agha declares, with reference to his grandson Krikor:

> I have here a written list
> Of girls about a score
> I'll read it and we'll select
> Approximately four
> For Krikor to decide
> The damsel for his bride.

The list is read, and the aunts begin to comment.

> AUNTIE SIRANOOSH –
> Mary Bedigian is the one,
> How that girl can cook;
> She isn't so dumb,
> She's reading some book,
> About souls and heaven and such
> By Burgoauree (sounds Dutch).
>
> …
> AUNTIE SIROOHI –
> Giragosians have a nice daughter
> Who looks pretty good to me,
> However, she may be stupid,
> I saw her climbing a tree;
> But then again I recommend
> Such profound agility.

It is narrowed down to semifinalists. Meanwhile, forty-year-old Tomas Domatesian takes the bride search into his own hands by paying a call on the parents of young Nevart to beseech her hand. When told of the prospect, she runs out of the room in tears, whereupon her mother assures Tomas, "Now, now, please understand, / She cries because she feels so grand." Nevart dutifully agrees to the betrothal, though the one she loves is actually the aforementioned Krikor. Krikor's family has, by this point, arranged for his betrothal to Mary Bedigian. Krikor and Mary, after they have been informed of the decision, privately exchange their affirmations of nonlove.

> MARY –
> I marry you just because
> I have to follow family laws.

I don't love you, you know that;
For Mama's sake you'd marry a cat.

KRIKOR –
I won't beat you or treat you bad,
But if I don't love you, don't feel sad.

Presently, a line ending with "good" is rhymed with Mary's offer to play the *oud*, a string instrument well known in the villages of old, which Krikor quickly declines. The playwright lets his own feelings about the *oud* be known when, in a subsequent stage direction, he calls it "the notorious instrument of torture." By the end of the play the young protagonists are paired with those they actually love. Pervading this lyrical odyssey is the collision of cultural norms, mainly between generations: the elders' desire to arrange the marriages, and the young people's desire neither to break their parents' hearts with outright rebellion nor to marry the mates of their parents' choosing.[25]

To be sure, some arranged marriages did take place in America. Vahram L. Shemmassian, in his study of Armenians from Musa Dagh, finds that the first generation in the United States tended to marry village compatriots, and that immigrant bachelors at times solicited help from family and friends in finding suitable brides for themselves. Robert Mirak additionally reports that, in the early twentieth century, some Armenian fathers in the United States were even "selling" their daughters' hands in marriage for $100 or $200, a practice that the press strongly condemned. As far along as 1926, a four-day civil trial was fought in Worcester in which one Mike Eretsian alleged—successfully with the court—that one Haji Krikor Ghazarian had promised to arrange for him to marry, sight-unseen, a young woman named Markrid Srabian, daughter of an acquaintance of Ghazarian. The plaintiff, naively convinced, had proceeded to purchase thirty pairs of shoes, furs, an overcoat, and a trove of fine food in preparation for the nuptial, incurring a price tag of $900— all this before discovering that the young lady in question was already betrothed. The court ruled for the unfortunate plaintiff. *Hairenik* reported the story, noting the embarrassment to the community from such a trial and exhorting readers not to emulate such an error.[26]

The youth culture of the larger society, of course, influenced Armenian immigrant society in the relaxing of the social codes. The agents of that cosmopolitan influence also included Armenians. Nelson found, in keeping with conventional wisdom, that older siblings who had grown up receiving the strictest upbringing often went forth into the more liberalized American adult world and then returned to the homestead as mediators, persuading their parents to be less strict with the younger offspring. In addition, apart from the transmission of ideas, the urban environment itself was an agent of change by being naturally less conducive to practices that were viable in rural villages. Arranged marriages had made more sense where families knew each other closely and could be readily introduced to each other through mutual friends, and where parents were in a position to take measure of suitability of marriage candidates for their own sons and daughters. The sheer population density and demographic heterogeneity of any urban neighborhood would make such practices unsustainable. Moreover, in an environment where the children were learning the prevailing language and customs faster than the parents, the authority of the parents inevitably suffered some erosion as well. At the same time, the consumer culture of movies, lipstick, and trendy fashion alongside the liberal ideas of romantic love and the companionate family did not take long to make their way into the world of the immigrants' growing children.[27]

For the immigrant generation, relaxing the traditions sometimes came in stages. Diana Keleshian, who grew up as the youngest of three sisters in an immigrant family, recalled that her oldest sister Alice, in her teenage years, was not permitted by their father to date boys, and thus had to resort to some surreptitious rendezvous. When Alice reached the age of sixteen or seventeen, the family suddenly began to be visited by Armenian families who were inspecting her as a prospective daughter-in-law. This was in the early 1930s. By the late 1930s, when youngest daughter Diana was an adolescent, their father had somewhat eased up: instead of actively forbidding Diana to date, he simply sat silently reading his newspaper when his daughter's male suitors came calling. In the mid-1940s, he did not attend the wedding of his middle daughter, May, because she had married an Armenian from a different region from their own; nor did he appear at Diana's wedding, offended that her husband had not followed the protocol of asking him for his daughter's hand in marriage. But in the 1960s, when his grandson introduced him to his fiancée who was not Armenian at all, the now-elderly man embraced the young woman immediately and declared, "Today I have four daughters!"[28]

- 4 -

Armenians who migrated to the United States from Turkey were, of course, looking for a haven from being treated as racial undesirables. Only up to a point did they enjoy that luxury. From 1921 to 1929, Congress passed a series of immigration restriction laws inspired, not only by the belief that space in the land of the free was limited, but that not all of the world's nationalities made equally good candidates for Americanization. Thus, while Armenian parents worried that the liberalizing American culture might be corrupting their youth, Armenian spokesmen strove to persuade America's lawmakers that the admission of more Armenian refugees would not corrupt America's culture. Here, they were up against the powerful influence of Madison Grant and his fellow racialists. In 1913, and in successive reprints up through 1923, Madison Grant's best-selling book *The Passing of the Great Race* warned that America, made great by northern and western European settlers and their spawn—the Nordics—was committing "race suicide" by letting in so many immigrants of racially inferior stock, namely the Mediterranean and Alpine races of southern and eastern Europe. A considerable number of Americans and their elected representatives in Congress had clearly come to agree with Representative Albert Johnson's remark in December of 1920 that "We are being made a dumping-ground for the human wreckage of the war." The acts of 1921, 1924, and 1929 reflected that belief. Grant, in fact, chaired the committee that designed the formula for the annual immigration quotas—2 percent of each group's 1890 population in America—that became the Johnson-Reed Act of 1924. (The Chinese, of course, had been subject to stringent restrictions dating back to 1883; the new law extended exclusion to Japanese and Koreans, among others.) The quota for Armenia under the 1924 law was 124 persons per year. More Armenians might enter from the thousand-plus persons allowed in annually from the Soviet Union; still, Armenian immigration to the United States fell to a trickle, after having been in the thousands annually in the years just prior.[29]

The 1921 act came just in time to slam the golden door in the faces of tens of thousands of Armenian and Greek refugees from the city of Smyrna and other parts of Anatolia who had escaped the brutal massacres of Turkish troops. Greece was bulging with those refugees, and in the fall of 1922 boatloads brought many to Ellis Island, far exceeding the quotas that the 1921 law established. As a result, many were detained on Ellis Island, and many detainees were ultimately shipped back, either to Greece or to Turkey. In the final months of 1922 and much of 1923, immigration officials received a barrage of letters from persons concerned for the welfare of the detainees at Ellis Island; those officials wrote many politely worded replies explaining that only Congress could enact exceptions to the law to allow these refugees entrance to the United States.[30]

The House Immigration and Naturalization Committee, chaired by the same Albert Johnson who was spearheading that decade's restriction laws, with others in its membership who also showed the influence of Madison Grant, held hearings in December 1922 on a modest proposal that would allow persons who had either gained citizenship or declared intentions of applying for it to bring family members whose lives were in danger into the country. In those hearings, the representatives heard graphic horror stories from Smyrna. They also heard testimony from purported experts on the racial desirability of Armenians. Lothrop Stoddard, author of books in the same vein as Madison Grant's, characterized the Armenians as Levantines, "the result of an extraordinary racial mixture which has been going on for at least 2,500 years." They were, he continued, very largely a parasitic population, living by their wits, by unproductive means of labor, by petty trading, by graft, and by similar equivocal methods. He artfully blamed the Levantines for the fall of the Roman Empire, as but one example of their "very baneful influence on whatever country they have entered." Asked about the Armenians' being Christians, Stoddard told the committee that the Armenian church, by virtue of having missed vital ecclesiastical councils (probably thinking of Chalcedon) and having kept itself separate from the main institutional bodies since the sixth century, practiced a backward and schismatic version of the faith.[31]

Another witness, Yale-based geographer Ellsworth Huntington, reached different conclusions. "The Armenians," he observed, "are to a peculiar degree a people who have been subjected to a very strong process of natural selection, and that is what produces the character of a people." An utterly astonishing exchange followed between Huntington and Representative William A. Vaile of Colorado, who was determined to believe that the fittest of the Armenians would surely have been the first whom the Turks killed off. When Huntington replied that many of the survivors had been those less vulnerable to massacre, and that the Turks would have logically sent the most desirable men into slavery and the most desirable women and girls into harems, Vaile did not appear satisfied. Huntington also reflected on the mixed personal qualities of the Armenians he had known while visiting Turkey.

> When I first met them they grated on me. After I had lived among them long enough to find their real good qualities, I had a kindlier feeling for them .... If I wanted a carpenter, I went and got an Armenian, because I knew he would do the job properly. I always got an Armenian. On the other hand, I had a most delightful time with the Turks when I was there.

Ultimately, Huntington opined, Congress should pass the bill in question. He conceded that he thought the ideal immigrants would be "high-grade Englishmen or Scots or Swedes or Irishmen," but "we cannot get that sort. We cannot get the top, but we can get people [above] the average."[32]

Secretary of State Charles Evans Hughes, whose name had been linked with pro-Armenian causes during the war years, was scarcely any friend to the Armenians now. He sent a message to Congress explicitly urging harsh quotas against Armenians. In the Caucasus, his note said, it was scarcely an exaggeration to say "that every Armenian family which has enough money to get away, or is not impregnated with Bolshevism, will ultimately endeavor to enter America," alongside Russians and Georgians. "Our restriction on immigration should be so rigid that it would be impossible for most of these people to enter the United States. Reference is especially made to Armenians, Jews, Persians and Russians, all of which"—and here he showed the familiar attitude that people can be fairly stigmatized merely on account of what has been done to them—"have been so driven hither and thither that they cannot be regarded as desirable populations for any country."[33]

When Congress tightened up the immigration laws in 1924, *Hairenik* and *Baikar* both responded in their distinctive styles. *Hairenik* read the immigration law as a lesson burned as if by fire into the brains of all Armenians, that the means of salvation for the Armenian nation was clearly not "the road to America" but rather "the road to Armenia," a fairly clear advertisement for its own homeland-centered agenda. The *Baikar* editorial, while treading lightly so as not to offend, voiced the hope that American authorities would take the Armenians' situation into account and thus "interpret and enforce the immigration law in a lenient and tolerant spirit," remembering America's traditional role as a haven for the oppressed and the Armenians' exceptional circumstances.[34]

Armenians in the 1920s also had to fight a case in federal court to prove their eligibility for naturalization; under the law still in effect at the time, that meant having to prove their whiteness. The first American naturalization law, passed in 1790, restricted eligibility to "free white persons." The Fourteenth Amendment to the Constitution, ratified in 1868, extended American citizenship to America's Black population, including the 4 million who were formerly enslaved, and the Reconstruction-era Congress also amended the 1790 law to allow for persons of African descent to become naturalized. Still, until the rule was finally abolished in 1952, "white" was still the criterion for naturalization for non-African immigrants, the main effect being to exclude Asians. In much of the pseudo-scientific and legal discourse, the notion of whiteness was freely conflated with the more performance-oriented qualities of "assimilability" and "fitness for self-government." To be "Asiatic," in the thinking of the day, was to be decidedly nonwhite. Japanese and Chinese immigrants were the law's clearest losers. One federal judge in 1923 wrote, "It is obvious that the objection on the part of Congress is not due to color, as color, but only to color as an evidence of a type of civilization which it characterizes. The yellow or bronze racial color is the hallmark of Oriental despotisms."[35]

Armenians, whose ancestral home straddled Europe and Asia, found themselves in that nether region of ambiguity between "white" and "Asiatic" in American racial thought. Whiteness cases were often exercises in semantic hair-splitting, and different rulings emphasized different elements of the popular construction of whiteness, some making "white" synonymous with "Caucasian" (another term open to varied definitions), others taking the hue of skin color more literally, others still relying unabashedly on sense of the popular will. In the one pre-1920s case involving Armenians, *In re Halladjian* (1908), the Supreme Court allowed for Armenian naturalization on the grounds that Armenians had not hitherto been customarily singled out for exclusion. Later the same year a federal court in Georgia allowed a dark-complexioned Syrian man to gain citizenship because a recent and acclaimed work, A. H. Keane's *The World's Peoples*, had called the Syrians Caucasians: "and this they are, so far as my information and knowledge go," concluded the judge. The question of whether "white" equaled Caucasian became more muddled when the Supreme Court lumped the two terms together to deny naturalization to Japanese on the grounds that they were non-Caucasian even though they were light-skinned (*Ozawa v. United States*, 1922), then separated the two terms the following year to deny naturalization to Asian Indians on the grounds that, even though most authorities of the day considered them Caucasian, their skin was too dark to call white (*United States v. Thind*, 1923). In that latter case, the Court also declared that, scientific and historical theories aside, the word *white* was "to be interpreted in accordance with the understanding of the common man." In other words, ordinary white Americans were the best judge of who should be allowed to join their club.[36]

Amid this backdrop, the Armenians found themselves called upon to defend their whiteness again in the 1924–5 case of *United States v. Cartozian*, which was decided in the Federal District Court of Oregon. The case began when the US government sued to strip Tatos O. Cartozian, a rug merchant living in Oregon, of his naturalization papers on the grounds that Armenians were Asiatic rather than European and white. Paradoxically, the Armenian spokespersons openly stated the belief at the time—which is supported by archived government correspondence—that Secretary of Labor James J. Davis claimed the desire to make a test case to help secure the Armenians' position. However, Cartozian's attorney William D. Guthrie, whose services were engaged by a group called the Armenian Naturalization Committee, expressed suspicion in his own correspondence that the real purpose of the suit was to pave the way toward excluding Eastern European Jews; he thus asked expert witness Franz Boas, famous anthropologist based at Columbia University whose work consistently challenged the prevailing racial theories, to stand ready to defend Jewish whiteness and assimilability in the event that it might be brought into question during the trial (which it was not).[37]

In the Cartozian case, two key witnesses secured by the Armenian Naturalization Committee were Boas and his fellow anthropologist Roland B. Dixon. Fitting in with what Matthew Frye Jacobson has demonstrated about the "alchemy" of race, Boas defended the Armenians' whiteness using both biological and behavioral evidence. For the biological, he prepared his case by writing to several doctors and nurses to inquire about a curious phenomenon called the "blue lumbar spot," "a temporary pigmented spot in the sacral region which lasts for about three weeks." As he explained in one of his letters, this was common among "children of parents of the Mongoloid race, such as Chinese and American Indians," while very rare in Europeans. Responses to his inquiry seem to have indicated that Armenian newborns had no tendency to exhibit this spot. Boas and Dixon used studies of early migration patterns to link the Armenians with the "Nordic" or "Alpine" races. Boas, who in other contexts frequently attacked the use of racial classifications to bestow ranks of inferiority, testified that the Armenians were of Alpine stock—not the highest grade on Grant's scale, but still clearly European and white. He found them racially akin to the Russians, with whom, he testified, Armenians amalgamated much more readily than they ever did with the Turks and other "Asiatic" populations.[38]

Dixon, with the map from Madison Grant's book in front of him, assented with only minor reservations to Grant's groupings and concurred that the Armenians were of the Alpine race. Remarks in Dixon's testimony went back to ancient times to affirm Armenians' racial prowess, including their representation as several Byzantine emperors and, during the Crusades, "the easy assimilation and easy union of Armenians with the European Crusading elements." Dr. Dixon went on to discuss Armenians' history of successful assimilation into northern European societies in modern times as well: that in France, Germany, Russia, and Italy they "mingled and mixed freely with the population and intermarried with them, and made themselves distinguished in letters, arts and sciences in one way or another." As for assimilation in America, he cited a study that found 17.5 percent of Armenian men who got married in the six years before the war to have married outside their own ethnic group, a figure to be compared with 17.4 percent for Irish, 14.8 percent for northern Italians (who would presumably be considered more assimilable than southern Italians), and 26 percent for Swedes.[39]

M. Vartan Malcom, president of the Armenian Naturalization Committee, testified at the trial that in a special inquiry of 257 married Armenian men, 125 were married to Armenian women and 132 to non-Armenians—the only context during these years in which a high rate of intermarriage could be a badge of triumph to Armenians. The court also heard testimony from Dr. Joseph Barton, long-time missionary leader and relief supervisor with the American Board of Commissioners for Foreign Missions, to the effect that, in his experience among Armenians, they had always been popularly understood to be white.[40]

In July 1925, federal judge C. E. Wolverton ruled that Armenians, though geographically Asiatic, were clearly of European descent and thus eligible for naturalization as "free white citizens." The government did not appeal the decision.

Armenians now had their permanent certificate of whiteness. Present-day students of racialist theory, imbued with an enlightened sense of its profound illegitimacy, may feel troubled that Cartozian's defenders were less interested in toppling Madison Grant's racial hierarchy than in securing for Armenians a favorable position within it. Indeed, as part of the reaction to the *Cartozian* decision, Arshag Mahdesian invoked Madison Grant to justify the Armenians' claim to whiteness, even seeking to go one better than Boas. "Eye color is of very great importance in race determination," he quoted Grant in a letter to the *Times*, "because all blue, gray or green eyes in the world today came originally from the same source, namely, the Nordic race of Northern Europe." Then, having cited this authority, he noted, "A great many Armenians have blue eyes and blond hair." However, while looking at such quotations, it is well to remember that it was the US government, not the Armenians, that decreed that the Armenians must defend their whiteness. Arguing that their whiteness or nonwhiteness did not matter was not an available option. (Racial restrictions on naturalization were finally abolished in 1952.)[41]

Armenian American thinkers did, in fact, develop some racialist ideas of their own, but of a different nature from the dichotomy of white and nonwhite. The phrase "the Armenian race" appeared in many of the newspapers of the 1920s and 1930s, with the argument that this "race" had characteristics, a heritage, and a legitimate claim to its young generation's loyalty. References to Grant notwithstanding, most Armenian discourse on race in the 1920s and 1930s fit a model of romanticism that John Higham used to characterize early Anglo-Saxonism: "Its vague identification of culture with ancestry served mainly to emphasize the antiquity, the uniqueness, and the permanence of a nationality. It suggested the inner vitality of one's own culture, rather than the menace of another race."[42]

Beyond the Cartozian case, how did Armenians fare amid the decade's notorious currents of xenophobia? A few general observations can be made here. First, as has been seen, the Armenians had managed, throughout the past several decades, to attract the solicitude of a not insubstantial number of the middle-class, Anglo-Saxon reformers who loom so large in that era's standard narrative. In the mid-1890s the Women's Christian Temperance Union, alongside its crusade for the prohibition of drink, worked to ensure a safe American haven for victims of the Hamidean massacres, and humanitarian luminaries Clara Barton, Julia Ward Howe, and others helped bring the plight of Armenians to the sympathetic attention of much of the American public. In the years just before and during the Great War, two different pro-Armenian lobby groups had attracted a distinguished line-up of notables to lend, at the very least, their names to the letterheads. A phrase in circulation at the time dubbed Armenians "the Anglo-Saxons of the Orient," an unalloyed compliment for those who subscribed to it.[43]

It would be inaccurate, however, to say that Armenians in America were entirely free from being victims of prejudice. It was particularly evident in Fresno. LaPiere, for his 1930 dissertation, surveyed the attitudes of 610 non-Armenians, having them complete a questionnaire as well as allowing them to offer their thoughts in prose. Of those who answered, 84 percent said that they would not admit Armenians to their private clubs as personal friends, 64 percent said that they would not hire Armenians, 61 percent said that they would not desire Armenians as playmates for their children, and 52.7 percent would unequivocally exclude Armenians from migrating to the

United States. Stereotypes gleaned from the interviews included dishonesty, greed in business, criminality, overuse of public charities, and internal contentiousness. Several officials involved with the dispensing of charity insisted that Armenians posed disproportionate problems with their demands on the system, and others stereotyped Armenians as having a high rate of criminality. LaPiere meticulously sifted through county records to test out a number of those stereotypes. He found that Armenians were notably *under*represented among those seeking charitable services and among those facing arrest. The only stereotype that had a slight tendency to surface in the statistics was the one that many Armenians themselves would guess: contentiousness. Armenians were slightly more likely than others to be involved in lawsuits and were somewhat overrepresented in charges of battery. Nonetheless, the stereotypes in general did not hold up to LaPiere's quantitative inquiry.[44]

The degree of anti-Armenian sentiment in Fresno appears to have been the exception nationwide. A US Immigration Commission report found that there was more intermarriage of Armenians in the eastern states because this was where "there is less feeling against the Armenian race." Even so, some degree of stereotyping does appear to have affected Armenians in other locales as well. An article in *Hairenik*, complaining that Armenians in business should be doing better than they were, alluded with irony to "those who regard our race as so 'commercially shrewd.'" Moreover, the short *New York Times* write-up that carried the news of Armenian victory in the *Cartozian* case offered a commentary that bespoke an ambivalent stereotype: "The faults ascribed to Armenians are natural to people long oppressed and forced to live by craft rather than strength. In safer environments they lose these characteristics, and many have done so already in the United States." Armenians also found themselves included in some areas on lists of undesirables, alongside African Americans and Jews, to whom real estate could not be sold in neighborhoods where restrictive covenants prevailed. Only in 1948 did the Supreme Court rule that court enforcement of such covenants violated the Constitution.[45]

Running in parallel with nativist hysterias were the intense efforts by white American civic groups, with help from parts of the corporate sector and the government, to accelerate the "Americanization" of immigrants. The Americanization movement was not a sinister monolith; it included some genuinely useful services such as English language classes. Nonetheless, much of the driving force came from the same fears that called for the immigration restriction laws: that foreigners with their non-American ways of life and thought could be a threat to America's character. The term "melting pot" had entered the language already, and many people's idea of the melting pot model came closer to what sociologist Milton Gordon later termed "Anglo-conformity."[46]

Yet Anglo-conformist thinking needs to be understood, not as the single voice that immigrants were hearing from their host society, but rather, one part of a debate being waged about them. Horace Kallen had made his case for cultural pluralism, the acceptance and full encouragement of ethnic diversity with the analogy of a symphony orchestra composed of many distinct instruments, as early as February 1915, in the two-part article in *The Nation*, "Democracy versus the Melting Pot," and was continuing to promote this view in the 1920s. In 1910 settlement worker Edith Terry Bremer had founded the International Institute movement, spawning the creation of

International Institutes. These numbered around fifty-five in the early 1920s, originally as departments to local YWCAs (Young Women's Christian Associations) and later becoming an organization of their own. A key feature of International Institutes was their employment of "nationality workers," members of ethnic communities who knew their groups' immigrant experiences firsthand and, at the same time, had been trained in social work in the United States. Cultural pluralism as a form of Americanization found greater mainstream acceptance in the 1930s, but already in the 1920s immigrants could organize and attend cultural events that affirmed the uniqueness of their heritage and fell under the auspices of a respected American social service network. Boston's International Institute had an Armenian Women's Club, founded in 1927 by nationality worker Olympia Yeranian, which sponsored lectures on both history and practical topics and ran Armenian-language classes for Armenian American youngsters. The discourse of the International Institute leaders showed an awareness of the "second generation problem," the propensity for the American-born children of immigrants to feel lost between two somewhat foreign cultures, and their programs and social services sought to alleviate this with an emphasis on affirming the ethnic heritage.[47]

For immigrants and their descendants, the question was not (as many have always imagined) how American they were willing to be, but rather, on what terms and by what means they would be American. Immigrant advocates often asserted a claim for acceptance as Americans with full participation in the heritage, as opposed to having to feel like probationary stepchildren to that heritage. Historian Orm Øverland has insightfully shone light on the paradox whereby native-born whites seemed to want immigrants to embrace the American identity while still feeling some sense of deferential outsiderhood, and it was against that sense of outsiderhood that immigrant leaders strove. The groups Øverland studied pointed up their contributions to the country's early development, to argue that they had helped to create the quality of Americanness rather than having just arrived late to receive its full-grown fruits. Consistent with that spirit, a *New York Times* announcement of a 1921 civil festival of New York's immigrant groups told readers, right after promising demonstration of the Dutch immigrants' influence on American silverware, interior decoration, and agriculture, "Armenian immigrants will show their introduction of silk culture to America in the old colonial days when we all lived under the king." Advocates also pointed to Armenians' current successes in integration as Americans. M. Vartan Malcom, in his 1919 book written to introduce Americans to their Armenian neighbors (and to lobby for an American protective mandate over Armenia), observed that Armenian Americans included a prominent Bellevue Hospital psychiatrist, a distinguished Philadelphia scientist, the inventor of an innovative photographic method, and the first soldier to land in the Philippines in the Spanish-American War.[48]

- 5 -

From the point of view of the immigrant generation bringing up the American-born second generation, being good Americans did not have to, and indeed should not, come at the expense of maintaining a distinctive Armenian identity. Among immigrant families with children, there was always a fear among the elders that the youth would lose their ethnicity and a sense of urgent need to prevent, or at least forestall, this calamity. In this context, the word *assimilation* often had negative connotations; the Armenian word for degeneration was sometimes used as well. Marjorie Housepian, looking back on the 1920s in her 1954 novel *A Houseful of Love*, recalled that pervasive sense of danger. "In thirty-five years what difference will it make?" a curmudgeonly uncle says on the subject of planning a picnic. "The young people are going to become so diluted in thirty-five years there won't be a need for picnics." Another guest at the same Easter Sunday dinner agrees, lamenting, "What our enemies failed to do in fifteen hundred years our friends succeed in doing in one generation." But still another voice pipes up, "That is why we need to bring the young people together, or the next thing you know they are off marrying Irishmen. What will *that* do to the culture, will you tell me?"[49]

Cultural markers of Armenianness were ever present in these years, as genocide survivors joined the more settled community. A key institution for immigrant men was the coffeehouse. Especially before the war, Armenians in America were a disproportionately male-majority population, many of the men being unmarried and others having wives across the ocean. Coffeehouses assuaged the loneliness: men communed with one another, caught up on the latest news and gossip from both conversation and the newspapers kept in stock, learned of job opportunities, and partook of various familiar ethnic foods and beverages. Worcester local historian Hagop Martin Deranian paints a picture of "an endless supply of thick, strong and pungent powdered coffee, delivered in demitasse cups and served with Near Eastern delicacies such as *paklava*" (a dessert made of flaky layers of dough with walnut filling) "and *lokhum*" (a type of candy made of sugar and flavorings). The specialty of many a coffeehouse proprietor, according to Deranian, was *kheyma*, "a mixture of raw meat and bulghur flavored with tomatoes and parsley."[50] David Kherdian, in his novel *Finding Home* based on his mother's true story, provides more detail on the inside of the coffeehouse, where some sets of men conversed intensely while others played cards, backgammon, or pinochle.

> The talkers never mixed with the players, although there was always an idler or two who would stand in silence behind one or another of the card players. The card players enjoyed the attention of an audience, for they were puffy and boisterous in victory, but in need of commiseration when they lost. But the backgammon players, perhaps because their game was played head to head, were a morose group whose only words were addressed to the dice, God, and fate, with an occasional choice expression for the devil.[51]

Coffeehouses were not exclusively bachelor enclaves. Levon Z. Boyajian, born of genocide survivors in New York City in 1929, reports that his father, while working night shifts, spent his weekends at home with his wife but frequented the coffeehouses on the weekday afternoons. "Golf widows have no idea what Armenian wives and mothers endured," he surmises.[52]

If male camaraderie was an important part of the cultural landscape of Armenian immigrants, so was family life. Accounts from the early twentieth century depict the Armenian father as authoritative, though not necessarily quick to use physical punishment. Mirak characterizes the classic Armenian father, in both the old country and early-twentieth-century America, as having such status that "his younger brothers deferred to him, young people stood when he entered the room, and he meted out punishment to errant children usually by an irritated glance." (Consistent with this, Levon Boyajian recalls that his father never hit him, but did send him to bed without supper when he complained about the food being served; his father's anger was probably affected by the fact that the exchange occurred during the Depression decade, possibly during his unemployed period.) The Armenian mother was considered legendary for her strength. Mirak observes that many Armenian women in America had arrived later than their husbands, and thus had less opportunity to learn English and keep company with English-speaking Americans. Still, he finds, many had developed an inner strength from the weight of the burden they carried, which included in many instances having to navigate their way along with their children to meet up with their husbands who were already in America, when the dangers of staying in Turkey became obvious. Two key features of family life that did not survive the voyage, scholars have found, were the authority of grandfathers and the central role of godparents in the life spans of their godchildren.[53]

Foods were a major part of the Armenian cultural world. Besides *paklava*, *lokhum*, and *kheyma*, favorite Armenian delicacies included *choreg*, a kind of bread made with eggs, and *lahmajoon*, meat pastry. Nuts and yogurt figured large in Armenian culinary life, as well. Helene Pilibosian notes that "no one ever imagined then that yogurt would become a commercial entity and enterprise with flavors, high-fat, low-fat, even frozen. It was simply a staple made in the safety of the family, an Armenian family in America."[54] Mesrobian's history of Syracuse Armenians emphasizes the interconnection between food and social interactions between families.

> Everyone prepared certain foods like rice pilaf and yogurt. The preparation of yogurt, called *madzoon* in Armenian, also provided an opportunity for social contact, because the housewife inevitably stopped to chat while seeking a starter culture from her neighbor. *Madzoon* was used in many ways: eaten straight at breakfast, lunch, or dinner, as topping for *dolma* (vegetables, especially tomatoes, peppers and eggplant, stuffed with ground lamb and rice) and *sarma* (meat and rice filling wrapped in leaves from wild grape vines), pressed to a soft paste by straining out the liquid and eaten as a dressing on moistened flat cracker bread, diluted in water and chilled with ice cubes for a cooling hot-weather drink called *than*, and *jajukh*, with chopped cucumbers and a sprinkling of crushed mint leaves.

The picking of wild grape leaves, she adds, was a family affair, typically in June and the beginning of July.[55]

It bears repeating, for all its obviousness, that, for those old enough to remember the genocide and the upheavals that followed—even if they experienced the whole ordeal safely on American soil—those memories occupied a large part of their shared mental world. The Armenians who savored their *paklava* and played backgammon in the coffeehouses and navigated the changing social codes in the homestead remained conscious of their identity as a national group that another nation had tried to exterminate. The grief, the anger, the consolation of brave stands at Musa Dagh, Van, and Sardarabad, the hope of seeing some kind of restitution in the future—these were all part of what the immigrant generation carried with them, and part of what the children of the second generation would not only hear about, but feel called upon to carry in their own internal worlds. Years later, psychiatrists Levon Boyajian and Haigaz Grigorian would report from their clinical experience that many survivors displayed a "survivor syndrome" comprising depression, anxiety, and guilt over having survived while others perished. Many of the children grew up with "the sense that there is an obligation … to be the bearers of the hopes and aspirations, not only of a given family but of a whole people," as well as the obligation to carry a sadness not only for family members who died but for "the total loss and wiping out of one's home and homeland, transportation to an alien land, and no foreseeable hope for a return to one's roots." Many Armenian American homes and coffeehouses in the early twentieth century had the picture, in painted or crocheted form, of Mother Armenia looking in grief over the ruins of her country. Pictures of Armenian military leaders were also common in homes; many Tashnag families had the Tricolor, the flag of the thousand-day republic, on their walls. The American-born youth grew up with all this for a backdrop.[56]

A constant fixture in the press during these years was the editorial or letter lamenting that Armenians in America were failing to preserve their sense of themselves as Armenians. Here, willingness to contribute money to Armenian charities was often at the center. Once upon a time, the editorial staff of *Baikar* suggested in 1925, Armenians had given bountifully even though they had little for themselves; they "hesitated to spend two dollars on the same day for their basic needs, fearing that they were sinning against the laws of charity." Now, after having become more prosperous from years of hard work and resourcefulness (a good thing, the editorialist hastened to opine), Armenian immigrants and their children had become complete "sports," caring supremely about having the sharpest and finest model of the Ford automobile. While taking pains to make clear that the intent was not to ask Armenian Americans to live ascetic lives and to forego personal enjoyments, the piece called upon them to maintain a deeply ingrained ethos that included feeling connected to their less fortunate Armenian brethren overseas and tempering their own desires for luxury in order to donate more to their care.[57]

Charity was just one facet of the identity-balancing question. A four-part series in the Tashnag party's *Hairenik* in 1926, titled *"Incha Sirenk Hayoutean?"* which roughly translates into "What is there for us to love about being Armenian?" (the title being a variant on a question that a boy had purportedly asked his father), brought this into sharper focus. Part three of this series complained that Armenians were not putting down roots in America and integrating themselves into the American economy effectively enough, while part four—*written by the same author*—warned of the dangers of assimilation. Part three stressed the importance of ability to speak English and the etiquette of using English when doing business with non-Armenians;

part four stressed with equal urgency the importance of Armenians' maintaining their native language and having social spaces in which they could speak it with one another. Central to understanding the balance that the author was calling for, alongside what Armenians should do, was how they should interpret what they were doing. Armenians should be materially successful in America, but why? The answer: because Armenia needed a materially successful Armenian colony in America. Even if Armenia became liberated from its oppressors and sizable numbers of Armenians from America repatriated, the *Hairenik* writer opined, the country's future would still require a sizable number of Armenians remaining in America and living prosperous lives in the American economy, all the better to help both Armenia at large and their own relatives in Armenia in particular.[58]

What numbers of Armenians in America in the 1920s had ideas of eventually returning to the homeland would be impossible to quantify at this point. What is clear, however, is that the author of this four-part series understood there to be some such sentiment among his readers. They thus needed to hear that, even if this was their aspiration, it should not preclude engaging in all the economic behaviors apropos to making America their permanent home. Nor did the behavior of putting down roots in America conflict with the internalized mythology of a future repatriation to the homeland. What is safest to conclude is that, partisanship aside, there existed in the readership of the Armenian press a desire to hear the ideal of a balance: a collective identity that included Armenians' enthusiastic participation in the much-heralded American prosperity and a sense of obligation to consecrate a portion of their material gain, as well as their emotional and psychic being, to the identity of Armenianness and the future of Armenia. Armenians, in the view of this consensus, erred if they neglected either calling.

Being Armenian also included having strong opinions about the status of the homeland and the memories of the war years, felt along the lines of Tashnag versus non-Tashnag. These contested memories, of course, mainly involved events that had happened in the homeland an ocean away. After 1933, however, Armenians in America did not have to look any farther back than July and December of that year, or any farther away than Chicago and New York, for bitter contested memories that would divide them. If anyone hoped that partisan fighting would die down with time, it did not, but rather grew more intense than ever, in 1933 and for several decades after.

The Tourian Affair

Contested Memories and an Archbishop's Murder

"In short, being a Dashnak is being an Armenian. Dashnaktzoutyoun is Armenian national consciousness."
—Sarkis Atamian, *The Armenian Community*, 272

"How in the world can we class Dashnags as Armenians? We might class them as an uncivilized group of Armenians, but I think we shouldn't even call them Armenians."
—Letter, *Armenian Mirror*, February 16, 1934, 2

A staple of history is the highly publicized criminal trial that divides a nation's population into two camps according to which verdict they desire to see. In such instances, the case represents more than its face value: people's political ideology, perception of how society is ordered, and sense of their own identity within that society determine how they view the case. While usually seen in the context of a nation-state (the Dreyfus affair in France, the Sacco-Vanzetti and O. J. Simpson trials in the United States), the same phenomenon can happen in an immigrant community. So it was for the Armenians, with the fatal stabbing of Archbishop Levon Tourian on December 24, 1933 (variations on his transliterated first name included Leon and Ghevont), and the trial and conviction of nine members of the Tashnag party that following spring and summer. For decades to come, one could count on Armenians of the Tashnag persuasion to insist that the nine were innocent scapegoats and that the archbishop was a traitor. Anti-Tashnag Armenians, in contrast, considered the nine defendants and the Tashnag party as a whole guilty of the heinous murder of a beloved leader. These divided sentiments related closely to the partisan divide over Soviet Armenia and over the contested memories from the First World War era of the Tashnag-dominated Republic of Armenia. These were not mere opinions and abstractions for many Armenians in America: they cut right to the core of their sense of national identity, their sense of who and what ultimately symbolized their diasporic nation.[1]

- 1 -

As noted, eastern Armenia had an independent republic from May 1918 to November 1920. Among Armenians in America, those who got their news from *Hairenik* and fraternized in Tashnag clubs regarded the republic's existence as a major milestone and considered "Armenia" and "the republic" interchangeable terms. They similarly regarded that republic's flag, the Tricolor, as the symbol of Armenia. Meanwhile, Armenians who read the non-Tashnag press and mingled in non-Tashnag circles barely talked or thought about the republic at all, and instead looked to Boghos Nubar Pasha, Paris-based diplomatic appointee of the Catholicos at Echmiadzin, to lead the way in the creation of a free and independent Armenia for the future. After the collapse of the republic and the absorption of Armenia into the Soviet state, non-Tashnag factions accepted their homeland's new status while the Tashnag party held to a strong anti-Soviet stance.

Across the factional spectrum, Armenian Americans viewed the newly Sovietized Armenia as their homeland. Some immigrants had actually lived in those eastern provinces of the Caucasus that czarist Russia once ruled, but most came from *vilayets* of the Ottoman Empire, the western portion of the historic homeland. Thus, many Armenians in America identified emotionally with a country in which they had never actually set foot. This made sense in some ways: the native population spoke their language, though a somewhat different version, and now it included thousands of refugees from the atrocities in Turkey. The party organizations, with the Tashnags and the Ramgavars emerging as the leading lights, defined themselves largely in terms of their relationship with the Soviet regime, one declaring its opposition, the other its cooperation. Largely through their partisan press, Armenians in the United States followed the developments of their homeland's life under Communism.

Both religion and nationalism, it is known, conflict with Marxist ideology, and the Soviet rulers in Armenia initially demanded that the people make instant and total breaks with both their national identity and all Western-capitalist orientations and liaisons. However, after the short-lived Tashnag rebellion of 1921, Soviet Premier Vladimir Lenin launched a more moderate program, the New Economic Policy (NEP), designed to allow for smoother transitions and some latitude for the Armenians' Armenianness. Particularly complex was the relationship between church and state. The peasantry still identified with Christian institutions, and curtailing their freedom of worship completely would clearly prove counterproductive to gaining their allegiance. The regime under Lenin, therefore, allowed church services to continue, though at the same time sponsoring much antireligious propaganda and forbidding the churches to do much more than perform their liturgies. The government seized nearly all of the Echmiadzin Monastery's land, though not the monks' living and worshiping space. The government also supported schismatic impulses within the church: as a means of weakening the spiritual influence of Echmiadzin, the Soviet government promoted a secularizing faction known as the "Free Church" movement (akin to the "Living Church" movement in the Russian Orthodox Church). The regime further sought to break the Armenians of some of their customs and traditions.[2]

For the entire Soviet Union, including Armenia, the 1920s constituted a decade of infrastructure building. While the government declared all land as nationalized as early as December 28, 1920, the real machinery of forced collectivization did not begin until 1929. By that time Lenin had died and the more ruthless Joseph Stalin had risen to power. Despite resistance, by the end of the 1930s virtually all Armenian peasants lived on government-controlled collective farms. In the process, local village leadership institutions dissolved, as did the merchant class. Moves toward industrialization, including the Shirak Canal, desert irrigation projects, and electrification, were begun in the 1920s and accelerated in the 1930s under Stalin's Five-Year Plan, greatly increasing the portion of the population that labored in factories, railroads, and construction sites.[3]

The Armenian community abroad followed all these developments as filtered through a very partisan press. Both partisan camps marketed a sense of Armenianness that centered on a specific narrative about what was going on in the homeland and how Armenians in the United States should feel about it. Armenian Americans of Tashnag persuasion felt the presence of their party, not merely as a social organization (though it certainly served that role as well), but as a government in exile. Reuben Darbinian, the republic's defense minister, moved to Boston in 1922 (after spending a year in Tabriz, Iran, after the republic collapsed) and served as editor-in-chief of the *Hairenik* press until his death in 1968.[4] Simon Vratzian, agriculture minister and then prime minister of the republic in its final days, also contributed regularly to *Hairenik*. This phenomenon continued over the next several decades. As will be seen, in the 1930s General Karekin Nejdeh took a strong hand in the founding of the party's youth organization *Tzeghagron*, General Dro toured the country in the late 1940s to promote the party's new summer camp, and in 1963 editor James G. Mandalian published his translation of the memoirs of Tashnag revolutionary Rouben Der Minasian, condensed to just the right length to capture the imagination of English-speaking Armenian teenagers with some good true adventure stories. All through these decades, the *Hairenik* press, through both its Armenian- and (starting in the 1930s) its English-language organs, rehearsed the memories of the republic, as did field workers touring the communities. Thus, even as Tashnag Armenians pursued middle-class American mobility and did middle-class American things (like sending their children to summer camp), they received—because they chose to be receptive to—steady reminders of an identity rooted in the bravery of the Tashnag party and the glory of the thousand-day republic.

All of this sharply divided the ARF from other Armenians. Because Tashnag Armenians felt a strong attachment to the thousand-day republic, they commemorated May 28, the date of its founding in 1918, as an important anniversary. That date had no meaning for most non-Tashnags. For the same reason, Tashnag Armenians considered the flag of that republic, the Tricolor, their national symbol, another allegiance that most non-Tashnags did not share. Closely related was the division over how to feel about, and relate to, the Soviet government of Armenia. In a number of issues that arose there, *Hairenik* took the role of the regime's prosecutor while *Baikar* and other non-Tashnag papers either defended or minimized oppressive Soviet actions.

The actions in question frequently involved the church. This posed a paradox: based on their respective historic lineages, one might have expected the Ramgavars, more than the Tashnags, to take unequivocal stands for the rights of the church and the powers of the church hierarchy. This did not prove so. As the massive confiscation of property from the Holy See at Echmiadzin got underway, it was the Ramgavar *Baikar* that editorialized in 1924 that ecclesiastics did not need to live like princes and that the resources of the church lands might well be better used to benefit "the people." So it was again in January of 1926, when it was reported that the Supreme Council of the Armenian Church at Echmiadzin had made a plea for the reopening of closed churches, the recognition of Echmiadzin's autonomy in the leadership of the Armenian Church worldwide as well as in Armenia, and the cessation of persecution and oppression. *Baikar* ran a front-page article downplaying the ostensible implications of this plea, seeing it more as a formality to legitimate the authority of the council and shore up its relations with the Soviet government, and chiding "these eleventh-hour defenders of the church" (meaning the Tashnags) who had seized upon the report as a source of ammunition against the Soviet government. *Hairenik*, meanwhile, chastised the Ramgavars for explaining away every manifestation of Soviet tyranny.[5]

Because both the Tashnags and the Ramgavars viewed Armenia as the homeland, with or without approving of its present government, their conflicted reportage had in common an emphasis on its identity as the Armenian nation, which put both of them in contrast with the doctrinaire Bolsheviks who viewed it merely as part of a greater workers' state. This was evident in a July 1925 editorial in *Baikar* that noted cheerfully the rapid progress being made toward the industrialization of Armenia, with the building of roads and electrical power plants in all of the major cities and towns—with the credit belonging to the Armenians. "A few years of peace have been enough time to show the world the results of the Armenian creative mind," the paper opined; the progress had come out of "this race's natural capabilities." To be sure, the editorial also included some friendly words for the Soviet regime. Anything that was missing from the current state of progress, the editorial maintained, resulted only from the government's similarities to a shrewd shopkeeper who, with limited capital, knew better than to stock up beyond his means on decorations and merchandise. Still, the paper's editor focused mainly on the virtues of the Armenians, in language transcending any issues surrounding the political system.[6]

Subscribers to *Baikar* thus generally read of a homeland under guardianship; readers of *Hairenik*, in contrast, received reports of a homeland under enemy occupation. The latter press played up all available horror stories about not just Soviet Armenia but the Soviet Union at large. A 1924 series featured a Georgian intellectual who had recently escaped from his country, who described life under Communism as "that hell," "that nightmare," and an order where "rights generally have no meaning." Like the Ramgavars, the Tashnags were willing to concede that improvements had taken place in Armenia, but not to give the Soviet government an ounce of credit for bringing these about. Thus, when at the end of 1923 *Hairenik* reported that the birth rate in Armenia for that year had exceeded the death rate in a reversal from the past several years of Soviet rule, the writer explicitly went to lengths to show that this was due to the strength of Armenians, *in spite of* the actions of their government.[7]

Voicing opinions of events was not, of course, the only involvement that the parties and press in America promoted. Both parties saw a role for themselves in the life of

Armenia, not only in the future but in the present, and thus they incessantly sought support from their constituents for current humanitarian projects. The Armenian General Benevolent Union (AGBU) cooperated with the Ramgavar party. The Armenian Red Cross (*Haygagan Garmir Khatch*), later renamed the Armenian Relief Society, largely administered by women in its early years, was an arm of the Tashnag party. Non-Tashnag Armenian Americans also helped their ancestral homeland through the Committee to Aid Armenia, the *Hayasdani Oknoutean Gomideh*, abbreviated as HOG and derisively nicknamed "the hogs" by some Tashnag critics. Among other causes, HOG raised money for relief when an earthquake hit in the Leninakan region of Armenia. The party organizations, in carrying on this rivalry, constantly impugned each other's motives and authenticity. Both these factions, having the Armenian press as their forums, promoted their programs in such a way as to keep their constituents feeling involved in their homeland. The difference was in how they packaged it. Here again, it went beyond the mere dimension of friendliness versus hostility to the Soviet Armenian government. The appeals contained all-encompassing visions of peoplehood.[8]

An example of that phenomenon comes from the Tashnags' spring 1924 fundraising campaign to transport ten thousand refugees from Near Eastern locales into Armenia, and a front-page article about it in *Hairenik* titled "The Patriotic Enterprise." Before getting around to introducing the particular venture (though it was ultimately the point of the article), the editors first walked readers through a catechism of what, exactly, the precepts of philanthropy vis-à-vis the homeland entailed. "What is the supreme political preoccupation of the Armenian people of our day?" was the opening question. The answer: it was to reunify the scattered Armenian people in the motherland, and then to ensure their security. This was "the national, collective, political interest," and "something which can only take place in the boundaries of an independent national republic." Thus were the goals that must comprise the motto of "all our national enterprises, large or small, local or international." Philanthropy by itself would accomplish nothing of note; any venture to fortify the Armenian people economically and culturally must also empower them politically.

With this philosophical rationale on the table, the article then turned to the more immediate purpose of the pitch: urging readers to attend the many local concerts and dances being held to raise money for the movement of these refugees into Armenia. This section, in fact, put considerable emphasis on one of the more sanguine aspects of such events: the opportunity for Armenian Americans to hear the singing talents of some of their deserving locals. While the venture itself included nothing revolutionary, and while the method of appeal decidedly served to satisfy immigrants' social needs and their musical aesthetic, supporters still needed to be reminded that this all fit into a struggle to liberate their homeland. For the duration of the campaign, *Hairenik* printed reports of local social events with recitals and auctions to help it along.[9]

As it happened, the Ramgavars at that very same time were earnestly working to raise funds for another enterprise, the University of Armenia. Their official organ *Baikar* ran a recurring column encouraging local initiatives and updating readers on progress made. The editors lavished particular praise on the Detroit ADL chapter for the money it raised with a performance of the opera *Anoush*. (Detroit's Tashnags also scored high marks in *Hairenik* for their involvement in the refugee campaign.) Rather than merely running as parallel campaigns, they appeared in rivalry with each other. A piece in *Hairenik*, after taking great pains to show that the Tashnags not only would never denigrate the University of Armenia but were actually responsible for its founding, accused the Ramgavars of diverting potential contributions from an urgent cause in order to finance one that, worthy as it was, could wait. Typically, the piece appealed to patriotism.[10]

Closely enmeshed with all the other homeland-related questions ran that of whether a Holy See located at Echmiadzin, within the borders of the Soviet state and wholly at the mercy of Moscow for its existence, could effectively lead the church worldwide. From 1921 to 1928, North America's Eastern Diocese had a primate who, unlike his embattled successor, was at odds with the Holy See. This made Archbishop Dirayr Der Hovannisian a darling of the *Hairenik* press and a target of criticism in *Baikar*. A Tashnag sympathizer, Archbishop Der Hovannisian angered the Catholicos by encouraging churches to observe May 28, the anniversary of the republic's 1918 founding, and to display the Tricolor, the republic's flag. Armenag Nazar, editor of *Baikar*, wrote numerous editorials blasting the primate for taking political stances, and at the 1927 Diocesan convention he presented a set of grievances that gave the convention the flavor of an impeachment trial. Der Hovannisian was not removed that year, but he resigned in August 1928. There was talk in various circles in 1929 about moving the site of the Catholicos of All Armenians to a non-Sovietized location. The elderly Catholicos Kevork V issued a statement opposing such an idea; *Baikar* approvingly printed his statement while *Hairenik* remarked that he was clearly saying what the Soviet authorities required.[11]

The church provided an important means of connection for America's *Hayoutiun* with the Sovietized homeland. After Kevork's death, Dicran Simsarian of Union City, New Jersey, served as one of the lay delegates to the National Ecclesiastical Assembly that convened at Echmiadzin from November 10 to 13, 1932, to elect Archbishop Khoren Mouradpegian as the new Catholicos of All Armenians. Meanwhile, as has been seen, the church in America had its own divisive politics. The Diocese, operating on a severely strapped budget, had only a locum tenens (temporary acting primate) for a leader, a married priest named Fr. Serovpe Nershabouh, after Archbishop Der Hovannisian's abdication. Fr. Nershabouh died in the summer of 1930. His chosen successor, Fr. Haroutune Sarkisian, also a married priest, became ill right after that and was unable to serve. At the start of February 1931, a Diocesan Assembly convened in New York to elect a new primate. From three candidates, the delegates called Bishop Levon Tourian from his duties as pastor of the Apostolic congregation in Manchester, England, to serve as the Eastern Diocese's new primate.[12]

The West Coast parishes, regarding the Eastern Diocese as too far away to meet their needs, formed their own separate Western Diocese at Fresno, California, late in 1927 and installed Bishop Karekin Khachadourian as their primate in 1928. It did not take long for partisan politics to divide the House of God there. When Bishop Khachadourian's term expired in 1932, he had the support of the Tashnags in his bid for reelection while being challenged by clergy and laity of the non-Tashnag persuasion, many of whom belonged to the ostensibly nonpartisan fraternal order the Knights of

Vartan, which informally had a very non-Tashnag cast. In the September 1932 session of the Diocesan Council, during a segment when Bishop Khachadourian was out of the room for the delegates to elect either him or a successor, the delegates instead voted 12–10 not to have any primate at all. Bishop Khachadourian declared the vote invalid, on the grounds that the council had exceeded what it was legally empowered to do in the bishop's absence and without a two-thirds quorum, and he announced himself to be still the primate pending more legitimate action. He also submitted the question to the Holy See at Echmiadzin. The Council reconvened in February, this time boycotted by the delegates who objected to Khachadourian's continued service as primate. Those left unanimously elected him to another four-year term. The Spiritual Council at Echmiadzin, however, reversed their decision the following summer. Meanwhile, a crisis in the Eastern Diocese was already occupying Armenian community attention, both east and west.[13]

- 2 -

As noted above, during the life of the thousand-day republic, the Tashnag press had painted the regime as synonymous with Armenia while the non-Tashnag press ignored it when not sharply criticizing it. Through the 1920s, the party organs continued to rehearse these contested memories. Thus, when the incident at the Chicago fair on July 1, 1933, took place, both the Armenians who were there to witness it and those who read about it in the papers in the coming days knew exactly how to feel about it, divided along the familiar ethnic partisan lines. This, in turn, ensured that the same would hold true when the primate was stabbed to death in a New York church on December 24 of that year.

Archbishop Tourian had already managed, during his first two years of service, to gain the scorn of the Tashnags as a defender of the Soviet regime and thus to constitute a focal point for the continued partisan tensions. In 1932, in preparation for the annual commemoration of Martyrs' Day on April 24, Tourian instructed clergy to keep observances confined to the churches, in order to avoid any perceived connections between Armenian Apostolic clergy in America and political rallies that might be perceived as anti-Soviet in character. This directive inspired an editorial writer in the Tashnag *Hairenik* to call him "the Bolsheviks' man." Conflicts over commemorations were becoming more frequent. In 1933, the same year that the Tourian controversy later erupted, conflict broke out at the church in Providence, Rhode Island, between the non-Tashnag church council and a Tashnag contingent over whether to have the Tricolor on the stage for a commemoration of Martyrs' Day on April 24. There do not appear to have been any physical fights here, but the Tashnags angrily walked out with the Tricolor while singing the national anthem "*Mer Hairenik*" ("Our Fatherland") and reconvened the memorial in their own nearby club hall.[14]

On July 2, 1932, a year before the blowup in Chicago, *Hairenik* fired a volley at the primate by printing on its front page an article with damning allegations about the churchman's conduct in the Greek city of Smyrna when he was a bishop there a decade earlier. The writer, identifying himself only as Izmirtzi (equivalent to

Figure 3.1 Archbishop Levon Tourian was a martyr in the eyes of anti-Tashnag Armenians and a traitor to his nation in the eyes of Tashnags. His assassination in 1933 intensified the partisan animosity among Armenians in the United States and worldwide. Photo from Wikipedia.

Smyrnan), alleged that Tourian had kept himself safe and fled the city while doing nothing to alert and assist fellow Armenians in the face of danger. Archbishop Tourian responded to the allegation by recalling that he had urged fellow community leaders to attempt to evacuate the Armenians, but that they had agreed rather with the Greek Metropolitan Chrysostom, who expected aid from the Allies if they stayed and resisted the Turkish onslaught. Tourian left when it was made clear to him that his presence would endanger those who were harboring him; the Greek churchman died a brutal death at the hands of the Turkish mob. Predictably, an exchange of editorials ensued that summer between *Hairenik* and the non-Tashnag press over which story was credible.[15]

And yet, a paradox needs to be noted here. Chapter 8 of this book will chronicle a drastic decline in partisan mudslinging in the mid-1960s, continuing into the 1970s, as the two leading parties, Tashnag and Ramgavar, especially on their editorial pages, showed more interest in Turkey than in each other as a focus of indignation. That chapter will note that, while the partisan differences did not entirely recede in those decades, the parties began to coexist more peaceably as other concerns, especially involving Turkey, came to play a larger role in Armenian American identity and in the selling of newspapers serving and nurturing that identity. The paradox is that during 1931 and 1932, the two years prior to the incident at the Chicago fair, one might well have thought this trend to be already underway. Combing through *Hairenik* and *Baikar*, one finds considerably less space devoted to internecine conflicts and more frequent editorials spotlighting Turkey's latest actions and decrying the overly friendly treatment that the Western powers were giving to Turkey. To be sure, there were still editorials critical of each other's stances, but they came as more of a sprinkling than a constant hammering.[16] However, the events of July 1, 1933, ensured that the intensity level of the partisan feud would shoot right back up, and stay up for the next several decades.

The incident that brought Archbishop Tourian and his non-Tashnag loyalists to irreconcilable differences with the Tashnags occurred on July 1, 1933, at the Century of Progress Exposition in Chicago. Arriving at the fair's Armenian Pavilion to deliver an invocation, the primate became aware that the stage where he was to speak had the Tricolor on display below the American flag. From Archbishop Tourian's point of view, appearing on stage with that flag would constitute an act of disrespect to the Soviet Armenian state; thus, he ordered that the flag be removed before he would ascend the stage. The official in charge of the event, Major Felix J. Streyckmans, called for a vote on whether to honor the primate's demand. Satisfied that a majority had agreed to his removing the flag, he did so. Immediately a melee broke out, with fists and even a few chairs flying between Tashnag and non-Tashnag Armenians.[17]

The accounts of that day's events, like so much before and since, circulated with a Tashnag and non-Tashnag version. Each faction, predictably, claimed to have represented a majority of those present at the exposition. The Tashnags insisted that

Figure 3.2 The Tricolor, the flag of the short-lived Armenian republic created during World War I, had deep meaning for those Armenians who had looked upon that republic as the hope of the nation, mainly those of the Tashnag persuasion. For others, it had little or no relevance. From top to bottom, the colors are red, blue, and orange.

only a language barrier had made the vote favoring removal of the flag possible; their opponents countered that a perfectly fluent and articulate translator had made the question clear to all who responded. Above all else, they differed over who was responsible for the violent fracas. From the point of view of the Tashnags, the archbishop had committed a heinous offense against his own nation by refusing to honor its true flag, and he should have thought about the passions that such an insult would stir up. Non-Tashnags, of course, considered the Tashnags to be solely at fault. A *Baikar* editorial remarked that the Tashnags must feel very proud of themselves for having gained so much attention, stirring up trouble at an otherwise peaceful affair and bringing such dishonor to the community.[18]

In the months that followed, Tashnag Armenians seethed with indignation against the archbishop, whom they now considered a traitor to his nation—or, using the more popular term of the time, his "race." Heated quarrels between the two factions became constant and ubiquitous. The affair received considerable space on the pages of the party-run newspapers. "Has our Archbishop forgotten why our nation has suffered through long centuries?" asked one contributor to *Hairenik*. "Has the blood of our one million martyrs been shed in vain?" While the Tashnag press railed against the primate, *Baikar* defended the archbishop for following the church's policy not to antagonize the Soviet government. One essay in *Baikar* expressed condescending pity for persons who had no more important concerns than a flag about which to agitate themselves.[19]

Because the controversy over the Chicago flag incident related closely to conflicting feelings about that flag, it did not take long for the partisan editorial pages to revive the old quarrels about the thousand-day republic of the World War I era. A July 19 editorial in *Baikar* charged the Tashnag rulers of the republic with having lost independence "by reason of their political mistakes and their absolute inability to conduct the nation's works," and with having squandered all their resources on bravado and self-aggrandizement. *Hairenik*, of course, ran articles and editorials praising and defending the Tashnag party's record of governance.[20]

In August at a church picnic in Massachusetts, a group of Tashnags physically assaulted the archbishop. The divided reaction to this attack foreshadowed what was to come: *Baikar* condemned the assault, as well as the ongoing persecution of the spiritual leader whom non-Tashnag Armenians continued to revere. *Hairenik*, while falling short of applauding it, found that the picnic incident showed Archbishop Tourian to be "a source of scandal for our community" and that the situation he had created made his removal from office a necessity.[21]

The new contested memories of 1933 continued to mount up when the annual Diocesan Convention took place in New York City on September 2 and 3. The assembly, with both the elected delegates and a crowd of spectators present, convened on September 2 at St. Illuminator's Church on East Twenty-Eighth Street. Archbishop Tourian ordinarily would have presided, but through a letter read by Bishop Hovsep Garabedian he announced that he was ill and unable to attend. Then, amid debate over whether the convention should remain open to the public or take place with only the delegates behind closed doors, the meeting adjourned for the evening. The following day it reconvened—in two different places. The gathering sanctioned by Archbishop Tourian from his sickbed occurred in the Grand Suite of the Hotel Martinique; the other was held at the original site, presided over by the same bishop who had opened the convention the night before, Garabedian. Archbishop Tourian, upon learning that Bishop Garabedian was not presiding at the Hotel Martinique as according to his instructions, appointed another church leader for the task, Rev. Mampre Kalfayan. Each convocation, of course, considered itself the authentic Diocesan Convention and the other a rump assembly of dissidents. The delegates at the Hotel Martinique voted to affirm Archbishop Tourian's leadership; those at St. Illuminator's voted to remove him from his seat. Both conventions reported their results to Echmiadzin, which promptly sided with Archbishop Tourian and the delegates at the Hotel Martinique.[22]

The anger and quarrels continued throughout the fall. Then, on December 24, the assassination of the archbishop occurred—in broad daylight, during the weekly service of Divine Liturgy at the Holy Cross Church in Manhattan's Washington Heights section. Archbishop Tourian was officiating that day. Preceded by an altar boy, a choir, and a bishop, with two deacons following, he walked in solemn procession from the vestry to the center aisle carrying a staff and a crucifix. He had a bodyguard, but the bodyguard accompanied the entourage only that far. As the archbishop and his attendants proceeded down the aisle, a group of men suddenly jumped up from the pews, surrounded the embattled primate, and stabbed him in the abdomen with a large kitchen knife. Archbishop Tourian tried to hold himself up with the staff, but quickly collapsed. While some congregants walked him to a nearby room, others lunged at the assailants and began beating them up. None of them, however, could be stopped from fleeing before the police arrived. The archbishop died within minutes.[23]

By the end of the day, police had two members of the ARF in custody for the murder. Within several more days, the number of arrested suspects reached nine. Meanwhile, the leading partisan papers reacted swiftly. In the December 28 *Baikar* editorial, written when the press knew only that five Armenians were in custody and that the police investigation had focused on the Tashnag party's New York club, the Ramgavar organ meditated over the question of who would choose the holiest of places on the holiest of days to commit such a horrid, fratricidal crime in the clear view of a multitude that included women and children. The answer was clear: the Tashnags would. The editorial noted, moreover, that *Hairenik* had continually stirred up rage on its editorial page ever since the Chicago incident and, even if for that reason alone, deserved a share of the blame. Only the wielders of the knife could go to jail, but "those who, with their inflammatory spoken and written words, spurred on the rage of the assassins" would bear the wrath of the Armenian people.[24]

The same morning's *Hairenik* reciprocated the accusatory sentiment. The editorial began by philosophizing about the lamentably divided state of the Armenian population.

> It can be said confidently that life in our colonies would have far more peace and harmony if we did not now have a government seated at the head of Armenia, run by a foreign power's tutelage and force, steeped in antinational and antireligious ideas, which carries out the work of systematic and boundless oppression, to divide and destroy all our national organizations … and sow discord in every phase of Armenian life in the name of worldwide revolution.

What was more, disquiet and dissension would not exist appreciably in the ranks of Armenians "if there were not among us whole organizations which, addicted to their blind hatred of the Armenian Revolutionary Federation, encourage in every way the plots and connivances of the Soviet government against international Armenian solidarity." The situation had grown graver, the writer continued, now that "the enemy Soviet government [had] decided to turn the international Armenian church into a tool to destroy the peace-loving Armenian nation and decisively bury the Armenian cause." It was from this resolution that had arisen "the past year's furious struggle against the Armenian Tricolor and all the national values which that flag symbolized." All those who aided and abetted this work of the Soviet enemy (a category in which Tashnags clearly held the felled churchman himself) shared in the moral responsibility for "Sunday's frightful event." So too, the editorial continued, did those Armenians (obviously including the editors of *Baikar*) who, instead of calling for the archbishop's removal after his misdeed in Chicago, had turned the affair into an anti-Tashnag crusade and intensified the disunity. This tragic spilling of blood, the writer concluded, should stand as a lesson to all those intent on making Armenians a divided community.[25]

The murder of Archbishop Tourian stimulated tensions, including some fistfights, throughout the Armenian community. One morning in mid-January, somewhere between seventy-five and one hundred Tashnag-affiliated merchants had placards nailed to their businesses that read: "Do Not Patronize This Store! It is a member of the Dashnag—A secret order that assassinated Archbishop Leon Tourian of the Armenians of U.S.A." In at least one apartment building full of Armenian families, on East Twenty-Fifth Street in New York, Ramgavars and Tashnags called each other murderers and Communists in graffiti on walls. Armenian school children called each other names, some having no comprehension of what they meant. In an Armenian grocery store in Washington Heights, New York, an anti-Tashnag mother, in the presence of her daughter of about five years old, menaced a Tashnag woman with one of her daughter's roller skates. Tashnags "became people with horns to the children," the daughter would later recall. The tension spread worldwide. On February 25, 1934, in a suburb of Athens, Greece, it was reported that seven Tashnags reportedly set upon a man known to have taken part in open expressions of outrage over the deed, and that the victim of the assault drew and fired a revolver, wounding one of the assailants and sending the others fleeing.[26]

Early April saw riots between Tashnags and anti-Tashnags break out in Boston and Chicago. The aftershocks of the murder spread to personal and family relationships as well. In some instances, siblings who had fled the genocide together stopped speaking to each other now. Congregations, meanwhile, became either entirely Tashnag or anti-Tashnag in their membership, with forcible expulsions and violent fights in some instances. In January 1934, St. Gregory's Church in Philadelphia saw the two factions take turns seizing control of the building and locking each other out of Sunday services, with local police and courts having to referee the mess. In Troy, New York, the anti-Tashnags ousted four trustees from the area church and announced plans to publish the names of Tashnags who lived in that part of the state, even appealing to the non-Armenians to assist in their social ostracism.[27]

The nine suspects, several of whom had fought as volunteers in the Armenian Legion in 1918, stood trial in New York from June 8 to July 14, 1934, with forty-two witnesses testifying for the prosecution and thirty-five for the defense. The courtroom was packed with spectators representing both political orientations, and a much larger Armenian American population followed the proceedings through the press. Anti-Tashnags, of course, considered the nine Tashnag defendants and the whole Tashnag party guilty of the cold-blooded murder of a man they revered. While Tashnags regarded the slain churchman as a traitor and many felt that traitors deserved to die, the nine men on trial denied any involvement in the killing, and the party stood by them, viewing them as innocent scapegoats. An editorial in *Hairenik* remarked skeptically on the number of witnesses who had cited either confusion or fear of Tashnag reprisal as their reason for having taken so long to bring their stories into focus for the authorities, and charged that they had been prompted, or even bribed, by the Archbishop Leon Tourian Committee that the Diocese had formed several days after the murder. (Future New York governor and presidential candidate Thomas Dewey served as that committee's private counsel.) When the jury convicted the nine, *Hairenik* ran an editorial accusing the judge of bias and opining that a truly impartial trial would not have produced such an outcome.[28]

The jury convicted the two leading suspects, Matios Leylegian and Nishan Sarkisian, of first-degree murder. The judge sentenced them to death, but Governor Herbert H. Lehman commuted their sentences to life in prison, regarding a death sentence for just two out of nine as an unfair inequality. The remaining seven—Osgan Yarganian, Martin Mozian, Juan Gonzales Tchalikian, Mihran Zadigian, Ohanes Andreassian, Harry Sarafian, and John Mirijanian—received shorter prison terms for first-degree manslaughter. Those seven were paroled at the start of the next decade; the remaining two got out in 1958.[29]

The Tourian affair created a new contested memory, and it fit snugly with those already in place. With the help of the partisan press, which had furnished reminders all through the elapsing decade, one set of Armenians remembered the thousand-day republic as the embodiment of their nation and viewed the Tricolor as its symbol; another set viewed Armenia in completely different terms. Thus, one set regarded Archbishop Tourian as having desecrated the symbol of Armenia, while others regarded the primate himself as their nation's most revered symbol. For decades to come, Tashnag Armenians believed the nine men who went to prison for the high churchman's murder to be innocent scapegoats, while non-Tashnags regarded both the nine defendants and the Tashnag party itself as guilty of the archbishop's murder.

- 3 -

On the surface, the point of contention between the Ramgavar and Tashnag parties with respect to the homeland was clear: the Ramgavars, like the other anti-Tashnag parties, accepted Soviet rule over eastern Armenia; the Tashnags did not. Much of the Ramgavar-controlled *Baikar* and *Armenian Mirror*'s coverage of the homeland emphasized the favorable direction the country was taking with respect to its industrial and cultural development. This is not to suggest that Ramgavar editors never criticized the Soviet regime, but they held back from pounding on the table in indignation about anything going on there, even the extreme oppressions of the Stalin era.[30] The Tashnag press, in contrast, incessantly reminded its readers of everything bad concerning the Soviet state.

This discourse fit into a larger dynamic at work in the Armenian community in the United States. These political parties, all of which operated internationally and aspired to influence the future of the ancestral homeland, depended for their sustenance on the allegiance of a population of immigrants and their descendants who, whatever they might think and feel about the homeland, had much about their lives in America to occupy them. Their relationship with America, the country where they lived, was inescapable and constant; their relationship with Armenia, especially for those who had never been to any part of the ancestral homeland, was more optional and took more effort to sustain. That these parties found the support they needed shows that at least a fair portion of their desired constituency was willing to make that effort, and indeed no argument is being made here that ethnic leaders and institutions manipulated immigrants and their progeny into doing anything contrary to their own desires and inclinations. Even so, one can see a symbiotic marketing relationship between the parties and the community, with a product line that included party membership, social and recreational events, and of course newspaper subscriptions.

Following on this train of thought, the product line also included ideas and emotions about Armenian identity, bound tightly with the questions of the ancestral homeland and one's ideal relationship to it. Simply put, the Tashnags, unlike their opponents, felt a sense of struggle surrounding the homeland. In the inaugural issue of the ARF English-language *Hairenik Weekly*, Vartouhi Calantar Nalbandian expressed the Tashnag position most directly. Although the Tashnags officially denied that the assassination of Archbishop Tourian was a Tashnag act, Nalbandian did incorporate it into her definition of the controversy by saying, at the outset of her three-part article, that the fight over the Tricolor flag "with its climax, the sensational assassination of a high dignitary of the National Church," had "brought to the fore two attitudes of the Armenian mind." The Armenian population, she proceeded to explain, was divided into "two distinct groups, two fighting camps—those who believe in Armenia, and those who do not." The latter category, comprising the Ramgavars, the Bolsheviks, and portions of the now-declining Hunchag contingent, could be characterized by "the self-deprecatory exclamation often used by them when speaking of the Armenian people: 'Who are we?'"

These are the very words with which our God-fearing and Turk-fearing elders of two generations ago used to phrase their expostulations against the feeble cry for "Reforms" of the infant Revolution: "Who are we to brave the wrath of the formidable Sultan?" Today the same people or the heirs to their tradition and temperament say: "Who are we to measure ourselves against the 'Colossus of the North,' the formidable Soviet?"[31]

Thus, according to the standardized Tashnag position, this conception of the homeland and the inherent sense of struggle for it were the defining marks of a strong sense of Armenianness. To lack that sense of struggle, that feeling of being illegitimately deprived of an autonomous homeland, was to have a weaker ethnic identity.

Articles and editorials in the *Hairenik* papers regularly reinforced the theme of homeland deprivation. *Hairenik Weekly* columnist John Melikian told readers in 1937 of one afternoon when he was walking to the movie *The Good Earth*.

> I started thinking of our earth, the place on earth we used to have and how we haven't got a grain of the earth. I felt kind of sad realizing that once we were a part of a part of the earth, that we put our hands into that soil, that we drank the water from the many streams, that we breathed our own air.

Presently, he stopped for a hamburger.

> It was different. It looked different. It was thick. Real thick. And it tasted different. Parsely taste. Taste like hamburger my grandmother used to make.
>
> Boy, this is swell, I said. Real Armenian Hamburger. And it seemed my sadness disappeared for a moment and I became happy.
>
> And when the girl came I looked at her and we both smiled.
>
> She knew then that I was Armenian and I knew that she was too. We didn't say anything because it wasn't necessary, but in our minds we embraced each other somewhere in Armenia, where the soil was fertile, where the good earth was waiting for us to go and plant our seeds.[32]

What surely looked to any observer like a waitress serving a patron a hamburger and exchanging courteous smiles was, in the diasporic imagination of the Tashnag, a moment of empathy between two exiles from their homeland.

It followed, logically, that this shared sorrow and this struggle should constitute an important part of what the young generation needed to be taught. Indeed Article 10 of the *Tzeghagron* creed for the Tashnag youth catechized, "He who thinks of the future of the Armenian race, must aspire to the liberation of the Mother Country [and] the rehabilitation of the race. The symbols of these ideals are *May 28th* [the date of the founding of the republic in 1918], and the *Armenian Tricolor*." Yet paradoxically, none of this translated into any sort of strategy, plan, or even immediate desire to attack the Soviet state or to upset the status quo. Tashnags grudgingly admitted that, for the moment, the Soviet regime was a lesser of two evils and, for that reason, could only be opposed in the long run rather than the short. Vartouhi Calantar Nalbandian, writing in *Hairenik Weekly* in 1935, explained, "The A.R.F. cannot eject the Soviets from Armenia, in fact, it does not want them to go at this time. Primarily concerned with the welfare of the country it is regarding with deep apprehension the possible withdrawal of the Red Army from Armenia in a military contingency." Such a withdrawal, Nalbandian was convinced, "would mean instead invasion by Turkey and fresh massacres." But, she hastened to add, "that is no reason why [the Tashnag party] should refrain from criticism of and opposition to an odious tyranny and cease laboring for a better day."

Similarly, at a 1937 meeting of a Brooklyn chapter of *Tzeghagron*, the Tashnag youth group (discussed in more detail in the next chapter), when somebody raised the question of when the ARF would realize its aim of an independent Armenia, the Tashnag guest speaker replied that "it is too early now to think of independence. First we must follow the ideals of political aspirations and follow the ideals of true Tzeghagrons before we think of that."[33] The Tashnag Party was thus asking its constituents, not to do anything to change the situation, but merely to feel a sense of identity as a people whose homeland languished under enemy occupation and a sense of membership in a struggle to liberate it. At least where the 1930s were concerned, the key verb was to feel.

- 4 -

The church and its institutional control remained an issue for partisan contention throughout the decade as well as after. As noted, the Catholicos at Echmiadzin who sided with Archbishop Tourian in the 1933 crisis, Khoren I, had succeeded Kevork V in 1930 as locum tenens and then secured the high post in the vote at the November 1932 assembly at Echmiadzin that the Soviet authorities permitted. Khoren's words in an interview with *New York Times* reporter Walter Duranty, printed in November 1934, carry the clear voice of a man struggling to say the right things while acknowledging the obvious. "You know the policy of the Soviet Government and the Bolshevik party on religious questions and so do I," he told Duranty, "but here in Armenia I am happy to say there has been no hot-headedness or fanaticism on either side in religious matters." Referring to the 1932 election, he observed that delegates from outside the Soviet Union (who had constituted a minority at the assembly) had initially held anti-Soviet views, "but when they saw what the Soviet was doing for our Armenian homeland … they became reconciled in a great degree." He credited the government with having given the Armenians, not only "peace and security in which to heal dreadful wounds," but also much financial and material support. He mentioned that a proposal to move the seat of the Catholicos from Echmiadzin to Jerusalem had gone down to defeat at the conference, though omitted the fact that a majority of delegates at the conference, by Soviet fiat, came from within Soviet borders. The Catholicos denied being under any restrictions regarding either communication with bishops or receipt of gifts from outside Armenia. "On the whole," he told Duranty, "I have little cause for complaint. The Bolsheviks understand my position and I understand theirs." A passage of the article also quoted him discussing the Tourian affair, where he praised the archbishop and spoke ill of the Tashnag party.[34]

Indeed, as Catholicos of All Armenians, Khoren enjoyed the unequivocal support of the anti-Tashnags and consistently took stances at odds with Tashnag wishes. Even so, when Khoren died four years later, it was the Tashnag press rather than its rivals that charged foul play most vocally. In an article in dated May 13, 1938, drawing upon "reports from travelers recently having left Armenia, transmitted in an exclusive communication dated April 20 to the Armenian Press Bureau in Boston," *Hairenik Weekly* reported that the Soviet government had assessed a tax of forty thousand rubles on the already impoverished church at Echmiadzin, and that the Catholicos had

Figure 3.3 Khoren I, Catholicos at Echmiadzin from 1932 to 1938. He appears to have been murdered by Soviet authorities. Photo from Lusamut.net.

"perished at the hands of the Cheka either by poisoning or sheer heart failure at sight of the outrages against his institution." According to the story, Khoren had pleaded in vain for time to raise the money from international contributions and then been arrested when he refused to give the *Cheka* the keys to the museum that housed the precious relics of the ages, including a sacred kettle of myrhh (holy oil). The article admitted the uncertainty as to whether the Catholicos had been strangled, poisoned, or driven to heart failure by the anguish of the situation; but in any case, an editorial in the same issue remarked, "the Armenian Spiritual Head died a premature death at the hands of the Soviet Cheka."[35]

Both the conclusion of the *Hairenik Weekly* editorial and the dismissive *Armenian Mirror* editorial that followed raise the question of whether Armenians, or at least Armenian editorial writers, were capable of discussing anything without partisan rancor. The *Hairenik Weekly* editorial closed by opining, "Now that no one has any illusions as to what actually is transpiring in Armenia itself, it were time that Armenians abroad rallied around the patriotic (realistic) faction which foresaw these conditions long ago; compose their differences; and lastly, look to a solution which will prevent the Soviet Government from further disrupting both the Armenian Church and the people abroad." (The Tashnag party's own solution would show itself in 1956.) The following week's *Armenian Mirror* responded to the charge of foul play, or at least the *Hairenik* press's version thereof, with singular ridicule. "The pages of the twin Haireniks," the editorial posited, "have been figuratively dripping wet with the poison—sufficient by now to kill a regiment—that was supposed to have been administered to the holy man by the Cheka." The paper quoted the line from *Hairenik* attributing the death "either by poisoning or sheer heart failure," and remarked, "under no circumstance can it be said that it was due to a combination of a half-hearted heart failure and half a dose of poison!" Then, in case anybody missed the message, the editorial concluded, "We think that Hairenik's exclusive 'poison' serial is sheer hokum."[36]

Actually, Khoren appears to have been strangled.[37]

The 1930s purges and other Stalinist atrocities reached such extremes that the Ramgavar press could scarcely ignore them. The *Mirror* took an unusually critical tone in 1936 when, in response to a new constitution, a Soviet Armenian official named Aghasi Khanchian committed suicide (or *harakiri*, the Japanese term for self-inflicted death for the good of one's nation). In 1938, that same issue of the *Armenian Mirror* that ran the dismissive "'poison' serial" editorial had a front-page story, "Purge Strikes Again: Convicted of Infecting Collective Cows!," which reported on the death sentences of three Armenian farmers for (in the words of the *Mirror* writer) "sowing bad seeds, disorganizing machine and tractor stations, infecting collective farm cattle, and other crimes, as part of the counter-revolutionary plot." An earlier *Mirror* editorial in 1938 had lamented that, "like all the other federated republics, Armenia will not be spared the great misfortune of a bloody purge as it was generally hoped," noting that eight former officials in the Armenian Communist party had been executed and seven more probably would be soon. An article in the same issue spoke of the Stalinist constitution, with its promises of a republic's right of secession, as disingenuous. The following year, the same paper, now merged into the *Mirror-Spectator*, noted ruefully that Armenian intellectuals imprisoned by the Soviet regime were no longer being allowed to communicate with the outside world from their incarceration.[38]

Still, the two leading parties maintained a sharp distinction from each other. The Ramgavar press might on occasion show regret, even anger, over a Soviet action, but only the Tashnags maintained a stance of fierce hostility toward the Soviet state. Overall, the Ramgavars viewed their ancestral homeland as having a temporary guardian and protector, while the Tashnags viewed the Soviet state as an enemy occupier. Moreover, they lost no opportunity to remind their constituents of each other's villainy. All of this grew even more intense in the 1950s, at the height of the Cold War. In these same years, the contested memory of the Tourian affair remained fresh in the discourse of both camps.

"To Supply Armenia with Architects"

The Coming-of-Age of the American-Born Generations

The April 21, 1951, issue of the *Armenian Mirror-Spectator* ran an advertisement from one Marderos S. Boghosian of Danbury, Connecticut, calling for an "Armenian girl to communicate with," toward the object of "Matrimony for his American-born grandson." The following week, a letter appeared from Karekin Martin of an unspecified locale, wondering whether Mr. Boghosian had received any replies and, if so, if he might spare a few.[1] One can only speculate as to how many young Armenian women replied and how much these two men's grandsons appreciated their efforts, but the ads bespeak the same concern on the part of the immigrant generation as that expressed by the uncle in *A Houseful of Love*: inducing the American-born generations to marry fellow Armenians.

But not all first-generation Armenians who harbored that concern thought they could sustain customs like arranged marriage in their new American environment. Indeed, as the US-born generations came of age, it was clear to most that even while a strong sense of Armenianness might persist, changes in culture and customs were inevitable. Young couples in the 1930s and after were less likely to solicit, or even tolerate, their parents' help in selecting their mates, though it remained customary for the families to visit each other and establish relations once the young couple had become engaged. Predictably, young American-born Armenians resisted interference with private dating prior to betrothal. This is certainly not to say that families never called on each other in matchmaking ventures, because this even happened on occasion in the 1940s; however, most considered it obsolete. Even more rare by the 1940s, though not quite nonexistent, was the pressured arranged marriage. Abductions and ceremonial stealing became less frequent and seemed increasingly silly as the years went on. Also, as anthropologist Harold Nelson's 1953 study notes, several mainstream American practices found their way into the Armenian marriage, including the holding of a shower for the bride to receive gifts from female friends and relatives, the superstition that it was bad luck for the groom to see the bride before the ceremony on that day, and the ceremonial kiss.[2]

Immigrant parents, of course, even while (sometimes reluctantly) adapting to liberalization of customs, cared deeply for their children to remember that they were Armenian. But this concern extended beyond the household: from the 1930s onward,

the major Armenian political parties and other diasporan institutions, in a clear effort
to ensure their continued existence in the long run, formed youth organizations,
through which they provided Armenian teenagers and young adults with a steady
calendar of dances, athletic tournaments, and lectures on Armenian history. They did
so in an effort, not to keep the young generation rooted in the world their elders had
known, but to bring the idea of Armenian identity up-to-date in a present-minded,
forward-looking context. They wanted the young generation to feel Armenian, to care
about the future of the ancestral homeland, and to fraternize with other Armenians,
but not at the expense of enjoying a fully integrated position in the American cultural
mainstream.

Indeed, while exhorting the youth to be good Armenians, ethnic leaders also
desired them to be good Americans, and boasted of their constituents' steadfast
loyalty to their host country. It would be a mistake to downplay this as obligatory
lip service. Given that the diasporan political parties aspired to influence the fate of
the ancestral homeland, and that this involved appealing to government officials,
their spokespersons needed to have behind them a solid constituency with a secure
position in their host country's society and economy as well as a firm commitment
to Armenian causes. The parties also needed to keep themselves relevant to persons
in the second generation who, with or without their approval and influence, *were*
becoming integrated as Americans. Thus, the partisan press took diligent notice when
young Armenians in the American schools became editors of high school yearbooks,
won music competitions, and graduated with honors.

Yet an enormous difference still separated the two camps from each other. On the
question of how to be a good Armenian, Tashnag and Ramgavar leaders had very
different messages to teach the youth. Analogous to the two parties' outlooks on
their Sovietized homeland discussed in the preceding chapter, where the one party
promoted a sense of struggle while the other did not, the Tashnags' conception of
Armenian ethnicity and their prescriptions to the youth concerning ethnic loyalty
and doctrinal conformity carried greater demands. They might be viewed as two very
different styles of ethnicity—militant versus celebratory ethnicity—analogous to the
way that the terms *challenge religion* and *comfort religion* have been applied by social
scientists to contrasting theological orientations of communities of faith.

- 1 -

While the Tashnags and their adversaries were more bitterly divided than ever in
the 1930s, one could still see clear similarities in the way their leaders approached
community life. Both the ARF and the Ramgavar party began publishing English-
language weekly newspapers alongside their Armenian-language dailies. The Ramgavar
party launched the *Armenian Mirror* in 1933 (which merged into the *Mirror-Spectator*
in 1939), and the Tashnags followed in 1935 with *Hairenik Weekly*. Through these
papers, elders had a forum to advise and instruct youth on what their priorities in life
should be, and the youth themselves, via letters to the editor, had a forum in which to
talk back to their elders and, at times, complain about each other.[3]

Such letters and editorials had a clear group-consciousness about them. When they referred to "our youth" and "the elders," they conjured up the notion of an Armenian American collectivity, a commonality transcending both regions of origin and individual towns and cities in America. Implicitly, one finds shared expectations among young Armenians about the role that their elders—not just their own parents, but the generation at large—should play in their lives. Side by side was the sense among older Armenians that the youth—again, a broad collectivity—needed to be taught certain requisite ideas and values, in order that they might keep and transmit their sense of identity as Armenians. The editorial pages of the partisan press, one might say, served as a virtual village square for conversations and quarrels on these issues, and played the added role of preserving large parts of the discourse for later historians to eavesdrop on and analyze.

Alongside the English-language weeklies, the parties also founded Armenian youth organizations, including the ADL (Armenian Democratic Liberal, i.e., Ramgavar) Juniors and *Tzeghagron*, later to be renamed the Armenian Youth Federation, launched by the Tashnag party. These organizations provided social outlets to keep young Armenians dining, dancing, and playing basketball with other young Armenians. They also sought to instill a sense of ethnic pride and a knowledge of Armenian history: they bombarded their young readers with profiles of Armenian generals and poets across the ages, and episodes that showed Armenian courage and tenacity. This notwithstanding, in their rhetoric these two leading youth organizations contrasted starkly: the Tashnag youth organization professed its mission with notably more militant language, while the ADL's approach to ethnic identity was more celebratory and less doctrinaire.

The way that *Tzeghagron* was founded says much about the philosophy behind it. On the initiative of the ARF's 1932 international convention held in Paris, General Karekin Nejdeh, one of the revered military leaders from the First World War era, visited the United States and toured around for two years, organizing *Tzeghagron* out of new and preexisting local groups of Tashnag youth. During his tour, he published a fiery essay in the daily *Hairenik* calling for the youth to practice "racial patriotism," which he defined as "devotional worship of the majestic past of our race," "the natural and logical reaction against the foreign environment which is threatening the very existence of our race." The organization adopted some of the vocabulary from the battlefield, including the use of the word *ookht* (meaning "pledge") for each chapter. The uniform included blue shirts and orange kerchiefs, both colors in the Tricolor flag. According to the organization's original creed, members were to "live and act as the warriors of the race wherever they may be, and what ever [sic] social rank they may command outside of Armenia." Alongside the mandate that a youth member must be "One who demands a free and independent Armenia," other items in the creed were a mixture of general platitudes like "Hard working," "Master of a strong will," "Temperate, virtuous, modest, disciplinarian [sic]," with others more specifically geared toward ethnic militancy. Article 3 called for the *Tzeghagron* member to be "*Manly and courageous.* The coward and the timorous can not [sic] become standard bearers of racial aspirations." Point 4: "Always attentive to the voice of his race." Number 6: "Ready to sacrifice himself." *Tzeghagron* had its first annual convention in June 1934.[4]

Frequently, contributors to the Tashnag press expounded on the type of cultural training that the youth should receive to keep them connected with their "race." One frequent writer clearly active in the Tashnag party's youth organization, Mrs. Annie Hatch Boornazian, believed that knowing the language and absorbing a repertoire of folktales, songs, dances, and heroic historical narratives would render to the young "the romance of Armenia," "that quality that has enabled it to live long past contemporary nations, and that lives in the present with an undiminished flame to light those days that are to come." "The individual," Boornazian told readers, "must not only assimilate knowledge, he must assimilate rhythm, as expressed in our dances; he must think in pictures, as in the theaters. He must enter the group and assimilate the group into his consciousness the better to understand Armenia. This is what I mean by culture." And, in a sentence that might be seen as implying group mind-control, Boornazian wrote of the individual Armenian youth that "His thought must be clarified."[5]

Gregory Torosian, in a front-page editorial subtitled "To Exist You Must Fight for Your Cause," put the mandate for clarified thought even more bluntly. Writing just months after the assassination of Archbishop Tourian, Torosian depicted true Armenians as living in struggle not only against foreign powers and pressures for assimilation, but also against fellow Armenians (ostensibly the anti-Tashnags). Thus, the training of Tashnag youth must include the sense of struggle against unpatriotic Armenians in the local sphere.

> In view of the existence of anti-national elements within our people, the national spirit of our new generation must be so developed that it easily manifests itself with constructive aggressiveness to meet destructive arrogance of the anti-national elements, be they organized groups or individuals. **The aggressive spirit of our youth must be a dominant state of mind.** This spirit of defensive aggressiveness must be developed from childhood or rather from early school age and kept alive and active by good and healthy literature.

Armenian boys, Torosian went on to suggest, should also learn boxing. "As 'sport' boxing is a brutal 'amusement,' but as a means of defense boxing should be taught to our boys as a necessity." Whether he meant that Tashnag boys should prepare for possible fistfights with boys of the "anti-national elements," Torosian did not specify. Still, he was clearly saying that the truly patriotic Armenian had enemies, both distant and local.[6]

Like the Tashnags, Ramgavar editors and group leaders also had strong convictions about what the Armenian youth should be taught. Ramgavar advocates wanted the young to remember that they were Armenian and keep connected with their heritage and, if possible, their language. Especially in the early part of the decade, Ramgavars saw the young generation as important to the future of the homeland. Like its Tashnag counterparts, the Ramgavar press celebrated the Armenian heritage, followed the contemporary developments in Soviet Armenia, and looked to a future independent Armenia in which descendants of the present generation in America were to play a part. "It is they," a 1932 editorial posited concerning the youth, "who are to supply Armenia with architects, mechanics, engineers, intellectuals, and artists tomorrow."

Absent, however, was the sense of a contemporary *struggle* for the homeland. The author of this same editorial referred to "the greatest reality of contemporary times, the reawakening of Soviet Armenia." Ramgavar youth were taught to care about the homeland's future and take pride in its past, but the rhetoric of the group did not imply any sense of mission vis-à-vis its present, or even its very near future. In contrast with the Tashnags, who saw their homeland as occupied by an invader, the Ramgavars saw their homeland as being taken care of by a custodian. The Ramgavars' homeland was more a part of their past and their future than of their present.[7]

The Ramgavar press also placed considerable emphasis on the question of how the assets of the Armenian heritage might help the young generation succeed as Americans. An editorial in the inaugural issue of the *Mirror* provides a good example of the Ramgavar tone. The writer referred to Armenian history as a heritage "which epitomizes the unfaltering spirit of a martyred civilization, a civilization which has **survived** despite the endless persecutions to which it has been subjected. It embodies the finest virtues of any age: idealism, courage, piety, and love of liberty and country." The piece went on to depict Armenianness as an intrinsic quality that worked its magic even for those who were barely aware of it.

It is this natural endowment of those who have grown up in the American community life, calmly unaware that their inheritance is of such fine stuff, that has spurred them to high intellectual attainments in American universities, to auspicious careers in the professions, to successful application of the principles of good citizenship. It explains the eagerness, resourcefulness, intelligence, and sturdiness of character that have marked their participation in American business and civic life. It explains their intense pride in the achievements and success of their countrymen.[8]

Amid all these differences, the youth outreach of the two major parties showed substantial similarity in certain basics. Both consistently promoted education and personal achievement, with *Tzeghagron* launching a college scholarship program in 1935. Both *Hairenik Weekly* and the *Mirror* proudly reported on achievements of Armenian students in the American public schools. Both youth groups emphasized sports and spawned athletic teams in their chapters, as well as frequently sponsoring ballroom dances.[9] In short, as young Armenian Americans from both the Tashnag and Ramgavar parties pursued social, educational, and recreational interests common to their American middle-class contemporaries, the youth organizers of both parties encouraged these to the fullest while providing avenues and arguments for the young generation to stay close to their identity as Armenians.

- 2 -

Inasmuch as the Tashnags tended to talk of the homeland with more of the language of struggle than did the Ramgavars, a similar contrast marked the two groups' approaches to the more generalized issue of how to maintain and express their Armenianness, the how-to-be-an-ethnic-group question. Here, it is important not to exaggerate the difference. Ethnic leaders in both camps held forth consistently on the need for Armenians to be good Americans while keeping mindful of their Armenian heritage, and both factions ran dances and athletic tournaments to keep the young generation connected as Armenians. Even so, the Tashnag party promoted an Armenianness that carried a higher tone of urgency and a more specific set of mandates for how to be and feel Armenian. Related to this, while both Tashnags and non-Tashnags referred to the Armenian population as a "race," its preservation carried more sense of high-stakes struggle for Tashnags. Generally, the use of the word *race* in this context tended to steer clear of branding other "races" as inferior, taking on a rather mystical and romanticized quality, connoting the image of Armenians as having particularly desirable traits and assets in their blood, traceable back by many centuries.

Sometimes, one can deduce what members of a community agreed upon by examining their disagreements. Such a window of opportunity, with respect to Tashnag Armenians' perception of "race," presents itself in the virtual village square through a series of letters that *Hairenik Weekly* ran in the summer of 1936 in response to the question the editors posed, "Are mixed marriages desirable?" Indeed, the respondents disagreed on the answer, but they all couched their views in the language of whether intermarriage was good for the future of the Armenian "race" and drew upon the assumption that the Armenians, as a race, possessed inherent personality traits. B. M. Kachadourian of Brockton, Massachusetts, for example, employed these notions to advocate *in favor* of mixed blood.

> For thousands of years we have kept practically free the Armenian blood that flows in our veins. Certainly no people has done more to keep its strain clear of other people. Has it improved our race? Has it made us any stronger? Have our men become better fighters? Have our girls become better mothers? I should answer flatly. No! We are suspended in a midway position. We are not strong enough to win and we are not weak enough to die—so we continue living, getting fat, talking, filling ourselves with our importance and if possible tell *[sic]* other people how important we are. We have to tell ourselves how good we are …
>
> If we continue this way we shall die as individuals [and] as a people. What we need is new blood—new blood brought in from other races. These new elements might spoil our stock—yet they might improve it.[10]

The letter went on to cite examples of how closed-clannishness leads a national group to fizzle out of existence.

One finds a more romantic mindset on the matter in a letter by Souren Melik Kanian, in the same issue. Also affirming the goodness of intermarriage, Kanian sought to assure readers that it was a good thing because it would not happen too often. "In the first place, there is no danger of our race being carried away by the tide. There will be very few intermarriages with other nationalities among us. Our provincialism will take care of that." Still, in a line reminiscent of the Kachadourian letter, Kanian noted that "cross-breeding improves the specie."[11]

Quite another view, though, came in a letter signed as Devrish of St. Paul, Minnesota, an extreme manifesto of Armenian exceptionalism. In terms that allowed for no variation, Devrish declared all marriages between Armenian and non-Armenian doomed to failure because

> the other party is a stranger to us in disposition, traditions, in physical harmony, in domestic mode of life, in food, in religion, in moral conception, and lastly in quality of love .... European races have a certain degree of affinity making intermarriage possible, but we Armenians are the children of the Orient and our centuries-old tradition and character makes it impossible for us to harmonize with those of European make up.

Lest the letter be construed as hostile to "European races," Devrish affirmed that in the typical doomed intermarriage, the non-Armenian party came with the best of intentions: "many non-Armenian girls who have married Armenian boys have sincerely tried to make them happy but they have not succeeded because 'clay will never change'; the Armenian is Armenian and will die an Armenian."[12]

The "European race" closest at hand, of course, was the dominant white American population with whom Armenians inevitably intermingled. Implicit in the intermarriage question was that of whether the Armenian soul was in danger of drowning in a sea of Americanness. Quite a Manichean picture of this concern comes through in Melik Shah's short story "Raxana," which ran in both the daily Armenian-language *Hairenik* and the English-language *Hairenik Weekly*. The protagonist Araxie (who in her later decline takes on the less salutary name of Raxana) has "true Armenian modesty" and "big black eyes, which, if you are really patriotic, you must set them down as Armenian eyes," but enters an American high school "where awaits strong temptation." Araxie accepts and courts the insincere admiration of her American peers, takes up with an American boyfriend, and consequently "looked down on Armenian boys with condescension." She becomes impudent, coquettish, and disrespectful to her family, and—in an abrupt conclusion to the story—is seen several years later looking "bent, twisted, and grown old." As if the story's message needed further articulation, Shah concluded, "May heaven protect us from evil!"[13]

Yet one should not infer, even from this, that any of the Armenian party leaders or newspaper editors advocated an Armenianness that would clash with their constituents' sense of Americanness. In January of 1937, a letter from Mihran Saroyan to *Hairenik Weekly* ironically queried whether Armenians should "adopt the new world with most of its cheap glimmerings" and whether one could "be the perfect American gentleman, and meantime remain the noble ancient Armenian," presently prescribing the solution of striving to be "perfect Armenian gentlemen" rather than "'slick' Americans." The paper ran the letter, but followed it with a response likely written by editor James G. Mandalian (who essentially represented the Tashnag party leadership to his readers) disclaiming any concurrence with the letter's pejorative implications about Americans. And yet, minus the idea that Americans had undesirable traits, the editorial response still maintained the notion of special qualities coming from the Armenian line.

> It may be true that there are some Americans who are slick gentlemen, and it may even be true that there are many Americans who come under that category, but we have a very high opinion of the typical American. And our aim in educating our Armenian youth in the high standards and the ideals of our race is only in order to further raise the average standard of the American and to bring our contribution to the culture of the country we have adopted.[14]

Being able to infuse virtues from their "race" into the veins of their host society fit perfectly with the general call for Armenians to be good Americans.

The intra-Armenian dialogue had a connection with some other dialogues of the time involving mainstream (essentially white) American civic and political leaders, on the subject of ethnicity and the socialization of second generations. Advocates of cultural pluralism were gaining the public ear, including anthropologist Franz Boas, who devoted much of his career to discrediting racialist hierarchical theories, and Horace Kallen with his symphony model (see Chapter 2). A flurry of best-selling books by Slovenic immigrant Louis Adamic in the 1930s and 1940s helped to reinforce the intensified challenge to rigid monoculturalism, and in 1938 and 1939 the federal Office of Education teamed up with the CBS radio network to produce a twenty-six-segment series called "Americans All … Immigrants All," which offered a contributionist celebration of individual ethnic groups, with a segment on "the Negro" and another that included the Armenians in combination with the Greeks and the Syrians.[15]

The model that allowed for immigrants' ability to be true Americans and preserve the best of their cultures of origin was not, in itself, new: a number of the social workers in the settlement houses had championed it decades earlier, Jane Addams most notable among them. Immigrant leaders had asserted it as well. What was new was the range of circles in which the idea now gained acceptance and currency. To be sure, these were mainly the circles where the prime motive vis-à-vis immigrants and their children was still to secure their loyalty to America and its government and, to be sure, their eventual assimilation. Even so, it still helped to create a friendly climate for the efforts of Armenian organizers. In turn, the latter parties took great care to show their efforts as being fully compatible with Americanness and Americanization. At the same time, the pronouncements of the Armenian leaders generally showed a realistic perception that the young generation possessed an essentially American orientation whether their elders desired it so or not. Thus, from different angles, the Armenian American and the merely American outreach organizers shared a concern that there was a "youth problem" or a "second generation problem," and that the problem centered on the need for guidance in finding just the right balance of their dual identities.[16]

Late in 1937, the Tashnags' *Hairenik Weekly* circulated a letter with a questionnaire to persons holding positions of apparent community leadership in a number of other ethnic groups—"the Jew, the Greek, the Italian, the German, the Albanian, the Syrian, the Assyrian, and the French"—to engage in fellowship on the well-understood "youth problem" that they were presumed to share. After summarizing the perceived problem ("They have lacked a distinct sense of national identity. They are neither Armenians nor Americans") and the strategies that the Tashnag party was taking, the letter inquired:

> How do you manage to impart to your young generation the sense of loyalty to the country of their adoption and at the same time a definite interest in your past racial culture and the present fortunes of your people as a race? How do you proceed to teach them your language, your history, your religion, and which of these do you consider the most important factor in the preservation of their racial identity? How do you manage to continue the racial bond?

Yet even that letter defined the mission of *Tzeghagron* as being "to facilitate the process of assimilation of our youth into desirable American citizens" as well as the more obvious one of preserving the Armenian dimension. For all the rhetoric of maintaining the "race," the leaders of the youth movements—Tashnag as well as Ramgavar—knew that an Americanization process was occurring with which they had no choice but to keep pace. Their challenge was not to try to halt or retard Americanization, but to incorporate Armenianness into it.[17] In the coming weeks the paper printed responses, which were generally consistent with the tone of the question.

The emphasis on Americanness in the Tashnag discourse was most marked at the end of the 1930s and after. Early in 1940, Mandalian addressed the Boston chapter of *Tzeghagron* on the characteristics of the "ideal chapter" for the party's major youth organization. In the passage on the qualities that individual members in the ideal chapter should possess, the analogies of an army shone forth. The *Tzeghagron* "must be a convinced soldier of the cause," because "[a] battalion which is made up of physical weaklings, ignorants, and adventure seekers is a mercenary mob and can never become an efficient fighting machine." A moment later, in expounding on the need for discipline and obedience to authority in the youth movement, he noted, "Suppose an army refused to obey its officers, its generals, its captains, its lieutenants, its majors. What would happen to an army like that? How far could they go? How many victories could they carry?" The language of race was also present. Armenian youth were "the descendents of one of the oldest and noblest races of history."

That much could just as likely have come from a 1933 speech. And yet, in other parts, something had shifted. Conspicuously absent in this speech was any reference at all to a struggle for the liberation of the homeland, even in the imagination. (To be sure, that struggle would be back with a vengeance after the Second World War.) Much of what Mandalian had to say to this Boston gathering, in fact, might just as easily come from a Ramgavar leader, speaking at any point in the decade. If they were fighting for a cause like an army, the cause as represented in this speech was not as militarily ambitious as that of Tashnag oratory five years earlier. It was, rather, that of making a good showing in the adoptive homeland ("the noblest and best country in the world—The United States of America"). He charged his listeners:

> Remember, the *Tzeghagron* organization was founded for the purpose of giving our young generation intelligent direction and to develop a class of clean, healthy,

intelligent and self-assured boys and girls. And the ultimate aim of this preparation is two: first to direct the proper integration of these youth with our adopted or natural, as the case may be, homeland of America; the second, to enrich them with their parental background so that they may become all the more useful citizens.

He then referred to the general ethnic mosaic that was the American population, the contributions that the Armenian "race" had made to this amalgam, and the relationship between Americanness and Armenianness.

There is much in you which is splendid and beautiful and charming which is American. Your dress, your language, your manners are American. You attend the American university, the opera, the football game; you cast your vote in an American ward, and you win your medals and scholarships in American institutions.

The free air which you breathe, the self-assurance, the sense of sportsmanship, the frankness, the straightforwardness and courageousness, the instinct to fair play, the initiative, and the opportunity to help lift yourself up and to succeed, all these you owe to America. But you also inherited the basic goodness, the insatiable love of freedom and truth and justice, and your poetic soul from our parent race—a poetry which is helping enrich the spiritual wealth of America.

He concluded with a surgically honed position statement on what loyalties and commitments Armenian American youth should display. "We do not ask much from you," he posited. "We do not ask any unsavory blandishments and swashbucklings that you are an Armenian." Moreover, "we do not ask you to volunteer in an army and fight the battles of Armenia, although that would be quite a proper thing did the opportunity come and did you have the inclination for it. We know that your first allegiance, devotion, and love belongs to America, first and last." Even so, he continued, his listeners should "become the friends of Armenia, the cause of your parent people." And by what means? "You can do this by making a small sacrifice, by writing an article in a newspaper, a letter to the editor, by putting in a good word for the Armenian cause when the opportunity comes, you can be helpful in a thousand and one ways." But to do so, they must be educated. "That," he surmised, "is the reason why we ask you to take a little of your time and study your people's language, its history, and its culture."[18]

Meanwhile, in the competing Ramgavar party's press, one occasionally heard voices of concern that some in the community might be *too Armenian* and *not American enough*. Thus, Nazareth Barsumian of Barrington, Indiana, opined in a letter to the *Armenian Mirror-Spectator*, printed February 8, 1940, that many Armenians in America were so concerned with their Armenianness that they were derelict in their Americanness. "We Armenian-Americans should NOW be awakened from our dormant stage of citizenry," he wrote, "and put to work to render service to our adopted country as any worthy citizen should." He saw a danger of immigrants being so intent on their ethnic loyalty that their loyalty to the host society might suffer. For him the ideal Armenian American would be "proud and happy in finding another love of equal merit in the service of his adopted country." A formal editorial in the same issue responded to the letter.

> There can be no question that there does exist in our midst an element of immigrant Armenians, who despite their long years of residence in this country, have acquired neither the language nor any other rudiment of American culture; who have moved about the width and breadth of this vast country without receiving a lasting impression of the tremendous environment about them. But is this a truly representative picture? We do not think so.[19]

In this exchange, what matters most is the concurrence between contributor and editor on the ideal: that Armenians in America *should* be as integrated as possible into the political life of their receiving country.

In that same issue, editorial staff regular Paul Norehad offered a case for "Virile and Helpful Armenianism: A New Definition." In a sharp contrast from those who had once feared intermarriage, Norehad suggested that some of the young Armenian Americans—specifically the young women—should become more viable for intermarriage, with the help of the Armenian youth organizations. The problem Norehad outlined was partly one of math, originating from the reality that some number of Armenian males were looking to the non-Armenian realm for their mates, making it necessary for young Armenian women to do likewise. But, he lamented, "our girls, because of an outworn code of modesty, do not have the same opportunity, and are destined to remain spinsters in an exact ratio to the number of marriages between Armenian boys and American girls." He continued:

> The competition of American girls in the marriage market is further aided by another internal attitude, namely the still quite prevalent notion that Armenian girls must not cultivate the charms (or shall I say, the feminine wiles?) of her [sic] American sisters. Therefore, on this one point alone, that is, because of our concern for our girls, the continuance of the Armenian Tradition is of primary importance. Let us hope that as time goes on these Armenian organizations would be instrumental in bringing on a splinter-less Armenian society in America.[20]

In the issue just the week before, Norehad had put forth an even more codified manifesto of the ideal function of Armenian American heritage, and with it the ideal function of the Armenian American community leadership, in the lives of the young.

> No social institution will survive unless it performs some useful function. The **Armenian Tradition** must prove its value to the young Americans of Armenian descent; it must in some way contribute to his social or economic advancement; in some tangible manner it must be conducive to his or her happiness, otherwise it can not [sic] hope to win a place for itself in contemporary American life.[21]

Thus, the marketers of ideas about ethnic identity in both the Tashnag and the anti-Tashnag camps knew that they were talking to a population whose everyday life was, of necessity, rooted in the American environment, and could ill afford to miss any of the benefits of inclusion and integration in that American mainstream. The question, then, had become one of how constituents might remember and express their Armenianness in the context of living a lifestyle which, especially for the American-born, was being shaped by the liberal ideas, modern technology, and consumer culture of the host environment. The challenge was to craft an Armenianness that, far from being a hindrance to the Americanness, would complement and augment it.[22]

Even so, one sees a clear and marked difference, one that directly paralleled conflicting feelings about the ancestral homeland. Social scientists Peter L. Benson and Dorothy L. Williams, as part of a 1982 study of the religious behavior of Congress members, in talking about the styles and intensities of belief that distinguish different denominations from each other, invoked the terms *challenge religion*, faith that centers on a sense of obligation to act, and *comfort religion*, which gives the devotion more of an elective quality.[23] Scholars of religious experiences appear to have done surprisingly little with those concepts, which, among other applications, could be employed to contrast a fundamentalist church, where strict devotion and doctrinal conformity are deemed necessary for the salvation of the soul (for which reason proselytizing is also deemed necessary), from a more liberal one where the message is the more salutary assurance of God's love and help. Scholars of ethnic identity might consider looking to this model for an analogous distinction: that between *militant ethnicity*, ethnicity with an inherent sense of a high-stakes struggle, versus *celebratory ethnicity*, that which demands less while still encouraging participation for the joy that it brings. As the Tashnag vision posited a homeland under enemy occupation while the non-Tashnags had a homeland under friendly temporary guardianship, the Tashnags had an ethnic identity that demanded work and practice (perhaps even boxing lessons) to defend and preserve, while those of the anti-Tashnag coalition, while still wanting the youth to attend Armenian dances so they could supply Armenia with architects, were a bit less doctrinaire and austere about it.

But across the partisan spectrum, the leaders were marketing their ideas and their products (including newspapers and dance tickets) to their constituents. To do so, they had to be in touch with what those constituents needed and wanted. Indeed, the young took part in the dialogue. Parts of that conversation have been preserved for posterity, on the letters-to-the-editor pages.

- 3 -

The typical Armenian elder remembered a village, a literal one, where many families knew each other and took part in the socialization of each other's children, including helping find them mates. In the 1920s and before, as has been seen, Armenians' activity as immigrants in the United States included involvement in compatriotic societies, wherein former inhabitants of a specific village kept in contact with each other and kept the memory of their village alive. At the same time, through their daily Armenian-language newspapers including *Baikar* and *Hairenik*, and through political parties that were nationally as well as internationally based, they created a virtual village transcending lines of both old-world and new-world geography. Now, in the 1930s, by the creation of youth organizations and the launching of an English-language weekly press, Armenian American community leaders expanded on their virtual village, giving it a multigenerational dimension. In that village, as noted, the editorial pages served as a virtual village square.

There was an enormous difference between the literal and the virtual villages. For the Armenian born into a literal village of old, there were no escape and no option. For young Armenian Americans in the 1930s, the virtual village of youth groups and newspapers might be more peripheral to their everyday lives as young urban Americans. Membership in that village, in fact, with the ideas to debate and the New Year's dances to participate in, could be described as a commodity being packaged and marketed, with editors and youth-group organizers as promoters and the second generation as the consumers. James Mandalian's 1940 speech to the Boston chapter of *Tzeghagron,* excerpted above, makes particular sense in that light: he was seeking to persuade potentially skeptical buyers that the brand of Armenian ethnicity he was selling, while certainly not free, was comfortably within their means; they would not have to hock their Americanness in order to buy into it.

In that virtual village square, there was much dialogue. Armenian American elders, as has been seen, had plenty to say about how the youth should think and act. The youth, at least those who wrote letters to the editor, had much to say in response. The message from the youth in these letters was not one of resistance to being taught, but rather a proffered critique of how the older generation might do a better job of teaching them. A young person writing to the *Mirror* in 1935, referring to young Armenians' alleged lack of interest in "their race," cited the "failure of parents to instill a desire in their children to develop such an interest." Many parents, this critic charged, complained of their children's lack of interest in Armenian language and history, but failed to speak Armenian with their children or talk to them about the names and dates of their heritage. Later that same year, when an article in the Armenian-language *Baikar* had criticized the youth for lack of interest in the New Britain parade for the Connecticut tercentenary, a reader named Haig Yossian wrote to the *Mirror* that the elders, with their perception of "our supposedly superior education and intelligence," were laboring under "the false and ridiculous conclusion that we shall unassisted lead them from the mire to the summit of Ararat …. Isn't it the first law of nature," Yossian went on to ask, "that parents must teach their children just as long as they are able?" Yes, he declared. "They are destined to guide us and teach us just as long as they are able to do so. It is their duty to their Creator just as it shall be our duty to perpetuate in our progeny what we have been taught."[24]

If the elders came under indictment for dereliction of duty as cultural teachers, they also took their knocks for the dividedness of the community. Editors and institutional leaders, of course, agreed that discord was terrible while regarding it as the exclusive fault of the opposing faction, but there were also voices that faulted the stalwarts of both sides of the schism for that schism's existence. Armenian youth, wrote Mardie Jay Bakjian, saw their parents "injecting antagonism and hatred and fear" into the Armenian identity at the expense of its claim to greatness. "If Armenians would regard their children with greater seriousness in respect to the future of the Armenian race" and "endeavor to help each other to make this life more endurable," then "not only would their children be satisfied and smile over the cooperative feeling present in their kind, but the earth, the solid earth itself would breathe with greater relief, and the race, the Armenian race would not have existed and struggled and bled in vain."[25]

One revealing volley in *Hairenik Weekly* exposes the varied perceptions among the youth as to how much cultural liberalization the typical Armenian parent was open to. As late in the decade as 1938, the regular *Hairenik Weekly* columnist who called himself The New Yorker generalized that many young Armenian men found the young women too much trouble to date, largely on account of their overly strict parents. "An Armenian girl enjoys as much privacy in her life as does the proverbial goldfish," he posited, proceeding then to paint the scenario wherein the hapless Armenian male suitor attempted to court an Armenian girl.

> His family tree falls subject to investigation under a "third degree" assault of interrogatives; and if his status proves satisfactory the daughter is permitted to accompany him. Still there's a catch to it. She must be back at a puritanical hour; and even though the boy and girl realize with sinking heart the unfairness of the ultimatum, both are willing to acquiesce for the sake of avoiding an argument which may jeopardize their chances for the evening.
>
> Thus becomes self-evident another reason why an Armenian boy will not take out an Armenian girl; he must also take her back home and face the music.[26]

He referred to a purported incident in which a father of a twenty-one-year-old Armenian girl chased a young man down the street with an ax for bringing his daughter back a few minutes after midnight. The New Yorker also found that, when two young Armenians began dating, the parents and neighbors quickly assumed that they were to marry, and saw shame in the failure to do so—another factor inhibiting Armenian males from choosing their coethnics as dates. "What a sad commentary," he concluded, "that a race with our potentialities should remain supinely fettered by the habits, customs and beliefs of an out-moded ancestry!"[27]

The responses that followed showed disagreement, not only over how pervasively such strictness reigned, but also over how much one should desire it. Artacky Berberian of Providence, Rhode Island, chided the generalization "that it is difficult to date an Armenian girl," insisting that no such difficulty existed "if the youth enjoys a good reputation." Furthermore, she went on, "we must not forget that we, as civilized people, adhere to certain and definite customs." She also pointed out that some American parents scrutinize their daughters' dates too, though many other American parents (though "not the average"), being "of somewhat indifferent attitude or loose morals," let their daughters do as they please. "I do admit," Berberian continued, "that there are many backwoodsman type of Armenian parents. But then, let us not forget that in the old country, conventions and customs were altogether different than those of America. We can't expect these parents to grasp new conventions overnight."[28]

The following week, the *Weekly* printed a letter from Setrak Minas, secretary of the *Tzeghagron* organization. Minas, clearly in line with the views of his party and many of the paper's readers, affirmed the importance of social modernism and lamented that many Armenian immigrant parents were clinging to old-world ways, believing—understandably though mistakenly—"that if racial identity was to be retained all racial habits and customs must be retained." Consequently, he explained, youth saw parents as narrow-minded while parents saw youth as unmindful of their heritage and its morality. "Instead of meeting around the conference table, they aligned themselves in separate warring camps. Impasse is the present result." As a result of that impasse, Minas found, Armenian youth had gone to the extreme of accepting indiscriminately everything modern and American while rebelling against everything Armenian. But in order not to appear disrespectful of the host society, Minas suggested that the more decadent forms of social life—including many of the era's dance styles—were not authentically American, but rather the imports of other, less civilized immigrant groups. Young Armenians, he found, had "accepted without question the vulgar product from the melting-pot ingredients contributed by the ill-bred people of many nations now residing in the United States. This product they think is modern and American. How horrible their error." Harkening back to the editorial that had launched the exchange, he noted that checking a male suitor's family tree was "the custom of well-bred people in every country in the world." Both generations, he ultimately believed, needed to compromise.[29]

Generational discourses frequently bespoke fundamental questions of where Armenians collectively saw themselves with respect to cultural change. The same holds true as one looks at those letters in which young Armenian men and women rendered critiques to each other's comportment. One series of such critiques appeared on the editorial pages of the Ramgavar party's *Armenian Mirror* in the summer of 1935.

It began when writer Albert Chakarian, in his column "The Talk of the Town," observed that many Armenian girls possessed superior looks, but "because of a lack of proper training in the art of make-up, hair dressing and in wearing clothes remain the usual Armenian types." Many Armenian men, he found, had good cause to lament, "Why is it that our girls can't carry themselves as American girls do?" He opined, "If our girls would only, besides copying the ordinary mannerisms of the so-called Americans, who are such in name only, cultivate a little sophistication, and add a little grace to their carriage, acquire a little taste, simple yet effective, in their dress, they could easily have things their own way." He then added that he, personally, would choose an Armenian girl anyway, being "an exception to the rule because of an inherent love for my race," but that other Armenian men were looking to American women rather than Armenian. Chakarian concluded his editorial with an invitation for "the fair sex to criticize Armenian males."[30]

The invitation was accepted speedily. A letter in the following issue signed only by "Two of the Fair Sex" called Armenian men conceited, and further charged that they neither knew how to wear clothes nor could cultivate "that certain nonchalance." A longer letter in the same issue, signed by "Elsie," who mentioned that she had been attending Armenian dances from ages fifteen to twenty-five, said of fashion tastes that "most of our Armenian boys wouldn't know the difference between a Paris creation and a Filene $3.95." As for how Armenian and American girls compared, "in every case where an Armenian boy brings an American girl, she is never dressed correctly. She generally wears a suit with sport shoes and looks as though she belongs in the State ballroom or at the Tent." Elsie also quoted a young American man who attended a dance of the Armenian Students' Association, as exclaiming that he "had never in all his life seen so many beautiful girls and so many gorgeous gowns," showing that "even if our Armenian boys do not appreciate us, others do." Of "our boys": "they are nothing as far as looks are concerned and they still insist on attending formal dances with brown and grey suits." In a coup de grace that showed a touch of self-deprecatory racialism, she added that in her ten years of attending formal dances, "I cannot recall … ever seeing an Armenian fellow that was tall, well-mannered and good-looking. Most of them have been about five feet tall, dark and homely, and still they think they do the girls a big favor when they talk with them … Let all Armenian boys take a good look in the mirror before deciding to pick the opposite sex apart."[31]

Participants in the virtual village square of the editorial page were ever conscious of comparisons in social style between young Armenians and the youth of their host society. Later that same month, S. R. of Worcester, Massachusetts, in a letter titled "A Staunch Defender of the Armenian Girl," wrote scornfully of "our 'American' sisters" for "forever dolling up like Easter bunnies" and praised Armenians for knowing that "fine birds don't need fine feathers." Yet she also appeared to concede that young Armenian women lagged behind their non-Armenian contemporaries in areas where they would need to catch up.

> It is quite right that our girls don't carry themselves as Americans do, but why say they 'can't'? Isn't it all a matter of time? Armenian ethnics, customs, mannerisms, and ideas weren't built overnight and cannot be changed so quickly as the shake of a lamb's tail …. The Armenian girl realizes her shortcomings and that is far more than the boys have done (masculine conceit, you know).[32]

And, in defense of their male counterparts, Nemra S. of West New York, New Jersey, wrote, "Perhaps the Armenian boys do not have that nonchalance that American boys possess but upon what comparison do our girls base their judgment?" He suggested that the young woman might use other immigrant groups for their comparisons. "Does a group of Italians, Germans, or Jews show more nonchalance than we Armenian boys do?" The writer added that the fashions of nonchalance cost money, which not every young Armenian man had. (Given that the year was 1935, the same was also true of many non-Armenian contemporaries.)[33]

These writers, generally speaking, appear to have agreed on what the ideals were, while either finding fault with each other for failing to realize those ideals or explaining why some patience on the subject was in order. Generally speaking, the shared ideal was to effect a blend of innate, traditional Armenianness and modern, sophisticated Americanness, that is, to be modern-American, Armenian-style. Implicit in the discourse was the shared self-perception as a group living at the crossroads of the Eastern and Western worlds. The East had the simple rural virtue and a touch of mystique, the West (as exemplified by American youth) had the sophistication, and the task of Armenians was to find just the right blend. That this principle was well understood can be most effectively gleaned from those letter writers who alluded to it with some irony, like the young woman who complained in the January 8, 1935, *Mirror* that the recent New Year's dance had featured music that was too American, while the ladies' coat check was "run on a basis characteristically à la armenienne."[34]

Fighting on Many Fronts

The Second World War and Its Aftermath

As the Second World War was winding down, editor Bedros Norehad of the *Armenian Mirror-Spectator* let his readers know how much a quotation in *Hairenik Weekly* had disturbed him. It was in a letter to the editor from a sailor serving in the war. "Being in a professional capacity as exterminator of undesirable characters," he quoted the sailor as having told readers in April of 1945, "I would deem it a great pleasure to see the name of John Roy Carlson added to the growing list of persons who should be methodically liquidated before the world can once again know the peace and contentment it previously enjoyed." In his commentary, Norehad remarked to readers of his own paper:

> I certainly would not have taken the trouble of writing these lines if the author of the foregoing deplorable statement had been an old-generation partisan zealot or a professional terrorist. But when a young Armenian-American, born and bred in this free country, comes out openly in favor of 'liquidating' the critics of a discarded old-country terrorist group it is time to stop and ask just why and how much such unmanly, vicious, and thoroughly unamerican ideas have found soil in the minds of our American-born generation.[1]

Avedis Derounian, known at the time by his pen name John Roy Carlson, was born in 1909 in Alexandropolis, Greece, and moved to the United States in 1921. He began his career in journalism in the 1930s, serving for a time as editor of the *Armenian Spectator* before its merger with the *Mirror*, and as a contributor to various publications. Having known Archbishop Tourian from childhood as a family friend, he covered the trial of the nine Tashnags accused of his murder and made his outrage clear at every opportunity in the years to come. Under the auspices of the firm for which he worked, he provided research for the CBS radio show "Americans All ... Immigrants All," and his files during this period show a broad interest in American ethnicity, among other subjects. Carlson gained national prominence in 1943 with the publication of his book *Under Cover: My Four Years in the Nazi Underworld of America—The Amazing Revelation of How Axis Agents and Our Enemies Within Are Now Plotting to Destroy the United States*. To research it, he had used a fake identity (George Pagnanelli), infiltrated numerous extremist groups, and even published, via crude mimeograph, an anti-Semitic newsletter, all to ingratiate himself with Nazi and fascist groups and gather evidence against them. This of course made both enemies and admirers in circles that had little to do with matters Armenian.[2]

But Carlson saw to it, with his first chapter, that his book would also win him the adulation of anti-Tashnag Armenians and the hatred of Tashnags. That chapter, titled "A Black Christmas," recounted the assassination of Archbishop Tourian—even though it had little relevance to the main purpose of the book—with no doubt in the telling as to the guilt of the Tashnag party. But given the broad readership that the book was intended for, he was not merely speaking as an Armenian to call the Tashnags bad Armenians. He was also addressing Americans, and calling the Tashnags bad Americans, as was Bedros Norehad when he took notice of a young Tashnag's fantasy of liquidating Derounian/Carlson.

If the anti-Tashnags knew how to equate their partisan cause with American patriotism and paint their Armenian rivals as bad Americans, the Tashnags more than held their own at the same art. In the 1940s and 1950s, Tashnags sang in the most militant choruses of American nationalism and anti-Communism. To be sure,

Figure 5.1 Avedis Derounian, also known as John Roy Carlson, a hero to non-Tashnag Armenians and a villain to Tashnags. Courtesy of Avedis Derounian Archive, National Association for Armenian Studies and Research (NAASR), Belmont, MA.

the party tempered the anti-Soviet rhetoric during the war in observance of America's tenuous alliance with the Soviet Union, but once wartime cooperation had given way to Cold War suspicion and alarmism in the United States, as the following chapter shows, Tashnag leaders became fiery Cold Warriors. They could now conveniently depict American patriotism and the Armenian struggle to liberate the homeland as interchangeable concepts—and, of course, paint fellow Armenians who failed to share this sense of mission as bad Americans. None of this could have occurred, of course, had the two opposing sides not shared the consensus that their constituents should be good Americans as well as good Armenians, and that to be a bad American was to be a bad Armenian.

During the war, the priority of Armenian Americans was to support the American quest for victory, by buying war bonds and by serving in the armed forces. The papers continually affirmed their constituents' service to their host country, and by this time increasingly referred to the *Hayoutiun* as "Americans of Armenian descent." After the war, as the victorious nations tried once again to craft lasting institutions of world peace, Armenians in America divided: not on how loyal they should be to their host country, or even on what they should ask their host country to do for their ancestral homeland, but on a number of issues that involved the migration of compatriots, including displaced persons trying to enter the United States and Armenians of the diaspora seeking to repatriate to the land of Ararat.

- 1 -

From 1941 to 1945, America was at war. The generation of Armenians now coming of age, which might later supply Armenia with architects and artists, had to supply America with soldiers now. The start of a new world conflict gave author Peter Balakian's mother flashbacks to the village massacres and death marches she remembered from 1915, bringing her to the point of nervous breakdown and temporary institutionalization. Most survivors did not lose their grip on reality, but nightmares were not uncommon. Many who remembered seeing their whole families, in some instances including their children, murdered in cold blood now faced the trauma of seeing their American-born sons go off to war, sometimes to die. Suzanne Basmajian wrote of this poignancy in *Hairenik Weekly*:

> I wonder at their spirit and courage, these women who have seen so much in their time, who have watched their homes burned and their mothers and fathers killed, who have left their villages and traveled on the road to an unknown place, and yet today they are faced with a similar problem, and they smile and take heart and comfort through one another.[3]

The ethnic institutions mobilized their resources on behalf of Armenian American servicepersons. The Women's Central Committee of the AGBU posted an ad inviting "all service men of Armenian descent" as guests at club social events and at the dinner table in private homes, to "enjoy the comfort and atmosphere of an Armenian home during their furlough or leave from camp." The press also sent copies of their papers to servicepeople of Armenian descent, posted addresses where readers might send letters, and ran stories on the efforts and accomplishments of individual Armenian Americans in combat against the Axis. Notices also ran, of course, when Armenians died in the war.[4]

As was the case in the First World War, Armenian editors and party coordinators sought every opportunity to display the steadfast American patriotism of their constituency. When the Treasury Department encouraged ethnic communities to vie with each other for high-volume purchases of war bonds, the Armenian American press strongly urged readers to turn out. The Armenian General Benevolent Union (AGBU) reported from its annual convention at the end of May 1942 that it had already invested $25,000 in war bonds and prepared a directory of Armenian American men serving in the war, titled *Our Boys*, with a copy tendered to President Roosevelt. In the fall of 1943, a front-page ad in the *Mirror-Spectator* called for readers to participate in the Third War Loan Drive to build a warplane that would be called the *Spirit of Armenia*. The following year the Tashnag-run Armenian Youth Federation, which had recently changed its name from *Tzeghagron*, raised money for the "Buy a Bomber" campaign, a move calculated both to increase US air power and to advertise the AYF's existence. The Pan-Sebastia Construction Union, a compatriotic society of Armenians from the town of Sebastia, bought war bonds and also donated for supplies to Soviet troops to help their countryfolk in Soviet Armenia. Other compatriotic unions did similarly.[5]

Some of the exhortations in the Armenian American press appealed to readers' Americanness without even making reference to their Armenianness, using first-person plural forms to denote the American nationality. "Our economic and material sacrifices have been tremendous and still mounting higher with no end in sight," observed a *Mirror-Spectator* editorial at the start of 1943, but still "incomparably lighter" than life after losing the war would be. "Our hope to beat the enemy in 1942 was dim and far away," but "1943 brings us brighter prospects for our arms on all fighting fronts." Winning the war must be "the all-important problem confronting us" in the year now beginning, having "our industrial and military might geared up for a knock-out blow at our enemies." The following week, the editorial writer praised President Roosevelt's "forceful and resolute tone" in responding to the challenges of "a newly elected radical and insurgent Congress, jealous of its prerogatives, poised and determined for a reshuffle of powers invested in the Chief Executive." Readers' full inclusion in both the American nationality and the war effort was automatically assumed, rather than in any way contextualized or asserted.[6]

However, Armenian Americans during the war years were also regularly reminded of their Armenianness, especially with calls for money to aid suffering Armenians overseas. In the spring of 1942, the AGBU actively solicited donations to help Armenian refugee populations, first in the Near East and then in Greece. *Hairenik Weekly* similarly printed a letter appealing for aid to the Armenian National Sanatorium of Lebanon. Repeated articles and editorials in the *Mirror-Spectator* also highlighted the importance of the common kinship between Armenians in America and abroad.[7]

As the Armenians navigated and negotiated their duties and benevolences during the war, it took little to unleash a contentious partisan exchange. For instance, encouraged by Stalin at the same time that the US government was naming bombers for Armenians, the Catholicos at Echmiadzin and high-ranking clergy in the United States spearheaded a fund drive to endow a "David of Sassoun Tank Column Fund" in the Soviet army, named after a probably fictitious seventh-century Armenian battlefield hero. The *Mirror-Spectator* promoted the drive, noting early in 1943, "the sons of Armenia are performing glorious and super human feats on the battlefields with many other peoples of the Soviet Union." Later in 1943, Ramgavar party notable Bedros Terzian met with the Soviet consul general, and reported to *Mirror-Spectator* readers, "I assured him of the loyalty and unreserved support of the Armenians for the Soviet Union, and apprised the consul of our aspirations and future expectations" (that latter reference presumably relating to Kars and Ardahan, discussed later in this chapter). The Tashnag press did not applaud the David of Sassoun Tank Column. Referring to the coalition of the Ramgavar party, AGBU, and the openly pro-Soviet Armenian Progressive League as "a pitiable minority" and "disregarding the overwhelming majority of the Armenian people, as well as the strongest and foremost Armenian organization, the Armenian Revolutionary Federation," a *Hairenik Weekly* editorial also opined that, with Americans helping the Soviets through the Lend-Lease program, and with two hundred thousand soldiers from Soviet Armenia fighting with the Red Army, Armenian Americans could better use their resources to help Armenians in need in Greece, Syria, France, and the Balkans, than to buy the Soviets a few extra tanks.[8]

Indeed, by no means did the World War II years see any truce between the Armenian partisan factions. Especially in Armenian-language forums, the Tashnags and Ramgavars still rehashed the contested memories from the First World War era, integrating them closely with the quarrels of the present. A key point of contention was the 1920 collapse of the Tashnag-dominated republic and the Sovietization of eastern Armenia. *Hairenik*, in several 1942 editorials arguing the importance of unity and solidarity in the Armenian community in this time of world war, chastised those Armenians who had not supported the republic against its Bolshevik enemies. *Baikar*, on its own editorial page, presented a far different memory of 1920 pre-Soviet Armenia: a population demoralized and discouraged, unhappy under Tashnag rule as well as in danger of being overrun by Turks, ultimately rescued by Sovietization. In a 1942 *Mirror-Spectator* article on the history of the AGBU, Leon Guerdan chronicled the events in the homeland during and just after the First World War without mentioning the republic at all.[9]

Partisan Armenians did not have to rely on the past for contested memories; the war years generated fresh new ones. Just after the war ended, it was disclosed that a group of Tashnags, including the celebrated General Drastamat "Dro" Ganayan, made a pact with Nazi leaders in 1942, with terms that included favorable treatment of Armenians living on Nazi-ruled soil and self-government for Armenia should Soviet rule collapse, all in exchange for Dro's efforts forming an Armenian legion to help the German war effort. The pact's existence was never disputed, but its significance was understood in polar-opposite ways by the two opposing factions. The *Mirror-Spectator* editorialized in 1945 that "These leaders and their blind followers can never be the liberators of the Armenian people .... They conspired with the Nazis in the darkest and most critical period in the history of our people." Just over a decade later, a starkly

Figure 5.2 Drastamat Ganayan, popularly known as General Dro, a hero to Tashnag Armenians and a villain to non-Tashnags. Photo from Wikimedia Commons.

different interpretation of that pact appeared in a Tashnag eulogy for General Dro written by familiar *Hairenik* editor James G. Mandalian. During the war, Mandalian wrote, "there were thousands of Armenians who became stranded" in Germany and the occupied countries of Europe, and "it was necessary to do something to prevent these unfortunates of sharing the fate of the Jews." Dro earned the trust of the German government on behalf of the Armenians, and "as a result of his intercession not a single stranded Armenian was harmed." Evidence does bear out that Dro's efforts saved thousands of Armenian lives, including those of Soviet Armenians from the Red Army held in Nazi POW camps (though some in that category later suffered a cruel and unjust fate when they returned to Soviet authority). A 1946 State Department report surmised, "Although some Armenian leaders, notably those in Nazi-dominated areas, were won over [to the idea of enlisting Nazi support for a post-Soviet Armenian republic], official central and regional bureaus as well as the overwhelming majority of the Tashnags refused to enter into such an alliance."[10]

Avedis Derounian, using the pen name John Roy Carlson, published the aforementioned *Under Cover* in 1943. Predictably, the Ramgavar press praised his book while *Hairenik* condemned it. An editorial in the *Mirror-Spectator* declared, "John Roy Carlson deserves the deepest gratitude of all Americans and Armenians for his courageous exposure of our enemies within." A front-page article the following week concluded, "Therefore it is with the greatest joy, the deepest pride that we of the Armenian-American community point to Derounian to say 'He is one of us.'" Of course, the Tashnags shared no such pride. A *Hairenik Weekly* editorial, contemptuously referring to Derounian as "the Armenian name-changer," equated his treatment of the Tashnags with an assault on the Armenian people themselves. Saying that the attack would be less hurtful if it came from a Turk, the writer summed up the emergence of Carlson by declaring, "a viper from within our own bosom has risen to sting us."[11]

The Armenian population in the United States, one can infer, continued to provide a market for this divided partisan press that interpreted events of the nation and the world for them in forms consistent with their merged Armenian and American identity. Part of that identity was the sense of being either Tashnag or anti-Tashnag, and that component included a strong sense of the opposing party's identity as both bad Armenians and bad Americans. If the war years brought Armenians of different factions together for a season, the Cold War ensured that the partisan animosity would endure for some time to come. Moreover, even when the exchanges concerned matters American, the underlying question was still that of which camp had the right to speak for the Armenian Americans.

- 2 -

For those Armenians in America who followed the news of problems in their ancestral homeland, a distinct Armenian cause existed in 1945 just as much as it had in 1919. In June of 1945, as delegates to the San Francisco Conference sifted through the appeals of myriad national and other groups while crafting a charter for a new United Nations Organization, the Armenians were among those nationalities from whom they heard. The planners at San Francisco were told that Armenians had lived for years under Ottoman oppression; that reforms had been promised at the Congress of Berlin in 1878 but never delivered; that Armenians had been massacred in huge numbers in 1895–6, 1909, and especially 1915 and after; that they had fought valiantly on the side of the democracies in both world wars; that they had received many promises and assurances from the Great Powers that had come to naught; that the boundaries drawn up by President Wilson in 1920 represented the rightful territory of the Armenian state that must now be fulfilled by way of forced land concessions from Turkey; and that Armenians now scattered around as refugees must have the opportunity freely to repatriate to their ancestral homeland. Yet the delegates at San Francisco might well have experienced some déjà vu as they read these arguments, because they received them in not just one memorandum, but two. One came from a Tashnag contingent called the Armenian National Committee, which of course presented itself as representing the Armenian people. Alongside that memorandum was another, from the Armenian National Council of America (ANCOA), headed by Rev. Charles A. Vertanes, which identified itself as representing "all the Armenian civic, social, cultural and religious organizations in the United States, except a small fascist faction known as Dashnags." The editorial pages of the party papers made sure their readers did not miss a note of it, and *Hairenik Weekly* devoted considerable space to mocking the writing and grammar of the anti-Tashnag memorandum. Yet for all the mutual labeling and recriminating, one still found no difference in the substance of their claims.[12]

Indeed, for a short time during and after the war, Tashnag and anti-Tashnag Armenian organizations seemed to agree on major goals and aspirations even as they continued to spar. This even briefly meant sharing some common cause with Stalin. During the war, by necessity, the Tashnag party relaxed its anti-Soviet rhetoric. *Hairenik* editorials, rather than pushing to make Armenian support for the Soviet war effort conditional on the meeting of its demands, stridently defended the Tashnag party against Ramgavar accusations that it took such a stance. At the same time, Stalin's ideological onus for nationalism and religion gave way to the pragmatic realization that he needed the cooperation of Armenians *as Armenians*, and of the church *as a church*, to help win the war. He also, as historian Felix Corley has shown, solicited the cooperation of the locum tenens at Echmiadzin, Kevork, for his plans to demand the return to Soviet Armenia of Kars and Ardahan, two provinces that Lenin had ceded to Turkey while creating the Soviet Armenian state.[13] As the war drew to a close, Armenian American organizations of both partisan stripes favored fulfillment of this demand. In August of 1944, *Hairenik Weekly* ran an editorial titled "No Apologies for Armenia," prevailing upon Stalin to make good on his government's implicit word.

> If since 1920 the Soviet has done nothing about the extension of Armenia's boundaries the usual objection offered was that the Soviet was too weak to be in a position to revive such issues. Today that objection has ceased to exist. Today the Soviet is in a position to settle the Armenian Question as based upon the unanimous consent of the Armenian people as well as upon indisputable factual and moral rights. Only after the completion of Armenia's natural boundaries will Stalin and his comrades have the right to repeat their statement of 1920:
>
> What burgeoise [*sic*] Europe was unable to do we have done, we have solved the Armenian Question.
>
> To do this will be a moral triumph of the first order for Soviet Russia.[14]

Such Tashnag editorials did not carry a tone of great friendliness toward Stalin, rather one of calling on him to make himself useful for a change. Even so, in stark contrast with the direction the party would take several years later, on this issue the ARF concurred with its adversaries, and with Stalin, on a specific desired action. It was in similar spirit that the Tashnag-founded Armenian National Committee (ANC) sent a telegram to Stalin in April 1945 asking him to remember the just cause of the Armenians with regard to territory controlled by Turkey.[15]

Those next few years, a spirit of optimism for the future of "Armenia"—an imagined entity transcending any existing state and its political situation—pervaded the community. As before and since, Armenians rallied hand in hand with sympathetic non-Armenian allies. Armenian American press and advocacy groups put much energy into the question of Kars and Ardahan, never losing an opportunity to invoke the name of Woodrow Wilson. Even so, the emerging geopolitical landscape worked against the Armenians' interests with respect to this territory.

One of the first noted events of the Cold War was the president's "Truman Doctrine" speech of March 12, 1947, where he asked Congress for aid to the government of Greece, for its civil war against Communist insurgents, and to Turkey, to help the regime fend off pressure from Stalin for land cession—that is, his call for the surrender of Kars and Ardahan—as well as joint control of the Bosporus and Dardanelles straits. (The Montrose Convention of 1936, superseding the Lausanne Treaty of 1923, had given Turkey control over these waterways, though with some stipulations.) The context in which the demands occurred put the Armenian cause in bad stead, because from the Western point of view Stalin's demands represented, not the return of Armenian territory to Armenia, but the transfer of territory from the "free world" to the Communist world. Stalin presently dropped his demands, including Kars and Ardahan, but in the meantime Truman delivered his speech, resulting in American aid to the governments of Turkey and Greece for their struggles against Communist challenges.[16]

Armenian spokesmen had no complaint about aid to the Greeks, but raised vociferous opposition to American money for Turkey. Once again, they attempted to draw on the good will they had earned with their support of the Allied war effort, as well as their status as good Americans. Turkey, they pointed out, had joined the war on the Allied side at the last possible minute and undoubtedly would have joined Germany had Germany been winning. Rather than let themselves seem unpatriotic to America, they would if possible suggest that the policymakers who favored Turkey were, in those brief, unthinking moments, being unpatriotic to America by neglecting the rights of some of its most special citizens.[17]

Late in March 1947, the ANCOA held a mass meeting in New York in which a speaker, making use of a newly coined word, charged Turkey with having initiated the "monstrous concept of genocide." From April 30–May 4, 1947, a World Armenian Congress met at the Waldorf Astoria in New York City with seven hundred delegates from points worldwide and speakers including US senator Charles U. Tobin. and Eleanor Wilson McAdoo, daughter of President Wilson. The Congress drew up a resolution addressed to the United Nations; Archbishop Tiran Nersoyan, primate of the Eastern Diocese of the Apostolic Church in America, presented it at Lake Success (the UN's temporary site on Long Island) in early June.[18]

Shortly after, some three thousand persons attended a related rally at Carnegie Hall, where Colonel Sarkis M. Zartarian delivered a speech that thoroughly enmeshed the expansion of Armenia, as chartered in 1920 with the Treaty of Sèvres and Woodrow Wilson's map, with the spirit of American patriotism. Zartarian quoted at length from a speech that the governor of Massachusetts, Robert F. Bradford, made several weeks earlier at an observance of Patriot's Day, which celebrated the 1775 battle of Concord and Lexington. In addition to the standard celebration of "those brave men," Bradford had particularly attracted Zartarian's notice by saying, "Today the small nations of the world look hopefully to us to preserve their liberties and to effect a just peace." Putting that together with Bradford's exhortation to "accept the responsibility of April 19, 1947" (the anniversary of Concord and Lexington), Zartarian felt able to claim a noble lineage for the "Armenian Question" and Armenia's entitlement to Kars and Ardahan. In this losing battle, the Tashnag and anti-Tashnag presses voiced identical views.[19]

- 3 -

Other issues found the Tashnags and the anti-Tashnags on opposite ideological poles. Early on in the postwar years, the case of a man who desired to repatriate with his children to Soviet Armenia received much Armenian attention. Hampartzoom Cholakian, who had fled from persecutions in 1913, had placed his five children in the care of the Catholic welfare facilities in New York in 1942 when his wife was seriously ill and his own resources could not support them. Later still, in 1947, he sought to reunite his family and move to Soviet Armenia. At this point three of the children were still in Catholic orphanages, and the facilities refused to release the children. Cholakian's appeals to the federal courts got him nowhere. Highly interested in the case was Rev. Charles A. Vertanes, who lobbied the State Department and helped to keep the issue visible to the public. The prelate of the Armenian Church, Bishop Tiran Nersoyan, was quoted as having remarked that the court ruling against Cholakian served to "destroy family life in the interests of ideology." The Tashnag press gave it the occasional brief mention in a tone that implied an unsympathetic stance to the cause of allowing the children to be taken to Soviet Armenia. The dispute continued until the children came of age, at which time they resolved the matter by opting to stay in the United States.[20]

Rev. Vertanes, Bishop Nersoyan, and the Ramgavar party represented the more optimistic and salutary view of the state of the homeland. Especially in matters concerning Soviet Armenia's desirability as a place to live, their positions contained elements of wishful thinking. Indeed, Vertanes's 1947 book *Armenia Reborn* greatly romanticized conditions in the Soviet state. As the decade of the Second World War gave way to the 1950s, the ARF stood increasingly in a position to put the anti-Tashnags on the defensive about their position vis-à-vis the Soviet state, and to align itself with American politicians who were fighting the Cold War.

Also divisive along Armenian partisan lines was the displaced persons (DP) issue. Right after the war George Mardikian, owner of the famous Omar Khayyam's Restaurant in San Francisco who had donated his services as caterer for the 1945 UN conference, traveled to war-ravaged Germany to advise and assist the US Army with its food distribution mission. While there, he learned to his surprise that there was a DP camp at Funkerkasserne housing two thousand Armenians who had been prisoners of the Nazis and were afraid after the war to return to their homes in Soviet-controlled territories. Including DPs at other sites, the number of Armenians turned out to be about four thousand. For the time being they were being sustained by the efforts of the United Nations Relief Administration Agency (UNRAA), but that agency was soon to be phased out. The refugees had cause to fear for their future. According to his memoir, Mardikian told inhabitants at Funkerkasserne,

> I can solemnly promise you this. I will see to it that our people in the United States are told about you. It is their duty to help you, to give you a chance to find homes for yourselves so that you can start building your *ojakhs*—your hearths and firesides—all over again. If it takes all of my fortune and all of my life, I will help you.

Mardikian returned shortly to San Francisco, addressed a gathering of local Armenian American prominente, and with the assistance of young attorney Suren M. Saroyan oversaw the founding of the American Committee to Aid Homeless Armenians (ANCHA). Though it was ostensibly a nonpartisan concern, it was Tashnag groups that supported it. Chapters of the Armenian Youth Federation, for instance, collected clothing to send. ANCHA also set about arranging for these DPs to be admitted to the United States.[21]

At least two of the most prominent anti-Tashnag Armenian Americans sounded alarms about the admission of these displaced Armenians into the United States. Avedis Derounian (John Roy Carlson) wrote an article on the subject in the short-lived *Armenian Affairs*, a quarterly published by the ANCOA and edited by council chair Vertanes. After reviewing the crimes and misdemeanors of the Tashnag party, including the assassination of Archbishop Tourian and the accord with the Nazis in Germany, Carlson reported that his visit to the main DP camp at Stuttgart, Germany, had shown him that its inhabitants were receiving heavy Tashnag indoctrination and that, claims to nonpartisanism notwithstanding, the funding and leadership of ANCHA were all Tashnag, alongside a handful of nonpartisans, apparently including Mardikian himself, who were essentially dupes of the miscreant party. Clearly including government officials among his desired audience, Carlson called for an inquiry into the nature of the persons being admitted. "In the interests of America, the investigation should disclose how many of these are European Dashnag Party members, or Dashnag-trained recruits …. It would establish whether non-Dashnags among the DPs were compelled, under duress, to pledge themselves to the Dashnagist cause on their arrival here." He also expressed concern that the present government officials might not know how to recognize which DPs were indoctrinated Tashnags: "It's insidious, and difficult to detect by untrained American officers. Expert non-Dashnag Armenian counsel" (perhaps alluding to himself) "should be called in to aid in the task of investigation." Derounian's correspondence files indicate that he made some attempts to influence refugee policy at the expense of Tashnag supplicants.[22]

The matter also came up in a letter by Vertanes himself to Bishop Nersoyan. Vertanes was responding to a concern expressed by the bishop that the quarterly seemed excessively caught up in Armenian partisanism. In the course of defending his editorial policies, Vertanes referred to a recent conversation he had had with Rev. Dr. Frank B. Fagerburg, pastor of the First Baptist Church in Los Angeles, "regarded by many as the greatest pastor here on the West Coast." The two churchmen talked on considerable common ground, Vertanes reported.

> Then, right in the midst of the discussion he said something about the disgraceful conduct of Armenians in Los Angeles who were bringing D.P.'s to this city. He said they were an "utterly unreliable, cheating, lying, thieving" group. These are his own words. He must have felt pretty badly about the situation, since Dr. Fagerburg is not given to the use of such language. To substantiate his charges, Dr. Fagerburg gave details of the conduct of the "Armenians," most recently in connection with the arrival of about two hundred Armenian D.P.'s.

Do you think it was wrong for me to have assured Dr. Fagerburg that the group he was referring to was a small ostracized faction, known among the Armenians as Dashnags, and that the ANCHA was solely their child, and had nothing to do with the vast majority of Armenians? Not to have done that would have been to betray our own people.[23]

The deep inner motives of Carlson and Vertanes are beyond the scope of this study, but it might be inferred that they did not wish to see any drastic increases in the percentage of America's *Hayoutiun* who felt beholden to the ARF. These men appear to have had at least some temporary influence on admission decisions, because DP Commission files show a letter from Mardikian to the commissioners dated January 9, 1951, complaining of reports that subordinate officials of the commission had taken it upon themselves to deny visas to some Armenian refugees on grounds of alleged Tashnag affiliation or orientation. How that particular complaint was resolved is not clear, but ANCHA's records indicate that it helped relocate 3,400 Armenian DPs, 2,551 of whom were granted entry into the United States.[24]

The postwar years were also the Cold War years. If the assassination of Archbishop Tourian ensured that partisan tensions would endure for at least some decades to come, circumstances of the Cold War helped increase their intensity level even further. The Tourian assassination occurred in a church, of course, dividing the house of the Lord against itself, and in the Cold War years the church continued to be one of the many arenas in which Armenians concurrently fought the Cold War and the Tashnag/anti-Tashnag battles. During these years of contest, the parties made sure their young generations knew the score.

The Armenian Americans' Cold War

In May of 1952, one John Arzoomian, age thirteen, whose Tashnak-affiliated father owned a grocery store in the Bronx, tried to run away from home. He was no ordinary runaway: he aspired to "join the Army" and help liberate Armenia from Soviet rule. "I'm out to fight Communism," he explained, "because my relatives in Armenia have been mistreated and I'd like to do what I can to help out."[1] The lad was of course rushing things a bit—even by Tashnag party standards—but he had apparently learned his lessons well. In keeping with the party's intent, he knew his identity as a member of a nation whose homeland chafed under enemy rule and in whose liberation he had a role to play. At any time since 1920, viewed through the Tashnag lens, this would have made him a good Armenian. Now, in 1952, it made him a good American as well.

The dawning of the Cold War could not have come at a more opportune time for the Armenian Revolutionary Federation (ARF) in America. The Tourian affair, the allegations of fascist leanings, and the controversy over General Dro's actions in Nazi Germany might, at first glance, appear to have put the *Tashnagtsiutiun* on the defensive with a reputation as precisely the sort of group that American patriotic societies would wish to target for some remedial assimilation lessons. On the contrary, events in the late 1940s and 1950s provided ARF leaders and their partisan constituents in the United States with golden opportunities to present themselves, not on the defensive, but on the march as the standard bearers of virile patriotic Americanism as well as authentic and virtuous Armenianness. The postwar political climate gave them much to work with.[2]

- 1 -

Winston Churchill announced in 1946 that "an Iron Curtain" had "descended across the Continent" of Europe, and in the years that followed, no American could escape the constant reminders of this. On May 1, 1950, citizens of Mosinee, Wisconsin, with help of the American Legion and with several penitent ex-Communists portraying the arch-villains, spent an entire day enacting the horrors of a Communist takeover of their town. The following year, *Collier's* magazine devoted its October issue to a set of articles fantasizing about the US-led reconstruction of a post-Soviet Russia, including a triumphal staging of *Guys and Dolls* at the Bolshoi Theater. Indeed, ordinary Americans at the dawn of the 1950s found themselves called upon at every turn to feel under siege by Communism, and to feel a sense of membership in the crusade to slay this dragon.[3] This climate helped the Tashnags, like the ethnic nationalist contingents of other immigrant populations, to present their love for the ancestral homeland and their American patriotism as not only uncontradictory but synonymous and mutually edifying. Government agencies and private civic groups, at least some of which received CIA funding, encouraged immigrant communities from Iron Curtain countries to feel a strong sense of mission to liberate their homelands from the Soviet yoke, and encouraged ethnic leadership cadres such as that of the ARF to see themselves as governments in exile.

Behind the scenes in Washington, the struggle was even more serious. On the surface, the public understood the Truman administration's anti-Communist policy as governed by the buzzword *containment*, and associated his Republican successor with more aggressive policies geared toward liberating captive peoples. Indeed, the Eisenhower campaign of 1952 made Truman's so-called "cowardly containment of Communism" an object of scorn. Even so, the notion of liberation did not start with Eisenhower. Truman's advisors were using the term "psychological strategy" as early as 1947. In 1948, the newly created National Security Council issued a report advocating "a coordinated campaign to support underground resistance movements in countries behind the Iron Curtain, including the Soviet Union." Also in the late 1940s, the CIA helped parachute several hundred anti-Communist émigrés into Albania and made similar efforts to destabilize regimes in Ukraine, Yugoslavia, and Rumania.[4]

In 1950, the same year that the National Security Council codified the liberation doctrine in its NSC-68 document, the Truman administration created the short-lived Psychological Strategy Board to advise upon means of destabilizing the Soviet empire by encouraging dissatisfaction and rebellion within. Famed journalist Tom Braden (the same one whose book about his family, *Eight Is Enough*, inspired a 1970s TV series by the same title) headed an agency within the CIA called the International Organizations Division, through which the CIA secretly dispensed money to ostensibly private anti-Communist groups. A key organization in this category was the American Committee for the Liberation of the Peoples of Russia (AmComLib), founded in 1951 and subject to multiple name changes, which began broadcasting to population groups within the Soviet ambit via Radio Liberation in 1953. (The nationalities represented on the committee had their tensions. Not all Russian nationalists agreed that the liberation of Russians from the Soviets should also entail the liberation of Armenians, Ukrainians, and others from the Russians.) Also in the broadcasting business were the National Committee for a Free Europe, jointly sponsored by the CIA and the State Department, whose Radio Free Europe targeted Eastern European satellite nations, and the State Department, which ran the Voice of America before turning it over to the United States Information Agency when that new bureaucracy was created in 1953.[5]

There were, of course, huge differences between what the general public perceived and what took place behind closed doors. Zeal for policies aimed at out-and-out regime change actually *subsided* after Eisenhower took office, and there was frequently a blurred line between purposeful plans for regime change versus containment called by a different name. The founding document of the United States

Information Service (USIS), drafted in 1950, articulated four objectives, the last of which was "helping to roll back Soviet influence, not by arms, of course, but by all means short of war." But a close look at the wording of one of the components of this objective—"keeping the Soviet bear so busy scratching his own fleas that he has little time for molesting others"—suggests that much of the rhetoric of liberating captive peoples was really a repackaging of containment: preventing the Soviets from gaining any more ground.[6]

Foreign policy goals aside, governmental and civic agencies clearly wanted Americans to *feel* a strong sense of participation in a liberation mission. As historian David S. Foglesong observes, "the campaign had a greater impact on how Americans felt about themselves than on conditions inside the USSR." One coalition in particular took care to keep the liberationist spirit burning: that between committed Cold Warriors in Congress and spokespersons for immigrant communities whose ancestral homelands lay behind the Iron Curtain. One audible voice in this coalition was Representative Charles J. Kersten of Wisconsin. When Congress deliberated passage of the Mutual Security Act of 1951, authorizing $7.5 billion in military and economic aid to friendly countries fending off Communist challenges, Representative Kersten moved quickly and successfully to attach an amendment allowing for $100 million to go toward helping anti-Communist exiles take up arms to liberate their countries from the Soviet yoke. On February 22 and 23, 1952, Kersten and his fellow Republican representative Orland K. Armstrong of Missouri convened a Conference on Psychological Strategy in Washington, with representatives of fifty different ethnic communities, as well as various governmental, religious, and educational establishments in attendance.[7]

Editor James G. Mandalian of *Hairenik Weekly* attended that Psychological Strategy Conference in February 1952 and reported to his readers that much of what he heard there mirrored what he and his Tashnag colleagues had been saying right along. Indeed, the politics of the Cold War provided the ARF with a climate made to order. Tashnag leaders' twin goals in the United States, one should remember, were to present themselves to Armenians as the epitome of true Armenianness and to present Armenians (especially Tashnag Armenians) to the larger US population as model patriotic Americans. Thus, the upsurge in such rhetoric that came with the intensification of the Cold War at the end of the 1940s and start of the 1950s required no stretch and no shift with respect to how and where the Tashnag party situated itself. Tashnag leaders, moreover, sought out every opportunity to align themselves with ethnic leaders who represented parallel struggles, especially Lev Dobriansky, economics professor at Georgetown University and president of the Ukrainian Congress Committee of America, and Charles Rosmarek, president of the Polish American Congress. Tashnag leaders made use of every possible photo opportunity in this coalition. For example, when representatives of eleven ethnic groups held a testimonial dinner in New York honoring Representative Kersten, *Hairenik Weekly* made sure its readers knew that Armenians were represented there.[8]

Reuben Darbinian, clearly a leading spokesman for the party in the United States after having been justice minister in the Armenian republic of 1918–20, used his position as editor-in-chief of the Tashnag press to deliver reminders of Soviet tyranny, accounts of Armenian participation in global anti-Communist efforts, and calls for more action by the American government for the cause of liberation. "It is not *the good example* of the United States," he declared in 1951, "but it is her *readiness to help the Soviet peoples in their struggle for liberation* which will insure their cooperation with the West and render them apt to make sacrifices for the liberation of entire mankind." In reference to the passage of the Kersten amendment funding aid to liberation struggles, Darbinian opined in 1952:

> Today, apparently, the leadership of the free world, at least in the United States, finally has come to realize that it is impossible to compete successfully with the Soviet's global conspiracy by adhering strictly to the traditional and antiquated policy of non-interference, and that it is imperative, at least to a certain extent, to set aside the motheaten policy and to match the Soviet conspiracy with the same revolutionary methods in order to rid mankind of its menacing scourge.

Along the same lines, the Tashnag press applauded when, in 1959, Congress and President Eisenhower declared an annual Captive Nations Week with a proclamation that Dobriansky drafted.[9]

One should not infer that the ARF influenced American foreign policy—or even that it received a great deal of attention from the larger coalition with which it aligned itself. Indeed, while the pages of the Tashnag press referred approvingly—as well as constantly—to Kersten, Dobriansky, AmComLib, aid to anti-Communist exiles, and Captive Nations Week, few references to Armenians in the anti-Soviet liberation campaigns appear in surviving records of these non-Armenian entities. Reuben Darbinian occasionally got his name in the *New York Times* and the *Washington Post*, but not nearly as often as Dobriansky and Rozmarek. Mandalian, in the *Hairenik Weekly* editorial where he discussed the Psychological Strategy Conference, expressed chagrin that the Armenian press only learned about it at the last minute and that the lone ostensible representative of the Armenians was someone obscure and unfamiliar to him. The ARF thus appears as a junior partner, perhaps even just a camp follower, in the coalition. However, this should not obscure the more salient point: in their own press, Tashnag leaders kept their constituents constantly mindful of their party's dedication to the struggle.

- 2 -

Efforts by the parties and other institutions to cultivate the youth and thus maintain their institutional existence continued in the postwar years. The Armenian Apostolic Church of America founded a new youth group, the Armenian Church Youth of America (ACYOA). The ACYOA, like other groups, ran dances, athletic competitions, and conventions. It had its first national gathering in 1947, and in 1948 launched a monthly newspaper, the *Armenian Guardian*. Bishop Tiran Nersoyan, one of the key organizers, articulated the organization's weighty purpose in the inaugural issue of the *Guardian*, where he wrote, "the aims of the ACYO are so highly important, that the work of the salvation of our communal church life as well as the souls of its members depends on the realization of those aims as effectively as possible." Even more explicitly, the bishop wrote in a letter to General Council Chairman Zaven Housepian, "It is a body which has to shoulder the burden of responsibility of passing on the Armenian Church tradition to the American youth of Armenian parentage, and thus assure the continued existence of the Armenian Church in America." The organization was closely supervised by church authorities, and its activities—like so much else in Armenian life in this period—showed an earnest blend of Armenian cultural pride (including the celebratory history features in the publications) and sense of membership in the mainstream American middle class. "I shall to the best of my ability," a young member had to pledge, "be a faithful son of the Armenian Church, shall be a devoted upholder of the Armenian cultural heritage, [and] shall be a loyal citizen of the United States." Bishop Nersoyan pointed out at the first convention that the logo of the group included Mount Ararat and the eagle, key symbols respectively of Armenia and America.[10]

Cultivating the growth of the third generation's Armenianness and Americanness was also the ostensible mission of the Tashnags' Camp Hayasdan (the word for Armenia), located in Franklin, Massachusetts. The year the camp was launched, 1952, James H. Tashjian explained in the *Hairenik Weekly* that the camp, while steeping its campers in Armenian language and history, was "a thoroughly 'Western' administered set-up," with "no bungling of the thing, that there is a regular program of orientation, indoctrination, recreation and study, that the young people will not roam around unministered, to get into scrapes and what not." Tashjian continued, "The entire Camp program is calculated to build good citizenship, provide healthy recreational facilities, teach the language and culture of the parent people, and build sound bodies and minds." After the camp opened, *Hairenik Weekly* promoted it faithfully. For a stretch of 1952, not a week went by without a letter from a happy camper to regularly featured columnist Uncle Bozo (Merton Bozoyan, a Massachusetts high school principal). "The best part of the day, in my opinion, was the Armenian class with Mr. Beglar Nevasardian, our teacher. I learned a great deal about Armenian history," wrote Bob Avakian in one such testimonial.[11]

Meanwhile the Tashnag party's Armenian Youth Federation (AYF), already a youth organization, gave birth to AYF Juniors, to cultivate children from ages ten to sixteen for membership in the AYF. Founded in 1948, the junior adjunct had 70 graduating members to pass along into the AYF in 1952, as well as 150 other members, inspiring an editorialist in *Hairenik Weekly* to write with somewhat wishful optimism, "We rest that much easier for the future of the Armenian struggle for independence in the knowledge that we have another generation of Armenians poised and ready to aid us in that struggle."[12]

The *Hairenik* press found ways of reinforcing that sense of struggle even when dealing with seemingly apolitical matters. A pair of obituaries in a 1952 issue illustrates this. Of the untimely death of a young Armenian American woman, Varsenig Sahangian of Selma, California, *Hairenik Weekly* described her as "endowed with all the inherent virtues of the Armenian woman which have identified her through the glorious ages of Armenian history," including the intent to pass along to what offspring she might have had "all the spiritual fortitude and strength which enabled the Armenians to maintain their identity even under the heels of the worst oppressors," along with "the high sense of moral values and family honor; and the undying love for the ancestral land and all national heritages with which the Armenian Woman seems to be born." In the same article, the writer observed that the recently deceased Zakar Najarian of Salem, New Hampshire, "remained unwavering and faithful to his heritage from his early childhood days to that last fateful night when his young heart was brought to a stop." Of the two together, the writer lamented that a large part of the tragedy was that they had died without seeing Armenia liberated. "They lived their young lives for the day when they too would be able to say that what they had worked for had come true. But this was not to be."[13]

Not all Armenian Americans, of course, looked to any Armenian party or press to speak for them or provide them with news. In 1949, *Baikar*, the Armenian-language newspaper serving the East and the Midwest for the largest anti-Tashnag party, reported a circulation of 3,020, while *Hairenik* reported 4,375. On the West Coast, the Tashnag's *Asbarez* that same year reported 1,261, while the Ramgavar *Nor Or* had an estimated figure of 1,500. In the English language, *Hairenik Weekly* that year showed a circulation of 1,700. While the digest printing these figures does not, for some reason, show circulation for the *Mirror-Spectator*, one can conjecture that it was probably less than 1,700, but not less than 1,000. If these circulation figures are accurate, then, taking the existence of other partisan papers with smaller circulations, some not preserved, into account, it can be said that no more than 10 percent of Armenians, combining immigrants and the American-born, were regular buyers or subscribers of partisan Armenian papers.[14]

Church membership and attendance figures are also elusive and imprecise, as is the number of "Armenians" (an imprecise term in itself) living in America during these years, but the general sense of the picture can be summed up as follows: there was, throughout these years, a core of Armenian Americans, including immigrants and their American-born children and grandchildren, who took part in institutions that reinforced their sense of identity as members of a global diaspora. Outside that core were those who found their social, spiritual, and political needs met either in part or in full by non-Armenian institutions, whose interest in Armenian affairs was moderate, slight, or nonexistent. Within the core, the institutions gave Armenians space and exhortations to rehearse their memories, both shared and contested. Their relationship with these institutions, including the press, the churches, and the social clubs, involved an element of marketing: that is, the elites who ran them had a vested interest in keeping Armenians around as constituents, hence customers. This does not imply manipulation or control, but rather, symbiosis: the elites had to provide something that would keep their constituents interested. That something included social activities, and also ideas. In that latter realm, ideas included the sense of a focus of indignation. Turkey was always present in that role, but up through the mid-1970s the marketers devoted at least as much attention to reminding their customers of what bad Armenians and bad Americans their partisan Armenian rivals were.

- 3 -

While in some ways the ARF fought the Cold War out in the open—and indeed clamored for the widest possible audience—some covert activity, or at least the making of plans for such, also took place. It involved a man both well-known and intensely controversial in the community, the aforementioned Drastamat Ganayan, or "General Dro." Ganayan worked for US Army Intelligence right after the Second World War and, from 1947 into the early 1950s, the CIA. A biography of the general by Antranig Chalabian reports some of his travels and his interactions with the US government after the war. Even more intriguing pieces of the puzzle appear in his CIA and FBI files. The availability of both of those files bears a significance in itself. They were declassified as part of a congressional investigation into the government's collusion with former Nazis in the gathering of intelligence against America's Soviet adversary. This does not make Dro a Nazi, but rather, reflects the fact that his degree of cooperation with the Nazi regime during the war—for whatever motives, benign or malign—made him a target for official American attention after the war, and that his willingness to provide service affected the level of friendliness of that attention. Moreover, the records of his interactions contain several names that overlap with the cast of characters in that larger and sometimes sordid story.

According to the Chalabian biography, Dro and his family were living in Heidelberg, Germany, when the Allies gained control early in 1945, and Allied troops acting on a tip arrested him. At that point he had a narrow escape from being forcibly repatriated to the Soviet Union, where officials earnestly desired to get their hands on him, and was saved by the intercession of a French officer who was also an Armenian and who held a high rank in the Tashnag party. Dro then traveled with official protection to the United States while his family remained in Germany. Upon arrival in Massachusetts, he met with a Tashnag delegation and then—still according to Chalabian's sources— "was flown to Washington, D.C., for debriefing by United States intelligence."[15]

The government files do not contradict any of this narrative, but they certainly supplement it. General Edwin Sibert (misspelled as Seibert in the FBI file) had asked one of his subordinates to arrange for both the State Department and Immigration and Naturalization Service (INS) to "look the other way" when Dro entered. A memorandum written the following year stated that Dro "had been brought to the United States for the secret purpose of recruiting a number of Armenians who allegedly hate Russia as he does to go into Russia, the Near East and elsewhere to act as secret intelligence agents for Seibert [sic]." The subordinate who made the arrangements, Colonel L. R. Forney, apparently harbored some misgivings and was discreetly sending reports to FBI head J. Edgar Hoover. That July 1946 memorandum, written while Dro was still in the United States performing services for the government, reports, "Colonel Forney stated that Kannayan's [sic] family is at present being held by General Seibert as hostages to guarantee Kannayan's [sic] present activities." (While one could scarcely expect General Dro to like that arrangement, it most likely did not shock him, given his own background.) General Sibert's name shows up in other accounts of the period; as head of Army Intelligence in Germany, he was busily scouting out persons from inside the German state who could help the US government with intelligence on the Soviets.[16]

The CIA formally came into existence in 1947. A document dated July 1949, with older entries taped or typed onto it, includes a note from December 11 to 15, 1947, saying, "Subject will round up as many Tashnaks as possible in Lebanon and Palestine in order to combat Armenian Soviet influence. His activities in Palestine will also be for the Arabs against the Jews." (No further elaboration on the conflict in Palestine appears in this file, and siding against the Jews in the Middle East was certainly not consistent with the administration's policies.) The first recorded formal dialogue between the new agency and General Dro appears to have taken place on December 1, 1948, when Dro and his translator and friend Dr. Daghlian met with a pair of agents at the Shoreham Hotel. The memorandum documenting this interview notes up top that the conversation presupposed an eventual war against the Soviet Union, and that the meeting was being held to plan for that eventuality. In that meeting, Dro took a strong part in proposing that strong anti-Soviet insurgencies be built up in Armenia, Georgia, and other affected countries, and that a strong American role in occupying those areas be promised, with Armenians contributing two thousand troops for the occupation of Armenia. He asserted that he himself was legendary only among Armenians, and that therefore the Americans would have to coordinate the efforts outside of Armenia. "The Armenians feel that their only hope lies with the United States," the memorandum noted (apparently viewing Dro as speaking for his nationality), "and the knowledge of the fact that American troops would be cooperating with resistance groups would have a tremendous effect upon the population." In exchange for those services, General Dro wanted the Americans to guarantee Armenia's independence and provide protection from any Turkish massacres. Dro further noted that he had already, for the past several years, been drawing on intelligence networks from Armenia for updates as to what was going on there.[17]

Subsequent documents, including one dated December 13, 1951, show an active relationship of General Dro, in association with several other Tashnag leaders, and the CIA, with Dro promising to recruit two thousand young party members to form a paramilitary organization, five dependable party members to receive training as intelligence officers, and twenty party members to be trained in sabotage. In return, General Dro wanted 250 firearms for the party: 70 for use in Iran, 70 in Syria, and 110 in Lebanon. The party would pay the appropriate salaries, but Dro needed the US government to pay the travel expenses. The memorandum shows the CIA as having said yes to nearly all of Dro's requests, the one exception being "newsprint" (presumably meaning textual content) for the party press. Later memoranda suggest even bigger plans, with Dro assisting in intelligence and preparations for ground fighting in Iran as well as in Syria and Lebanon. The main quid pro quo in these talks seems to have been that Dro would provide specialized Armenian personnel and, in exchange, he wanted firearms supplies for the Armenian forces.[18]

Dro's intentions and those of his interlocutors in the CIA were not, by any means, always in synchrony. In a document dated November 1953, preparatory to a meeting with Dro about plans for a ground war involving Iran, reference was made to the fact that Dro would want American assurance that a whole unit of several hundred

Armenians would be safely evacuated in the event that the territory should fall to Soviet forces. The CIA, that document made clear, would only be interested in evacuating those twenty or thirty Armenians who would have valuable information that the Soviets could obtain by capturing them.[19]

Exactly what came of all these arrangements is unclear. Memoranda do credit Dro with having provided agents with intelligence reports on Communist activities throughout the Middle East, and being paid $1,000 a month for it over a thirteen-month period. Moreover, some preparation by Dro seems to have taken place in Iran, based on a line in that November 1953 memorandum to the effect that Dro might want reimbursement for the $2,000 he had apparently already spent on arms there. But by 1952, internal memos were showing some wariness, and some disappointment. In any case, the talk by both sides of organizing fighting and sabotage units appears to have been mostly that: talk. If one remembers that the US policy in this time period had more to do with keeping the Russian bear scratching at its fleas than with actual goals of regime change, and that the whole Armenian question lay in the periphery of most Cold Warriors' field of vision, one can infer that the CIA contacts gave General Dro an exaggerated picture of how much they valued his contribution and how much help he could expect to receive in return. At some point—the date is not clear—Dro purportedly said to CIA director Allen Dulles, "You son of a bitch. We kept our end of the bargain. You haven't kept yours."[20]

The files show one final intrigue. On November 20, 1955, Lt. Col. Joseph J. Caprucci of Air Force Counter Intelligence Division sent word to J. Edgar Hoover that, according to information furnished by the 7050th Air Intelligence Service Wing, HQ, USAFE, "One DRASTMAS KANAYAN, also known as 'GENERAL DRO,' is a possible Soviet agent. He is supposedly connected with an American agency and possibly resides in the United States." After receiving this communication, Hoover wrote on November 30 to both the CIA and the State Department for information on Dro. A reply from the chief of the Near East and Africa Division of the CIA told Hoover that the matter was under control and "It is requested that the FBI discontinue further investigative action on its own behalf."[21] The present author has seen no evidence consistent with that allegation.

Dro was already receiving treatment in Boston for cancer by this time; he died on March 8, 1956. Tashnag Armenians came out by the thousands to mourn him; anti-Tashnags paid him no such honor.[22]

- 4 -

As the Cholakian case, discussed in the preceding chapter, made evident, Tashnag and non-Tashnag community leaders had very different views, not only on how friendly to be with the Soviet state, but also on whether any persons in their right mind could desire to move from outside of Soviet Armenia to inside. That question received large-scale play with the postwar repatriation campaign. While the number of Armenians in America who desired to relocate to Armenia was negligible, both they and the more numerous Armenians from elsewhere in the world who made the move attracted much Armenian attention and inspired many quarrels.

The war had crippled the Soviet state and much reduced its population. To augment its productive workforce, Stalin in the war's aftermath launched a repatriation program to attract Armenians from the diaspora to move "back" to their homeland (though most First World War refugees in the diaspora had known the Turkish-ruled western Armenian provinces, rather than Russian-ruled eastern Armenia, as their home). As he had done with the David of Sassoun Tank Column and the claim on Kars and Ardahan, Stalin solicited the propaganda support of the locum tenens of the church at Echmiadzin, Kevork. On December 2, 1945, the Soviet government formally announced that it was inviting Armenians of the diaspora to move into Soviet Armenia, allowing them exemption from the usual customs assessments as well as access to subsidized housing. This spurred great excitement worldwide. The Armenian General Benevolent Union (AGBU) went right into action raising funds to assist repatriates with transportation expenses, setting a one-million-dollar goal, though its vice president and chief fundraiser Leon Guerdan confided to his diary that he was "hardly enthusiastic" about this task and considered the movement "too closely pegged to Russian policy goals." Though only a small handful in the United States wished to repatriate, many more supported the effort.[23]

Some Armenians in America made the move for purposes of helping their homeland, like Hovhannes and Beatrice Mugrditchian, who organized a leather workers' guild, sold their house in Los Angeles, and made the voyage. Some also had highly romanticized notions of what to expect, like Sonia Meghreblian's father Dajad, who had moved from France to upstate New York with his family in 1939 and held favorable perceptions of Soviet Armenian life for years. When his wife Marie expressed

Figure 6.1 Farewell reception for first group of repatriates from the United States to Soviet Armenia, held at the Hotel Diplomat in New York on October 29, 1947. Many among them would profoundly regret this decision. Photo from MSY Collection, National Association for Armenian Studies and Research (NAASR), Belmont, MA.

alarm over the letters coming back from her sister who was, with coded references, clearly warning them not to make the move, Dajad explained the sister's discontentment away and retained his faith in the Communist utopia they were heading to. Sonia, for her part, strongly wanted to stay in the States and attend the New York State Teachers' College at Albany (now the University at Albany, State University of New York). She was aware that local relatives also considered the move a bad idea, but her father was going blind and had convinced himself that the cure to restore his eyesight was to be found in the Soviet Union, and Sonia could not bring herself to argue with his one source of hope. "With a heavy heart," she recalls in her memoir, "I began to participate in the preparation for our move."[24]

Compatriotic unions embraced the program as an expansion of what they had begun in the 1920s; thus, for example, did the Pan-Sebastia Construction Union complement AGBU's fundraising efforts through a series of festive picnics and gala banquets attended by survivors who had fled the Ottoman town of Sebastia during the First World War, to help their Sebastatsis in Syria and Lebanon as well as various Eastern European countries, places where living conditions were considerably less desirable than those in America, to relocate to the town of Nor (New) Sebastia that the union has earlier founded and funded. The Tashnag party started out in concert with the effort but reversed course when it became clear that the Soviet government, associating the Tashnag party with challenges to its rule (a perception that did not take any great paranoia to entertain), was severely restricting the number of ARF members in the ranks of the repatriates and the influence of the ARF in the course of repatriation. From this point onward, the ARF sought to expose the whole venture as a hoax, abetted in this effort by some of the actual events that transpired in Soviet Armenia as the movement proceeded.[25]

Though the vast majority of postwar repatriates to Soviet Armenia hailed from countries other than the United States, approximately 300 from the American Armenian community did make the move. In mid-July of 1948, the Meghreblian and Mugrditchian families were among the 162 Armenian Americans who gathered in New York City expecting to board a ship called the *Pobeda* bound for Armenia, only to learn—after they had left jobs, sold homes and some belongings, packed everything for the voyage, and officially traded American citizenship in for Soviet—that there was to be a six-week delay due to some purported safety issues with the vessel. At the end of August came the report that the *Pobeda* had caught fire in its journey and would not be taking the repatriates at all. As the many families stayed lodged in limbo at a New Jersey hotel, this was where it really got hairy: it was learned that the Soviet government had halted reception of new migrants. Presumably these 162 would still be allowed to sail, having already done the citizenship paperwork and begun the journey, but not until January of 1949 did real assurance come. On January 21, they departed on the S.S. *Sobieski* and, after being stalled again at Naples, sailed aboard the Romanian cargo ship *Arteal* to their new life in Soviet Armenia.[26]

The Soviet government, having encouraged repatriates to bring their belongings with them, confiscated most possessions shortly after they arrived. The regime also changed the financial terms in mid-process, forcing AGBU to pony up more money to make good its original expenditure. Catholicos Kevork, who had helped sell the venture, took heat when some of the repatriates, especially priests and seminary students, attempted to stand up for more church freedom and found themselves exiled to Siberia. Repatriates also encountered resentment, and sometimes violence, from Soviet Armenians who felt their country was crowded enough as it was. On top of it all, though the 162 on the *Sobieski* got in, the sudden cutting off of repatriation left many others who had given up jobs and property stranded.[27]

The Tashnag press in the United States paid particularly close attention to the reports of undesirable conditions facing the repatriates. As James G. Mandalian reported in 1951 to readers of the quarterly *Armenian Review*, repatriates, knowing that Soviet censors scrutinized their correspondence, wrote in code to loved ones back in America. "One man, for example, upon his departure, had agreed with his confidant that when, upon his arrival in Armenia, he found life tolerable, he would send his picture standing. If life was bad, he would be seated in the picture. Six months later his confidant received a picture in which his relative was lying down on his back." Another mentioned the name of a mutual acquaintance and said he hoped one day to have a home as large as that man's home; as the recipient of the letter had to know, that home was a grave. A woman wrote, "Soviet Armenia is a wonderful land, exactly as you described it to me," in a letter addressed to her Tashnag sister who had tried to warn her that she would have poverty and no freedom there. Sonia Meghreblian's father, who had been so enthused for the move before he made it, found himself spending much of his waking life standing in line with his bad eyesight at various food stores.[28]

Within several years of making the voyage, some number (no precise figure is knowable) regretted the decision and desired to return. In the early summer of 1956 a group of repatriates approached a team of visitors to Yerevan referred to as the American Housing Delegation and gave them a letter addressed to President Eisenhower. Having made the journey, not out of disrespect to the United States, but as "self appointed ambassadors of good will," the repatriates, according to the letter, had "gone thru all manner of hardships and discrimination," suffering especially "the lack of Freedom and Justice." The letter concluded, "We now appeal to the magnanimity of the government of the United States, to forgive us, her errant children, who want to return home. We feel we have paid the penalty of our mistakes and we did our American born children a great injustice in depriving them of their right to live as Americans."[29]

Reports in State Department files show that, while some repatriates successfully contacted the American consulate, others found themselves blocked, with some being sent to Siberia for attempting—or even appearing to contemplate attempting—contact with American officials. The records show State Department personnel as sympathetic, and in some instances successful in obtaining release for repatriates, though they show no statistics on success rates. The State Department could only request, not demand, Soviet cooperation, and a number of memoranda show an effort to tread gingerly in the matter. Because repatriation had meant giving up American citizenship and submitting to Soviet authority, the task of repatriates and sympathetic officials often boiled down to claiming that they had not entirely understood what they were doing (somewhat analogous to annulling a marriage) or, especially in the case of children being taken by their parents, had not had a real choice.

The Soviet government, in its response to American intercessions, appears to have found a middle ground by applying a law allowing nationals to leave if they had close family members awaiting them abroad. This required a letter of invitation. In one case, four children named Palakian whose father had taken them to Armenia and died, and whose mother languished in frail mental condition in a hospital on Long Island, wished desperately to return. State Department officials first inquired of the hospital staff as to whether Mrs. Palakian was capable of writing a letter of invitation. Learning that she was not, they sought out other relatives, which also yielded little. The Palakian children gained release in spring of 1963, apparently the result of State Department officials and the private charity Church World Service drafting a letter for the mother to "sign" to create the fiction that her health was improving and that she would be able to care for them.[30]

The files only show continuous follow-through and outcomes for a small handful of cases, thus yielding little that is quantifiable for statistics. The Harootian family occupy much space with their story. Agnes Harootian, apparently a teenager in 1947, had refused at the time to migrate to Soviet Armenia with her parents and her three sisters Mary, Grace, and Rosie. She went there for the first time as a visitor when the mother died in 1960. By that time her three sisters were married, two of them had children, and at some point early that decade their father remarried. Apparently, the whole family in Armenia desired to leave for America. Helping them was Virginia H. James, international relations officer at the State Department's Office of Soviet Affairs. Mrs. James showed much compassion and concern, allowing members of this family (especially Agnes, who lived in New Jersey) to call her at home. "One aspect of the case is worrying me very much," she wrote to Dexter Anderson at the embassy in Moscow.

> [Agnes] informed me that her father has $6,000 in United States money in his possession. Please, most emphatically, impress on them that they should not try to smuggle any American money out of the Soviet Union. I have the terrible feeling that the exit visas might have been issued to them knowing that the father has this money and that he will be arrested at the border.

In the same letter, she added, "I only hope that their cases can be successfully processed and that after their arrival in the United States there will not be a family blowup. You can well imagine what turmoil will take place when 10 Armenians join their Armenian sister in a small apartment." The Harootians appear to have come through successfully. In a number of instances, part of the challenge was that, when the Soviet government issued an exit visa, it came with a close expiration date, not convenient for all the bureaucratic procedures that the American side required to bring the repatriates in.[31]

- 5 -

The division between the two partisan camps made itself most evident through differing commemorations of anniversaries. Among the most effective devices by which the Tashnags made Armenian ethnic nationalism and American patriotism synonymous—and drew the approving attention of prominent American political figures—were the February 18 celebrations. They continued, of course, to observe May 28, the anniversary of the founding of the thousand-day republic, and to display proudly the endorsements these observances garnered from non-Armenian notables. But now, from 1948 onward, the ARF gave equal emphasis to commemorating the uprising in February 1921 in which the Tashnag party in Armenia, albeit with only temporary success, shook off Soviet rule—the first anti-Communist rebellion ever by a Sovietized nationality. As with May 28, the *Hairenik* press proudly displayed resolutions by city councils and speeches by mayors, governors, and legislators praising the uprising and commending Armenians (as represented by the Tashnags) for standing on the forefront of the fight for freedom against Communism. In 1953, Governor Thomas Dewey of New York officially declared, "The Armenians of America rededicate themselves to work for the final emancipation not only of the Armenian people but all the subjugated minorities of the world suffering under despotic rule." Senator Styles Bridges of New Hampshire similarly noted, "This valiant revolt by a new and small republic against a despotic occupation fills us with pride and renews our faith in human determination even today." On February 18, 1955, Representative Alvin M. Bentley of Michigan read a statement into the *Congressional Record* marking "the 34th anniversary of the temporary establishment of freedom in the Armenian Republic." Annually throughout these years, the *Hairenik* press proudly quoted such proclamations, which made the February 18 celebration not only an Armenian affair but an American one.[32]

During those same years, the anti-Tashnag coalition observed yet another anniversary: November 29, 1920, the founding of the Soviet Armenian state. Over fifteen hundred reportedly showed up on December 12, 1948, to mark the twenty-eighth anniversary of "the founding of the Armenian Republic," as the *Mirror-Spectator* article called it. Speakers included Dr. Hewlett Johnson, Dean of Canterbury and an unabashed apologist for the Soviet government, and Bishop Tiran Nersoyan, primate of the Armenian Apostolic Church of America. A pair of musicians performed both the American and the Soviet Armenian national anthems, among other selections. On November 23, 1952, the Armenian National Council of America (ANCOA), the group helmed by the aforementioned Rev. Vertanes, observed the thirty-second anniversary of the "emancipation of Armenia from tyranny, insecurity and the threat of annihilation." Archbishop Mampré Calfayan greeted the reportedly "large crowd," and Vertanes was among the orators.[33]

Shortly after, the Ramgavar-controlled *Baikar* published an editorial in Armenian, reprinted in English in the *Mirror-Spectator*, suggesting a balance sheet for the years after Sovietization, with the good outweighing the bad. "During these 32 years Armenia has enjoyed security and peace—in the sense that no attack or invasion against her has occurred … Reconstruction, industry and agriculture made great advances. Great progress was made culturally, in the arts, and all branches of science." Were there negatives as well? Yes, the editorialist continued:

> The debit side of the balance sheet is not all white: harsh lines are present if the word freedom is taken at its classical meaning. During these years Armenia has

remained under the domination of one kind of thinking. She has not allowed free traveling to those who would have liked to visit their native land, or those who would have liked to see the outside world.

However, the writer continued, one must not lose sight of the balance sheet, which still shows that "the 32nd anniversary finds the balance heavy on the credit side for our people returning to life from the grave."[34]

While many, probably most, spokespersons for the anti-Tashnag coalition held anti-Communist beliefs and maintained their stance of friendly accommodation toward the Soviet state for pragmatic reasons only, it is difficult to draw such a conclusion about Charles A. Vertanes. His papers, housed in the NAASR library in Belmont, Massachusetts, suggest a genuine ideological sympathy with Soviet Communism. One folder in particular contains a set of typewritten papers with quotations from anti-Communist sources followed by commentary bearing Vertanes's initials, answering those anti-Communist critiques—not even with any special attention to Armenia. Throughout these papers, Vertanes refers to the Communist regimes as "people's democracies," abbreviated in places as "PDs." In one spot, Vertanes quotes an unspecified anti-Communist article criticizing a Bulgarian church law of 1949 prohibiting correspondence between Bulgarian churches and any organizations outside of Bulgaria; Vertanes then writes:

> And why not? How does the attitude and practice of the churches in the eastern democracies differ at this point from the policies and attitudes of the western states toward their churches? The only difference is that in the west these things are done more subtly, more hypocritically, so that the vast majority of the people do not know what goes on behind the scenes with respect to the control and thinking of the church.

Unlike Bishop Nersoyan, who (as discussed in the next chapter) lamented the persecution of religion in the Communist countries, Vertanes appears to have dismissed this factor entirely.[35]

In March 1951 the *Mirror-Spectator* expressed embarrassment when Vertanes, in his capacity as executive secretary of the ANCOA, attended the Second World Conference of the Partisans of Peace, widely regarded as a Communist event, in Warsaw, and suggested that the ANC should disband: "The Armenian National Council was expressly formed for the purpose of winning, not alienating, the friendship and sympathy of the American government and people for our cause." This prompted an editorial in *Hairenik Weekly* accusing the Ramgavar organ of tiptoeing around the real reason why the ANCOA should disband: "because, essentially and basically, it has been and still is a COMMUNIST FRONT, just like a host of fronts which at present clutter the American scene." Tashnag leaders also missed no opportunity to castigate the anti-Tashnag institutions as pro-Soviet. Noting that these organizations had started to find themselves on the defensive on the subject in 1947, Darbinian remarked in 1953, "They could not understand that by having favored the Soviet regime for the past thirty years they had jeopardized their position, rendering themselves suspects in the eyes of the authorities. No matter how badly they wanted it, they could not conceal their real identity nor *[sic]* to efface their record of long years."[36]

During these years, the Tashnag/anti-Tashnag rivalry crescendoed. Paradoxically, with the exception of the Armenian Progressive League's stances, which were overtly Bolshevist, the conflict had nothing to do with any debate about capitalism. The fiercely anti-Soviet Tashnag party, it should be recalled, had always identified itself as socialist, and even now it claimed membership in the Second International; even so, the closest the *Hairenik* press came to espousing socialism in America was to express approval of the New Deal and American liberalism—though at times speaking in concert with some very anti-New Deal politicians and pundits in its anti-Soviet crusade.[37] The Ramgavar party, the leading component of the anti-Tashnag coalition, had been founded with a bourgeois-clerical character and explicitly disavowed any Communist ideologies. It defended its Soviet-friendly position exclusively in practical terms. It was, even so, in a coalition with the APL, and identified most closely with the Apostolic church hierarchy, which at this point fully answered to the Catholicos at Echmiadzin. Thus, while the Ramgavar party rejected the label "pro-Soviet," it participated in a coalition with other elements that did not, and identified with stances that opened it up to that charge.

As noted, Ramgavar and other anti-Tashnag voices—with Avedis Derounian among the loudest—accused the ARF of having a fascist orientation. The ARF had no trouble answering that. "Has it occurred to anyone," *Hairenik Weekly* asked its readers in 1951, as part of a series of responses to Ramgavar allegations,

> that the men who are the most vociferous about the fascists and the Nazis invariably are Communists or Soviet sympathizers? The words fascist and Nazi have long since lost their original connotations. For sometime *[sic]* they have become synonymous with Enemies of the Soviet. That accounts for the virulence of certain Armenian factions in their persecution of the Dashnags as fascists. The accusation identifies the accused, not necessarily as a fascist but as an enemy of the Soviet, while conversely, it identifies the accuser either as a Communist or a Soviet sympathizer.[38]

The climactic point of the Tashnags' efforts at putting the Ramgavars on the defensive over appearing "pro-Soviet" came in 1955 when, on June 24, a woman named Stella Andrassy, who had held a position with the New York Civil Defense Office that brought her into close contact with the immigrant press, told the Senate Subcommittee on Internal Security that thirty-four foreign-language newspapers in the United States hued to the Communist line, *Baikar* among them. The Tashnag Press capitalized on this right away. Reuben Darbinian, writing in the quarterly *Armenian Review*, contrasted the two parties, choosing his words carefully (as usual) to confine the charge to the leadership and to hold back from calling those adversaries Communist even while unabashedly calling them pro-Soviet. "True," he wrote:

> The followers of the Ramgavar Party are not communists at heart; most of them are conservative people. But unfortunately their minds have been poisoned for

years by the Ramgavar editors who, although not card-bearing members, have consistently promoted and preached such ideas which are in perfect keeping with the Soviet line, and which have been dictated by secular and ecclesiastical agents in disguise.

He then noted the contrast in the anniversaries observed:

Ramgavar papers to this day have considered the Soviet takeover as a great blessing to the Armenian people and each year they zealously observe November 29, the infamous day of Armenia's enslavement, as the "Day of Armenia's salvation"! On the other hand, the same papers deride May 28, the birthday of Independent Armenia. The Ramgavar editors do not even want to preserve the memory of Independent Armenia's freedoms which were abrogated by the Communists and regard the Dashnaks, the builders of those freedoms, as their mortal enemies, meanwhile glorifying the Soviet regime which enslaved the Armenian people.

Darbinian proceeded to cite passages from *Baikar* praising speeches by Stalin and criticizing Truman for calling the eleven prosecuted Communist leaders traitors.[39]

Whether a Ramgavar contingent ever did testify before the Internal Security Subcommittee is not clear. What is on record is that the editorial staff of *Baikar*, along with Avedis Derounian (though he did not identify himself as a Ramgavar), made contact with the committee, expressed a strong desire to testify, and were given to expect such an opportunity. The files of the committee also show that senators were in touch with one Beglar Navassardian of the ARF, who reported to them on ostensibly pro-Soviet activity in the non-Tashnag coalition. Clearly, Armenian partisan leaders no longer maintained even the fiction of keeping their divisions in the family.[40]

A number of high-profile Cold War events not specifically centering on Armenians gave Tashnag leaders material with which to remind their constituents of their membership in an international struggle and to affirm their party's credentials as a beacon of American patriotism. The same sagas gave the anti-Tashnag coalition exercise in articulating a finely honed position that neither condemned nor cheered the Soviet Union but that decisively opposed the Tashnag stance and took care not to antagonize either the Soviet or the US government.

The fall of 1956 saw two challenges to Soviet domination of Eastern Europe: Polish October and the Hungarian uprising, the latter of which culminated in a brutal crackdown. As background to these episodes, one should note that Soviet control over Eastern Europe had never operated without some challenges and contradictions. Czechoslovakia's attempt at a government independent of Stalin's control had ended decisively with a Soviet-run coup in early 1948, but Yugoslavia's determined leader, Josip Broz, popularly known as Marshall Tito, had successfully established an independent national Communist regime. Stalin could sometimes temper his megalomania with a pragmatic cost-benefit analysis, especially when he was busy on other fronts (like Korea), and thus he reluctantly opted not to use force against Tito. In the countries that he did control, however, he saw to the purging of many suspected Titoists. After Stalin's death in 1953, Nikita Khrushchev—solidifying his own position as

Stalin's successor after a brief interregnum—visited Yugoslavia in 1955 and apologized for Stalin's earlier obstinacy. He delivered his famous "Crimes of Stalin" speech to the Twentieth Congress of the Soviet Communist Party in February 1956 and, in May of that year, made the surprising move of cooperating with the Western allies by withdrawing troops from Austria, allowing for an independent non-Communist regime to take hold there.[41]

All of this raised hopes among Poles and Hungarians for the loosening of Soviet control over their countries. In both instances, the world observed mass demonstrations in the streets and wondered whether these would lead to fulfillment of demands or a bloody crackdown. The results were the former for Poland and the latter in Hungary, though some blood also got spilled in Poland along the way to resolution. Radio Free Europe egged on the Hungarian rebels and implied, very recklessly, that they could expect Western help if they kept up the fight, delivering a challenge to Khrushchev as well as encouragement to the insurrection. The results were tragic. After a brief moment of appearing to withdraw, Soviet troops under Khrushchev's orders moved in and crushed the rebellion, with an estimated twenty-five thousand Hungarians falling dead and two hundred thousand survivors fleeing westward.[42]

All this happened with the world watching closely—Armenian partisan leaders included. At the end of October, the Tashnag party sent Eisenhower a telegram noting that Armenians, being the first nation to revolt against Soviet tyranny in February 1921, had good cause for sympathy with the people of Poland and Hungary and entreating "THAT ALL OFFICES OF UNITED STATES GOVERNMENT BE MOBILIZED TO SUPPORT THE HEROIC STRUGGLE OF POLAND AND HUNGARY FOR FREEDOM." An editorial in *Hairenik Weekly* during the uprising found a connection, not only with the Armenian revolt of 1921 but with another show of Armenian resistance, the fifth-century Battle of Avarayr against the anti-Christian Persian king, and opined that the events in Poland and Hungary disproved the myth "that the peoples of the Soviet Union and her satellites were happy under the regime of the so-called 'people's democracies.'"[43]

An even more sterling example of Armenian immigrant history intersecting with American political history comes with the polarized reactions to the 1959 visit to the United States of Anastas Mikoyan, that high-ranking Armenian in the Moscow government—foreign secretary at that time—who had miraculously survived the Stalin purges. Mikoyan arrived in the United States on January 4, 1959, for a two-and-a-half-week tour. True to form, the anti-Tashnags applauded and the Tashnags, through editorials in the *Hairenik* press, booed. Both Armenian camps, in their respective responses, were in chorus with sectors of the larger American society and could indeed, on the pages of their newspapers, quote from ideological allies. The US government extended an official welcome to Mikoyan, including a personal meeting with Secretary Dulles. His critics also had their say, including a delegation of Hungarians who met him at the airport to call him a "murdering dog."[44]

In the Tashnag view, Mikoyan deserved no welcome and no respect. Referring in his headline to "The Man We Are Wining and Dining" (in the ethnic press's familiar practice of referring to the American nation as "we"), editor James H. Tashjian wrote in a mid-January issue of *Hairenik Weekly*, "He ought rather to be relegated to the status of a pariah. He ought to be an outcast among free men. He ought to be shunned like the biblical plague." Tashjian slammed much of the mainstream American press for matching the "pathological devotion to anyone or anything emanating from or smacking of the Soviet Union on the part of certain Armenian circles" and equated the welcoming of Mikoyan with the idea of extending such courtesy to Ribbentrop or Goebbels from Nazi Germany in 1939. He further charged Mikoyan with falsifying his pre-Soviet background, presiding over the purging of thousands of Armenians in the 1930s, and helping suppress the Hungarian uprising by deceptively luring rebel leaders into captivity. On the *Mirror-Spectator*'s suggestion that Mikoyan was a true Armenian who had looked out for his nation's interests, Tashjian asked, "How silly can we get?" An editorial in the same issue called the friendly treatment of Mikoyan "a tragic commentary on American reception in morality." Subsequent issues followed the Mikoyan tour with further disapproval and continued reminders of his past and recent treachery. The paper approvingly cited an anti-Mikoyan gathering in Detroit composed of representatives from multiple nationality groups who opposed Communist control of their homelands, and editorials in non-Armenian papers concurring with their objections to the American hospitality being extended to Mikoyan. *Hairenik Weekly* also reprinted a *Baikar* editorial praising Mikoyan, under the all-caps headline "HERE'S WHY MRS. ANDRASSY TERMED RAMGAVAR 'BAIKAR' A PRO-SOVIET PAPER."[45]

Religion figured heavily into both the American and the Armenian Cold War discourses. After all, many Americans—certainly including their secretary of state—liked to think of their country as a Christian nation, while the Soviet Union unabashedly espoused atheism and did much, albeit with exceptions and contradictions, to force that mindset on its populace. In the case of Armenians, both Tashnags and anti-Tashnags tended strongly to identify with the churches. The intensity of the Cold War helped unleash a series of new conflicts and contested memories in the Apostolic Church, especially in the 1950s, to which the next chapter will turn.

A House of God Divided

The Formalization of the Church Split

It was natural that the Cold War–era partisan conflicts should involve the church. Much of Armenian community life centered there, and the climactic event in the Tashnag/anti-Tashnag feud in the 1930s not only took place in a church but also came as part of a broader quarrel over the loyalties of the church hierarchy. Armenians of both camps belonged to the Apostolic Church and accordingly held opposing visions of their church's proper allegiance. Armenians of the smaller Evangelical denomination, if politically active, tended to be anti-Tashnag and respected the Catholicos at Echmiadzin while not being members of his flock. To anti-Tashnag Apostolics, the Catholicos at Echmiadzin represented the highest spiritual authority, and the hierarchy in the United States should fall in line. In the Tashnag view, the same Catholicos, by virtue of living under the Soviet thumb, had no ability to speak freely for the Armenian nation or its church. After coming to a head with the Tourian affair of 1933, this struggle reached a further climax in the mid-1950s.

- 1 -

In America's Eastern Diocese, after Archbishop Tourian's 1933 murder, the Central Executive Committee installed Fr. Mampré Calfayan, a priest not yet consecrated as a bishop, as the Archdiocese's locum tenens. Fr. Calfayan served until September 1938 when the Diocesan Assembly elected Archbishop Karekin Hovsepian, legate of the Catholicos at Echmiadzin, as primate of the church in America. From 1944 to 1953, Archbishop Tiran Nersoyan held the post, succeeded by Mampré Calfayan, now a fully consecrated archbishop. Meanwhile, the fallout from the Tourian assassination, as has been seen, had hastened the rupture in the Apostolic Church at the local level. Each individual congregation in the United States became either Tashnag or anti-Tashnag, with members of the controlling faction forcibly driving their partisan adversaries from the Lord's house. Churches under Tashnag control now seceded from the Diocese and became loosely confederated under an executive committee, though nominally professing allegiance to the Holy See at Echmiadzin in matters purely spiritual.

At the same time, the international dynamics of the Cold War continued to affect the struggle for the soul of the church. In 1943, the year before he assumed office as primate of the church in America, Archbishop Nersoyan published a book titled *A Christian Approach to Communism,* which played a part in the controversies surrounding his name over the next two decades. In this book, after a close study of the dialectical materialist theory on which Marxism was based, and with the deep knowledge of Christian theology that he of necessity possessed, Nersoyan put forth the finding that the two belief systems had much more compatibility than their respective practitioners realized. True, both the authors of Marxist theory and the rulers of the Soviet state heaved superlative vitriol at religion of every kind, and true, the present generation of Communists showed no signs of changing this stance; but in the longer run, he foresaw a different picture. Marxist theorists, correctly seeing the church as having historically sided with ruling classes, and incorrectly seeing Christianity as dogmatically unscientific and as a hindrance to oppressed people's struggles against their oppressors, had hastily dismissed Christianity and, indeed, all forms of religion and spirituality as counterproductive to Communist revolutions. However, Nersoyan opined, closer examination of both dialectical materialist theory and Christian theology showed them to share much in common in their beliefs and their goals. "The Christian attitude towards possessiveness and possessions," for instance, "is in full accord with the Communist attitude. It faces the eventual freedom of man from the fetters of 'gold and silver.'" Moreover, dialectical materialism had such intrinsically prospiritual implications, Communist ideology had so much in common with the teachings of Christ, and human nature had such a powerful urge toward spiritual realization that the antireligious nature of Marxist society could not possibly last forever. An enlightenment would eventually dawn, whereby religion would have a place in Communist society. Until that day, the Christian church must bear the task of positioning and preparing itself for Christianity to emerge as the prevailing faith.

Much in this book might trouble some readers. For one thing, it carries the clear, pervasive implication that Marxist theory and the Soviet state have the right idea on every count except for that one blind spot, their stubborn insistence on atheism. In one place, he remarks that Communism has triumphed "because in those spheres where it has a positive and constructive teaching it is in possession of truth. Its method of dealing with the material universe and with the things of this world is logical and imposing." Consistently with this, he concludes a section on Lenin's unfair views on Christianity: "Lenin was a great man, but he does not show an adequate knowledge of religion," and indeed he depicts the revolution and the subsequent Communist state as having made awe-inspiring achievements. He calls the state "a 'benevolent dictatorship,' in spite of all its incidental cruelties, and ... based on the will of the majority."

Perhaps most jolting is that, fairly early on in the pamphlet, he addresses the bad press that the Soviet state has received for its brutal punishment of dissenters. "Freedom," he explains, "is the ultimate ideal of Communists," and they intend to bring it about after class distinctions and privations have been eliminated, analogous to the Christian theology of being temporarily under the law while awaiting the liberating power of the spirit. Yes, the state impinges upon individual conscience and free will, but sometimes, for the health of the whole body, it is necessary for a surgeon (i.e., the state) to remove an unhealthy organ (as in an individual whose conscience works at cross purposes with that greater good). He further implies, in one spot, that, in holding up their fair share in the necessary dialogue, Christians need to become anticapitalist. "Christians as a whole," he wrote, "will have to make their position clear; either with or against Capitalism as this word is commonly understood at present. They cannot stand aloof in a world faced with gigantic social problems."[1] Attitudes toward Nersoyan and interpretations of his intent in writing this book ranked among the many issues of the 1940s and 1950s that had a Tashnag and an anti-Tashnag position.

As previously noted, partisan debates in America notwithstanding, religious oppression in the Soviet Union and the Soviet bloc countries *was* a fierce and bitter reality. The Soviet state, after all, predicated its claim to legitimacy upon a belief system whose charter document called religion the opiate of the masses. Perhaps more to the point, totalitarian states customarily seek to control thought and feeling as well as action. Even so, that control was neither absolute nor neatly linear. From the start, Soviet authorities under Lenin moved to limit activities of churches to weekly worship services, expropriate land from churches and monasteries, and bathe the populace in antireligious propaganda. Like other aspects of the dictatorship, this went from bad to worse when Stalin succeeded Lenin, with the 1930s seeing a nadir in religious freedom as well as other forms of free expression: numerous intellectuals and creative artists suffered persecution or death during these years. Only nine Armenian churches and only a few hundred churches of any kind (in contrast with thousands before) existed in the entire Soviet Union in 1940, and in 1948 the faculty of the Theological Academy were dismissed, ostensibly due to lack of funds. In the midst of this nadir, it appears, Soviet operatives brutally murdered Catholicos Khoren in 1938.[2]

However, the same Stalin who presided over the crackdown of the 1930s showed some semblance of moderation in the 1940s. Right after the untimely death of Khoren, Khoren's deputy Kevork, who fully expected to be arrested any day, was allowed to serve as locum tenens, effectively the acting Catholicos. Historian Felix Corley notes that, for reasons not altogether clear, Stalin began somewhat to ease up on the Armenian church even before the Nazi invasion. The war itself made for some serious religious revival activity within Soviet borders. Stalin started to realize that, in the short run, churches loyal to the government could support the war effort, and in the longer run they could help with propaganda efforts, as the Soviet Union drove the Nazi occupiers out of Eastern Europe and created Communist satellites. Starting in 1942, Kevork spearheaded the international Armenian fundraising campaign for the David of Sassoun Tank Column. (Stalin also modified his stance toward the Russian Orthodox Church: he met with its three top leaders in 1943 and allowed the election of a patriarch, which he had previously barred, and ordered the creation of a Department of Foreign Affairs within that church structure to help propagandize Soviet legitimacy.) In 1945 he allowed an election for the Armenian Holy See at Echmiadzin, in which Kevork VI became Catholicos of All Armenians. Stalin also allowed ten new churches and four monasteries to open in Armenia after the war.[3]

Between the authorities in Echmiadzin and the church in America existed an ongoing dynamic of control and negotiation. Ironically, if Nersoyan's book attempting to reconcile the Christian and the Communist world drew him criticism from Tashnags, he also scored low with Echmiadzin and Moscow during his tenure. When he began maneuvering for the church in America to join the National Council of the Churches of Christ in the United States (NCC), Hratchya Grigoryan, chairman of the Council for the Affairs of the Armenian-Gregorian Church, objected, calling the NCC a "most reactionary body entirely serving the interests of the imperialist circles of America," run "with the backing of the Rockefellers." Shortly after, in response to Nersoyan's desire to invite Catholicos Kevork to New York to lay the cornerstone for the new cathedral being built on Second Avenue at East Thirty-Fourth Street, Grigoryan called Nersoyan "an active agent of American imperialism." Now that the Armenians had a homeland, Grigoryan reasoned, building new Armenian churches abroad should be deemed "an unpatriotic act." For both of these plans, Nersoyan was instructed to "study more thoroughly the desirability of these intentions." Soviet officials also showed some wariness of Kevork, as when they vetoed his wish to take an international tour of Armenian churches, on the grounds that "interested organs and persons ... could exploit him and seriously compromise him."[4]

Significantly, Corley has also found that the Soviet regime in the 1950s felt increasingly threatened by the international politicking of the Tashnag party and saw the church at Echmiadzin—the spiritual center for anti-Tashnag Armenians worldwide—as a useful counterweight in the propaganda war.[5] Indeed, one can see the mid-1950s as the apex of that propaganda war, especially with the holding of two globally significant catholical elections.

- 2 -

When Kevork VI died in 1954, the Soviets allowed a council, with delegates from Armenian congregations worldwide, to convene the following year at Echmiadzin and elect a new Catholicos. Soviet authorities exercised tight control over the candidate nominations, and influenced the outcome. Out of 170 eligible delegates from around the world, 140 attended, with Tashnags boycotting the proceedings. Out of the 140, 108 came from within the USSR and 5 more from other Communist countries. The favored candidate, Bishop Vasken Baljian of the Armenian Church in Rumania, had established his Soviet-friendly credentials in 1954 through authorship of a book titled *Under the Sun of the Homeland*, where he wrote, "Armenians abroad must understand, once and for all, that only Soviet rule and only the Russian people can guarantee prosperity for our people, can guarantee the further development of our country and peaceful progress, and can guarantee the attainment of a golden future for the Armenian nation." He was elected with 126 out of 137 votes cast. In the final meeting of the ecclesiastical assembly, Vasken received Soviet citizenship, which he called "my dream now for years."[6]

The election of a new Catholicos at Echmiadzin represented a major event for Armenians worldwide, including those in the American community. An American clerical and lay delegation flew out, headed by Archbishop Mampré Calfayan, and also including Dickran Boyajian and Avedis Derounian (John Roy Carlson), both of whom published reports of the journey. Boyajian, in particular, rendered a detailed

Figure 7.1 Cathedral of the Holy See of Echmiadzin, Armenia. Photo from Wikimedia Commons, licensed under the Creative Commons Attribution-Share Alike 3.0 Unported license.

report of conditions in Soviet Armenia, describing both problems and improvements, through his 1958 book *A Light through the Iron Curtain*. In this volume, Boyajian recalled sorrowfully how he had been elected to take part in the previous election, in 1945, and then preempted from going by a Soviet bureaucratic snag. He mentioned the purges and the long bread lines of earlier years, happily noting that these days were over. Boyajian took the reader on a guided tour of the things he saw, both pleasing and troubling. In Yerevan he found an acute housing shortage with both a feverish construction of new houses and the deplorable sight of old, rotting ones. In the town of Sovetashen (formerly Nubarashen, initially founded and funded by Boghos Nubar Pasha), where his sister lived, he observed, "Many of the people I came in contact with were in need of many things, such as clothing, shoes, and ordinary household goods—the lack of which causes concern in any home in the United States. Meat and sugar were not plentiful. They had forgotten the word extravagance and tried to be satisfied with what they had."

A high point for the delegates, in their tour of the ancestral homeland, was the cathedral at Echmiadzin, which had stood in all its glory through the turmoil. As described in Boyajian's account, an oil painting of Mary with the baby Jesus in her lap was set amid the ornate altar.

> The facade of the altar platform is of marble and has fifteen sections on which are painted in beautiful colors the twelve disciples of Christ flanking the Holy Virgin Mary and the Infant Jesus on both sides, with deacons Stephen on the left end and

Philibbos on the right. Each picture is bordered in gold. Since 1720 these paintings
have kept their originality without being touched.

An elaborate design with much gold adorned the walls, ceiling, and arches. Close by
was the manmade Nersessian Lake, 350 feet long, 150 feet wide, and 30 feet deep,
surrounded by trees and flowers, "rendering splendor and charm to the place." The
group toured some other religious sites as well, including the church of St. Ripsimé and
the ancient monastery at Keghart. Ultimately, Boyajian concluded, "I can now state in
all fairness and sincerity that *Armenia is neither hell nor heaven*."[7]

Tashnag Armenians viewed the whole thing in a far more negative mood.
With a handful of exceptions, Tashnag party members boycotted the proceedings
(Avedis Derounian reported having exchanged pleasantries with a Tashnag couple,
not something Derounian and Tashnags usually made a habit of). An editorial
in *Hairenik Weekly* noted both the speed of the resolution and the disproportional
weight of delegates from inside the Soviet state, this despite the near nonexistence of
Armenian Church congregations behind the Iron Curtain. The writer remarked, with
uncharacteristic restraint for the subject, "It is to be hoped that the new Catholicos will
make a supreme effort to accomplish what his predecessors have failed to accomplish,
namely, the restoration of the unity of the Armenian Church."[8]

A year and a half later, another Catholical election served as the locus for even
greater contention.

- 3 -

Before the genocide, the Armenian church had two Holy Sees, Echmiadzin and Sis
(in Cilicia), and three additional patriarchates: at Constantinople, Jerusalem, and
Aghtamar (in the Ottoman Empire near Van). After the First World War, the Aghtamar
patriarchate ceased to exist. Catholicos Sahag II relocated the Holy See of Sis to the
coastal village of Antelias, in the newly constituted nation of Lebanon. The postwar
reconfigurations brought several dioceses in Lebanon and Syria into the jurisdictional
ambit of this Catholicosate.

Lebanon had an unusual political structure for a twentieth-century nation-
state: religions and ethnicities within its citizenry had special designations of status,
including proportions of representation in the legislature. Thus, Apostolic Armenians
had a fixed position: a small and periodically changing number of designated seats in
the Chamber of Deputies, alongside the larger Maronite Catholic, Shiite and Sunni
Muslim, and other confessional contingents. Among other things, this meant that
the government of Lebanon paid close attention to the proceedings of the churches,
including elections for Catholicos. By the mid-1950s, helped partly by the movement
of many non-Tashnags to Soviet Armenia under the repatriation movement, the
Tashnag party dominated Armenian community political life in Lebanon.[9]

In May of 1943, Karekin Hovsepian, hitherto serving as primate in America, was
elected to the position of Catholicos of the Holy See at Antelias. At that time, the two
Holy Sees did not quarrel, and in fact assisted each other in elections and consecrations.

When Karekin died in 1952, however, rumblings of conflict began to make themselves heard. The Tashnags at the international level began openly and overtly mobilizing to ensure the election of their own man for the position. Among other effects, this would mean a separate hierarchical structure for Tashnag-dominated congregations to align with. "The Armenian churches," Reuben Darbinian wrote in 1953 to his readers in the United States, "must be rescued from Soviet agents, and this is possible only if and when the throne of the Cilician Catholicosate is occupied by a man who is capable and courageous, independent-minded, and completely free of Soviet influence." Once that was achieved, he continued, "the churches for the Dispersion can sever their ties with Etchmiadzin for the time being and rally around the Catholicos of Antilias [sic] (Cilician See) who will be in a position to protect the interests of the Armenian church in the free world without the Soviet's invervention."[10] At the time, Tashnag-affiliated sociologist Sarkis Atamian was at work on his extensive book on Armenian Americans, which when published in 1955 contained this concurring passage:

> The Dashnak church will become legitimate on the basis of ecclesiastical recognition, as it has been factually, as soon as a duly authorized ecclesiast grants it such recognition. Since the Dashnak church has only lower-level pastors who will never be ordained to upper-level positions by the "true" church, the Dashnak church cannot be recognized or sanctioned as "legitimate" outside of the jurisdiction of either Echmiadzin or Sis ... But a pro-Dashnak or anti-Communist Catholicos occupying the vacancy in Sis left by Karekin's demise, makes it a forgone conclusion that: the basis for recognizing the Dashnak churches might become a reality, and the Eastern churches, at least, can be freed from the Echmiadzin-Moscow control.

He unabashedly acknowledged that this would mean a schism in "the unified national Armenian church, one of the oldest in Christendom," but "its present impasse will have been solved ... A segment of the Armenian people being led by the Moscow-Echmiadzin nexus will be lost to the present Soviet attempt to utilize the church as an ideological or political weapon." The monthly magazine *Echmiadzin* ran an editorial in October 1953 which, without mentioning the Tashnags by name, made clear its sense of the importance of not letting the ARF faction take over the See at Antelias; editorials in the Armenian partisan press in the United States ensured that Armenian Americans knew that the battle for the soul of that portion of the church was about to begin.[11]

The Tashnag party by the mid-1950s had amassed significant influence in the Dioceses that Antelias served. High clergy aligned with the ARF helped the process along for the Tashnags by reviving the centuries-old, though now dormant, argument that the See of Cilicia could and should assert its spiritual independence from Echmiadzin; they included Bishop Khoren Paroyan, prelate of Beirut now serving as locum tenens at Antelias, and Bishop Zareh Payaslian, prelate of Aleppo, the leading candidate in the pending election. An old spiritual rivalry had thus now merged with a comparatively newer political one, and the stage was set.

Between 1952 and 1956, Apostolic Armenians in Lebanon made several abortive attempts at scheduling elections for a new Catholicos. Right after the installation of

Catholicos Vasken at Echmiadzin, a vote at Antelias was set for February 14, 1956. Anticipating a partisan struggle, a *Hairenik* editorial just the week after the election at Echmiadzin made sure readers knew which side to see partisan agitators on. A constitution drawn up at Antelias back in 1941 called for Echmiadzin to send two voting delegates, one clerical and one lay, to take part. Shortly before the election, Catholicos Vasken, more successful than his predecessor in getting travel privileges from the Soviet government, announced that he would accompany that delegation, making him the first Echmiadzin Catholicos in centuries to leave Armenia. When he arrived in Beirut on February 12, Armenians turned out by the thousands to welcome him at the airport and along the route to the monastery at Antelias.[12]

As delegations arrived for the election, some behind-the-scenes communications and murmurs were taking place, especially over a complication with one of the delegations. In the city of Aleppo, a Communal Council had functioned as the voice of the Armenian community since the nineteenth century under Ottoman rule. Though the council's constitution required that a fifth of its membership must come up for election every two years, in recent times those elections had only been held every *four* years. That council had chosen a seventeen-man delegation to represent Aleppo at Antelias, but anti-Tashnag elements in Aleppo had contacted the government of Syria to challenge that delegation's constitutional legitimacy. The concern had then reached Lebanon's government. Because the church and its authorities had a sanctioned status in both countries, Syria's government could have blocked the delegation from traveling to Lebanon, and Lebanese rulers could have forced a postponement; instead, governing officials approached the gathering churchmen and presented the idea of postponing the election as a strong suggestion.[13]

On February 14, Catholicos Vasken made an impassioned speech to the full gathering urging postponement of the election until the following week. Implicit in his entreaty was the idea that no official proceedings connected with the election should take place until the dispute over delegate credentials had been resolved. "In case of the contrary situation," he told his listeners, "our religious life will be imperfect and without meaning. We will plunge into common troubles, disputes and quarrels; we will cease to be the honored servants of the church." He would, moreover, be "grieved to death" and could not stay to take part. Locum tenens Khoren allowed the delegates to decide the matter. The majority of the delegates voted to form a Provisional Committee to move ahead with the election. Ten delegates loyal to Vasken walked out at that point, and the Provisional Committee officially validated the legitimacy of the delegates in question. As an apparent courtesy gesture to Vasken, the assembly voted to postpone the election until February 20. The Catholicos, however, replied that "all the possibilities of arriving at an understanding have been exhausted," and announced his intention to leave Lebanon before the vote was taken.[14]

In the days leading up to the vote, efforts to rescue the Armenian Church from a worldwide schism continued in earnest. Archbishop Yeghishe Derderian, locum tenens of the Patriarchate of Jerusalem whom Vasken appointed as his surrogate in Lebanon, held meetings with delegates and bishops. The elderly and venerated Patriarch of Istanbul (Constantinople), Archbishop Karekin Khatchaturian, paid a visit to urge reconciliation. The prime ministers of Syria and Lebanon demonstrated their

Figure 7.2 St. Gregory the Illuminator Armenian Cathedral at the Holy See of Cilicia, located in Antelias, Lebanon. Photo from Wikimedia Commons, licensed under the Creative Commons Attribution 2.0 Generic license.

concern by having a face-to-face meeting on the matter, though they still declined to exert any peremptory power.[15]

By February 20, civility had given way, not only to acrimony, but to violence. The day before, just after locum tenens Khoren had escorted Vasken to his plane, a crowd gathered at the airport to throw stones at Khoren and even try to abduct him, possibly (as Khoren believed) to obstruct the election by preventing him from officiating. On the day of the election, a band of women hostile to Bishop Zareh numbering somewhere between sixty and three hundred occupied the church, mistakenly thinking that the election ceremony could only be held inside the edifice. Moreover, the Christian mandate to love their neighbors as themselves did not stop mobs from physically assaulting Zareh and several of his allies, putting them briefly in the hospital. Deployment of gendarmes by Lebanese president Camille Chamoun ensured that the vote went through. On February 20, 1956, delegates elected Zareh, the favored candidate of the Tashnag party, as Catholicos of the Holy See of Sis at Antelias.[16]

Catholicos Vasken now intended to convene a conference of bishops in Jerusalem. However, because Jordan, which still controlled the eastern half of the city, did not have diplomatic relations with the Soviet Union, Vasken could not obtain a visa. Egypt's president Gamal Abdel Nasser solved that problem by cordially inviting the churchmen to Cairo. The General Episcopal Synod, meeting March 5–8 with Vasken's ally Yegishe Derderian of Jerusalem serving as chair and with eleven out of the sixteen bishops aligned with Vasken on the matter at hand, issued a statement affirming the superior spiritual authority of Echmiadzin over Antelias and calling the election results "defective and unacceptable." Even so, the bishops of the majority side showed a clear willingness to recognize Zareh as the new Catholicos if he would take a pledge of deference and subordination to the See at Echmiadzin in all matters spiritual (as opposed to administrative, where Echmiadzin did recognize Antelias as independent). In his written reply, Zareh refused to take any such pledge, insisting—even as he respectfully referred to Vasken by his customary title of Catholicos of All Armenians—on the mutual independence of the two Sees in all matters and calling for a set of agreements of reciprocal courtesy and cooperation as equals. Communications went back and forth between the two camps throughout the spring and early summer. In late June the efforts appeared briefly to have succeeded in healing the rift, but they ultimately came to no avail.[17]

Though Khoren's partisans had comprised most of the election delegates, Vasken's loyalists represented the majority in the Brotherhood of the Catholicosate of Cilicia. This ensured continued tension on the church grounds. In July a volley of high-handed pronouncements flew in both directions, neither side recognizing the other's actions as legal, and late in the month a physical fight occurred over possession of the keys to the secretariat office. Opponents of the Catholicos-elect continued to petition the president of Lebanon to intervene. Another complication also remained: by the rules of the church, the new Catholicos had to be consecrated to take office. (Bishop Khoren was still serving as locum tenens.) The consecration ceremony required a minimum of three bishops to officiate. Under normal circumstances, Catholicos Vasken and every Armenian bishop anywhere near would have done the honors, with the ceremony most likely taking place at Echmiadzin. As it happened, under these *ab*normal circumstances, in all of Armenian Christendom only two eligible bishops—Khoren, locum tenens at Antelias and prelate of Beirut, and Ghevond of Cyprus—were willing to oblige. This seems to have given *Mirror-Spectator* editor Varoujan Samuelian some amusement, judging from an editorial mockingly titled "Wanted: One Bishop." "Once he becomes a catholicos," Samuelian jeered from his office in Boston, "he can consecrate bishops by the dozens, but he cannot consecrate any one until he himself becomes consecrated. He is in quite a dilemma, we would say." Armenians were not the only interested parties here: cable traffic shows that British diplomats in Amman and Jerusalem sought to help find an anti-Communist bishop who would oblige the pro-Zareh Armenians. Finally, Tashnag-supported church officials broke the logjam by arranging for an elderly Assyrian Orthodox bishop, Prelate of Antioch Severios Yacoub, to join Khoren and Ghevond in conducting the ritual, an expedient whose legitimacy the opposing camp would challenge for years to come. The consecration took place on September 2, 1956, in front of a crowd estimated at thirty thousand. Lebanon's president and prime minister and a host of Lebanese and Syrian officials took part.[18]

In the midst of the consecration crisis, the Tashnag religious authorities announced that a number of sacred relics had mysteriously disappeared from the Holy See at Antelias, apparently stolen by high-ranking men of the cloth loyal to Vasken: the *Sourp Atch* (holy right arm) of St. Gregory the Illuminator, those of Patriarchs Nicholayos and Seghbesdros, bone relics of Barsama the Hermit and St. Keghart, and a piece of wood from the actual cross. Tradition had made the presence of the *Sourp Atch* necessary in some minds to legitimate the See's authority. Pro-Zareh clergy and the Tashnag press promptly indicted the anti-Tashnag church hierarchy for the thefts; one priest loyal to Zareh made a case that Echmiadzin had stolen the *Sourp Atch* from Sis once before, in 1443, evidence of a pattern of bad faith in such matters. (He and other clergy also assured their followers that, contrary to myth, the legitimacy of the See at Antelias did *not* require the physical presence of those relics to endow it.) Samuelian at the *Mirror-Spectator*, in the same editorial quoted above, wondered how "people who would commit murder in a church" could "let a little thing like stealing bother them." The editorial proceeded from there to reminisce about how the Tashnags had blamed the 1933 Tourian murder on a mysterious Mr. X, and suggested, "While Bishop Zareh is looking for his one bishop, he can keep his eyes open for 'Mr. X.'" The relics resurfaced and were returned to Antelias the following year. The Tashnag press reported widely that the thieves had been Archbishop Karekin Khatchaturian of Istanbul and the aforementioned and ubiquitous Archbishop Tiran Nersoyan, both loyal to Echmiadzin and desirous of delegitimizing Zareh's election. They had been housed at Jerusalem by Patriarch Yeghishe, who over time had thought better of the deed and arranged for their return.[19]

Right away, the proponents and opponents of the election's results scrambled to gain recognition for their version of events in the non-Armenian world. The British Foreign Office embraced Zareh right away, but Lambeth Palace, seat of the Church of England, snubbed him until 1960, declining to congratulate him and ceasing to exchange Christmas and Easter greetings (the aforementioned Hewlitt Johnson, notorious Soviet apologist, was still Canterbury's dean). The factions campaigned intensely in the United States, each regarding its own spiritual institution as the authentic church. Moreover, by the lights of each camp, it was the other camp that was politicizing the church. When the *New York Times*, in language with which the Tashnags concurred entirely, reported that Catholicos Vasken's February visit to Lebanon represented "the Russians … trying to use the Armenian Orthodox Church as a means of injecting Soviet influence into the Middle East," a letter to the editor by North American Acting Primate Father Vartan Megherian countered that Vasken exerted solely spiritual and not political leadership and had been recognized as such, in his role as Catholicos of All Armenians, in a recent American assembly.[20]

With the new Catholicos in place, congregations of the Armenian Apostolic Church of America controlled by Tashnag worshipers formally broke with Echmiadzin and, in affiliation with the Prelacy (constituted in 1958, originally located in Boston, now on East Thirty-Eighth Street in Manhattan), aligned themselves with Antelias. Each American denomination tried to gain membership in the NCC; when the Diocese loyal to Echmiadzin prevailed, the Diocese interpreted this action as an official NCC endorsement of it as the true Armenian church, while the Tashnag-aligned Prelacy denounced its rival as "the dissident church." In 1958 each faction printed up an English-language pamphlet arguing for its own legitimacy, with the pro-Antelias pamphlet calling its rival "an unworthy, disloyal *pro-Soviet political party* masked as a church organization." Unlike in the First World War era, Armenian politics did not stop at the water's edge: each camp now actively pled its case to the mainstream American society and its institutions.[21]

From the anti-Tashnag point of view, supplanting Echmiadzin's place of primacy over all other Holy Sees assailed centuries of tradition and flew in the face of all authenticity.

To Tashnags, the only assault on authenticity came from the degree of control that the Soviet regime exercised over Echmiadzin, and the legitimacy of the church worldwide could only be restored through the leadership of a primate who operated under no such constraints. All through the following decade, the competing party presses repeatedly ran retrospectives retelling their versions of the story in intricate detail. Each faction, at the leadership level, needed its constituents to remember the bad faith of the other side, and the legitimacy or illegitimacy of the 1956 election results and the affiliation of America's Tashnag-dominated churches with the Cilician See. This took its place in what by now was a very long parade of contested memories that the factions continually rehearsed.[22]

Armenians, of course, were not the only nationality with an international hierarchical church whose spiritual center lay behind the Iron Curtain and whose highest spiritual leader worked under Soviet restrictions. Since 1924, a breakaway institution of the Russian Orthodox Church known as the Metropolitan District had supplanted the Patriarch of Moscow as the authority over those congregations so inclined. Since 1945, two factions of the St. Nicholas congregation in New York had struggled for control of that church, bringing forth a case that danced back and forth between the state appeals court and the US Supreme Court. The state court, ruling in favor of the breakaways in both 1952 and 1960, applied a statute precluding an agency of a foreign government from controlling a church; the Supreme Court, ruling in 1954 and then with full finality in 1960, found the New York statute to violate the constitutional guarantee of free exercise of religion by setting eligibility standards for spiritual authority. Prior to that resolution, the Tashnags hoped and the anti-Tashnags feared that an anti-Moscow outcome would strengthen the Tashnag hand in prying North American Armenian churches away from the hold of Echmiadzin.[23]

In the course of the travails over the church in the 1950s, the Armenian American press never let its readers forget the controversies surrounding one well-traveled churchman in particular, Bishop Tiran Nersoyan—an incorrigible cheerleader for the Communists according to the Tashnags, and a long-suffering victim of Tashnag persecution according to the Ramgavars. Tiran Nersoyan and his family hailed from Cilicia and fled the genocide by way of Syria. He studied theology at the seminary in Jerusalem in the 1920s and was serving as pastor to the Armenian community in London during the Second World War, when he wrote his controversial *Christian Approach to Communism*. After his 1944 election to the primacy of the church in the United States, he was consecrated as a bishop in 1945 and then archbishop in 1953. In the process of serving as primate, he became a naturalized citizen of the United States. As noted, he received round condemnation from the Tashnag press for his role in encouraging several hundred Armenians in the United States to repatriate to Soviet Armenia.[24]

Archbishop Nersoyan, well known to both his admirers and his critics in the Armenian American community, was a key player in a protracted drama at Jerusalem that got underway even while the crisis at Antelias played itself out. Since the October 1949 death of Patriarch Guregh Israelian, Archbishop Yeghishe Derderian had served as locum tenens. In late 1955, Nersoyan arrived in Jerusalem to lead a campaign to have Derderian investigated for some alleged fiscal chicaneries. The feud caused a split among the voting members of the Brotherhood of St. James, which administered this historic spiritual site, with one faction loyal to each contender. The government of Jordan, at that time exercising authority over East Jerusalem while rocked by internal problems of its own, took an increasingly strong hand in supporting Derderian; by 1961, the Jordanian government had exiled Nersoyan and several clergy loyal to him, and now took peremptory measures to ensure Derderian's election as patriarch.

Resemblance between this saga and the familiar Cold War alignments held up only to a point, however. While much of Jordan's Cold War activity during these years conformed to Anglo-American expectations and prodding, in this instance, according to research by historian Ara Sanjian, the State Department showed more concern over the abrupt deportation of an American citizen, which Bishop Nersoyan indisputably was. The influence therefore would appear to have come from Tashnag advocates. Moreover, while Derderian enjoyed Tashnag support for long stretches of the protracted affair, and while the Jordanian government consistently justified its actions against Nersoyan on the grounds of his authorship of *A Christian Approach to Communism* and other alleged pro-Soviet actions, Derderian's loyalty appears to have been to himself (and perhaps God, on some level): upon his election as patriarch, he appealed to Catholicos Vasken at Echmiadzin to lift an earlier suspension from the episcopate; once recognized as patriarch by Echmiadzin, he remained cooperative with same, much to the anger of his erstwhile Tashnag supporters. Meanwhile Nersoyan retired from international controversies, returned to the States, and founded St. Nerses Seminary in New Rochelle, New York, which he administered until his death in 1989.[25]

- 4 -

The conventional wisdom in Armenian and Armenian-friendly circles has understandably assumed that the partisan schism weakened the Armenian community and made for a plethora of missed opportunities: *if only* there had been unity instead of division. Certainly, the division did much damage, especially when Armenians actually killed each other, as happened in Lebanon in 1958 when Tashnags and anti-Tashnags took sides in the civil war between the Lebanese government and rebels and continued exchanging retaliatory assassinations even after the larger war had ended.[26] However, especially where the newspaper wars in America are concerned, lamentations of the "if only" variety run the risk of missing some of the point. Several paradoxes emerge that make the schism, while still not something to celebrate, a factor worthy of study as more than just missed opportunities.

It has already been observed, with credit to Felix Corley's incisive research, that the Soviet state of the early 1950s, in contrast with that of the 1920s and 1930s, made modest but real efforts to resurrect the church that its own earlier leaders had all but snuffed out. Records of internal discourse show that the Soviet leaders felt the need to counter Tashnag propaganda in the diaspora. They saw Catholicos Kevork and, to an even greater extent, Catholicos Vasken as important tools for that effort. This led to greater freedom of movement for the Catholicos and greater freedom of worship and national identity (though still within limits) for the Armenian populace. Thus, the combination of pressure from the international Tashnag network combined with solicitude from the anti-Tashnag coalition seems to have induced modest reforms that might not have happened otherwise.

A second paradoxical feature of the partisan divide is that the editorial writers of the respective presses, for all their lamentations about the lack of Armenian unity, appear to have mastered the art of using the schism as a marketing tool, at times with relish. Armenians did not by any means invent this practice. In nineteenth-century America, most of the major city newspapers served as organs for the parties—Whigs, Democrats, Republicans, Know-Nothings, Populists—with their editors crafting an art form out of not only political polemics but ad hominem attacks on rival editors. Students of this phenomenon, in the American national context, recognize the parties and the press organs as having served a function in the growth of the nation, as opposed to merely representing the lamentable absence of unity. Might not the same be said for a diasporan nation and an immigrant community? The behavior patterns of the partisan editors certainly show a parallel: especially in the 1950s, subscribers to either the *Hairenik* or the *Baikar* papers, both English and Armenian, could count on steady updates on the other side's treachery. Moreover, each faction, by selling newspapers and sustaining itself as the voice of a portion of the *Hayoutiun*, was playing an important part in sustaining among its readers a sense of identity as Armenians, even while using other Armenians (or at least other Armenian leadership cadres) as a common enemy. (It should be remembered that party elites generally attacked opposing party elites, not the populace within the offending party.)

Yet a third paradox comes with the question of Americanism and Americanization. Armenians, it has been noted, were nearly unanimous in their consensus about the importance of being good patriotic Americans and appearing as such to observers. From this standpoint, one could scarcely see their public fighting and their appeals to their non-Armenian neighbors to take sides as anything but an embarrassment. Even there, however, a comparison with that larger society quickly reminds us of a basic fact: if one group of Armenians was caught up in Cold War hysteria and a mission to liberate the Communist world, while another group felt less threatened by the Soviets than by Cold War excesses in their own midst, and if these two groups mutually accused each other of being unduly influenced by totalitarian extremists while considering themselves the true defenders of democracy, this hardly made them different from the larger society to which they were being assimilated. Armenians fought the Cold War as Armenians and Americans, and they did it through their partisan schism.

Author Michael Bobelian argues that the partisan schism caused a delay in the coming together of the Armenians to demand recognition of the genocide by the world and atonement for it by Turkey.[27] The present work, as has been seen, takes a somewhat different angle, though our approaches may well be reconcilable. It is undisputed, however, that from the 1970s onward, the campaign for genocide recognition took center stage of Armenian American ethnic political life, and during those same years, the intensity of the feud between Tashnag and anti-Tashnag diminished. The following chapter addresses this phenomenon.

The Power of a Word

Naming and Claiming the Genocide

"Tonight is New Year's Eve," Leon Surmelian contritely told readers of *Common Ground* magazine in 1940, "and I'm drunk again. I realize that I'm a disgrace to this society, of which I have the honor of being a member." But, he continued, now invoking his title, "I ask you, ladies and gentlemen, what can I do, when once upon a time the world was no larger than the little side street where I was born? Where I led my armies to incredible victories on my spirited broomstick horse?" Fleeting but vivid images follow: of vegetable venders with very premodern scales; of village women carrying jars and pitchers of clay, filled with milk and yogurt, in baskets on their backs; of boys carrying lanterns singing hymns door to door at night; and of tables lined with figs, almonds, cakes, and old-world-style meats. Then comes the source of his pain.

> I ask you, what can you do on New Year's Eve in free and happy America, when your playmates and schoolmates, the kids you grew up with, your companions in grief and joy, in hunger and misery, fellow dreamers during your dream age, are gone, lost? … When you see the old swimming hole in far-away Pontus, seeds of ripe pomegranate, the purple cascade of noble wistaria over porches and doorsteps, yellow roses climbing garden walls, and hear the melancholy cry of popcorn vendors on winter nights? When the pretty girls you loved in kindergarten and grade school are dead and their bones lie unburied, or they are in captivity, forgotten by their own nation?

Surmelian apologizes again for his inebriation, assuring the reader it is not his habitual condition; but "once in twelve months, on New Year's Eve, I must forget my past, the New Years of long ago."[1]

He was, of course, not forgetting his past at all, but rather remembering it vividly, and making his memories accessible to a non-Armenian readership. His 1945 autobiography *I Ask You, Ladies and Gentlemen*, which contained that essay as a chapter, was published before the newly coined word *genocide* had entered general usage. Even so, the book was among the first and most cogent of English-language genocide narratives, describing village life before the massacres, the horrors of seeing loved ones die, the terror of knowing he might die, the ordeal of living in an orphanage, and the years lived as an immigrant in the United States. From the time that the word came into existence, it did not take any time for Armenians and many others to apply the word to what had taken place during the First World War. However, the use of the term as an actual *name* for what had happened—"*the* genocide"—took longer. Later still came the practice by many Armenians of insisting that "the genocide" was the *only* acceptable term for the mass murders of 1915, and that any other term constituted a euphemism and thus denial. In these same later years, Armenians began to wage a focused campaign for recognition that a genocide had taken place, calling upon the United States and other countries to declare it and the present-day government of Turkey to acknowledge it.

- 1 -

As in all immigrant communities, major social as well as economic transformations were taking place with the Armenians during these postwar years. The young who had been so fussed over in the 1930s were full-grown adults by the late 1940s, many of them owning houses and parenting the next generation. Increasingly, social integration coincided with physical movement. Armenians living in Worcester, Massachusetts, began making their way from the more urban east side to the more residential west side of the city, and to the nearby towns of Shrewsbury and Holden. Others simultaneously streamed from the blue-collar neighborhoods of Union City, Hoboken, and Paterson, New Jersey, to houses in towns such as Cliffside Park, Teaneck, Tenafly, and Clifton. Armenians in the less affluent sections of Boston and Watertown, Massachusetts, began buying houses in nearby Belmont and Waltham. The construction of new Armenian churches and the movement of existing church congregations in the late 1950s and the 1960s reflected this trend. Movement of New York Armenians to outer Queens led to the founding of the Holy Martyrs Apostolic Church in 1958. St. Leon Armenian Apostolic Church congregation moved from urban Paterson, New Jersey, to suburban Fair Lawn in 1965. The congregation of the First Armenian Evangelical (Protestant) Church of Boston, founded in 1908, purchased a plot of land in nearby suburban Belmont in 1955 for a new colonial-style structure and began services at the new location in 1958.[2]

As early as 1939, writer Garo Massis observed a shift of style, as well as of location, of women's shopping habits. In the Washington Heights section of uptown Manhattan, he informed readers of the *Mirror-Spectator*, "a whole community has sprung up, a smart and modern community that flocks to up-to-date markets rather than the Oriental shops of Third Avenue. They have lost the old flavor, and the substitute is a tone you can find in any A. & P." He contrasted the older Armenian community "down on Third Avenue" with this newer one uptown. In the downtown stores, he recalled "the smell of dried egg-plant which mother used to stuff with rice and meat and raisins" as well as "the huge displays of 'halvah'" and "the 'wedding candy' in high jars that bring back all the colors of the Orient." Where the Third Avenue ethnic grocers had "raisins in all shapes and sizes," the uptown stores had merely the modern boxed raisins from California. "Even the lowly prune had a glamour of its own in the stores of Third

Avenue; but in the stores of Washington Heights, it's just another box of merchandise waiting for a customer."[3]

As the second generation brought up the third, cultural change continued. Harold Nelson found, in his Fresno study, that the immigrants' grandchildren were more inclined to *date* rather than *court*, and some even engaged in that ultimate expression of modernity, *sassing* their parents. Outspokenness with opinions by the young was more prevalent by this time, and use of cosmetics had mostly ceased to be a subject of contention. Sociologist Mary Bosworth Treudley and a team of undergraduate students from Wellesley College, visiting some middle-class Armenian households in the Boston area, found a wide range of styles of ethnicity. Her report depicted families as facing together the dilemma of "in-group or out-group participation," with some families appearing "parent-centered or child-centered," but many on neither extreme.

> Because there is a balance between the generations, the children know and like a whole circle of older Armenians, while their own non-ethnic friends are equally welcomed by their parents. Sometimes schools tips *[sic]* the balance somewhat to the American side. The parents join the Parent-Teacher's Association and make acquaintances at their own age level with non-ethnics.

Treudley found the exigencies of economic mobility to be a strong pull toward integrated Americanness. At the same time, she took notice of ethnic dances and other such social activities that seemed to function as "mating agencies," "an American answer" to parents' quandary over how to influence their children toward marriage with fellow Armenians. "The young people," she found, "seem to be tolerant of such parental attitudes and desires. Some of them, who have been isolated from the ethnic group, even welcome the chance to come to know members of their own generation who have been brought up in the ethnic community." Treudley also noted that some Armenian Americans lived, worshiped, worked, and fraternized almost entirely in America's non-Armenian milieux, their only Armenian contacts being family. She implied that this was particularly common among successful professionals and businessmen, noting that "men of this type are often race heroes to the ethnic group, though they maintain very few contacts with its members."[4]

Much of the publicly aired discourse of the time also suggested continued tension between generations, with many of the young feeling neglected by their elders with respect to their ethnic socialization, and the elders viewing the young generation as insufficiently loyal to their heritage. An editorial in the *Mirror-Spectator* in July 1950 opined, "It seems to us that the older generation has long since abandoned the bulk of its responsibilities toward its youth, save what it apparently regards as its proprietary right of criticism." Robert Meliksetian of Detroit, writing in *Hairenik Weekly* in 1949, observed more charitably, "They provided for us and sent us to American schools; now we ask questions they cannot answer," but also characterized the elders as possessing a "gnawing and neurotic hopelessness." The older generation also had its defenders. An editorial in the Fresno-based newspaper *Nor Or* ("New Day") called the elders "eternal targets of unjust, sometimes monstrous criticism," and offered the analogy of a house being overtaken by the waters of an overflowing river: one would not expect to see the father and son of that house blaming each other for the plight of it.[5]

Editorial-page jousts did not, of course, entirely reflect what took place among grandparents, parents, and children in the individual household. Family dynamics varied, of course; but in the rising postwar Armenian middle class, it was not unusual for three generations to take vacations together. One American consumer phenomenon in particular facilitated such intergenerational fraternizing: the resort hotel industry. As American families enjoyed the postwar resort vacation boom, sizable numbers of Armenian Americans could be found taking sojourns in each other's company. Several spots became associated with Armenian-owned resort hotels catering to largely Armenian clienteles. In the Catskill Mountains of upstate New York, the towns of Lexington, Tannersville, and Hunter contained a cluster of such hotels. The Pine Tree Inn in Onset, Massachusetts, and the Hotel Idlewild on Cape Cod also placed their notices in the Armenian press. In New Jersey, the resort town of Asbury Park gained popularity. As depicted in recent memoirs, these resort communities, often involving cramped and spartan accommodations, brought the three generations together. Diana Alexanian Jalelian, whose family stayed at the O'Hara House hotel in Lexington, New York, recalls seeing the immigrant elders "playing rummy, poker, pinochle, and *scambeel* at the card tables in the specially designated, smoke-filed 'card room.'" She writes of "much conversation in Armenian, Turkish, and English in a nostalgic atmosphere during which people shared stories of their prior lives before their immigration." The younger set was also exposed to traditional Armenian music and folk dances. Some not-insubstantial number of enduring romantic liaisons, as well, appears to have begun in such vacation settings. Vacationing in these resort towns could be experienced as both a very Armenian and a very American thing to do. It was postwar American prosperity that made a resort industry and its market possible. At the same time, the atmosphere reinforced participants' sense of Armenianness.[6]

Another source of cultural Armenianness during these years was the popularity of music composer Alan Hovhaness. For a sizable number of Armenians, including the American-born, an Alan Hovhaness concert provided expression for a collective identity rooted simultaneously in the old-world Armenian past and the middle-class American present. According to musicologist Arnold Rosner, Hovhaness expressed little interest in Armenian matters prior to the early 1940s, when he entered the "Armenian phase" of his ever-changing musical career. At that point his composing inspirations began incorporating elements of eastern mysticism as well as his own Armenian heritage. Between 1943 and 1950, he produced a body of work that has been classified as distinctively Armenian. Both he and various other musicians—including Maro and Anahid Ajemian, two sisters who appeared together playing piano and violin, respectively—made the rounds performing his pieces.[7]

Assessments of his work in the ethnic press credited him with having re-created ancient eras of Armenian history in the compositions. Nona Balakian, major *New York Times* literary critic, wrote in 1946 in the *Armenian Mirror-Spectator* that Hovhaness had answered "the challenge to prove the dynamic and universal values of a culture that has survived the loss of national power and the most tragic vicissitudes of history"; he had learned the laws of ancient music and updated them for the Western-conditioned aesthetic. A writer for *Hairenik Weekly* observed with delight in 1946 that Tashnag, Ramgavar, and Progressive (Bolshevik) Armenians sat side by side at a Hovhaness concert at Town Hall in Boston, "rubbing elbows during the intermission and talking to each other as if they were all the members of one family." The observer suggested that such unity represented the true Armenian spirit, which after years of being overshadowed by the contrivances of "a few unworthy editors and political leaders" who were lacking that spirit had been revived by Hovhaness's "reproductions of Armenian's ancient culture." That same year a contributor told readers of the *Mirror-Spectator* that Hovhaness's compositions were "so full of the wealth and beauty of our Armenian cultural heritage" as to "stir dormant memories in all Armenians uprooted from their native soil."[8]

The Hovhaness phenomenon illustrates much about the position of Armenian Americans, as an ethnic group, in the years just following the Second World War. Audience members, according to the accounts, sat in the concert halls and felt as if they were connecting with Armenian ancestors across both many centuries and a globe. During these early formative years of the man's musical career, the concerts were funded by a circle of Armenian businessmen who had achieved affluence in the American market. Thus, for both promoters and auditors, the ancient and the modern were fused through an exercise in a style of ethnic identity that fit comfortably with the integrated American lifestyle. The sense of a rich heritage and a mystical connectedness with pious peasants and clerics of centuries past could be enjoyed in a modern American concert hall by middle-class Americans living in middle-class American homes. And, as Nona Balakian noted, Hovhaness had updated the musical aesthetic so that, while it gave forth an air of authenticity, it also held accessibility to ears that had themselves come of age in 1930s America.[9]

If Armenians in America could express nostalgia for memories of the world they had known before the genocide, as well as suffer from the memories of the genocide, these immigrants and their American-born descendants now also carried memories of their earlier years in America. Marjorie Housepian's novel *A Houseful of Love*, published in 1954, provided a fictionalized recollection of the author's childhood years in the 1920s in the East Twenties of Manhattan. Housepian was in real life the daughter of a physician noted for his humanitarian work during the World War I years, and in the 1920s he had a medical practice in the neighborhood, as does the father of Housepian's young protagonist-narrator. Uncle Pousand also lives in this fictional household and owns a restaurant nearby. Numerous other family members, whether sojourning or living locally, enter the pages with their various eccentricities and opinions. The old country is never far from this family's consciousness, with both the house and the restaurant serving as intake points for migrants. Ethnic self-satire dots the pages as well. At dinner on Easter Sunday, an archbishop observes that "If there are two Armenians there will be three parties—one for A, one for B, and one to give them something to argue about"; not long after, another dinner guest balks at the idea of calling a meeting and starting it on time: "Doctor, please, in all the years of your experience, tell me, has an Armenian ever arrived at three o'clock for a meeting called for three o'clock?"[10]

Hovhaness's music and Housepian's novel were also accessible and of interest to persons with no Armenian blood or heritage. Another link between Armenian Americans and the host society was William Saroyan, who established himself in the 1930s and early 1940s simultaneously in Armenian venues such as *Hairenik Weekly* and the broader American literary scene as a playwright and fiction writer. His 1961 autobiography *Here Comes, There Goes, You Know Who* brought the memory of boyhood in an Armenian family in Fresno into public view. The creations of artist Arshile Gorky and theater director Rouben Mamoulian further enhanced the Armenian image as a population with contributions to make.[11]

Indeed, Americans of Armenian descent could not only feel their Armenianness but share it with their fellow Americans who were not Armenian. Book reviewer Orville Prescott cheerily took up the host intelligentsia's part of the dialogue when he told *New York Times* readers about *I Ask You, Ladies and Gentlemen*, Leon Surmelian's memoir, in 1945. "And everyone knows," Prescott wrote, "that Armenians are unusually talented people, sad with poetic sorrows and glad with a divine joy of living. Words rise to the tops of their minds like the bubbles in carbonated water; the milk of human kindness is their natural drink." Presently, he remarked on how exquisitely "Armenians stick together," referring to William Saroyan's lavish introduction. Prescott then proceeded to note the serious and tragic content of Surmelian's childhood story, calling the milieu from which he came "a corner of the world little known to most of us"; he added that place-names like Trebizond and Erzurum had "a poetry of their own." A decade later the same reviewer found in Marjorie Housepian's novel that "one almost smells garlic and onions, almost hears the loud lamentations, the eloquent curses, the toasts and songs." One might well have found his words patronizing, especially with Surmelian's book. However, his characterization consisted with the image that many Armenians, or "Americans of Armenian descent," were seeking to cultivate in the United States: good Americans, but with distinctive traits, and with tragedies and triumphs of their own that they wanted to share with the larger society.[12]

Thus, even while negotiating and quarreling among themselves, Armenians were engaged as Americans, with their fellow Americans, in the telling of their story as Armenians. That story could not be told without reference to what had been done to them in 1915. The evolution of the word *genocide* in vernacular usage played a big part in this dialogue.

- 2 -

Rafel Lemkin, while still living in Poland and dealing with discrimination as a Jewish lawyer, submitted a paper in 1933 to the League of Nations' official publisher in which he proposed the identification and punishment of two crimes in international law: barbarity—defined as attempts to wipe out ethnic, social, and religious groups by either physical violence or economic restrictions—and vandalism—destruction of such artistic and literary properties as would do injury to a group's cultural identity. As a refugee and a faculty member at Duke University, Lemkin, now spelling his first name Raphael, coined the word *genocide*, meaning murder of a race, in 1943, and introduced it into public currency with the January 1945 publication of his book *Axis Rule in Occupied Europe*. This nearly seven-hundred-page work chronicled not only the mass murders of Jews and other minority groups by the Nazis but also the assaults on nationality and culture inherent in Nazi occupation of invaded European countries. This book influenced the proceedings at Nuremberg, and Lemkin himself joined the research staff of the War Crimes Office of the Judge Advocate General's Office.[13]

Lemkin played a key role in shepherding through the United Nations (UN) a resolution passed in December 1946, declaring genocide an international crime, and then the more elaborate Convention on the Prevention and Punishment of the Crime of Genocide, which the General Assembly passed in December 1948. Though Lemkin had favored inclusion of provisions against *cultural* genocide, and though the Syrian delegation, sympathetic to Palestinians recently displaced from homes in Israel, had attempted to insert a clause citing forced relocations and deportations, the final version more narrowly defined genocide as:

Any of the following acts committed with intent to destroy, in whole or in part, a national, ethnical, racial, or religious group, as such:
  (a) Killing members of the group
  (b) Causing serious bodily or mental harm to members of the group
  (c) Deliberately inflicting on the group conditions of life calculated to bring about its physical destruction in whole or in part
  (d) Imposing measures intended to prevent births within the group
  (e) Forcibly transferring children of the group to another group.

The Genocide Convention was to become binding as an instrument of international law as soon as twenty member nations out of fifty-eight had ratified it.[14]

Getting twenty ratifications happened relatively quickly: the Genocide Convention became official in January 1951. One nation, however, despite the strong role that its own UN delegation had played in shepherding the document to passage in the General Assembly, and despite strong lobbying efforts from within its population, took several more decades to ratify it. That nation was the United States. A number of factors got in the way, including some little-understood idiosyncrasies of the American constitutional system and some very well-known facts about the country's own situation with regard to race.

Like any other treaty, the Genocide Convention needed a two-thirds vote in the Senate before the United States could call itself a signatory. Of all the hearings held on this question in the Senate, the most lengthy and elaborate took place in the first round, beginning in January and February of 1950 and concluding that following September, conducted by the Foreign Relations Committee's Subcommittee on the Genocide Convention. Brien McMahon of Connecticut chaired the subcommittee, which also included Elbert B. Thomas of Utah, Claude Pepper of Florida, Bourke B. Hickenlooper of Iowa, and Henry Cabot Lodge, Jr., of Massachusetts. A long parade of witnesses testified, including representatives of various Christian and Jewish organizations, labor, the legal profession, and other affinities. "Genocide is the insidious foe of civilization," Mrs. Irving Engel, president of the National Council of Jewish Women, told the lawmakers. "When a group is destroyed much more is lost than the men, women, and children who make up that group. With their destruction the world loses the creative energies, the cultural and the religious contributions which they had to offer." Dana Converse Backus, vice chairman of the International Law Committee of the New York City Bar Association, suggested, "we have used the treaty power of the United States to protect migrating birds, and it is now time to use the treaty power of the United States to protect men." Dr. Joachim Prinz, representative of the American Jewish Congress, argued that if the United States did not ratify the Convention, whatever legalistic fine points might affect the decision, it would give the world the impression that the United States condoned the atrocities under discussion.[15]

Witnesses also included familiar players in the ethnic Cold War. Both Charles Rosmarek and Lev Dobriansky testified, representing Poles and Ukrainians, respectively, speaking of atrocities by both the Nazis and the Soviets. Indeed, like Lemkin in his book, a number of witnesses emphasized actions by Stalin during and after the war that smacked of suppression of non-Russian ethnic identities within Soviet territory. From the amount of importance that some witnesses gave American ratification, they appeared to believe—mistakenly—that by ratifying the Genocide Convention the United States would be assuming a world police power and thus coming to the rescue of their beleaguered nations. Oddly, in light of the wide variety of witnesses, the senators did not hear testimony from any Armenians, though to be sure they heard repeated references to the Turkish massacres of Armenians in 1915, paired with the Nazi Holocaust as clear examples of the crime of genocide. The Armenians were, however, represented in the form of a printed statement from the Armenian National Council of America, which Rev. Charles A. Vertanes headed. The ANCOA statement, while predictably not talking about Soviet atrocities (as a Tashnag petition undoubtedly would have), reviewed the plight of the Armenians under the Turks, citing the massacres spanning from the 1890s through the early 1920s, and invoking a now-famous quotation in support of the argument that more international attention to genocide might deter it in the future.[16]

> An incontrovertible evidence of this is what Hitler did and said in 1939, just before the invasion of Poland, when he sent to the East his Death's Head units, with the order to "kill without pity or mercy, old men, women, and children of the Polish race and language," because, he explained, "only in such a way will we win the vital space we need." He felt sure at the time he would not be called personally accountable for the heinous order, for he argued, "who still talks nowadays of the extermination of the Armenians?" When informed of the threat of the Allies concerning the personal responsibility of public criminals, he put the question cynically, "What Allies? The same that threatened against the Turks?"
>
> Hitler was right. The Turks who had plotted the Armenian genocide were not personally called to account for their monstrous deeds, a failure for which the world paid very dearly.[17]

The statement then reviewed events following the First World War, including the fact that the Allies had at first held eighty-two men at Malta for trial for atrocities against Armenians, but then released them, and that many of these criminals had subsequently held positions in the Kemalist regime, including the then president of Turkey, İsmet İnönü, formerly Ismet Pasha. Noting that the Convention made genocide a crime subject to extradition for individuals, Vertanes and his colleagues told the subcommittee, "Henceforth it will not be possible for people guilty of the crime of genocide to be at large without the apprehension that the organized will and judicial machinery of international society has condemned them as public criminals subject to punishment in due time."[18]

Amid all the moral logic rallied in favor of ratification, the senators also heard arguments against it, presented with particular strength by representatives of the American Bar Association's Special Committee on Peace and Law through the United Nations. Though these arguments did not hold sway with McMahon's subcommittee, they did stop the larger Committee on Foreign Relations, which Tom Connally of Texas chaired, from bringing it to a vote and sending it on to the full Senate. Some of the arguments against ratification centered on the clause in the Constitution that included treaties as "the supreme law of the land." This bore a couple of scary implications. First, a treaty could be self-executing: even without follow-up domestic legislation putting its provisions into effect, American courts might begin basing rulings on it. Second, though the Constitution limited Congress to enumerated powers (powers specifically listed in the Constitution) and reserved all other prerogatives to the states, the Supreme Court—again, using the "supreme law of the land clause"—had ruled that a power otherwise off limits to Congress could become permissible if the United States signed a treaty calling for it. (The case involved migratory birds. The court had previously ruled that Congress had no constitutional power to restrict which birds hunters might shoot. After the United States signed a treaty on the subject with Great Britain on behalf of Canada in 1918, and Congress passed a law consistent with that treaty, the court allowed that law to stand in *Missouri v. Holland*, in 1920.) Critics of ratification thus feared that the Genocide Convention might both encroach on Congress and allow Congress to encroach on the states. Critics also raised concerns about what constituted "mental harm" and how large-scale an attack on a group had to be for the word *genocide* to apply.[19]

For those who harbored such concerns, the matter was not abstract. Both national attention to the civil rights of African Americans and white southern defenses of Jim Crow segregation had reached an all-time high (and continued rising in the years to come). Would it be possible, a number of people worried, for lynchings and race riots to be construed as genocide and for US citizens to be tried in some yet-to-be-created international tribunal for their involvement in such? Mrs. Eunice Carroll, testifying for the Convention on behalf of the National Council of Negro Women, attempted to assure the subcommittee, "The situation of the Negro people in this country is in no way involved. The lynching of an individual or of several individuals has no relation to the extinction of masses of peoples because of race, religion, or political beliefs." Adrian Fisher, legal advisor in the State Department, affirmed in his testimony that, for as serious a problem as lynching was, "This convention does not deal with all of the ills or evils in the world, and that is one of them." A number of witnesses, however, were not persuaded.[20]

As noted, the majority on the subcommittee in 1950 favored ratification. To satisfy the concerns of critics, the subcommittee recommended that the Senate ratify the Convention with four understandings (as opposed to reservations, which would require renegotiations with the other signatories). Those understandings were: (1) that the definition of genocide involved an intent to destroy an entire group; (2) that mental harm meant "permanent physical injury to mental faculties" (as opposed to merely adverse psychological effects from living in a discriminatory environment); (3) that complicity meant aiding and abetting the crime of genocide (an answer to concerns about freedom-of-speech issues in the American context); and (4) that, while the Convention called for Congress to exercise its constitutional power to punish offenses against the laws of nations, it did not create any new powers for Congress. Subsequently, the subcommittee suggested calling these out-and-out reservations, and adding a fifth, essentially an amplification of the fourth: "the provisions of this convention shall not be considered as enlarging the powers of the Federal Government with respect to any matters recognized under the Constitution as being within the reserved powers of the several states." Even so, neither the full Committee on Foreign Relations nor the full Senate brought the Genocide Convention up for a vote that decade. Indeed, though the Truman administration had favored signing the Convention in the first round and sent representatives to testify accordingly before the McMahon subcommittee in 1950, Eisenhower announced not long after taking office that he would not be asking the Senate to act on it anytime soon.[21]

Disagreements over the UN Genocide Convention notwithstanding, the word *genocide* had entered the language, and over time became widely understood to apply to what had happened to the Armenians in Turkey in 1915.

- 3 -

Armenians and their sympathizers right along had commemorated components of the 1915 experience. Early on, April 24 took on the name of Martyrs' Day as a remembrance of the execution of influential men in Istanbul and in Armenian towns and villages, which occurred mostly on that date. Heroic stands at Van and Musa Dagh also received attention, especially with the 1933 publication of Werfel's *Forty Days of Musa Dagh*, which many non-Armenians as well as Armenians read. Compatriotic societies kept memories from their particular villages and regions alive. In September of 1949, for example, Armenians from Musa Dagh began holding annual commemorations of the Musa Dagh saga in Saint Leon Church in Paterson, New Jersey, at times more festive than solemn, as they represented not just commemoration of an event but celebration of an identity.[22]

While it took no effort on the part of Armenians to understand that a horrible crime had been committed against them in 1915, giving that crime a formal name, defining its parameters, and incorporating that more focused understanding into a larger narrative of identity involved more of a process, one of naming and claiming. One might expect—and rightly so—that for Armenians to share any sense of historical memory and of common identity would have to entail some easing of the tensions between Tashnag and anti-Tashnag. To be sure, the bitterness over the Tourian affair would continue to feel fresh for some decades to come. As late as the early 1990s, an eighty-three-year-old woman who had witnessed the archbishop's stabbing told researcher Gregory Doudoukjian, "I cursed the Tashnags and I still do." Even so, the 1960s and 1970s saw a shift—subtle and ambiguous in the former decade, but clear and decisive in the latter—entailing a decline in the intensity of the partisan feud.[23]

The years 1965 and 1975 are important checkpoints in the chronology for both their similarities and their differences. Both represented important round-numbered anniversaries, and in both instances one heard both Tashnag and non-Tashnag partisans express the importance of laying aside the feud so as to honor the fallen martyrs properly. Moreover, in both those years there was much to command united Armenian attention regarding indignation against Turkey and the world's overly friendly behavior to that enemy country. The 1965 anniversary gave Armenians a nudge in the direction of easing up the partisan animosity between themselves and refocusing their attention onto a campaign for genocide recognition from the world and atonement and restitution from Turkey. A decade later, the sixtieth anniversary—with the help of other shifting circumstances—gave them an even greater nudge.

At every step, as before, the behavior of newspaper editors made a difference. The argument has been made here that partisan tensions played a part over the decades in sustaining the political parties and, in close tandem, selling newspapers. The attacks between the opposing presses carried such predictable consistency that, if an Armenian had fallen asleep in 1952 and awoken in 1962, or even (to a slightly lesser degree) 1972, that Armenian upon waking might reliably have asked to see the latest copy of *Baikar* or *Hairenik* in order to catch up on what mischief those treacherous Tashnags or Ramgavars, respectively, were up to now. The church had been split since 1933, with the schism formalized in 1956, and Armenians aligned with either faction could scarcely escape the steady reminders of how right their own side had been. Thus, the main outlets for reinforcement of Armenian identity—the social clubs, the newspapers, and the churches—had Armenian identity enmeshed with either Tashnag or non-Tashnag identity.

Though it was probably not articulated precisely this way, in retrospect the question facing Armenian Americans at the start of the 1960s appears to have been whether partisan animosity could decline without pulling Armenian identity down with it. If this sounds like a convoluted way of asking whether there could be unity rather than division, there was a problem with this: each camp had particular memories and ideologies that it had no intention of relinquishing, and each camp's sense of Armenianness was caught up in those views. The two sides had, moreover, depended for decades upon each other's perceived misdeeds to promote themselves as political parties. Thus, the formula for easing the partisan acrimony was not so much a matter of the parties' deciding to come together and be united, as rather in their coming to depend less on each other to supply them with a focus of indignation. This may seem paradoxical, as obviously they had always had Turkey for that. What changed in the 1960s and even more in the 1970s was not the level of indignation against Turkey, but the level of focus.

The 1960s started out with the partisan tensions at an all-time high. The bitterest strains of intra-Armenian partisanism had, after all, just received a booster shot from the formal church split in 1956, causing Apostolic Armenians in both camps to feel the partisan division as acutely as ever in their religious lives. At the dawn of the new decade the ink was still wet on the pamphlets that Tashnags and anti-Tashnags had printed up to explain, not only to Armenians but to the outside world, which Apostolic denomination was the true versus the "dissident" church. All through the 1960s, the partisan presses still reminded their readers of each other's bad faith in the church schism. In fact, much of what one saw in the partisan press of the early 1960s seemed to show an almost frenetic determination to make clear that *nothing* was changing in the party wars.

In November 1963, Catholicos Vasken I of Echmiadzin visited Jerusalem, invited the newly elected Khoren I (Khoren Paroyan) to visit him, and extended recognition to him as the legitimate Catholicos at Antelias. The two Catholicoi appeared for all to see in a photographed fraternal embrace. For as nice as this picture appeared, the partisan papers quickly made sure that their readers knew how to understand this gesture. "Thus did the Catholicos of Etchmiadzin," the editorial writer of *Hairenik Weekly* explained, "bestow on his peer, the Catholicos of Cilicia, the traditional syllogism of recognition which has been delayed through seven stormy years." The editorial also observed that, apparently, the Ramgavars were not very happy with this. Whether happy with it or not, the Ramgavar party's *Mirror-Spectator* also made sure its readers did not misconstrue what they were seeing. After reviewing the misdeeds of the Tashnag-aligned See at Antelias, the editor surmised, "The historic embrace in Jerusalem was but a magnanimous act of good will, Christian humility and forbearance, but never an act of surrender." The demands for the return of the dioceses "which had been taken away from Holy Etchmiadzin through political manipulations" still stood. (Readers of *Armenian Church*, published in both Armenian and English by the Diocese, saw the same commentary.)[24]

That following April—the forty-ninth anniversary month of the genocide—*Mirror-Spectator* editor Varoujan Samuelian felt moved to assure his readers—on the front page, no less—that no truce was in effect with the ARF. "I have been asked," he wrote, "why of late I have been 'taking it easy' on the Dashnags. Perhaps I have been, but I can assure you that it was not from any humanitarian instincts. It was just that the simpletons were behaving themselves." He then proceeded to make up for lost time by lobbing reams of righteous ridicule at the ARF for the recent contents of "their poor excuse for a newspaper." His main point, though buried in the broader caricaturing, was that the *Hairenik* press had seized upon a *New York Times* story about repatriates unhappy in Soviet Armenia and trying to return to the United States. Samuelian, in this essay at least, took a dismissive tone toward the concern about the discontented repatriates themselves, as well as toward the *New York Times* journalists who were reporting on them. To make sure he did not seem to be going easy on his partisan rivals now, he wrote near the end of the piece, referring to the Tashnags' anti-Communist credentials, "No one could have possibly been more anti-Communist than Adolf Hitler, who caused millions of them to be killed. That the Dashnags were active allies of the Nazis is a matter of historical record."[25]

Even as the fiftieth anniversary of the genocide approached, the church wars continued. The *Mirror-Spectator* devoted a large chunk of its editorial page, for many weeks in late 1964 and early 1965, to an exchange of letters between Catholicos Vasken I at Echmiadzin and Khoren I at Antelias, alongside fresh pieces of prose from Samuelian making sure readers did not mistakenly perceive the conflict between the Sees as being over. Prompted by Khoren's dispatch of an archbishop to Marseilles to serve as primate in southern France, a unilateral move that Vasken took as an affront to his own prerogatives, the letters made clear that both sets of heels that had been dug in before were still firmly dug in. "It is true," Vasken wrote, "that our embrace [at] Jerusalem was unconditional, but it is clear that that embrace was destined to be a condition for the unity and peace of Our Church life ... If the malfeasances will continue ... how can we still talk about unity, brotherhood and reconciliation?" Khoren's replies made clear that he would not defer to Echmiadzin in any decision-making matters. "The honorary preferred position of the August pontiff of Holy Etchmiadzin," he wrote, "is respected and must be respected, though without comprehending it with the meaning of legal sovereignty ... Dear Brother in Christ, we would fervently request that Your Holiness ... forbid the adoption of a limiting and negative attitude toward the Holy See of Cilicia." Newspapers editors being less fraternal in Christ than catholicoi, Samuelian remarked to his readers that Khoren's embrace of Vasken at Jerusalem "was obviously a ruse to obtain more power," and added: "It is not new for Antelias and the ARF to declare loyalty to one side one day, and upon the next to slander it beyond belief."[26]

Yet even as the opposing sides kept up the feud, they paid increasing attention to matters involving Turkey. As Armenians were observing the forty-ninth anniversary of the genocide in 1964, they observed with alarm that the United Nations Educational, Scientific, and Cultural Organization (UNESCO) seemed more interested in the twenty-fifth anniversary of the death of Mustafa Kemal, or Atatürk, and had sent out a call to member nations to issue commemorative stamps for the man. Obviously, honoring Atatürk made no more sense to Armenians (or to Greeks) than honoring Hitler. *Hairenik Weekly* called this move "a somber commentary on the morality of the world today," and noted that Atatürk, "rather than demonstrating regret and contrition for what his nation had done in the awful year of 1915, proceeded to compound the crime of his people" by killing 226,000 more and then "going on to consign about 500,000 others either to murder or deportation." The *Mirror-Spectator* expressed similar sentiments, calling Atatürk "a man who only deserves to be listed on the blackest pages of history" and lamenting that UNESCO, an agency so widely associated with promoting world justice, could see any justice in paying homage to such a man.[27]

In preparation for the fiftieth anniversary of the genocide, Armenian advocates called upon members of Congress to make statements. They encountered resistance. When Representative Adam Clayton Powell of New York asked Assistant Secretary of State Frederick G. Dutton how he should respond to one such solicitation, Dutton replied, "A statement making current tragedies of the past could have a negative effect on our relations with a faithful American ally in NATO, needlessly aggravating an ancient animosity—perhaps to the negative interest of Armenians in a number of countries—without repairing the violations of human rights which may have occurred." Still, a number of individual governors and lawmakers, state and federal, responded favorably. Massachusetts Governor John A. Volpe, for example, declared the whole period from April 24 to May 31 as the Fiftieth Anniversary of the Armenian Massacres, "urg[ing] all citizens of the Commonwealth to join with those of Armenian descent in commemoration of this event." Meanwhile, Armenian advocates continued to reaffirm their demands for territorial concessions from Turkey. On January 30, 1965, the *Mirror-Spectator* printed a declaration from the Temporary Central Committee for the Pursuit of the Armenian Territorial Cause that the Armenian people "expect that their official and unofficial bodies, their entire leadership will continue to pursue Armenian territorial rights with new vigor and courage, **demanding the liberation of Armenian territories now occupied by Turkey and their unification with the present Armenian Republic.**"[28]

In the weeks leading up to April 24, 1965, the churches and the partisan presses observed a tenuous truce. While the papers did not change their stances on issues (*Hairenik Weekly*, for example, ran an editorial on April 15 recalling Soviet participation in some of Turkey's atrocities), they took a hiatus from overtly attacking each other. Reminders of the fiftieth anniversary were constant, and commemorations were ubiquitous wherever Armenians lived. Churches held special masses on Saturday, April 24. In New York, that day, two different processions marched to the UN: one organized privately by Charles Metjian in cooperation with the Diocese (non-Tashnag) between 10 and 12, and a second organized by the Prelacy (Tashnag) that began at 12 and emanated from St. Illuminator's Church on East Twenty-Eighth Street. There were also commemorative instrumental and choral concerts, including one sponsored by the Diocese at Lincoln Center on April 25. There were other kinds of observance as well. A consortium of Armenian Youth Federation (AYF) chapters in New England held a mock trial for Talaat Pasha and found him guilty (though Soghomon Tehlirian had already executed him). The Hamavasbouragan Compatriotic Union of Greater Boston held a commemoration on May 2 of the defense of Van.[29]

- 4 -

The 1970s constituted a decade of change: a diminution of the tensions that ran along partisan lines of Tashnag and anti-Tashnag, and an increased sense of common cause in relation to the genocide. A combination of global, regional, and local factors drove that change. Global factors included the behavior of party elites in the diaspora, as well as the increased migration of Armenians from the Middle East to the United States. Regional factors entailed the changing behavior of church and party leaders in the United States. It should also be remembered that by this time many in the community were at least third-generation, which connoted a degree of integration into the American cultural mainstream that made it harder to be preoccupied with ethnic hostilities, even if the Armenian identity still carried weight. The imminence of the sixtieth anniversary of the genocide, as well as awareness of events in the news involving Turkey, led to both the creation of a new lobbying organization and an increase in lobbying efforts by the existing ones. In the realm of ethnic journalism (bearing in mind that the parties had to sell newspapers alongside everything else that they did), the presence of a new nonpartisan English-language Armenian paper affected the competitive relationship between the partisan papers. And, at the local level, church congregations began taking the initiative of commemorating the genocide without segregating themselves along lines of Diocese (non-Tashnag) and Prelacy (Tashnag), even before the top leadership opted to work together. Many of those church congregations, meanwhile, were finding themselves dealing with a new cleavage, that between old-generation American Armenians and the new Armenian immigrants.

Back in 1924, as has been seen, Congress enacted an immigration restriction act that imposed restrictive quotas on nationality groups, shutting out most Asian groups completely and sharply limiting the number of Armenians who could enter. During and after the Second World War, the United States began rethinking the racial aspects of its immigration laws, allowing small numbers of Japanese and Chinese to enter the country and eliminating the racial qualifications for naturalization. In 1965, Emmanuel Celler, representative from Brooklyn of German Jewish immigrant descent, who had served in Congress long enough to have voted against the 1924 act and other laws of its ilk, cosponsored the Hart-Celler act, which totally revamped the immigration laws, completely dispensing with national origins quotas. For Armenians, this meant a fresh influx of sons and daughters of Ararat coming into their communities and dramatically altering their cultural character.

Claudia Der-Martirosian, from her study of the census, reports that in 1980 there were 50,225 adult Armenian immigrants in the United States. Of these, 17,810 had come from Turkey, 14,376 from Soviet Armenia, 9,734 from Iran, and 8,305 from Lebanon. By this time, California was the state receiving the largest influx, especially of Armenians from Iran (72 percent). Of the 93,890 American-born citizens of Armenian descent, 28 percent lived in California, 17 percent in Massachusetts, and 10 percent in New York. In 1990, the total number of foreign-born Armenians in the United States was 76,897, including 15,542 from Lebanon, of whom fully 72 percent lived in California. The concentration of new Armenian immigrants in California was even greater at century's end.[30]

Armenian community institutions, especially churches, became meeting grounds— at times battlegrounds—for the old-line Armenians, including immigrants from years back and their descendants, and the new immigrants from the Middle East. In a discourse reminiscent of the legendary German Jew / Russian Jew conflicts in turn-of-the-century New York, while some in the longer-settled generations regarded the newer immigrants as needing Americanization lessons, some among the latter thought the former needed some remedial Armenianization. Most overtly, many new immigrants felt scornful of the lack of retention of the western Armenian language by the American-born generations they encountered. The new immigrants, after all, came from countries where their ethnicity had an official relevance to their position in the larger society's polity. Immigrant Garabed Koujian, living in Watertown, told a reporter of his new neighbors in 1978, "Most of them don't know our language, and to me that means they can't call themselves Armenian." Around the same time, an informant talking to anthropologist Ingrid Poschmann O'Grady remarked, "There is a sort of snobbism, elitism occurring in the church … These people coming over from overseas are more Armenian than we are because they've had to be. They really were minorities in 'foreign countries' whereas we're at home here and we don't feel that." The largest influx of new Armenian immigrants settled in Los Angeles. As scholar Vahe Sahakyan notes, Middle Eastern Armenian immigrants began opening schools and clubs "to recreate the club-church-school trinity in the United States" that had been their method of "nation-building" in Lebanon.[31]

There were thus lines of division developing among Armenians which, while not seeming at first glance like harbingers of unity, at least had the attribute of being different from Tashnag versus anti-Tashnag. As one sign of this phenomenon, in Watertown, Massachusetts, as the Prelacy-affiliated (thus Tashnag-dominated) St. Stephens Church began filling up with new immigrants from Syria and Lebanon, a number of parishioners started going to St. James Church, which was Diocese-affiliated (non-Tashnag). The need for cultural similarity thus surpassed the need for partisan agreement, not a pattern that one would have foreseen decades earlier. Not all old-line Armenians saw the new influx as a bad thing. Barbara Merguerian, editor of the *Mirror-Spectator*, was quoted in 1978 as observing, "It has given an impetus to the community. The conflict is good. It has generated competition and there are many more events." Those events, of course, included genocide commemorations.[32]

At the same time that demographic changes were providing diversions from partisan conflicts, the parties at the global leadership levels were changing their approach. In December 1972, the ARF held its Twentieth World Congress in Vienna. Here, a new generation of Tashnag partisans made its presence felt, and the body passed a series of resolutions shifting the focus of its enmity from the Soviet Union to Turkey and calling for an Armenian cultural revival throughout the diaspora with demands for recognition of the genocide as a major component. Three years later, the central committees at Beirut of the three major Armenian parties—Tashnag, Ramgavar, and Hunchag—started working together to keep the Armenian community as a whole from becoming unduly caught up and divided in the civil war that broke out in Lebanon. All of this coincided with, and reinforced, the large amount of activity worldwide that brought Armenian indignation against Turkey into sharper and more articulate focus.[33]

Armenians also followed the Cyprus crisis. Cyprus, an independent island state independent since 1960, with a Greek majority and a Turkish minority, had been the scene of recurring tensions and skirmishes between the two historic enemy groups. On July 15, 1974, a Greek-orchestrated coup overthrew the government of Archbishop Makarios III and installed a more virulently anti-Turkish regime. Turkey landed its troops on the island July 20. A ceasefire was arranged at the end of July, but the peace collapsed by mid-August and the Turkish military incursion took off in earnest. The conflict on Cyprus led to a conflict in Washington, with members of Congress objecting to Turkey's use of US-supplied weapons for this invasion and demanding a cut-off of aid to Turkey, and the Ford administration, guided in its foreign policymaking by Secretary of State Henry Kissinger, insisting otherwise.[34]

The Armenian press continued the practice of attempting to explain to American politicians how supporting the Armenian cause would also best serve the true American interests. When President Ford vetoed a bill embargoing aid to Turkey, the

ARF's *Armenian Weekly* (formerly *Hairenik Weekly*) opined, "It seems to us that the President was the victim of the same dangerously tiresome State Department overthink and misjudgment which continues to portray Turkey as an 'important and contributing ally' even after a span of 15 years … a period during which Turkey has insulted, scorned, condemned and caricatured the U.S. and its generosity." US policy was driven by not wanting Turkey to be "a ripe plum in the hands of Moscow"; policymakers should recognize that Turkey was a "rotten plum" that "stinks up the whole NATO barrel" (because aid was about to expire anyway, Congress was still able to force an embargo; Ford reluctantly signed a bill conditionally extending aid through December 10). In the same vein, a *Mirror-Spectator* editorial in March cited US government statistics showing that 80 percent of the heroin and morphine entering the United States came from Turkish opium, and opining that the aid money the United States had given Turkey to help make a transition away from such a drug-based economy constituted "throwing good money after bad."[35]

Again, criticizing the friendliness of America's policies toward Turkey in the Armenian party-run papers was not a new development, but it occurred more frequently now, representing a new focus of indignation that was replacing the partisan feuds as the standard fare of the press. To be sure, the opposing camps had not stopped criticizing each other or viewing history and current events differently. The older generations still remembered the murder of Archbishop Tourian and maintained their conflicting interpretations of it. However, the emphasis was changing. By the mid-1970s, one no longer looked at the editorial page of one's party newspaper to find out what new, outrageous shenanigans the scoundrels in the opposing faction were trying to pull now. A weekly series that the Tashnag *Armenian Weekly* ran in 1974–5, "What Every Young Dashnakstakan Should Know," lauded the ARF and all its great patriotic deeds, but did not disparage the other parties.[36]

Closely related was a shift in the way Armenian observers spoke of the political parties. There was now a greater tendency to use that plural phrase, "the political parties," to refer to a collectivity with attributes of its own, and to defend that collectivity against critics. Representative of this shift was an article by Noubar Dorian that ran in the *Armenian Reporter* late in 1974. "It is sad to behold," Dorian wrote, "that a large segment of the Armenian community characterizes the person who belongs to a political party in America as a fanatic, a fool, a fantasizer." Many Armenians, he continued, associated parties with all manner of undesirable behavior, division, "and on occasion, murder." Yes, he conceded, some party men pursue power and sow discord, but still "the future of the Armenian-American community would have been bleak indeed without the invigorating presence of our political parties. It is impossible to visualize a viable and healthy future for our community in America without them. Who else would give substance and meaning to our ethnicity? Who else would keep the Armenian cause alive?"[37] The novelty lay in the notion that one could speak of the parties together, as opposed to one or another specific party, as an entity to praise or critique. Implicit was the idea that, in the years to come, the parties could promote themselves and justify their existence by means other than condemning each other.

Though this article appeared in the seven-year-old nonpartisan weekly paper the *Armenian Reporter*, some contemporaries apparently saw the *Reporter* itself as a challenge to the parties. In January of 1975 *Armenian Weekly* ran a lengthy letter from a doctoral student in mathematics at Syracuse University named Artin Boghossian that rendered a scathing critique of the *Reporter*, to which he was now cancelling his subscription. The letter writer opened with his dissatisfaction with the nonpartisan paper's handling of a specific story (an AGBU dance event), then proceeded to accuse the *Reporter* of claiming to champion unity while categorically attacking the parties. "The stimulation of increased disenchantment within our community towards our institutions may increase your clientele. Here in may be found the basis of your policy—a policy of 'divide and conquer' while pretending to be an advocate for unity."[38] Here again, the point was not the Tashnag, Ramgavar, or Hunchag party, but rather, "the parties." While this might seem like one division replacing another, that was not quite so: because the *Armenian Reporter* did not serve as a surrogate for a specific sector of the Armenian populace, but rather, was competing for subscribers in all sectors, a slam at the *Reporter* was not a slam at an ideological faction; it was, purely and simply, a slam at a newspaper—and a defense of "the parties," plural.

Amid all this came the sixtieth anniversary of the genocide. Though the genocide itself had done little or nothing to bring Armenians together across party lines, the commemoration of it sixty years later did play a part in moving the *Hayoutiun* toward at least some semblance of unity. In the years leading up to 1975, when churches commemorated the tragedy at the local level, some cooperative efforts took place. These had to be finessed because, while clergy affiliated with the Diocese and the Prelacy had certainly been known to develop cordial relations and attend the same unofficial events, the Echmiadzin-affiliated Diocese forbade its member clergy to take part formally in events that implied recognition of Antelias-aligned churches. Thus, seven hundred Armenians including Tashnags and non-Tashnags observed Martyrs Day together in 1972 at Sts. Vartanantz Armenian Apostolic Church in Ridgefield, New Jersey, with clergy of both alignments officiating; significantly, the program did not list the names of participating churches. Archbishop Torkom Manoogian, primate of the Diocese, told the *Armenian Reporter* that, though meetings were taking place to discuss the prospect of church unity, "until such time as unity is set as a goal and the steps leading to this unity are defined, formal joint affairs and announcements have to be deferred."[39]

In September 1974, the central committees of the Tashnag, Ramgavar, and Hunchag parties issued a joint "Appeal to All Armenians" from Beirut, declaring "that the time has come to present a united front to the world on the occasion of the Sixtieth Anniversary of the genocide executed on the Armenians." The statement, which included a demand for territorial cessions from Turkey, called it important "that no government may use our internal differences as an occasion to ignore the voice of the Armenians." That December, the American centers of the same three parties echoed the appeal. "It was high time," the editorial page of *Armenian Weekly* declared, "that all Armenians said to one another, 'Hey, listen, I'm a Dashnak, you're a Ramgavar, or you're a Huntchak, but what difference does this really mean in terms of the Great Wrong?'"[40]

It looked briefly as if the factions might still deadlock over whether to display the Tricolor in the 1975 commemorations, but after some honest brokering from the Armenian Assembly, they agreed to march and rally without any national flag at all.

The three parties formed a United Committee, which held a set of smaller-scale events in Boston on April 12 and 13, then chartered a fleet of buses to transport Armenians from the Boston area to New York for the larger, central observances on April 23–25. The two church bodies did not go so far as to merge their own observances. The Diocese organized a march on Wednesday night, April 23, with a route that took three thousand marchers by the UN headquarters and then to St. Patrick's, where the size of the crowd swelled by another two thousand. The Diocese also hosted a three-day conference of religious leaders and scholars, "Religion's Role in a Violent World," with cosponsorship of a number of major non-Armenian religious entities. The Prelacy, meanwhile, took sixty genocide survivors on a "Survivor's Pilgrimage" to the Statue of Liberty on Thursday morning, April 24, and presented a silver chalice to the Museum of Immigration, and then that evening had a symposium at Madison Square Garden's Felt Forum featuring a keynote address by Barbara Tuchman, Pulitzer Prize–winning historian and granddaughter of Ambassador Morgenthau. But the three political parties ran an unprecedented joint commemoration that Thursday afternoon, which was also a protest demonstration against contemporary human rights violations by Turkey as well as its continued denial of the genocide. Tashnags, Ramgavars, and Hunchag marched in concert from Twenty-Sixty Street and Madison Avenue up to UN headquarters. They presented a petition to the UN addressed to Secretary General Kurt Waldheim (whose role in another genocide had not yet been revealed).[41]

Indeed, the 1915 campaign of mass murder in which over a million Armenians in Turkey perished, though longer ago than the 1933 Tourian assassination, bore more immediate relevance for Armenians in the 1970s, so many of whom had been born much later in the century. While the genocide itself was six decades old, the naming and claiming of it was very current. Genocide, in the language since 1943 as a descriptive term applicable to the events of 1915, was increasingly the *name* of those events, now understood as a complete and singular package, and Armenians more fully understood episodes like the martyring of influential men on April 24, the forced marches of women and children, the defense of Van, and the forty-day holdout at Musa Dagh as components of that package. From this understanding arose a more focused campaign for recognition by the world's powers that a genocide, *the* genocide, had taken place, for official acknowledgement of same by the government of Turkey, and for land cessions from Turkey to Armenia on the principle that no nation had the right to reap benefits by wiping out the population of another.

- 5 -

As noted, US leaders regarded Turkey as an important Cold War ally. Obviously, this clashed with Armenian demands for formal genocide recognition. In 1965, in fact, even while Armenians were calling on the US government to acknowledge and condemn the mass murder of Armenians in 1915, employing the word *genocide* in the process, the government of Turkey was trying to get the US government to clamp down on Armenian protests and on the display of genocide memorials on private property. The State Department actually did ask federal officials to take care not to offend Turkey, though it had little control over the remarks of individual federal officeholders and even less influence over the actions of local governments and groups of private citizens (a fact that the government of Turkey did not always seem to understand). In 1968, the town of Montebello, California, erected a seventy-five-foot-tall, eight-column monument with arches and a dome, dedicated to Armenian genocide victims and "to men of all nations" ("men" still meant "people" at that time) "who have fallen victim to crimes against humanity." Though the wording on the plaque did not explicitly mention Turkey or say everything that Armenian advocates would have liked, it was enough to rankle the Turkish government and its representative who had attempted to lobby it down. Ceremonies on April 24 at the Montebello monument became an annual event. The State Department did succeed in stopping some events from happening. In April of 1971, plans had been made for a US Marine Band to perform at the commemoration at Montebello but then their performance was canceled. As Representative George E. Danielson of Los Angeles related to his colleagues in the House not long after, he inquired with the Marine Corps on behalf of his Armenian constituents and was told that the band needed to rehearse for another performance. Regarding this as a weak excuse, he pressed further, whereupon he learned that the State Department, in accordance with President Richard Nixon's wishes, had asked the Marine Band not to perform there "because we are fearful there may be demonstrations and that a certain other nation might resent it."[42]

It should be remembered that these were years in which ethnic group consciousness in America was enjoying an all-around renaissance, with much youth participation, and indeed the young generation of Armenian Americans was well-represented in the struggle for recognition of the Armenian genocide. In 1965, a group of AYF members got ahead of their Tashnag leadership and staged a demonstration at the office of Turkey's permanent representative to the UN, resulting in their expulsion from the group. Protests directly aimed at Turkish consulates became more frequent in the 1970s. Vartkes Yeghiayan, a lawyer, organized such a demonstration, about two thousand strong, at the consulate in Los Angeles in 1971, on the April 24 anniversary. Historian Gerard Libaridian, who was serving as editor of the ARF paper *Asbarez* at the time, took a major part in this action. He and others returned the following year, forcibly entering the consulate office and reading a list of grievances against the nation and government of Turkey. In April 1971, about four hundred Armenians of all ages staged a boisterous demonstration at the Turkish embassy in Washington, DC, carrying a symbolic coffin as well as hanged effigies of Talaat and Djemal Pasha, chanting "Justice for Armenians" and handing out leaflets to passing motorists and pedestrians; they also placed a wreath at the Woodrow Wilson Memorial Home. In November of 1972, a contingent of young Armenians crashed the party at the Bel-Air Hotel in Los Angeles where smartly attired Turks were celebrating the founding of the Turkish republic. Here, ARF member Levon Kirakosian rushed the stage and read a prepared proclamation, while others formed a shield to prevent celebrants from stopping him. The uninvited guests were eventually arrested by police, but not before they had made their feelings known.[43]

The year 1972 was significant in a number of other ways. That year Dickran Boyajian, veteran of the Armenian Legion of the First World War and a Boston attorney, published his book *Armenia: The Case for a Forgotten Genocide*. It was announced in August of that year that a Committee for Armenian Rights was raising funds to secure copies of that book for UN delegations, American lawmakers, college and town libraries, and other influential individuals and institutions. Also circulating after its publication the previous year was Marjorie Housepian's book *The Smyrna Affair*. As noted, the September 1922 Turkish massacres of Armenians and Greeks in that city were logically viewed as a continuation of the genocide and a good reason to object to any honors being paid to Atatürk. The year 1972 further saw the founding of the Armenian Assembly of America. Initiated by, among others, Prof. John Hanessian, Jr., of George Washington University and Stephen Mugar, founder of the New England chain Star Markets, its mission included bringing conflicted segments of the Armenian community together under one umbrella, promoting cultural identity within the diaspora, and political lobbying. The organization took shape at a three-day convention in Airlie, Virginia, in early May of 1972, and had similar conventions in each of the next two years.[44]

The crusade was, of course, an international one. In 1971, a division of the UN Commission on Human Rights called the Sub-Commission on Prevention of Discrimination and Protection of Minorities began drafting a report, "The Question of the Prevention and Punishment of the Crime of Genocide," which, in an early version, contained as part of "Paragraph 30" a reference to "the existence of relatively full documentation dealing with the massacres of the Armenians which have been described as the 'first case of genocide in the twentieth century.'" After intervention by Turkish delegates and much wrangling over the next few years, that reference was ultimately omitted. Armenians followed the issue. Several hundred Armenians protested outside UN headquarters in August of 1974; soon after, Archbishop Manoogian addressed a letter to the UN missions appealing for them to use their influence to keep Paragraph 30 in the report, insisting that the genocide had been thoroughly proven and not merely by relying on Armenian sources.[45]

The US Senate took up ratification of the UN Genocide Convention again, but a filibuster kept it from coming to a vote in early February of 1974. Senator Sam Ervin, Jr., led the blockage, seeing it as surrendering national sovereignty and opening the way for international tribunals to overturn rulings of the US Supreme Court. Armenian advocates, including Harry A. Dorian addressing the Philadelphia Branch of the Armenian Students Association, rejected those arguments as specious; indeed, Dorian recalled that critics of joining the UN to begin with had used similar arguments. "The United States must affirm it to add its strong voice to those who oppose calculated, planned destruction of groups of human beings," he told the gathering. "If such a stand had been taken after the Armenian Genocide, no other genocides may have occurred thereafter."[46] (Ratification finally happened in 1988.)

In 1975, Armenians scored a major, though fleeting, victory in Congress. It helped that House Majority Leader and later Speaker Thomas "Tip" O'Neill had an Armenian staff member working for him, Linda Melconian, whose grandmother years earlier had gotten married at Ellis Island to protect herself from being forced back to Turkey. O'Neill also had a friendship with Stephen Mugar, and his Massachusetts House district included the heavily Armenian-populated towns of Watertown and Belmont. Despite a personal appeal from Turkey's ambassador, O'Neill supported a resolution for which the Armenian Assembly, represented for this cause by historian Dennis R. Papazian, lobbied, declaring April 24 a day of remembrance "for all the victims of genocide, especially those of Armenian ancestry who succumbed to the genocide perpetrated in 1915." The State Department did succeed in talking O'Neill out of including a reference to Turkey as the perpetrator, but that hardly created any ambiguity: the unequivocal acknowledgement that a genocide against Armenians had occurred was still potent, and energizing for future Armenian campaigns.[47]

The Armenian Assembly, it should be noted, had shifted focus after 1974 from holding conventions to operating an office in Washington, through which it engaged in lobbying efforts with the government for a greater priority to Armenian issues in American foreign policy. A key moment was when the Assembly induced the House Subcommittee on Future Foreign Policy Research and Development of the Committee on International Relations to hold hearings on the specifics of the Armenian genocide in 1976, with the Assembly's executive director Prof. Dennis Papazian among those who testified. Attorney Dicran Simsarian gave eyewitness testimony as a survivor and advocated formal action by the United States calling upon the UN to convene an international tribunal on the matter.[48]

- 6 -

A new complication arose during the 1970s and 1980s. On January 27, 1973, a seventy-seven-year-old California land developer named Gourgen Yanikian, a genocide survivor who had lost numerous family members in 1915, lured two Turkish consular officials to his hotel room in Santa Barbara under false pretenses and gunned them down. Unlike the Young Turk leaders assassinated right after the First World War, these two men were born long after the genocide; their only offense was working for Turkey's current government. Yanikian confessed to the killings on the spot—in fact he called the hotel switchboard and said "I have just killed two men"—but pleaded not guilty to murder, claiming that he was justifiably rooting out evil (for which reason he declined an attorney's suggestion of an insanity plea). He received a life sentence, but was paroled early in 1984 due to ill health and died shortly after.[49]

Yanikian's deed turned out to be the opening shot in a decade-plus of Armenian terrorist activity. The Armenian Secret Army for the Liberation of Armenia (ASALA) was founded in the early 1970s and began its overt attacks in 1975. With some of its leaders having cut their teeth in the Palestinian movement, ASALA carried out assassinations of Turkish officials and bombings of not only Turkish targets but also those it regarded as enemies to the Armenian cause. Its first bombing, in fact, was of the World Council of Churches' headquarters in Beirut. The council had worked cooperatively with the American National Committee to Aid Homeless Armenians (ANCHA) to help Armenians migrate to the United States, and ASALA believed that such activity was weakening Armenian identity because Armenians in Western countries would become rapidly assimilated, thus less distinctively Armenian and less attached to the fate of their homeland. It did not take long for a competing terror group, the Justice Commandos of the Armenian Genocide (JCAG), to take shape; it began assassinating Turkish diplomats, starting with Turkey's ambassador to Austria in October of 1975. Though the Tashnag party officially denied being JCAG's founding entity, it was understood by many to be precisely that. It has been widely argued that ASALA's successful appeals to the youth of Beirut gave the ARF the sense of necessity of competing in that arena.[50]

For the most part, the leaders and members of the Armenian terror groups hailed from the Middle East. An exception was Monte Melkonian. Born in Visalia, California, in 1957 to two American-born parents, Melkonian enjoyed a childhood replete with Little League, Boy Scouts, water balloon fights, and summers at an uncle's ranch. His skin was sufficiently dark to make him subject, at times, to racial prejudice. After a sojourn with the family in Europe that included a visit to where his maternal grandparents had once lived in Turkey, after absorbing stories of the 1915 genocide and other past atrocities, and after being asked by a teacher where he was "from," he developed a consciousness in his teen years that blossomed into full-scale militancy by young adulthood. He took only two-and-a-half years to earn a degree from the University of California, Berkeley, and then enrolled briefly in Oxford University's doctoral program in archaeology for the express purpose of running reconnaissance in Turkey in the guise of academic fieldwork. In the late 1970s he spent time in Iran and Lebanon, becoming caught up in Lebanon's civil war and carving out a niche for himself as a revolutionary. He fought briefly with Tashnag militia in Lebanon, and then connected with ASALA in 1980, quickly rising into its leadership before breaking away and creating a rival outfit, ASALA–Revolutionary Movement (RM). On one occasion in Athens, he fired into a car with tinted glass, knowing only that it had Turkish diplomatic plates, killing Turkish diplomat and intelligence agent Galip Osman and his fourteen-year-old daughter while wounding the man's wife and sixteen-year-old son. He later expressed regret about the girl's death.[51]

In 1981, in an operation that Melkonian was involved in planning, four ASALA members laid siege to the Turkish consulate in Paris, killed one guard, and held as many as sixty hostages for fifteen hours before surrendering to French authorities. This was one of forty-one Armenian terror attacks that year. On July 15, 1983, the group ASALA detonated a bomb at Orly Airport near Paris, killing four French persons, two Turks, one American, and one Swede, as well as wounding over fifty others. (Many more would have died if the bomb had exploded in flight, which was the actual plan.) The recklessness of this attack and the number of innocent (i.e., non-Turkish) victims played a part in ASALA leader Monte Melkonian's decision to part ways with the group and form ASALA-RM. On July 27 the Armenian Revolutionary Army (ARA, the JCAG's changed name), having assassinated Turkey's ambassador to Yugoslavia in March, now launched a five-man attack on the Turkish embassy in Lisbon, Portugal. It appears to have been an attempt to take over the embassy, but it ended with an explosion that decimated the residence of the chargé d'affaires. In the course of it, a Portuguese security officer, the wife of the chargé d'affaires, and all five young Armenian attackers died.[52]

Responses to such events in the Armenian press and in Armenian public opinion varied. The Tashnag press showed more than a little bit of sympathy for members of the JCAG and the renamed ARA when they stood trial and were convicted for particular actions. For instance, when ARA member Hampig Sassounian was convicted in Los Angeles at the start of 1984 for the assassination of Turkish consul general Kemal Arikan, *Armenian Weekly* called the verdict a "mockery of justice" and showed clear signs of agreeing with the Sassounian Defense Committee's communiqué that "Hampig is being used as a scapegoat and a vehicle to deter Armenians from actively and peacefully pursuing our cause. We are concerned that forces outside the American justice system" (clearly alluding to political pressure from the Turkish government) "played a role in this trial and that justice was not fully served." In January of 1985, multiple chapters of the AYF-YOARF (the latter initials standing for Youth Organization of the Armenian Revolutionary Federation) held memorial rallies for the Lisbon Five. At the one held at Sts. Vartanantz Church in Ridgewood, New Jersey, attended by more than four hundred, youth lit a candle for each of the "heroes" and placed a folded Tricolor flag on each man's portrait; keynote speaker Ohan Balian called the Lisbon operation "a logical step in the process of the new Armenian revolution" and a strike against Armenians' former "slavish mentality."[53]

On the subject of ASALA attacks, the Tashnag press was more circumspect. Other press organs kept varying levels of distance. "The vast majority of Armenians," the *Mirror-Spectator* observed, "agree that the indiscriminate use of violence is not an appropriate means for Armenians to express our frustrations or to achieve our political goals." However, in reviewing commentaries on the subject in the mainstream press, many of which condemned the terrorist acts while also expressing sympathy for the Armenians' situation, the *Mirror-Spectator* also noted that some suggestions of what alternatives would achieve the goal would be helpful. Many Armenians, maybe even most, appear to have agreed with that sentiment.[54]

From the mid-1970s to the mid-1980s, much of the public discourse about the Armenian genocide was enmeshed with Armenian terrorism. In 1982 the State Department issued a bulletin discussing Armenian terror attacks, concluding with a paragraph calling the record of 1915 "ambiguous" and saying "the Department of State does not endorse allegations that the Turkish Government committed a genocide against the American people," though bipartisan pressure from Congress induced the department to disclaim that paragraph as representing its official position. The House passed a resolution commemorating the genocide in 1984, but the following year President Ronald Reagan, who while governor of California and also as president (in 1981) had openly acknowledged the genocide more than once, asked Congress with this statement not to pass any resolutions of commemoration that year:

> I know this is a deeply emotional issue, and I sympathize with all those who suffered during the tragic events of 1915. I also profoundly regret that Turks and Armenians have so far not been able to resolve their differences. Nevertheless, there is no question regarding my opposition to terrorism. On those grounds alone, my Administration opposes Congressional action on the kind of resolution to which you refer. We are concerned such resolutions might inadvertently encourage or reward terrorist attacks on Turks and Turkish Americans. We also oppose them because they could harm relations with an important ally.

That year and in subsequent years, resolutions were blocked from passage.[55]

If 1984 was a banner year for Armenian terrorism, it was also its last such year. As various scholars have observed, the Orly airport bombing of 1981, with its indiscriminate wasting of lives by no means limited to Turkish ones, shocked many Armenians worldwide out of wanting to be identified with groups like ASALA. (Shortly after his breakaway from ASALA, Melkonian received a six-year prison sentence in France, of which he served four, being released in 1989. He ultimately died in 1993 in the struggle for Nagorno-Karabagh, discussed in the epilogue.) With the decline of ASALA came the decline of JCAG/ARA as well. Though the two groups were very different in their operations, the latter strictly limiting itself mostly to Turkish targets (with the occasional rival Armenian target), the non-Armenian public lumped them together as "Armenian terrorism," putting Armenians in general on the defensive and causing them to suffer both embarrassment and, in some countries (such as Iran), political repression. Laura Dugan and colleagues attribute the swift decline of Armenian terrorism to this factor. Historian Gerard Libaridian suggests an alternate explanation for the end of the terror attacks: the groups had achieved their goals, not of extracting reparations and territory from Turkey, but of raising public awareness of the genocide and orienting the Armenian diaspora toward viewing Turkey, and not the Soviet Union, as the main enemy.[56]

- 7 -

Campaigns to induce the US government to recognize the genocide at official levels—with the unequivocal use of precisely that word—continued. Barack Obama, as a presidential candidate in 2008, openly used the word *genocide* on the subject. As president in 2009, he avoided using the actual word, calling it the *Medz Yeghern*—which had been Armenians' own term for it in past years. He noted separately that he was aware that negotiations were taking place between Armenia and Turkey and that he was "not interested in the U.S. tilting these negotiations one way or another" while they were in progress. Notwithstanding, his statement—with or without the desired word—left no doubt as to what he understood had taken place. "Ninety-four years ago," Obama said in 2009, "one of the great atrocities of the twentieth century began. Each year, we pause to remember the 1.5 million Armenians who were subsequently massacred or marched to their death in the final days of the Ottoman Empire. The *Meds Yeghern* must live on in our memories, just as it lives on in the hearts of the Armenian people." Despite Obama's invocation of the number that Armenians agree upon and his description of the action, to many Armenians the omission of that one key word made the commemoration inadequate, even an incident of denial.[57]

What, exactly, does *Medz* (or *Meds*) *Yeghern* (Մեծ եղեռն) mean? *Medz* means "great." As for the word *yeghern*, as historian Vartan Matiossian points out, different Armenian-English dictionaries have translated it differently. Some understand *Medz Yeghern* to mean "Great Catastrophe," which of course has a more generic meaning than "genocide." However, it has alternately been understood—and with greater

Figure 8.1 Annual commemoration of the Armenian genocide in Times Square, most likely April 25, 1988. Project SAVE Armenian Photograph Archives, courtesy of Tina Hazarian.

authoritative support—to mean "Great Crime." In fact, that very same year as Obama's first presidential statement there were some announcements of commemorations, where the English version said "Genocide" and the Armenian version said "Yeghern," and some Armenian-language publications continued to refer to the genocide as the *Medz Yeghern*, using the term interchangeably with the ցեղասպանութիւն (*tseghasbanoutiun*, which translates precisely as the killing of a race). In any event, one could make a case that in wording his statement as he did, President Obama made it possible for Armenian newspapers, had they so desired (which generally they did not), to run the headline "Obama Commemorates Armenian Genocide," intermix his words with the word *genocide* in such a way as to make the two terms appear synonymous, and leave it to Obama or anyone else to refute or dispute the interpretation. Turkish commentators, it should be noted, fully resented Obama's remarks.[58]

The annual ritual continued with seven more years of Obama followed by four years of Donald J. Trump. It fell to Joe Biden to break the pattern; his statement paired the familiar Armenian term with the words "the Armenian Genocide," and he expressed his support for a congressional resolution and legislation formalizing recognition. The Armenian Genocide Education Act, authorizing funding to the Library of Congress for promoting education about the Armenian genocide and condemning Turkey's actions against Armenians and others during and after the First World War, was introduced in the House in 2022, but when this book went to press no such measure was moving forward.[59]

At present, there are annual commemorations at New York City's Times Square and elsewhere. Speakers typically call for recognition and public education on the subject of what took place, insisting on explicit use of the word *genocide*. There is yet another dimension to their demands, which was also a stated goal of the terror groups of the 1970s and 1980s, a demand that, though sensible on its face given what was done in 1915, is not particularly realistic: for Turkey to be compelled to relinquish the historic Armenian territory that she currently holds, including that historic symbol of Armenia, Mount Ararat. Somewhat more realistic, though with very limited results, have been attempts through litigation against museums, insurance companies, banks, and the Turkish government for the return of stolen artworks and restitution for other lost property occasioned by the genocide. Attorney Vartkes Yeghiayan, until his death in 2017, was instrumental in these efforts.[60]

Epilogue

Response to a New Armenia

On the evening of March 10, 1985, Soviet General Secretary Constantin U. Chernenko, in office just over a year and known to be in failing health, died at the age of seventy-three. The Kremlin swiftly announced the choice of his successor: Mikhail Gorbachev. In the seven years that ensued, events played out that fit perfectly with Alexis de Tocqueville's famous observation that "the most dangerous moment for a bad government is generally that in which it sets about reform."

- 1 -

Just two months in office, Gorbachev began using the term *perestroika*, meaning restructuring or reconstruction, declaring that "all of us must undergo reconstruction" and "everyone must adopt new approaches and understand that no other path is available to us." Early in 1986, Gorbachev began saying that Soviet society needed more *glasnost*, or openness. The immediate expression of this new policy was an easing of censorship over the press, the arts, and scholarship. That December Gorbachev invited exiled scientist, Nobel laureate, and human rights activist Andrei Sakharov back to Moscow. In 1989 Gorbachev allowed elections to a Congress of People's Deputies, whose televised deliberations that spring allowed Soviet citizens unprecedented exposure to ideological debates and criticism of leadership. The following year, in the face of worsening economic crisis, he even toyed with the idea, though not for long, of instituting a free enterprise system.[1]

The changed atmosphere emboldened non-Russian nationalities in the Soviet empire to start making demands. In Soviet Armenia, among the first protests, in 1987 and continuing into 1988, were those of an environmental nature: calls for the closing down of the Nairit rubber plant, which discharged toxic chemicals on a grand scale, and of the Medzamor nuclear plant, which had given cancer and birth defects to many while threatening even greater disasters down the road. Armenians also protested against the planned construction of a new chemical plant in the town of Abovian.[2] But what really got Armenians exercised, as well as leading to a bloody and protracted armed conflict that is still not resolved, was a dispute over territory and irredentist rights with the neighboring Muslim country of Azerbaijan.

It is a well-known fact that the boundary lines of nation-states have often not coincided neatly with where nationalities resided. This phenomenon has led more than a few times to ethnic conflicts that turned deadly, even genocidal. Within the borders of Azerbaijan, there exists a mountainous region known as Nagorno-Karabagh. Its population in 1988 was 160,000, of whom three-quarters were Armenian. Both Armenians and Azerbaijanis claim historical precedence there. Under Soviet rule, from 1923 onward it held the status of an autonomous region, or *oblast*, which essentially meant that it was culturally and linguistically Armenian while under the political control of Soviet Azerbaijan, with neither nationality entirely happy about the arrangement. In 1987, emboldened by the spirit of *glasnost* and *perestroika*, Armenians in Karabagh began calling for their region to be detached from Azerbaijan and joined to Armenia. The protests become more formal early that following year. The Karabagh Soviet of People's Deputies passed a resolution in February 1988 requesting this transfer; there was a massive street demonstration in the *oblast*'s capital, Stepanakert, on February 13; and multiple delegations of Armenians petitioned Moscow to this effect, including one led by popular Armenian actress Zhanna Galstian. Armenians in Armenia proper also took to the streets to demonstrate on behalf of their conationals.[3]

Armenians in the United States quickly did likewise. A daily silent vigil was begun in front of the Soviet mission to the United Nations. On Saturday, February 27, amid snowfall and frigid temperatures, over a thousand persons of all ages demonstrated half a block from the mission, with signs reading "Karabagh Is Armenian," "Return Karabagh to Armenia," and "*Miatsum*" (unification). On March 13 the crowd was even larger, as two marches led by the normally competing Armenian Apostolic church organizations converged on the mission and joined forces. Archbishop Torkom Manoogian, primate of the (non-Tashnag) Eastern Diocese, and Archbishop Mesrob Ashjian, prelate of the (Tashnag-dominated) Eastern Prelacy, exchanged an embrace, with the former calling the latter his "spiritual brother" to thunderous applause. No less a personage than New York mayor Ed Koch addressed the crowd of over five thousand, declaring "Karabagh is Armenian" and noting that the Armenians and the Jews (himself being among the latter) shared a common bond as victims of genocide. Large rallies were also held in Los Angeles and elsewhere. A delegation from the Armenian Assembly of America met with the Soviet ambassador in Washington to urge favorable resolution of the Armenians' entreaty.[4]

In other times, what the Armenians wanted might not have been such a big deal for the Soviet government at Moscow to grant, but assertions of national identity from Ukrainians, Belarusians, and Georgians were causing the central government to feel its grip on power being challenged. Moscow balked, and Azerbaijanis responded to the demands with a wave of pogroms against Armenians in late February and early March, killing at least thirty-one persons before Soviet troops intervened. Conflict between Armenians and Azerbaijanis continued for the next several years, leading the Soviet government to shepherd the migration of one hundred seventy thousand ethnic Azerbaijanis out of Armenia and three hundred thousand Armenians out of Azerbaijan. (Nagorno-Karabagh continued to have an Armenian majority, though displacements occurred in certain sections.) In 1989, Azerbaijan began blockading rail transport to Armenia and Nagorno-Karabagh, with Turkey following suit. Readers of the Armenian press in the diaspora saw horror stories of the experiences of compatriots who fled from war-torn areas.[5]

The three major parties in the diaspora, it should be remembered, were the Ramgavars, the Hunchags, and the Armenian Revolutionary Federation (ARF) or Tashnag party. At this point the ARF, after decades of viewing the Soviet Union as an enemy occupier of the homeland, had adopted the position long held by the other two that Armenia needed the protection of Russia, even Soviet Russia, in the face of the menace of Pan-Turkism. In October 1988, the three diasporan parties issued a joint statement urging Armenians in Armenia and Karabagh "to avoid such extreme measures as strikes and extremist appeals and expressions which disrupt law and order, and which cause serious damage to the economy, industry, education and culture, and undermine our people's good reputation." Nationalists in Armenia, having expected little right along from the other two parties, felt let down by the ARF and from that point held no desire to bring it into power in their future independent republic.[6]

Amid the turmoil, on December 7, 1988, Armenia was hit with a massive earthquake, killing at least twenty-five thousand people and displacing hundreds of thousands more from their homes. At the time that it struck, exiles were moving in both directions between the two rival countries, and in fact the deportations saved many Azerbaijanis from perishing in the earthquake. Some Azerbaijanis helped the Armenians while others shot off fireworks to celebrate that their enemy was getting punished. Some Armenians, receiving a shipment of medicine from across the border, thought the Azerbaijanis were trying to poison them. Aid came from the government of Turkey as well. The earthquake exacerbated tensions between the Communist authorities and the recently formed, increasingly militant Karabagh Committee. Moscow held all eleven members of the Karabagh Committee in prison from December to June; after their release, the protest leaders rechristened their organization as the Armenian National Movement (ANM).[7]

Armenians in the diaspora, of course, were called upon to donate. Governor George Deukmejian of California, the highest-ranking Armenian American elected official, announced that he was donating $100,000 from his campaign fund and an additional amount of his own money, and he took part in a telethon that raised $1,200,000 for earthquake relief. In New York, the Antranig Dance Ensemble turned the proceeds from a December 17 Christmas dance over to the cause. Both the Armenian Relief Society and the American Red Cross flew in medical supplies from the United States. Armenian American philanthropist Hirair Hovnanian chipped in a million dollars. In the weeks that followed, Armenians worldwide received steady reminders that their help was needed.[8]

In Soviet Armenia, political change continued to play out. The ANM, believing that Armenia's destiny should be controlled by Armenians, grew with popular dissatisfaction over the lack of Soviet protection in the conflict with Azerbaijan as well as the government's ineffective response to the earthquake and the corruption inherent in its relief efforts. The drive for independence was fed further in April of 1990 when the Supreme Soviet of the USSR revised an article in the constitution, allowing Soviet republics to secede by referendum. Elections held in the spring and summer of 1990 gave the ANM a plurality in the Armenian parliament, enabling the ascent of a scholar named Levon Ter Petrosian as the parliament's president. Though Armenia was still formally a Soviet republic rather than an independent state, it was already coming increasingly close to being the latter. Ter Petrosian took care to include members of the Communist Party, including his own chief opponent, in the new governmental structure. In August of 1990 the Armenian parliament issued a Declaration on (not *of*) Independence that, while falling short of repudiating Armenia's membership in the Soviet Union, asserted the right to make policy and to assure free speech, free press, and a multiparty system, clearly laying the foundation for a totally independent state in the not-so-distant future.[9]

As the power of the Soviet state declined and Armenia moved closer to full independence, ethnic conflict between Armenians and Azerbaijanis continued to rage. The spring of 1991 saw a Soviet-Azerbaijani military coalition violently drive Armenians out of fourteen villages just north of Nagorno-Karabagh. There were also some Armenian attacks on Azerbaijanis. Though Armenians and Azerbaijanis had exchanged gunfire before, they had coexisted peacefully, or at least grudgingly tolerated each other, for most of the Soviet years, with each country having the other nationality as a sizable minority. In the mid-1980s there had been about three hundred fifty thousand Armenians in Azerbaijan and about two hundred thousand Azerbaijanis in Armenia, living in peace. Now, refugees were crossing the border in both directions. The stakes got higher in November when the parliament of Azerbaijan—which back in August had declared itself independent from the Soviet regime—now voted to revoke Karabagh's status as an autonomous region: as far as the Azerbaijani government was concerned, Nagorno-Karabagh was simply part of Azerbaijan, with Armenians having no special rights. Close to the same time, the Armenian majority in Karabagh voted to secede from Azerbaijan and make their region a state of its own. Armenians and Azerbaijanis were thus farther apart than ever in their very definition of the disputed region.[10]

It should be noted, of course, that not all Armenians and Azerbaijanis hated each other. There were some instances of mutual help between the two groups and of peaceful exchanges of homes between border crossers. There was even an unconfirmed report of an exchange of mental patients between two psychiatric hospitals. Still, many were driven out of their homes by armed gangs, and deaths in a single year were in the hundreds. The central Soviet government in Moscow, while it still existed, was trying to quell the conflict while still adamantly forbidding the transfer that the Armenians desired.[11]

In the early part of 1991, while it may not have been clear that the Soviet regime was about to collapse completely, it was clear that it was undergoing a rapid transformation, and one not entirely under the control of its leaders. In March of 1991, the Soviet government ran a nationwide referendum on maintaining the USSR with continued reforms. The government of Armenia, however, declined to have its republic take part, opting instead for an Armenian referendum on independence. In September, Armenians voted overwhelmingly for independence. Meanwhile, the Soviet system was unraveling. In August, Kremlin hardliners placed Gorbachev under house arrest. It briefly looked as if the Soviet regime had reverted to its former austerity. However, intense popular resistance forced Gorbachev's release, and the collapse of the whole system followed fast. By the end of 1991, the Soviet Union was no more.[12]

- 2 -

Independence was hardly an unmixed blessing for Armenia. "It was transformed," Nora Dudwick writes, "from a province of the powerful Soviet state, to a tiny—the size of Belgium—landlocked, resource-poor, and vulnerable republic bordering hostile or unstable neighbors." Where the conflict over Karabagh was concerned, the conflicting enactments in the fall of 1991 ensured that, with the fall of the Soviet Union, an ethnic conflict within a larger empire was now a full-fledged war between two distinct national polities. The conflict continued to take a heavy toll on civilians, in death and especially in displacement.[13]

The main stretch of the Karabagh war ran from the start of 1992 through May of 1994. Even then, when the warring parties agreed to a ceasefire, much remained unresolved. Karabagh held the precarious status of a de facto (or one could say quasi) republic that neither Azerbaijan nor the international community recognized, and Armenian forces held about 10 percent of Azerbaijani territory not including Karabagh, including the Lachin Corridor, the land connecting Karabagh to Armenia proper. In the years that followed, both negotiations and skirmishes took place, with no shortage of outside mediators trying to find terms of lasting peace that the opposing camps could agree upon. It was, as one congressional briefing memorandum put it, "a clash between the principles of territorial integrity [the Azerbaijani point of view] and self-determination [in the eyes of Armenians]."[14]

Levon Ter Petrosian was Armenia's first president. Among his priorities was cultivating relations with the global Armenian diaspora. He included several diasporans in his administration, including historian Gerard J. Libaridian and Raffi K. Hovannisian, son of historian Richard G. Hovannisian. Diasporan financial support was considerable, well into the tens of millions of dollars, and it was sorely needed. Armenia's economy for the first several years was in severe crisis, with a large share of the population experiencing a drop in standard of living. Having previously gotten most of its oil and gas from Azerbaijan, Armenia now faced an acute energy shortage from the Karabagh conflict and the resulting blockade, making for several miserable winters for Armenians. The areas hit by the 1988 earthquake were also still in dire need of reconstruction.[15]

There were controversies, and the political parties in the diaspora took sides. The Ramgavar and Hunchag parties and the Armenian Assembly of America generally stood by the Ter Petrosian administration, though not always uncritically. The Tashnag party, which had unsuccessfully run its own candidate in the 1991 presidential election, was a voice of opposition. On two areas—Nagorno-Karabagh and relations with Turkey—the government of Armenia preferred a cautious approach, its top priority being the immediate economic and security needs of the country. The ARF,

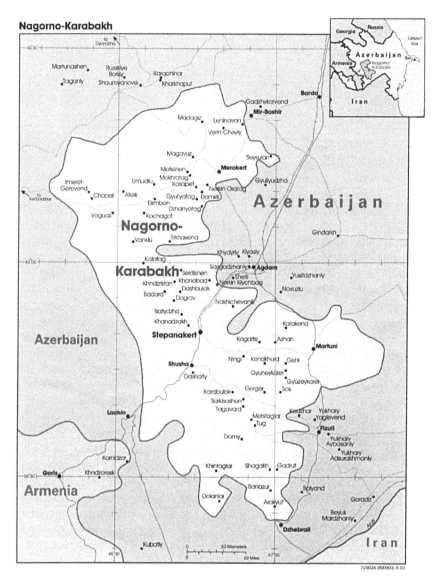

Map E.1 Nagorno-Karabagh as of 1993. With each new flare-up of the war, the borders change. Map courtesy of University of Texas Libraries, University of Texas at Austin.

in contrast, wanted the regime to take unequivocal stands on both matters, assertively recognizing Nagorno Karabagh as either an independent republic or part of Armenia and demanding that Turkey acknowledge the genocide before any business could be done between the countries. Tashnags also felt rankled by the president's remarks on the subject of diasporan political parties in a spring 1994 interview, calling their existence "unnatural" and opining that leaders of diasporan organizations needed to "come to terms with the reality that policy is determined here" (meaning within the country's own borders).[16]

Friction between the ARF and the Ter Petrosian administration, as well as between the ARF and other diasporan parties in the United States, was in evidence in August of 1994 when Armenia's president paid the United States a visit. The Tashnag press chose this occasion to run editorials sharply critical of Ter Petrosian, showing among other things the party's resentment at his underappreciation of Tashnag efforts over the decades to keep the diaspora loyal to the goal of national independence. When Ter Petrosian spoke in Los Angeles, local Armenians coming out of church found flyers on their windshields urging them not to participate in the president's "self-propaganda." (The Armenian Assembly, in contrast, took out a full-page advertisement to welcome him to the United States in 1994 and honored him with a banquet when he returned in 1995.) The tensions with the ARF were even greater in Armenia itself. At the end of that year the government banned formal political activity by ARF/Armenia, accusing its leaders of complicity in terrorist- and drug-related activity and of being dominated in its leadership by noncitizens of Armenia. (Ter Petrosian remarked on numerous occasions throughout his time in office that he regarded the nation-state and the diaspora as two different polities and did not think diasporan political parties should be wielding influence in Armenia. Tashnags, having historically considered themselves the very essence of Armenia and Armenianness, responded to this position with strong indignation.) In the fall of 1996, the party teamed up with factions in Armenia that questioned the legitimacy of Ter Petrosian's reelection. The non-Tashnag press in the United States consistently criticized Tashnag positions and actions.[17]

For the most part, the partisan conflicts did not stop the Armenian government, the parties, the churches, and other diasporan entities from working cooperatively in fundraising, though the ARF was only fully on board starting in 1998. Throughout the republic's first decade (as well as after), hundreds of millions of dollars flowed from the diaspora into Armenia in the form of both personal remittances within families and philanthropic donations for humanitarian aid and various construction and reconstruction projects. Especially with the energy crisis, as exacerbated by the war, the country needed all the assistance it could get. Armenian American billionaire Kirk Kerkorian, with his Lincy Foundation, was among the leading donors and fundraisers, as was famed French Armenian singer Charles Aznavour, with *Aznavour pour l'Armenie*. Armenians in America, as well as elsewhere in the diaspora, were regularly called upon to donate. A major conduit was the Hayastan All-Armenia Fund, whose administration included representatives from religious, charitable, and party groups and leaders in Armenia, Nagorno-Karabagh, and the diaspora. The ARF withdrew from the Fund in 1995 but rejoined in 1996; even while participating in the Fund, it ran its own competing Artsakh Fund. The Armenian General Benevolent Union continued its worldwide charitable operations, as did most other Armenian organizations.[18]

The Armenian Americans' two major Washington-based lobby groups, the Armenian Assembly of America and the Tashnag-run Armenian National Committee, consistently advocated for policies favorable to Armenia and Armenians. That included, of course, genocide recognition and aid to the republic, and indeed Congress maintained an annual minimum of $90 million to Armenia and Karabagh throughout

Figure E1 Levon Ter Petrosian, Armenia's first president after independence. Photo from Wikimedia Commons, Creative Commons Attribution-Share Alike 4.0 International license.

the 1990s and after. Also maintained, starting in 1992, was Section 907 of the Freedom Support Act, denying aid to Azerbaijan as long as she was blockading Armenia. That provision met with disapproval from, among other entities, the editorial board of the *Washington Post*, which opined in early August of 1996 that the policy represented "punishing the loser, comforting the conqueror, occupier and evident winner of the war." Armenians, of course, did not consider themselves conquerors of anything.[19]

The partisan quarrels in the United States, though still in evidence at century's end, did not at this point match the levels of vitriolic intensity that had so dominated the Armenian American community in earlier decades. Moreover, although the two worldwide Armenian Apostolic churches were no closer to reuniting than before, and although each still officially regarded the other as dissident, relations were friendlier, or at least more tolerant. A rather peculiar thing happened in 1995: After the death of Catholicos Vasken I at Echmiadzin, the Catholicos of the rival Holy See at Antelias, with the overt endorsement of President Ter Petrosian, was elected to the position, constituting a very out-of-the-ordinary crossover. While Tashnags voiced resentment and anti-Tashnags voiced suspicion, Karekin I (formerly Karekin II) was well received when he visited the United States in January 1996. While in New York City, on invitation of the prelate, Archbishop Mesrob Ashjian, he made an appearance at St. Illuminator's Church, precisely the church that would have been hostile to his presence in earlier times. Relations also warmed between the ARF and the homeland's government after President Ter Petrosian resigned and Robert Kocharian took the helm, early in 1998.[20]

Tragically, war between Armenians and Azerbaijanis flared up again in 2020, with Azerbaijan retaking those districts outside of Karabagh that Armenians had controlled since the ceasefire, as well as a portion of Karabagh itself. Further skirmishes broke out during the next two years. In all instances, readers of the Armenian American press saw regular updates, with reaffirmations of the rightness of the Armenian position, indignation at the actions of the Azerbaijani adversary, and solicitations for donations. When this book went to press, real peace between the two countries and amicable resolution of the Karabagh question remained elusive.

- 3 -

Ever since Benedict Anderson suggested that nations are "imagined communities," scholars have invariably invoked his book whenever discussing nationhood and nationalism. On the subject of the Armenian diaspora, historian Razmik Panossian observes, the sense of peoplehood requires a "double imagination," because "for this diaspora, national identity—that is, the sense of belonging to an imagined community—does not necessarily, or even predominantly, emanate from a specific kin-state or even an ancestral homeland; nor is it entirely rooted in the host country." Rather, he writes, it hovers between the two. Moreover, the imagined identity "is, by and large, quite removed from its everyday life and, necessarily, from its geographic location … making it not once, but twice removed from the reality of its physical existence."[21]

The present work is about Armenians as an immigrant group in the United States. It is intended as a contribution to American immigrant history as well as Armenian history. Every immigrant group to the United States, like every nation-state and other communal entity, has its own exceptional story. Moreover, within each group, opinions and orientations will differ widely as to what membership in this group signifies. Any search for a one-size-fits-all explanation of what immigrants and their descendants either *tend to want* or *should want* would be not only futile but counterproductive. Differences both between and within groups happen for a reason, and the study of any given community must take variations into account as well as commonalities, both between a group's members and between that group and somewhat comparable communities.

In the case of Armenians, the partisan conflict between Tashnag and anti-Tashnag has always played a conspicuous role in community life. As this book has shown, it also for a number of decades played a significant role in the marketing of newspapers, association memberships, activities, and ideas about identity. It was, however, but one component. Armenian immigrants to the United States and their progeny all had in common the necessity of navigating life in the United States and finding their place within the larger society. In the American context, the parties and other ethnic organizations, even as they encouraged ethnic loyalty and feared loss of ethnic identity, also shared a consensus that Armenians in America should be good Americans as well as good Armenians. Through both political activism and artistic expression, Armenians shared the knowledge of their presence and their story with their non-Armenian neighbors. The Armenian story in America is as much one of integration within the cultural mainstream as of sporting a distinct cultural identity.

And where does the word *assimilation* fit into the discussion? The word has generally tended to carry the connotation of the decline of *ethnicity*, broadly understood as the maintenance of culturally distinctive traits and orientations common to the ethnic group and different from those of the host society. The connotation of assimilation as coming at the expense of ethnicity has certainly been evident in the discourse of ethnic leaders who viewed it as an evil to be fought against or at least slowed down— though, to be clear, they were not discouraging either loyalty to or participation in the host society. But the connotation is also apparent in the work of sociologists who seek to rescue the term from reductionist understandings. Milton Gordon, in his chart of assimilation variables in his 1964 work, included "identificational assimilation" and defined it as "development of sense of peoplehood based exclusively on [the] host society." He painted "structural assimilation," or integration with the social institutions of the dominant population, as the key factor that led to the other types of assimilation, "like a row of tenpins bowled over in rapid succession by a well-placed strike," at the price of "the disappearance of the ethnic group as a separate entity and the evaporation of its distinctive values." More recently, Richard Alba and Victor Nee defined assimilation as "the decline, and at its endpoint the disappearance, of an ethnic/racial distinction and the cultural and social differences that express it," though making clear that this conception was not limited to the scenario of one group changing and being culturally absorbed by another. Matthew Ari Jendian, in his study of Fresno Armenians, categorizes assimilation as cultural, structural, marital, and identificational, and measures "cultural assimilation" in terms of lesser tendencies toward using the Armenian language, eating Armenian food, reading Armenian literature, and attending an Armenian church.[22]

Jendian's ultimate point, though, is that assimilation does not have to come at the expense of ethnicity, but rather, as his book title suggests, "Becoming American [and] Remaining Ethnic" is very much an existent scenario. This is certainly borne out in the experience of the American-born generations who remained close to their Armenian community. As they came of age, they were tacitly embracing and asserting their Americanness by the sheer acts of being American in much of their everyday life: being educated in the public schools and colleges, working jobs in the American economy, and having opinions on issues in the American political scene. Many were doing all this while also worshiping in Armenian churches and taking part in Armenian dances, picnics, and political rallies. Especially in the 1940s and after, editorials in the Armenian American press, especially the English-language weeklies, clearly addressed readers who, whatever their opinions, cared about presidential elections, congressional investigations, and the general landscape of international relations. When Armenian editors criticized measures in Congress or editorials in other papers that showed either chauvinistic stances toward immigrants or overly friendly stances toward Turkey, they did so by way of asserting the place of Armenians as full and rightful participants in the American nationality.

The term *diasporic nationalism* has received much play in this study. Basically, it refers to members of an ethnic community caring deeply about their ancestral homeland, not only feeling sentimental about it but having strong opinions about what its political status should be and how it should be governed. It is, obviously, closely intertwined with *ethnicity*. This study has emphasized two distinctive aspects of Armenians' diasporic nationalism in America. One is the partisan conflict, whereby different groups of Armenians were not only holding different opinions of what was going on in Armenia but actually believing different narratives. Closely intertwined is the theme of a symbiotic marketing relationship between community leaders—including priests, field workers, and newspaper editors—and their constituents. Structured organizations seeking to keep themselves in existence and to maintain a support base for their efforts to influence the homeland's future marketed their ideas, as well as events and newspapers, to the general Armenian American public. Level of interest in what was being marketed as well as style of response and participation, of course, always varied from one Armenian American individual to another.

Armenian community leaders and influencers certainly hope that succeeding young generations will maintain a sense of Armenianness alongside their Americanness, and indeed the Armenian American press still runs editorials and letters lamenting the dangers of this not happening—which will undoubtedly continue to be the case for some time to come. The present work makes no efforts at prescription or prognosis. For questions concerning what's in store for the future, having traveled through an odyssey of decades of Armenian life in the United States, the tragedies, trials, and tribulations, joys and sorrows, Sabina's concluding lines to the audience in Thornton Wilder's play *The Skin of Our Teeth* would seem to apply: "We have to go on for ages and ages ... The end of this play isn't written yet."

Notes

Introduction

1 In the mid-1980s, the word conjured up might have been "terrorist."

2 Leading works on the broad contours of Armenian history include George A. Bournoutian, *A History of the Armenian People*, 2 vols. (Costa Mesa, CA: Mazda Publishers, 1994); Richard G. Hovannisian, ed., *Armenian People from Ancient to Modern Times* (New York: St. Martin's Press, 2004), 2 vols. A. E. Redgate, *The Armenians* (Oxford: Blackwell, 1997). On the religious denominations, see Aharon Sapsezian, *Armenian Christianity* (Paramus, NJ: Armenian Missionary Association of America, 1996).

3 Bournoutian, *History of the Armenian People*, 2: 7–8; Hagop Barsoumian, "The Eastern Question and the Tanzimat Era," in Hovannisian, *Armenian People from Ancient to Modern Times*, 2: 182–8. For a cogent synthesis of Armenian life under three imperial powers in the nineteenth and early twentieth centuries, see Aram Arkun, "Into the Modern Age, 1800–1913," in *The Armenians: Past and Present in the Making of National Identity*, ed. Edmund Herzig and Marina Kurkchiyan (London: RoutledgeCurzon, 2005), 65–88.

4 Hagop Barsoumian, "The Dual Role of the Armenian *Amira* Class within the Ottoman Government and the Armenian *Millet* (1750–1850)," in *Christians and Jews in the Ottoman Empire*, ed. Benjamin Braude and Bernard Lewis (New York: Holmer & Meyer, 1982), 171–84, 192–5; Barsoumian, "Eastern Question and the Tanzimat Era," 191–5; Barsoumian, *The Armenian Amira Class of Istanbul* (Yerevan: American University of Armenia, 2007); Bournoutian, *History of the Armenian People*, 2: 9–10, 85–8. Kurdish villagers bore heavy tax burdens and suffered other indignities as well. However, the Kurds in many instances did as the poor whites of the Jim Crow South in America did vis-à-vis the African-Americans: identified with the power elites in their sense of superiority over the group that was cast as an *Other*: a racial Other in the American case, a religious Other in the Ottoman.

5 Arkun, "Into the Modern Age," 72–3.

6 Richard G. Hovannisian, "The Armenian Question in the Ottoman Empire, 1876–1914," in Hovannisian, *Armenian People from Ancient to Modern Times*, 2: 203–6.

7 Louise Nalbandian, *The Armenian Revolutionary Movement: The Development of Armenian Political Parties through the Nineteenth Century* (Berkeley: University of California Press, 1967), 28–9; Hovannisian, "Armenian Question," 206–12; Arkun, "Into the Modern Age," 77–9.

8 Hovannisian, "Armenian Question," 212–8; Bournoutian, *History of the Armenian People*, 2: 92–4; Nalbandian, *Armenian Revolutionary Movement*, 104–31; 151–76; Robert Mirak, *Torn between Two Lands: Armenians in America, 1890 to World War I* (Cambridge, MA: Harvard University Press, 1983), 241–52.

9 Hovannisian, "Armenian Question," 222–38; Bournoutian, *History of the Armenian People*, 2: 96–8; Arkun, "Into the Modern Age," 82; Vahakn N. Dadrian, *The History of*

the Armenian Genocide: Ethnic Conflict from the Balkans to Anatolia to the Caucasus
(New York: Berghahn Books, 2004), 182–3; Bedross Der Matossian, *The Horrors of
Adana: Revolution and Violence in the Early Twentieth Century* (Stanford, CA: Stanford
University Press, 2022), esp. 209–11. For the dynamics of the ARF's attempts at
cooperation with the CUP, with a strong argument against the notion that Armenians
posed any threat to the regime, see Dikran Mesrob Kaligian, *Armenian Organization
and Ideology under Ottoman Rule* (New Brunswick, NJ: Transaction Publishers, 2010).

    The Ramgavar party would later reconstitute itself by merging with splinter
groups from other parties in both 1919 and 1923. For purposes of this study,
however, "Ramgavar" (capitalized, as distinct from the generic Armenian word for
"democratic" in lower case) can be understood in all time periods to refer to the
strongest partisan voice of opposition to the Tashnag party and, with respect to the
status of the homeland, the voice of allegiance to the positions of Boghos Nubar
Pasha in Paris (an allegiance of memory after the First World War years).

10   Kaligian, *Armenian Organization and Ideology*, 121–222.

11   Susie Hoogasian Villa and Mary Kilbourne Matossian, *Armenian Village Life before
1914* (Detroit: Wayne State University Press, 1982), 22; Vatche Ghazarian, ed.,
A Village Remembered: The Armenians of Habousi (Waltham, MA: Mayreni Publishing,
1997), 25–8; Vahé Tachjian, "Agn—Foods," *Houshamadyan*, www.houshamadyan.org;
Tachjian, "Reconstructing Armenian Village Life: Manoog Dzeron and Alevor, Unique
Authors of the 'Houshamadyan' Genre," in *Ottoman Armenians: Life, Culture, Society*,
ed. Vahé Tachjian (Berlin: Houshamadyan, 2015), 1: 214–17.

12   Ghazarian, *A Village Remembered*, 6; Vahé Tachjian, "Dersim—Schools,"
Houshamadyan, www.houshamadyan.org; Hoogasian Villa and Matossian, *Armenian
Village Life*, 71; Mirak, *Torn between Two Lands*, 174; Tachjian, "Reconstructing
Armenian Village Life," 230. For more detail on life in the Armenian villages, see
Vahan Hambartsumian, *Village World (Kiughashkharh): An Historical and Cultural
Study of Govdoon*, trans. Murad A. Meneshian (Providence, RI: Govdoon Youth of
America, 2001; original printing, Paris: Daron Publishing House, 1927).

13   Mirak, *Torn between Two Lands*, 105–22.

    The Armenian enclave in the Oriental rug business was also big in the Canadian cities
of Montreal and Toronto. Isabel Kaprielian-Churchill, *Like Our Mountains: A History of
Armenians in Canada* (Montreal: McGill-Queen's University Press, 2005), 363–72.

14   Mirak, *Torn between Two Lands*, 36–44; Hagop Bogigian, *In Quest of the Soul of
Civilization* (Washington, DC: self-published, 1925), 71–82.

15   Deranian, *Worcester Is America*, 18, 151; S. Hagopian, "The Armenian Community of
Providence, Rhode Island, up to 1937," originally printed in three parts in *Hairenik
Monthly*, June-July-August, 1937, also included in Varoujan Karentz, *Mitchnapert
(The Citadel): A History of Armenians in Rhode Island* (Lincoln, NE: iUniverse,
2004); Oshagan Minassian, *A History of the Armenian Holy Apostolic Orthodox
Church in the United States (1888-1944)* (Monterey, CA: Mayreni, 2010), 145; Gary
A. Kulhanjian, "From Ararat to America: The Armenian Settlements of New Jersey,"
Journal of Armenian Studies 3 (Winter 1986–87): 36; *Hairenik Weekly*, April 1,
1952, 1; Vahram L. Shemmassian, *The Musa Dagh Armenians: A Socioeconomic
and Cultural History, 1919–1939* (Beirut: Haigazian University Press, 2015), 190–1;
Mirak, *Torn between Two Lands*, 86. On chain migrations drawn by information
about jobs, see Alan Kraut, *The Huddled Masses: The Immigrant in American Society,
1880–1921*, 2nd ed. (Wheeling, IL: Harlan Davidson, 2001), 86–95.

16   Mirak, *Torn between Two Lands*, 95–9.

17   Mirak, *Torn between Two Lands*, 112; Berge Bulbulian, *The Fresno Armenians: History of a Diaspora Community* (Fresno: The Press at California State University, Fresno, 2000), 16–45; George Kooshian, "The Armenian Immigrant Community of California, 1880–1935" (PhD diss., University of California, Los Angeles, 2002), 40–6; *Hairenik*, October 16, 1925, 1.

18   Mirak, *Torn between Two Lands*, 180–201; Minassian, *History of the Armenian Holy Apostolic Church*, 65–90; Christopher Hagop Zakian, ed., *The Torch Was Passed: The Centennial History of the Armenian Church of America* (New York: St. Vartan Press, 1998), 3–12.

19   Mirak, *Torn between Two Lands*, 247–52.

20   Mirak, *Torn between Two Lands*, 150–4; Knarik Avakian, "The Early History of Armenian Emigration to the USA: Evidence from the Archives of the Armenian Patriarchate of Constantinople," *Journal of the Society for Armenian Studies* 17 (2008): 112–13.

21   Matthew Frye Jacobson, *Special Sorrows: The Diasporic Imagination of Irish, Polish, and Jewish Immigrants in the United States* (New York: Cambridge University Press, 1995). Two prime examples of that old, critical historiography are Louis L. Gerson, *Woodrow Wilson and the Rebirth of Poland, 1914–1920: A Study in the Influence on American Policy of Minority Groups of Foreign Origin* (New Haven, CT: Yale University Press, 1953) and Robert L. Daniel, "The Armenian Question and American-Turkish Relations, 1914–1927," *Mississippi Valley Historical Review* 46, no. 2 (September 1959): 252–75.

22   Anna D. Jaroszyńska-Kirchmann, *The Polish Hearst: Ameryka-Echo and the Public Role of the Immigrant Press* (Champaign: University of Illinois Press, 2015), 6.

23   Jaroszyńska-Kirchmann, *Polish Hearst*, 2–3.

24   Herbert J. Gans, "Symbolic Ethnicity: The Future of Ethnic Groups and Cultures in America," *Ethnic and Racial Studies* 2, no. 1 (1979): 1–20; June Granatir Alexander, *Ethnic Pride, American Patriotism: Slovaks and Other New Immigrants in the Interwar Era* (Philadelphia: Temple University Press, 2004), 70–90.
        An example of immigrants offering patriotism lessons to their not-always-welcoming hosts came in late 1925 when it was learned that the president of the Allied Patriotic Societies had proposed at the annual meeting that the foreign-language press should receive greater scrutiny and constraints from the federal government. The New York Italian *Corrierre d'America* wrote, "Do the Allied Patriotic Societies fear, perhaps, that these languages cover the irresistible political influences of their respective countries of origin? But then the English language ought to have the same effect. In using it the American people ought to feel themselves English. But do they? To pretend that Americanism must be garbed in English in order to be genuine is to deny the very patriotism we would defend. In reality all our foreign languages in America, except the Iroquois and the Sioux." *The Interpreter*, January 1926, 11.

Chapter 1

1   Christopher J. Walker, "World War I and the Armenian Genocide," in *Armenian People from Ancient to Modern Times*, ed. Richard G. Hovannisian (New York: St. Martin's Press, 2004), 2: 244–6.

2   Dramatic accounts of these events include, among numerous others, Elise
     Hagopian Taft, *Rebirth* (Plandone, NY: New Age Publishers, 1981), esp. 33–66;
     Alice Muggerditchian Shipley, *We Walked, Then Ran* (self-published, 1983), esp.
     50–69; Florence M. Soghoian, *Portrait of a Survivor* (Hanover, MA: Christopher
     Publishing House, 1997), esp. 19–34; Naomi Getsoyan Topalian, *Dust to Destiny*
     (Watertown, MA: Baikar, 1986), esp. 9–24; Topalian, *Breaking the Rock of Tradition:
     An Autobiography* (Watertown, MA: Baikar, 2000); Aliza Harb, with Florence
     Gilmore, *Aliza: An Armenian Survivor Torn between Two Cultures* (Belmont,
     MA: NAASR, 2003); Serpoohi Christine Jafferian, *Winds of Destiny: An Immigrant
     Girl's Odyssey* (Belmont, MA: NAASR, 1993); Abraham H. Hartunian, *Neither to
     Laugh nor to Weep: A Memoir of the Armenian Genocide* (Boston: Beacon Press,
     1968), esp. 51–117; Boghos Jafarian, *Farewell Kharpert* (published independently
     by Claire Mangasarian, 1989), esp. 83–109; Khachadoor Pilibosian with Helene
     Pilibosian, *They Called Me Mustafa: Memoir of an Immigrant* (Watertown, MA:
     Ohan Press, 1992), esp. 10–29; John Minassian, *Many Hills Yet to Climb: Memoirs
     of an Armenian Deportee* (Santa Barbara, CA: Jim Cook, 1986); Kerop Bedoukian,
     Some of Us Survived (New York: Farrar Straus Giroux, 1978), esp. 15–57; Hannah
     Kalajian, as told to Bernadine Sullivan, *Hannah's Story: Escape from Genocide in
     Turkey to Success in America* (Belmont, MA: NAASR, 1990); Robert Mirak, *Genocide
     Survivors, Community Builders: The Family of John and Artemis Mirak* (Arlington,
     MA: Armenian Cultural Foundation, 2014); and of course Leon Z. Surmelian, *I Ask
     You, Ladies and Gentlemen* (New York: E. P. Dutton, 1945), discussed at the opening
     of Chapter 8 of the present work. Scholarly studies of the genocide include, but are by
     no means limited to, Raymond Kévorkian, *The Armenian Genocide: A Comprehensive
     History* (London: I.B. Tauris, 2011); Vahakn N. Dadrian, *The History of the American
     Genocide: Ethnic Conflict from the Balkans to Anatolia to the Caucasus* (Providence,
     RI: Berghahn, 1995); Ronald Grigor Suny, *"They Can Live in the Desert but Nowhere
     Else": A History of the Armenian Genocide* (Princeton, NJ: Princeton University Press,
     2015); and Vahé Tachjian, *Daily Life in the Abyss: Genocide Diaries, 1915–1918* (New
     York: Berghahn, 2017).
3   Walker, "World War I," 260–73; Bournoutian, *History of the Armenian People*,
     2: 102–3; Dadrian, *History of the Armenian Genocide*, 219–26 (including Riza
     references); Manoug Joseph Somakian, *Empires in Conflict: Armenia and the Great
     Powers, 1895–1920* (London: Tauris Academic Studies, 1995), 131–77. The American
     ambassador to Turkey at the time, Henry Morgenthau, records his horror at the
     events he witnessed and the cavalier remarks made to him by Turkish officials about
     their aims in Henry Morgenthau, *Ambassador Morgenthau's Story* (1918; repr.,
     Detroit: Wayne State University Press, 2003), 301–24.
4   Walker, "World War I," 246–60; Bournoutian, *History of the Armenian People*, 2:
     101–2; Peter Balakian, *The Burning Tigris: The Armenian Genocide and America's
     Response* (New York: HarperCollins, 2003), esp. 175–216.
5   Vahram L. Shemmassian, *The Armenians of Musa Dagh: From Obscurity to Genocide
     Resistance and Fame, 1840–1915* (Fresno: The Press, California State University,
     Fresno, 2020), 323–78; Edward Minasian, *Musa Dagh: A Chronicle of the Armenian
     Genocide Factor in the Subsequent Suppression, by the Intervention of the United States
     Government, of the Movie Based on Franz Werfel's "The Forty Days of Musa Dagh"*
     (Nashville, TN: Cold Tree Press, 2007), 3–22.
6   Levon Z. Boyajian, *Hayots Badeevuh: Reminiscences of Armenian Life in New York
     City* (Reading, England: Taderon Press, 2004), 11–12; Arpena S. Mesrobian, *"Like*

One Family": The Armenians of Syracuse (Ann Arbor, MI: Gomidas Institute, 2000), 50–1; *Azk*, July 6, 1918, 3; *Hairenik*, May 2, 1916, 2. California local historian George Kooshian echoes the observation on the constancy of musical recitals at local fundraising events and at meetings of political import. George Kooshian, "The Armenian Immigrant Community of California, 1880–1935" (PhD diss., University of California, Los Angeles, 2002), 321, 344, 347.

7   Kooshian, "Armenian Immigrant Community," 147–50.

8   *Boston Sunday Herald*, May 9, 1915, C-1. Gulesian had an interesting career. Arriving in New York penniless and spending his first three nights in America on a park bench, he became wealthy in Boston's copper manufacturing trade. He was involved in Armenian lobbying in the mid-1890s and, in 1905, distinguished his American patriotism in a campaign to save the historic U.S.S. *Constitution*, or "Old Ironsides," from official plans to scrap it and use its body for target practice. Irene H. Burnham, *Not by Accident: The Story of Moses H. Gulesian's Career* (Boston: Christopher Publishing House, 1938), esp. 158–9. For the Plattsburgh movement, see J. Garry Clifford, *The Citizen Soldiers: The Plattsburg Training Camp Movement, 1913–1920* (Lexington: University Press of Kentucky, 1972). Gulesian's name appears in the *Roster of the First Training Regiment (Plattsburg), August 10th to September 6th, September 8th to October 6th, 1915*, available in both hard copy and digital form at various libraries, including the Boston Public Library.

9   Nubar to Armenian National Union of Egypt, October 6, 1916; Meeting of Boghos Nubar with Mr. Malcom, October 23, 1916; Meeting of Nubar with Sir Mark Sykes, October 24, 1916; Meeting of Boghos Nubar with Mr. Picot, October 24, 1916, in *Boghos Nubar's Papers and the Armenian Question, 1915–1918*, ed./ trans. Vatche Ghazarian (Waltham, MA: Mayreni Publishing, 1996), 372–4, 380–6; Akaby Nassibian, *Britain and the Armenian Question, 1915–1923* (New York: St. Martin's Press, 1984), 109–10.

10 Another volunteer force that had members of an American immigrant community fighting as members of a diaspora to liberate an ancestral homeland was the Polish Army, which the French government organized with tacit cooperation from the United States. See David T. Ruskoski, "The Polish Army in France: Immigrants in America, World War I Volunteers in France, Defenders of the Recreated State in Poland" (PhD diss., Georgia State University, 2006); Joseph T. Hapak, "Recruiting a Polish Army in the United States, 1917–1919" (PhD diss., University of Kansas, 1985); Hapak, "Selective Service and Polish Army Recruitment During World War I," *Journal of American Ethnic History* 10, no. 4 (Summer 1991): 38–60.

11 Kooshian, "Armenian American Community," 164; Boghos Nubar Pasha to Secretary of State James Lansing, September 12, 1917, in *Papers Relating to the Foreign Relations of the United States (FRUS), 1917, Supplement 2, the World War* (Washington, DC: Government Printing Office, 1932), 795–6.

12 David M. Kennedy, *Over Here: The First World War and American Society* (New York: Oxford University Press, 1980), 63–6; John Higham, *Strangers in the Land: Patterns of American Nativism, 1860–1925* (New Brunswick, NJ: Rutgers University Press, 1955), 195–212; Desmond King, *Making Americans: Immigration, Race, and the Origins of the Diverse Democracy* (Cambridge, MA: Harvard University Press, 2000), 90–8; Alan M. Kraut, *The Huddled Masses: The Immigrant in American Society, 1880–1921* (Wheeling, IN: Harlan Davidson, 2001), 203–7.

13 *New York Times*, October 13, 1915, 1, 5; July 5, 1918, 20; Florence Kellor to
    Commissioner of Education Philander Claxton, March, 1918, quoted in King,
    Making Americans, 94.

14 June Granatir Alexander, *Ethnic Pride, American Patriotism: Slovaks and Other New
    Immigrants in the Interwar Era* (Philadelphia: Temple University Press, 2004), 18–38;
    King, *Making Americans*, 45; *Azk*, July 4, 1918, 2; *Hairenik*, July 3, 1918, 1; October
    18, 1918, 2; *Gotchnag*, June 22, 1918, 2217–18. George Creel, head of the propaganda-
    generating Committee on Public Information, worked with ethnic leaders to set
    up Loyalty Leagues in the ethnic communities, which facilitated dissemination of
    pamphlets in the respective languages. Kennedy, *Over Here*, 65.

15 *Hairenik*, July 2, 1918, 2.

16 *Hairenik*, June 26, 1918, 1; event reported in *New York Times*, June 20, 1918, 1.

17 *New York Times*, May 2, 1918, 3.

18 *Azk*, July 6, 1918, 2.

19 *Armenian Herald*, February-March-April, 1919, 163–5, 167–72. Hughes would
    later lose his credibility with Armenians when, as President Warren G. Harding's
    secretary of state, he supported the quick normalization of relations with Turkey. For
    all the times that Hughes's name appears in rosters of friends of the Armenians, it is
    interesting that his papers at the Library of Congress scarcely show any references
    to them. It should also be noted that Bryan, who had the misfortune of being most
    remembered in popular history for his strident defense of the Christian-creationist
    biology curriculum (with all its implications for an established Christian religion
    in the United States) in the 1925 Scopes Monkey Trial, addressed the dangers of
    established religion in this speech, with respect to Turkey. See also *New Armenia*,
    the full range of issues during these years. For more on Hughes's role, see Mark
    Malkasian, "The Disintegration of the Armenian Cause in the United States,
    1918–1927," *International Journal of Middle East Studies* 16, no. 3 (August 1984):
    357–60; On TR, see Balakian, 310–12.

20 Harry N. Howard, *The Partition of Turkey: A Diplomatic History* (1931; repr., New
    York: H. Fertig, 1966), 200–1.

21 Richard G. Hovannisian, *Armenia on the Road to Independence, 1918* (Berkeley:
    University of California Press, 1967), 106–85. The Batum accord required the
    Armenians to pull out of the city of Baku, which had been governed by a coalition
    called the Baku Commune since Russia's March Revolution of 1917. Turkey gained
    control over Baku in September of 1918, unleashing a fresh round of massacres
    on those Armenians who had not fled; about thirty thousand perished. Antranig
    Chalabian, *General Antranik and the Armenian Revolutionary Movement* (self-
    published, 1988), 379–92. The famous General Antranik rejected the terms of Batum
    and led an army that continued fighting in Turkish-controlled territory. Chalabian,
    General Antranik, 407–40.

22 *New York Times*, June 29, 1918, 3 (misspelling of Khatissian's name in original).

23 *Hairenik*, June 30, 1918, 1; July 4, 1918, 2; *Azk*, July 7, 1918, 2. I have previously
    written of the republic in "Divided Diaspora: Armenian-American Responses to the
    Republic," *Armenian Review* 56, no. 3-4 (2019): 25–42.

24 *Azk*, August 6, 1918, 2; August 8, 1918, 2; *Hairenik*, August 15, 1918, 2; August
    16, 1918, 2; October 9, 1918, 1; Kooshian, "Armenian Immigrant Community,"
    176–81; Jenny Phillips, *Symbol, Myth, and Rhetoric: The Politics of Culture in an
    Armenian-American Population* (New York: AMS Press, 1989), 81–4.

25 *Hye Heghapokhagan Tashnagtsiutiun Hiusisayin Amerigayi Mech* 2: 399–400; *Azk*, October 17, 1918, 2.

26 Kooshian, "Armenian Immigrant Community," 181–5.

27 Kooshian, "Armenian Immigrant Community," 185–93; *Azk*, January 9, 1919, 2; January 25, 1919, 2; January 28, 1919, 2; *Hairenik*, January 24, 1919, 1, 2.

28 Taking the disputed returns into account, the number of Armenian Americans who went to the polls on April 1 and 2, 1919, to influence the future of their homeland falls somewhere between 19,955 and 23,435. But what was the total Armenian population at the time? This is harder to calculate with precision. The 1920 census showed 36,628 persons who listed "Armenia" as their place of birth, but how many more Armenians called their birthplace "Turkey" is unknowable. Another piece of data is the 52,840 who were listed as "Armenian-speaking," irrespective of birth. Left out of these figures are whatever number of second- and third-generation Armenians who might have been from the earlier waves of immigration who did not maintain the Armenian language. It should be noted, however, that the principal newspapers of the parties apparently did not consider the non-Armenian-speaking population substantial enough to campaign to them in English, at least not on the pages of the newspapers themselves; indeed, a real English-language Armenian American press waited until the 1930s to come into existence. If we round the population of Armenian Americans, with or without the language, up to 60,000, and then consider that as many as a quarter of them may have been children ineligible to vote, that brings the broadly overestimated eligible population down to 45,000. If we then split the difference on the low side and say that around 20,000 actually voted, we can say that at least 44 percent of the eligible voters appear to have gone to the polls. While most of the participants probably voted in straight-ticket style, it would appear that at least several hundred did otherwise. More than half the voters apparently voted for at least one Tashnag candidate, and almost all voted for *either* the Tashnag *or* the "bloc" ticket, with approximately a thousand (about 5 percent of the voters) favoring one or more Reformed Hunchag candidates. Thus, it can be inferred, a critical mass of Armenian American adults held the persuasion that they could help shape the future of their ancestral homeland, and this critical mass was fairly evenly split between Tashnag and non. Election figures (contradictory, of course) appear in *Hairenik*, February 5, 1919, 1; February 6, 1919, 1; and *Azk*, April 5, 1919, 4. Population figures are gleaned from Schnorhig (Beatrice) Balayan, *The Armenians in the United States of America* (MA thesis, University of Chicago, 1927), 2–4.

29 Gregory Aftandilian, *Armenia, Vision of a Republic: The Independence Lobby in America, 1918–1927* (Charlestown, MA: Charles River Books, 1981).

30 Vartkes Yeghiayan, *Vahan Cardashian: Advocate Extraordinaire for the Armenian Cause* (Glendale, CA: Center for Armenian Remembrance, 2008), 1–34; James H. Tashjian, "Life and Papers of Vahan Cardashian," *Armenian Review* 10, no. 1 (Spring 1957): 3–15.

31 *Papers Relating to the Foreign Relations of the United States (FRUS), The Paris Peace Conference, 1919* (Washington, DC: Government Printing Office, 1943), 4: 147–57, https://history.state.gov/historicaldocuments/frus1919Parisv04/d8; Margaret MacMillan, *Paris, 1919: Six Months That Changed the World* (New York: Random House, 2001), 377–80.

32 For an extensive explanation of both the concept of postwar mandates and the discourse about a mandate for Armenia, see Edita Gzoyan, "The Plan to Solve the Armenian Mandate Question through a Non-State Organization," *Armenian*

Review 56, no. 3–4 (2019): 55–79. On the Armenian cause and lobbying efforts overall, see Malkasian, "Disintegration of the Armenian Cause," 349–65.

33 *Maintenance of Peace in Armenia: Hearings before a Subcommittee of the Committee on Foreign Relations, United States Senate, Sixty-Sixth Congress, First Session, on S.J.R. 106: A Joint Resolution for the Maintenance of Peace in Armenia* (Washington, DC: Government Printing Office, 1919), esp. 7–11. The Williams resolution would recognize Armenia's rightful borders as including the six vilayets of Turkish Armenia, the provinces of Russian Armenia, and Cilicia; allow the president to commit "such military and naval forces of the United States as in his opinion may seem expedient for the maintenance of peace and tranquility in Armenia" pending official settlement by treaty; and authorize the president to suspend restrictions on foreign enlistment in order to let still more Armenian Americans don uniforms and go to the service of their ancestral homeland.

34 *Hairenik*, October 2, 1919, 2. Editorials of October 3, 4, and 7, 1919, continued the vituperation.

35 *New York Times*, April 11, 1917, 2; *Azk*, May 18, 1917, 2; *Hairenik*, September 21, 1918, 2.

36 Kooshian, "Armenian Immigrant Community," 195–201; *Hairenik*, January 4, 1920, 2; January 6, 1920, 2; January 7, 1920, 2; January 8, 1920, 2.

37 *Bahag*, October 8, 1918, 1; November 8, 1918, 1–4.

38 Inquiry Document No. 887, submitted December 22, 1917, printed in full in *FRUS 1919: Paris Peace Conference* 1: 41–53; Foreign Office memorandum quoted in Richard G. Hovannisian, *The Republic of Armenia* (Berkeley: University of California Press, 1971–1996), 1: 267. See also Simon Payaslian, *United States Policy toward the Armenian Question and the Armenian Genocide* (New York: Palgrave MacMillan, 2005), 73–141; Nassibian, *Britain and the Armenian Question*, 67–119; James B. Gidney, *A Mandate for Armenia* (Kent, OH: Kent State University Press, 1967), 41–73; Lawrence E. Gelfand, *The Inquiry: American Preparations for Peace* (New Haven, CT: Yale University Press, 1963), 214–15, 244–8; Laurence Evans, *United States Policy and the Partition of Turkey* (Baltimore: Johns Hopkins University Press, 1965), 71–5; Marc A. Mamigonian, "'Armenia Will Call upon Us in Vain': U.S. Relations with the First Republic of Armenia," *Armenian Review* 56, no. 3–4 (2019): 81–97.

The December 22, 1917, Inquiry memorandum reflected an intense concern for preventing Germany from having a Berlin-Baghdad axis, a contiguous stretch of influence that would allow it to strike even deeper into the east, and the ostensible idealism concerning Armenia came in that context, calling the Armenians "the one people of Asia Minor capable of preventing economic monopolization of Turkey by Germany." *FRUS* (1919): 1:43. Notably, the Inquiry treated Turkey with finesse, depicting it primarily as a victim of Germany's overpowering. The memorandum called for the cancellation of Turkey's war debts to Germany as "the one method by which Turkey can be given a new start, considerably reduced in size, without power to misgovern alien races, and therefore free to concentrate upon the needs of her own population." 53.

Wilson's right-hand man "Colonel" Edward House noted in his diary, "After the Turkish paragraph had been written, the President thought it might be made more specific, and that Armenia, Mesopotamia, Syria and other parts be mentioned by name. I disagreed with this, believing that what was said was sufficient to indicate this, and it finally stood as originally framed." *Papers of Woodrow Wilson* (PWW), ed. Arthur S. Link (Princeton, NJ: Woodrow Wilson Foundation, Princeton University, 1966–94), 45: 553.

39   Nassibian, 120–50, quotations on 131. The terms negotiated at Mudros appalled
     British officials sympathetic to the Armenians, including Arnold Toynbee, famed
     historian working in the Political Intelligence Department, and Sir Mark Sykes of
     Sykes-Picot fame.
40   Vahakn N. Dadrian and Taner Akçam, *Judgment at Istanbul: The Armenian Genocide
     Trials* (New York: Berghahn Books, 2011), esp. 23–7, 33–52, 195–7, and passim;
     Marian Mesrobian MacCurdy, *Sacred Justice: The Voices and Legacy of the Armenian
     Operation Nemesis* (New Brunswick, NJ: Transaction Publishers, 2015), 110–11.
41   Hovannisian, *Republic of Armenia* 1: 133–44; *Republic of Armenia* 2: 317–22; Payaslian,
     United States Policy, 148–53; James L. Barton, *Story of Near East Relief (1915–1930):
     An Interpretation* (New York: MacMillan, 1930), 3–19, 104–27; Gidney, *Mandate for
     Armenia*, 168–91; Harbord Report in *FRUS* (1919) 2: 841–89, esp. 857–60.
         The Harbord report noted, "The Armenian is not guiltless of blood himself. His
     memory is long and reprisals are due, and will doubtless be made if opportunity
     arises," and stated that there had been large-scale massacres in Baku by both
     Armenians and Azerbaijanis against each other in March 1918. Harbord Report
     in *FRUS* (1919) 2: 860. Stephen Bonsal, American journalist serving as personal
     secretary to Wilson, wrote in his diary on March 19, 1919, "I do not close my eyes
     to the crimes which the Armenians have since committed … against the diabolical
     Kurds and the Turkish irregulars …. Indeed, I approve of them." Stephen Bonsal,
     Suitors and Suppliants: The Little Nations at Versailles (New York: Prentice-Hall, Inc.,
     1946), 186.
42   See, for example, Wilson's speeches at Kansas City on September 6, 1919, *PPW* 63:
     71, and at Salt Lake City, September 23, 1919, *PWW* 63:458. See also Payaslian,
     United States Policy, 161–4; and John Milton Cooper, "A Friend in Power? Woodrow
     Wilson and Armenia," in *America and the Armenian Genocide of 1915*, ed. Jay Winter
     (Cambridge, UK: Cambridge University Press, 2003), 108–9. The larger story of the
     treaty fight is in all the standard U.S. history textbooks and books about Wilson's
     life and presidency. A concise treatment of it appears in Robert H. Zieger, *America's
     Great War: World War I and the American Experience* (Lanham, MD: Rowan and
     Littlefield, 2000), 215–25. Among the many full-length books on the subject is John
     Milton Cooper, *Breaking the Heart of the World: Woodrow Wilson and the Fight for
     the League of Nations* (Cambridge, UK: Cambridge University Press, 2001).
43   Gzoyan, "Plan to Solve the Armenian Mandate Question"; Wilson to Congress,
     May 24, 1920, *PWW* 65: 320–3; Gidney, *Mandate for Armenia*, 222–39; Concurrent
     Resolution 72, *Congressional Record*, June 1, 1920, Congress 66, Session 2 (1920),
     8073. Hovannisian discusses the U.S. political dimension in *Republic of Armenia*
     4: 1–44.
44   Syria, Mesopotamia, and Palestine were to become Allied mandates. Armed conflict
     between French forces and Syrian nationalists ensued promptly, with defeat for
     the local resistance and exile for Faisal. Smyrna was to be in a state of limbo for
     five years, but essentially governed by Greece, with a plebiscite to follow. The
     Bosporus and Dardanelles Straits and the Marmora Sea would be governed by an
     international commission (of which the United States, in its classic unilateralism,
     claimed the perpetual right to be either a member or a nonmember as it saw fit).
     Howard, *Partition of Turkey*, 242–9; Evans, *United States Policy and the Partition
     of Turkey*, 245–9, 269–91; MacMillan, *Paris, 1919*, 406–9; Hovannisian, *Republic
     of Armenia*, 1: 296–8 and 3: 90–105; "Treaty of Sèvres, August 10, 1920," in *Major
     Peace Treaties of Modern History, 1648–1967*, ed. Fred L. Israel (New York: Chelsea

House, 1967), 3: 2055–213, esp. 2084–88; Erik Goldstein, *The First World War Peace Settlements, 1919–1925* (London: Pearson, 2002), 59–60.

45 Gidney, *Mandate for Armenia*, 246; Woodrow Wilson, *Boundary between Turkey and Armenia: As Determined by Woodrow Wilson, President of the United States of America* (Washington, DC: Department of State, 1920).

46 Ralph Elliott Cook, "The United States and the Armenian Question, 1894–1924" (PhD diss., The Fletcher School of Law and Diplomacy, Tufts University, 1957), 150–287; Levon Marashlian, "The Armenian Question from Sèvres to Lausanne: Economics and Morality in American and British Policies, 1920–1923" (PhD diss., University of California, Los Angeles, 1992), 52–62; Hovannisian, *Republic of Armenia* 3: 71–93; 4: 1–44, esp. 40–4; 180–236; 373–90; Balakian, *Burning Tigris*, 299–318, 349–62.

47 Gidney, *A Mandate for Armenia*, 243–44.

48 Cook, "United States and the Armenian Question," 277, 283; Hovannisian, *Republic of Armenia* 4: 373–408; Mary Kilbourne Matossian, *The Impact of Soviet Policies in Armenia* (Leiden, Netherlands: E. J. Brill, 1962), 29; Gidney, *Mandate for Armenia*, 246–50.

49 Matossian, *Impact of Soviet Policies*, 30, 36. The dictatorial regime that took hold now showed a modicum of forbearance and tolerance, heeding Lenin's admonition that "Nothing delays so much the development and consolidation of the proletarian class solidarity as national injustice." Further adjustments of boundary lines were made that year as well, including the transfer of the Armenian-dominated province of Nagorno-Karabagh and the Muslim-dominated Nakhichevan section of Yerevan province, to the neighboring Muslim Soviet republic of Azerbaijan. Decades later, starting with the decline of the Soviet government in the late 1980s, Nagorno-Karabagh would be a spot of bitter Armenian-Azerbaijani conflict.

50 MacMillan, *Paris, 1919*, 429–34.

51 Hovannisian, *Republic of Armenia* 3: 20–86; Stanley E. Kerr, *The Lions of Marash: Personal Experiences with American Near East Relief, 1919–1922* (Albany: SUNY Press, 1973), 30–1, 61–71, 95–174; Bernard Lewis, *The Emergence of Modern Turkey*, 3rd ed. (New York: Oxford University Press, 2002), 239–53.

52 Howard, *Partition of Turkey*, 260–8.

53 Marjorie Housepian Dobkin, *Smyrna, 1922: The Destruction of a City* (New York: Newmark Press, 1998), esp. 145–208.

54 Evans, *United States Policy*, 390–403; Howard, *Partition of Turkey*, 277–314; Joseph C. Grew, *Turbulent Era: A Diplomatic Record of Forty Years*, ed. Walter Johnson (Boston: Houghton Mifflin, 1952), 1: 475–585; *New York Times*, July 26, 1924, 1; August 5, 1924, 16.

55 Thomas A. Bryson, "The Armenian American [*sic*] Society: A Factor in American-Turkish Relations, 1919–1924," *Armenian Review* 29, no. 1 (Spring 1976): 57; Nubar to Gerard, April 16, 1921, attached to note from Gerard to Cardashian, May 1, 1921, Gerard Papers, ACIA file, University of Montana; *Azk-Bahag*, May 22, 1922, 2; *Hairenik*, April 30, 1921, 2.

56 Grew, *Turbulent Era* 1: 530–3. On one issue, for example, that of honoring prewar Turkish concessions to European businesses that would undermine America's Open Door policy by giving countries economic spheres of influence in Turkey, Joseph Grew proudly recalled in his memoir the way that he—the representative of a country that was theoretically just observing the proceedings—coached Ismet Pasha to stand firmly against the demands of the European leaders, assuring Ismet that, if he did not back down, the Europeans would. Grew, *Turbulent Era* 1: 559–60.

57   Grew, *Turbulent Era* 1: 603–5.
58   Democratic Platform 1924, in *History of American Presidential Elections, 1789–2001*, ed. Arthur M. Schlesinger, Jr. (Philadelphia: Chelsea House, 2002), 2501.
59   *New York Times*, June 30, 1926, 16; January 25, 1924, 21; April 6, 1923, E2; April 23, 1926, 8.
60   *New York Times*, June 28, 1925, XX10; August 23, 1925, E6; May 3, 1926, 28; *Baikar*, May 26, 1927, 2.
61   *New York Times*, January 19, 1927, 1; Cardashian to Coolidge, March 23, 1927, and May 7, 1927, quoted in Yeghiayan, *Vahan Cardashian*, 313–14.
62   Edward Minasian, *They Came from Ararat: The Exodus of the Armenian People to America* (Lafayette, CA: Big Hat Press, 2018), 213; *New Republic*, June 29, 1921, 142–3.

Chapter 2

1   *Hairenik*, March 17, 1921, 1; March 19, 1921, 2; Edward Alexander, *A Crime of Vengeance: An Armenian Struggle for Justice* (New York: Free Press, 1991).
2   Marian Mesrobian MacCurdy, *Sacred Justice: The Voices and Legacy of the Armenian Operation Nemesis* (New Brunswick, NJ: Transaction Publishers, 2015), 78–80, 116–28. See also Jacques Derogy, *Resistance and Revenge: The Armenian Assassination of the Turkish Leaders Responsible for the 1915 Massacres and Deportations* (New Brunswick, NJ: Transaction Publishers, 1990); Eric Bogosian, *Operation Nemesis: The Assassination Plot That Avenged the Armenian Genocide* (New York: Little, Brown, 2015).
3   John Cooper, *Raphael Lemkin and the Struggle for the Genocide Convention* (Basingstoke, UK: Palgrave Macmillan, 2008), 15.
4   Edward Minasian, "The Armenian Immigrant Tide: From the Great War to the Great Depression," in *Recent Studies in Modern Armenian History*, ed. National Association for Armenian Studies and Research (NAASR) (Cambridge, MA: Armenian Heritage Press, 1972), 106.
5   Leon Surmelian, *I Ask You, Ladies and Gentlemen* (New York: E. P. Dutton, 1945), 256; *New York Times*, May 30, 1921, 15; Helene Pilibosian, *My Literary Profile: A Memoir* (Watertown, MA: Ohan Press, 2010), 40–1. On the entry policies, see Alan M. Kraut, *The Huddled Masses: The Immigrant in American Society, 1880–1921* (Wheeling, IN: Harlan Davidson, 2001), 69–70.
6   David Kherdian, *The Road from Home: The Story of an Armenian Girl* (New York: Greenwillow Books, 1979), 211–39; David Kherdian, *Finding Home* (New York: Greenwillow Books, 1981), 4–116; Isabel Kaprielian-Churchill, "Armenian Refugee Women: The Picture Brides, 1920–1930," *Journal of American Ethnic History* 12 (Spring 1993): 3–29; *New York Times*, August 3, 1922, 32; Arpena S. Mesrobian, *"Like One Family": The Armenians of Syracuse* (Ann Arbor, MI: Gomidas Institute, 2000), 90–1; Pilibosian, *My Literary Profile*, 4–5; Khachadoor Pilibosian, *They Called Me Mustafa* (Watertown, MA: Ohan Press, 1992), 43–5.
7   *New York Times*, August 3, 1922, 32; Michael Bobelian, *Children of Armenia: A Forgotten Genocide and the Century-Long Struggle for Justice* (New York: Simon and Schuster, 2009), 175. Bobelian, drawing in part from his interview with Van Z. Krikorian, whose grandmother was one of the picture brides, writes,

"The desperation of the times led to many strained nuptials. The age gap between the men and women typically reached twenty years. People of different socioeconomic backgrounds, who would have never crossed each other's social circles prior to 1915, found themselves flung together. Armenians from different parts of the Ottoman Empire, who rarely interacted in the past, checked their provincial inclinations. The marriages were a crapshoot, particularly for the women, who were often at the total mercy of the men. Those with overbearing in-laws or abusive husbands had no avenues for escape. Some forged loving families while others had no luck in this bizarre lottery."

8 Douglas C. Baynton, *Defectives in the Land: Disability and Immigration in the Age of Eugenics* (Chicago: University of Chicago Press, 2016), 126–9; *New York Times*, September 16, 1921, 10; September 18, 1921, 13; Edward Minasian, *They Came from Ararat: The Exodus of the Armenian People to America* (Lafayette, CA: Big Hat Press, 2018), 153–4.

9 Isabel Kaprielian-Churchill, "Changing Patterns of Armenian Neighborhoods," in *Armenians of New England*, ed. Marc A. Mamigonian (Belmont, MA: National Association for Armenian Studies and Research, 2004),18; Robert Mirak, "Armenians," in *Harvard Encyclopedia of American Ethnic Groups* (Cambridge, MA: Harvard University Press, 1980), 141; Minasian, "Armenian Immigrant Tide," 110–13; Noubar Dorian, interview by the author, October 19, 2002; Vahram L. Shemmassian, *The Musa Dagh Armenians: A Socioeconomic and Cultural History, 1919–1939* (Beirut: Haigazian University Press, 2015), 190–1; Nouritza Matossian, *Black Angel: The Life of Arshile Gorky* (Woodstock, NY: Overlook Press, 2000), 127–30.

10 Mesrobian, *"Like One Family,"* 97–100; Helene Pilibosian, *My Literary Profile*, 27; Khachadoor Pilibosian, *They Called Me Mustafa*, 46–8; Edward D. Simsarian, email to the author, January 14, 2016; Hovhannes Mugrditchian, *To Armenians with Love: The Memoirs of a Patriot* (Hobe Sound, FL: Paul Mart, 1996), 107–9.

11 Souren A. Papazian, *Odyssey of a Survivor* (self-published, 2002), 97–114; Kaprielian-Churchill, "Changing Patterns," 18; Kherdian, *Finding Home*, 32.

12 *Hairenik*, October 16, 1925, 1; *Hairenik*, January 23, 1926, 3. The significance of the compatriotic societies is discussed further in Anny Bakalian, *Armenian-Americans: From Being to Feeling Armenian* (New Brunswick, NJ: Transaction Publishers, 1996), 184, and Mirak, *Torn between Two Lands*, 174. For a broader comparative perspective, see Jose C. Moya, "Immigrants and Associations: A Global and Historical Perspective," *Journal of Ethnic and Migration Studies* 31, no. 5 (2005): 847–50. Moya observes that hometown associations were larger and more numerous among larger immigrant communities such as the Italians, where there were sizable subgroups from a common town or region of the sending country within a major American city.

13 On American cultural change in the 1920s, see Steven Mintz and Susan Kellogg, *Domestic Revolutions: A Social History of American Family Life* (New York: The Free Press, 1988), 107–31; Paula S. Fass, *The Damned and the Beautiful: American Youth in the 1920s* (New York: Oxford University Press, 1977), 53–118; and Kathy Peiss, *Hope in a Jar: The Making of America's Beauty Culture* (New York: Metropolitan Books, 1998), 97–133. Primary source material about the consternation of conservative elders can be found in many of the major magazines of the decade; see, for example, "Is the Younger Generation in Peril?," *Literary Digest*, May 14, 1921; John R. McMahon, "Unspeakable Jazz Must Go," *Literary Digest*, January 6, 1922.

14   Susie Hoogasian Villa and Mary Kilbourne Matossian, *Armenian Village Life before 1914* (Detroit: Wayne State University Press, 1982), 72–8; Vatche Ghazarian, *A Village Remembered: The Armenians of Habousi* (Waltham, MA: Mayreni Publishing, 1997, a publication of the Compatriotic Union of Habousi), 45–7; Vahé Tachjian, "Reconstructing Armenian Village Life: Manoog Dzeron and Alevor, Unique Authors of the 'Houshamadyan' Genre," in *Ottoman Armenians: Life, Culture, Society*, ed. Vahé Tachjian (Berlin: Houshamadyan, 2015), 1: 217.

15   Hoogasian Villa and Matossian, *Armenian Village Life*, 78–9. The married life that followed was no less regulated by ritual. The bride, now living with her in-laws under the prevailing patrilocal system, had to observe silence with the groom's parents for a period that could range from a few months to a few years. Even after, her life entailed trappings of subservience. Years later, however, she might rise to the position of the being the wife of the head of the household, which would give her substantial prerogatives—including a strong voice in the selection of marriage partners for the young. The groom's father, if still alive, headed the household, a position his eldest son inherited when he died. Younger sons, around the time their own children began to marry, moved out and became patriarchs of their own households. Most of the betrothal and family structure traditions appear to have remained fairly intact right up to the upheavals. It was observed that village girls who attended Protestant schools had a higher average marriage age, but it does not appear that the introduction of Protestantism threw the wedding rites off kilter to any appreciable degree.

The powerful role that rituals and rules played in village life is illustrated in the extreme example of how the parents of chef-author George Mardikian "met," if the version handed down to and retold by their son is to be believed. Young Magar Mardikian had taken notice of Haiganoush Amirian, but whenever he bowed and tipped his hat to her, her stern and disapproving family "pulled her along and forbade her to look back." One evening when Haiganoush was attending a wedding, Magar sent Haiganoush a forged message tricking her into leaving the gathering. As she walked, Magar suddenly galloped by on his horse, scooped her up, and carried her out of the village. When members of her family got word, they mounted their own horses and took up chase. When they were caught, the verdict delivered by some unspecified member of her family was, "Either you will marry her—or we shall kill you both." This was exactly the life sentence Magar wanted. This was 1894; the marriage endured until 1915 when Magar perished in the genocide. George Mardikian, *The Song of America* (New York: McGraw-Hill, 1956), 1–6, 14–15.

16   *Hairenik*, January 22, 1926, 1; Mesrobian, *"Like One Family,"* 130–2.

17   *Hairenik*, January 22, 1926, 1; Ewa Morawska, "In Defense of the Assimilation Model," *Journal of American Ethnic History* 13 (Winter, 1994): 76–87. On family adaptations in the urban environment, see John Bodnar, *The Transplanted: A History of Immigrants in Urban America* (Bloomington: Indiana University Press, 1985), 71–83.

18   Richard Tracy LaPiere, "The Armenian Colony in Fresno County, California: A Study in Social Psychology" (PhD diss., Stanford University, 1930), 217–20, 237–41.

19   LaPiere, "Armenian Colony," 228, 237, 245–6.

20   LaPiere, "Armenian Colony," 256–7.

21   Fass, *Damned and the Beautiful*, 276.

22   LaPiere, "Armenian Colony," 241. A fringe benefit of stricter parenting for girls may have been higher scholastic achievement. In the graduating classes of 1927 and 1928 at Fresno High School, thirteen Armenian girls (constituting 30 percent of graduating Armenian girls) graduated with honors, alongside zero Armenian boys.

LaPiere cites both their constricted social lives and the pressure to defend the value of their being educated to their parents as reasons for girls' superior school work. LaPiere, "Armenian Colony," 278. As will be seen in Chapter 4, Armenian dances were a prime vehicle of cultural transition, as formal institutions that needed to ensure a self-replenishing constituency for themselves sponsored such social events to bring the cosmopolitan practices of consensual romantic love into an Armenian context, to maximize the number of such consensual unions between Armenians.

23 Harold Nelson, "The Armenian Family: Changing Patterns of Family Life in a California Community" (PhD diss., University of California, Berkeley, 1953), 179–210.

24 LaPiere, "Armenian Colony," 190–7.

25 Harry A. Sachaklian, *Marriage by Ballot*, unpublished, copy given to the author by Arpena Mesrobian, n.d.

26 Shemmassian, *Musa Dagh Armenians*, 204; Mirak, *Torn between Two Lands*, 152–4; *Hairenik*, January 11, 1926, 2.

27 Nelson, "Armenian Family," 61–2, 94; Elizabeth Ewen, *Immigrant Women in the Land of Dollars: Life and Culture on the Lower East Side, 1890–1925* (New York: Monthly Review Press, 1985), 208–24; Selma Cantor Berrol, *Growing Up American: Immigrant Children in America, Then and Now* (New York: Twayne Publishers, 1995), 91–5; Nancy Foner, *From Ellis Island to JFK: New York's Two Great Waves of Immigration* (New Haven: Yale University Press, 2000), 114–15.

28 Diana Keleshian, interview by the author, June 5, 2002.

29 Madison Grant, *The Passing of the Great Race* (New York: Charles Scribner's Sons, 1916, with successive revisions through 1923); Matthew Frye Jacobson, *Whiteness of a Different Color: European Immigrants and the Alchemy of Race* (Cambridge, MA: Harvard University Press, 1998), 83; Desmond King, *Making Americans: Immigration, Race, and the Origins of the Diverse Democracy* (Cambridge, MA: Harvard University Press, 2000), 199–223; John Higham, *Strangers in the Land: Patterns of American Nativism, 1860–1925* (New Brunswick, NJ: Rutgers University Press, 1955), 308–24; Elliot Barkan, *And Still They Come: Immigrants and American Society, 1920 to the 1990s* (Wheeling, IL: Harlan-Davidson, 1996), 8 (for Johnson quote); Roger Daniels, *Guarding the Golden Door: American Immigration Policy since 1882* (New York: Hill and Wang, 2004), 48.

30 *New York Times*, September 18, 1921, 13; Minasian, *They Came from Ararat*, 134; "General File: Armenians detained in excess of quota," in Records of the Immigration and Naturalization Service, Subject and Policy Files, 1893–1957, record group 85, box 4516, folder 55166/229, National Archives and Records Administration, Washington, DC (NARA-DC). The *New York Times* reported on one particular boatload of fifty-one Armenians that got sent back to Turkey by order of Immigration Commissioner Robert E. Tod even though Tod knew that a writ of habeas corpus had been issued for those Armenians by federal judge Learned Hand. Judge Hand apparently declined to take any follow-up action on behalf of those unfortunate refugees. *New York Times*, February 11, 1923, 1; March 3, 1923, 4.

31 *Admission of Near East Refugees: Hearings before the Committee on Immigration and Naturalization, House of Representatives, Sixty-Seventh Congress, Fourth Session, on H.R. 13269* (Washington, DC: U.S. Government Printing Office, 1923), esp. 13, 17, 19, 73.

32 *Admission of Near East Refugees*, 79–81.

33 *New York Times*, April 20, 1921, 1; Minasian, "Armenian Immigrant Tide," 106.

34 *Hairenik*, April 12, 1924, 2; *Baikar*, April 5, 1924, 2. The California-based *Nor Or*
    ("New Day") was less restrained, blaming the volume of Armenian refugees to
    America on the failure of the powers (including America) to stand by Woodrow
    Wilson's territorial award to Armenia of 1920; the powers "forsook them to become a
    wandering people." *Literary Digest*, May 17, 1924, 18. The *Literary Digest* ran excerpts
    from all three of these Armenian papers, but very brief and omitting much of import.
35 *Terrace v. Thompson*, 274 F 841, 849 (W.D. Washington 1921), cited in Ian
    F. Haney-López, *White by Law: The Legal Construction of Race* (New York: NYU
    Press, 1996), 55–6.
36 *In re Halladjian*, 174 F. 834 (C.C.D. Mass. 1909), cited in Jacobson, *Whiteness
    of a Different Color*, 230–5; *In re Najour*, 174 F. 735 (N.D. Ga. 1909), cited in
    Haney-López, *White by Law*, 68; *Ozawa v. United States*, 260 U.S. 178 (1922) and
    United States v. Thind, 261 U.S. 204 (1923), cited in Haney-López, *White by Law*,
    80–92, and Jacobson, *Whiteness of a Different Color*, 235–7.
37 Letter by Arshag Mahdesian printed in *New York Times*, December 28, 1925, 14.
    Attorney General John G. Sargent to Secretary of Labor James J. Davis, October
    7, 1925, File 38-701, Item 18, Papers from the Department of Justice on *Cartozian
    v. United States*, United States Government, National Archives and Records
    Administration, College Park, MD (NARA-CP); William D. Guthrie to Franz Boas,
    March 27, 1924, in Franz Boas papers on Cartozian case, American Philosophical
    Society (APS), Philadelphia, PA. Labor Secretary Davis, it might be noted, was also
    the author of a letter to President Coolidge in 1924 urging him to sign the very
    racialist Johnson-Reed immigration restriction bill, saying "We have enough trouble
    now with our racial groups without adding to it." Davis to Coolidge, May 20, 1924, in
    Calvin Coolidge Papers, Labor Department, 1923–29, Series 1, Case File 15 Microfilm
    accession #12,731 (Reel 20), Library of Congress, Washington, DC, available online at
    "Prosperity and Thrift: The Coolidge Era and the Consumer Economy, 1921–1929,"
    American Memory series, Library of Congress, http://memory.loc.gov/cgi-bin/query/
    D?coolbib:2:./temp/~ammem_09bk:, images 31 and 32.
38 Boas to Dr. Harold Bailey, April 17, 1924, and ensuing correspondence, in Franz Boas
    papers on Cartozian case at APS.
39 Deposition of Roland Burrage Dixon, cited in court decision *United States v.
    Cartozian* (6 Fed. Rept., 2nd Ser. 919, Dist. Court of Oregon), 20–3, in Franz
    Boas papers on Cartozian case at APS. When asked to define a "white person,"
    Dixon—after rattling off his impressive credentials—replied, "one who, on ordinary
    examination, one would classify as of white skin, and obviously similar to the bulk of
    the population of Europe."
40 Franz Boas papers on Cartozian case at APS. See also Earlene Craver, "On the
    Boundary of White: The *Cartozian* Naturalization Case and the Armenians,
    1923–1925," *Journal of American Ethnic History* 28, no. 2 (Winter 2009): 30–56.
41 *New York Times*, July 29, 1925, 20; August 3, 1925, 14. Interestingly, Madison Grant's
    name shows up on in the 1919 membership rolls of the American Committee for the
    Independence of Armenia (ACIA). That notwithstanding, his life's work fully earns
    him a place in the annals of twentieth-century America's most notorious racists.
    He was also an avid botanist, but in 2021 his name was removed from a section of
    the Prairie Creek Redwoods State Park in California, in response to a petition from
    212 scholars including the present author.
42 Higham, *Strangers in the Land*, 133. Chapter 4 contains further discussion of this
    theme.

43 Mirak, *Torn between Two Lands,* 68–71; Balakian, *Burning Tigris,* 63–80, 93–102; *New Armenia,* January–February 1925, 6–7.

44 LaPiere, "The Armenian Colony," 365–86 and Appendix, 101.

45 Mirak, *Torn between Two Lands,* 155; *Hairenik,* January 24, 1926, 1; *New York Times,* July 29, 1925, 20; Orville Vernon Burton and Armand Derfner, *Justice Deferred: Race and the Supreme Court* (Cambridge, MA: Belknap Press of Harvard University Press, 2021), 156. Writer Mardie Jay Bakjian observed anti-Armenian prejudice still to be rampant in Fresno as late as 1945. *Armenian Mirror-Spectator,* October 20, 1945, 1, 4. Edward Minasian echoes the finding that anti-Armenian prejudice was pervasive in Fresno and came in occasional incidents elsewhere. Minasian, *They Came from Ararat,* 226–8. See also Bakalian, *Armenian-Americans,* 19.

46 Milton Gordon, *Assimilation in American Life* (New York: Oxford University Press, 1964), 88–114. For details on the monoculturalist impulses, see John Higham, *Strangers in the Land: Patterns of American Nativism, 1860–1925* (New Brunswick, NJ: Rutgers University Press, 1955), esp. chaps. 8, 9, and 10, and Desmond King, *Making Americans: Immigration, Race, and the Origins of the Diverse Democracy* (Cambridge, MA: Harvard University Press, 2000), esp. chaps. 4 and 5.

47 For the rise of cultural pluralist thought and the International Institute movement, see Horace Kallen, "Democracy versus the Melting Pot," *The Nation,* February 18, 1915, 190–4; February 25, 1915, 217–20; Horace Kallen, *Culture and Democracy in the United States* (New York: Boni and Liveright, 1924), esp. 67–125; Raymond A. Mohl, "The International Institute Movement and Ethnic Pluralism," *Social Science* 56 (Winter 1981): 14–21.

48 Orm Øverland, *Immigrant Minds, American Identities: Making the United States Home, 1870–1930* (Urbana: University of Illinois Press, 2000), 54–86; *New York Times,* September 11, 1921, 81; M. Vartan Malcom, *Armenians in America* (Boston: Pilgrim Press, 1919), 97–8. See also James H. Tashjian, *The Armenians of the United States and Canada* (Boston: Hairenik Press, 1947), 54–9. Consistent with this theme is John Higham's observation that ethnic leaders promoted an "inclusive Americanism" by pointing up their own groups' historic contributions to the larger society. Higham, "The Ethnic Historical Society in Changing Times," *Journal of American Ethnic History* 13, no. 2 (Winter 1994): 33–4.

49 Marjorie Housepian, *A Houseful of Love* (New York: Random House, 1954), 126.

50 Deranian, *Worcester Is America,* 183; Mirak, *Torn between Two Lands,* 172.

51 Kherdian, *Finding Home,* 1981), 34.

52 Boyajian, *Hayots Badeevuh,* 23.

53 Mirak, *Torn between Two Lands,* 157‑61; Boyajian, *Hayots Badeevuh,* 26.

54 Pilibosian, *My Literary Profile,* 35.

55 Mesrobian, *"Like One Family,"* 108–9.

56 Levon Boyajian and Haigaz Grigorian, "Psychosocial Sequelae of the Armenian Genocide," in *The Armenian Genocide in Perspective,* ed. Richard G. Hovannisian (New Brunswick, NJ: Transaction Publishers, 1986), 177–85; Mirak, *Torn between Two Lands,* 159; Mesrobian, *"Like One Family,"* 104–5.

57 *Baikar,* July 29, 1925, 2. The philosophizing did not stop there; the writer also saw fit to deliver a paragraph-long catechism on the importance of acquiring wealth by way of humble and honest work rather than through greed and chicanery. Ill-gotten gain, the writer told readers, makes one wealthy for a time, then leaves one poor and ultimately destroyed; humbleness and hard work may not be a fast ticket to great wealth, but over time they are what lead to true success. While those sentiments are

hardly unique to Armenians, the inference can be drawn that the editorialist and some share of the readers considered it important for Armenians to display some noteworthy qualities of virtue in their economic behavior.

58　*Hairenik*, January 22, 1926, 1, 2; January 23, 1926, 1, 2; January 24, 1926, 1, 2; January 25, 1926, 1, 2. Yet if the future of Armenia depended on a vibrant Armenian community in America, paradoxically, the Tashnag editors of *Hairenik* also believed that it depended on some displaced Armenians *not* migrating to America. When Congress passed the Johnson-Reed immigrant restriction law in April of 1924, that aforementioned *Hairenik* editorial, which in the opening lines smoldered at the injury to national honor and bristled at the privileging of Anglo-Saxon immigrants at the expense of those of southern and eastern European descent, went on to suggest a silver lining in that it would keep down the number of Armenians in danger of losing their Armenianness in the American melting pot. "The farther from America the Armenian refugee stays," the unabashedly bitter editorial observed, "the closer he will be to the motherland, and the less will be the danger to his nation's existence." *Hairenik*, April 22, 1924, 2. Further discourse on the effects of American life on Armenian cultural life appears in *Baikar*, January 24, 1928, 2. The rights and obligations of American citizenship for Armenian and other immigrants are discussed in *Baikar*, January 15, 1928, 2.

Chapter 3

1　I have previously written of this saga in "Contested Memories, Divided Diaspora: Armenian Americans, the Thousand-day Republic, and the Polarized Response to an Archbishop's Murder," *Journal of American Ethnic History* 27, no. 1 (2007): 32–59. For a fictionalized account, see Terry Phillips, *Murder at the Altar* (Bakersfield, CA: Hye Books, 2008).

2　Mary Kilbourne Matossian, *The Impact of Soviet Policies in Armenia* (Leiden, Netherlands: E. J. Brill, 1962), 62–70, 78–95; Simon Payaslian, *The History of Armenia: From the Origins to the Present* (New York: Palgrave Macmillan, 2007), 175–9.

3　Ronald Grigor Suny, *Looking toward Ararat: Armenia in Modern History* (Bloomington: Indiana University Press, 1993), 142–3, 151–3.

4　On Reuben Darbinian's journalism, see Gregory Aftandilian, "The Cold War Writings of Reuben Darbinian in the Armenian Review," *Armenian Review* 56, no. 3–4 (2019): 1–25.

5　*Baikar*, March 11, 1924, 1; January 19, 1926, 2; *Hairenik*, March 20, 1924, 2; January 22, 1926, 2.

6　*Baikar*, July 28, 1925, 2. The editorial concluded by making clear the paper's ultimate interest, being the vehicle by which its readers saw themselves as connected to the homeland, by posing and then answering the question of what Armenians in America might do to help Armenia's industrialization: form societies to build new factories in Armenia. Noting that Armenia had both the finest-quality wool and a population particular gifted in the fine arts, the editorialist wondered why a group of Armenian rug merchants in the diaspora could not take the lead in founding a rug factory in the old country, one that would inevitably produce the most durable and beautiful rugs on the world scene.

7　*Hairenik*, April 30, 1924, 1; December 19, 1923, 1.

8   Hovhannes Mugrditchian, *To Armenians with Love: The Memoirs of a Patriot* (Hobe
     Sound, FL: Paul Mart, 1996), 113–15.
         By the 1930s there was a full-scale Armenian Progressive League, openly
     Bolshevik, claiming its own market share of supporters among the American
     Hayoutiun. George Kooshian, "The Armenian Immigrant Community of California,
     1880–1935" (PhD diss., University of California, Los Angeles, 2002), 331–8.
9   *Hairenik*, May 4, 1924, 1.
10   *Baikar*, May 1, 1924, 1; *Hairenik*, May 4, 1924, 2.
11   Oshagan Minassian, *A History of the Armenian Holy Apostolic Orthodox Church
     in the United States (1888–1944)* (Monterey, CA: Mayreni, 2010), 245–9; *Baikar*,
     May 22, 1927, 2; May 24, 1927, 2; August 18, 1929, 1; *Hairenik*, May 19, 1927;
     August 20, 1929, 4.
12   Christopher Hagop Zakian, ed., *The Torch Was Passed: The Centennial History of the
     Armenian Church of America* (New York: St. Vartan Press, 1998), 26–30.
13   Kooshian, "Armenian Immigrant Community," 413–27; *Nor Or*, October 21, 1932, 4.
14   Gregory Doudoukjian, "Oral History: An Intergenerational Study of the Effects of
     the Assassination of Archbishop Leon Tourian in 1933 on Armenian-Americans"
     (Master of Divinity thesis, St. Vladimir's Orthodox Theological Seminary, Crestwood,
     NY, 1993), 25–27; *Hairenik*, April 30, 1932, 4; *Hairenik Amsakir* (Monthly), May
     1933, 169–70.
15   *Hairenik*, July 2, 1932, 1, 3; August 2, 1932, 4; *Baikar*, August 7, 1932, 2; *Gotchnag*,
     October 8, 1932, 1021; Minassian, *History of the Armenian Holy Apostolic Orthodox
     Church*, 273–75. A book chronicling the career of Archbishop Tourian from a
     decidedly critical, pro-Tashnag view is A. Partizian, *Hay Ekeghets'voy tagnapĕ ev anor
     pataskhanatunerĕ* (Boston: Hairenik Press, 1936).
16   For example *Hairenik*, September 22, 1931, 4.
17   Minassian, *History of the Armenian Holy Apostolic Orthodox Church*, 276–79.
18   Minassian, *History of the Armenian Holy Apostolic Orthodox Church*, 279–80; *Baikar*,
     July 7, 1933, 1, 2; *Hairenik*, July 8, 1933, 1, 2, 4.
19   *Hairenik*, July 11, 1933, 2; *Baikar*, July 12, 1933, 2.
20   *Baikar*, July 19, 1933, 2; *Hairenik*, August 24, 1933, 1.
21   *Hairenik*, August 17, 1933, 4; *Baikar*, August 24, 1933, 2; *Gotchnag*, August 26, 1934,
     797–98; Minassian, *History of the Armenian Holy Apostolic Orthodox Church*, 280–81.
22   *New York Times*, September 5, 1933, 19; *Hairenik*, September 6, 1933, 1; September
     7, 1933, 4; *Baikar*, September 7, 1933, 2; Minassian, *History of the Armenian Holy
     Apostolic Church*, 282–92.
23   *New York Times*, December 25, 1933, 1, 3.
24   *Baikar*, December 28, 1933, 2.
25   *Hairenik*, December 28, 1933, 4.
26   *Armenian Mirror*, January 19, 1934, 1; March 30, 1934, 1; Doudoukjian, "Oral History," 72.
         The split was also felt in Canada's Armenian community. Isabel Kaprielian-
     Churchill, *Like Our Mountains: A History of Armenians in Canada* (Montreal:
     McGill-Queen's University Press, 2005), 308–10.
27   Doudoukjian, "Oral History," 50–54, 79; *Armenian Mirror*, February 1, 1934, 1, 3; Jenny
     Phillips, *Symbol, Myth, and Rhetoric: The Politics of Culture in an Armenian-American
     Population* (New York: AMS Press, 1989), 121–33; *Armenian Spectator*, January 18,
     1934, 1, 4; January 25, 1934, 1, 4; *Armenian Mirror*, February 19, 1934, 1, 3.
28   *Hairenik*, June 17, 1934, 3; June 23, 1934, 4; July 17, 1934, 4; *Baikar*, June 19, 1934, 1;
     June 24, 1934, 2. See also the general coverage in *Hairenik*, *Baikar*, and the *Armenian
     Mirror* between June 8 and July 31, 1934.

29   *New York Times*, July 14, 1934, 1; July 25, 1934, 36; April 10, 1935, 7; Phillips, *Murder at the Altar*, 231–2.
30   *Armenian Mirror-Spectator*, January 25, 1939, 1.
31   *Hairenik Weekly*, March 1, 1934, 3.
32   *Hairenik Weekly*, October 8, 1937, 2.
33   *Hairenik Weekly*, July 10, 1936, 5; March 29, 1935, 3; October 29, 1937, 2. For further thought along these lines, see *Hairenik Weekly*, January 15, 1937, 2.
34   *New York Times*, November 11, 1932, 26.
35   *Hairenik Weekly*, May 13, 1938, 1, 2, 3.
36   *Hairenik Weekly*, May 13, 1938, 2; *Armenian Mirror*, May 18, 1938, 2.
37   A servant of Khoren's later reported having seen possible strangulation marks on Khoren's deceased body. Felix Corey, "The Armenian Church under the Soviet Regime, Part 1: The Leadership of Kevork," *Religion, State & Society* 24, no. 1 (March 1996): 48n7.
38   *Armenian Mirror*, August 19, 1936, 1; May 18, 1938, 2; January 5, 1938, 2; January 25, 1939, 1.

Chapter 4

1   *Armenian Mirror-Spectator*, April 21, 1951, 7; April 28, 1951, 2.
2   Harold Nelson, "The Armenian Family: Changing Patterns of Family Life in a California Community" (PhD diss., University of California, Berkeley, 1953), 179–210. While change was taking place in both the Apostolic and Protestant communities of faith, Nelson's inquiries found, it happened more rapidly among the latter.
3   Some of the information in this chapter was previously published in "'To Supply Armenia with Architects': The Press, the Parties, and the Second Generation in the 1930s," *Journal of the Society for Armenian Studies* 17 (2008): 189–206.
4   Ara Caprielian, "The Armenian Revolutionary Federation: The Politics of a Party in Exile" (PhD diss., New York University, 1975), 187; Arpena S. Mesrobian, *"Like One Family": The Armenians of Syracuse* (Ann Arbor, MI: Gomidas Institute, 2000), 166–7; *The AYF Legacy: Portrait of a Movement in Historical* Review, *1933–1993* (Watertown, MA: Armenian Youth Federation, 1994), 8; *Hairenik*, January 7, 1934, 4; *Hairenik Weekly*, July 10, 1936, 5 (italics in original).
5   *Hairenik Weekly*, October 29, 1937, 2.
6   *Hairenik Weekly*, May 24, 1934, 1 (bold type in original).
7   *Armenian Mirror*, July 8, 1932, 2. For further insight on the connection between the partisan ideology and cultural orientation of the Tashnag and anti-Tashnag factions, see Anny Bakalian, *Armenian-Americans: From Being to Feeling Armenian* (New Brunswick, NJ: Transaction Publishers, 1996), 133–7.
8   *Armenian Mirror*, July 1, 1932, 1 (bold type in original).
9   *Hairenik Weekly*, December 4, 1936, 1; *Armenian Mirror*, January 1, 1935, 1, 2; June 5, 1935, 2; *Hairenik Weekly*, June 5, 1936, 2; June 4, 1937, 1; October 8, 1937, 2.
10   *Hairenik Weekly*, August 7, 1936, 2.
11   *Hairenik Weekly*, August 7, 1936, 2.
12   *Hairenik Weekly*, August 14, 1936, 2.
13   *Hairenik Weekly*, February 1, 1935, 1, 2.
14   *Hairenik Weekly*, January 8, 1937, 2.

15   A general treatment of this phenomenon comes in Stephen Weiss, "Ethnicity and Reform: Minorities and the Ambience of the Depression Years," *Journal of American History* 66 (December 1979): 566–85, and a close-up study of pluralist programs in Detroit is provided by Anne Brophy, "'What of Youth Today?': Social Politics, Cultural Pluralism, and the Construction of Second-Generation Ethnicity in Detroit, 1914–1941" (PhD diss., Cornell University, 1999). Weiss points up the distinction between the positions of Kallen and Adamic: Kallen celebrated distinctiveness, whereas Adamic believed in the eventual, gradual melting pot–style amalgamation of the immigrant groups into a homogenous whole and castigated the hardline Americanizers for impeding rather than assisting this process. Brophy, based on a meticulous combing of archives of numerous civic organizations in Detroit, views programs in the 1930s that promoted ethnic pride for the American-born children of immigrants as part of a lineage of efforts designed, ultimately, to secure the loyalty of immigrants and their progeny to the American nationality. Here, what is most significant is that civic and government movement in the 1930s created a more conducive climate for the stance of Armenian American advocates that their constituents could reasonably see themselves as simultaneously Armenian and American, with the one not coming at the expense or contradiction of the other. See especially Chapters 4 and 5 of Brophy. Reference to Armenian segment on "Americans All—Immigrants All" in *Armenian Mirror-Spectator*, March 8, 1939, 1. See also Louis Adamic, *From Many Lands* (New York: Harper & Brothers, 1939), esp. 132–46, and *A Nation of Nations* (New York: Harper & Brothers, 1944), esp. 1–17.

16   Brophy, "'What of Youth Today?,'" 73, 76–87. A further expression of the pluralist climate of the 1930s, as promoted by the intellectual community, comes from a speech by immigrant historian Marcus Lee Hansen to the Augustana Historical Society in Rock Island, IL, in 1937. While historians have shown the most interest in this speech for its articulation of the "third-generation thesis" and its place in the theoretical literature on immigrant generational patterns, it can also be seen as an expression of the intellectual climate of the times with regard to the value of ethnic identity, the main thrust of the speech having been the desirability of ethnic preservation among the third generation. Peter Kivisto and Dag Blanck, eds., *American Immigrants and Their Generations: Studies and Commentaries on the Hansen Thesis after Fifty Years* (Urbana: University of Illinois Press, 1990), 191–203 (for text of Hansen speech).

17   *Hairenik Weekly*, October 29, 1937, 1, 2. Responses appeared in the weeks that followed.

18   *Hairenik Weekly*, March 8, 1940, 1, 3. Clearly, Mandalian did not expect the Armenian youth in America to live like the Tashnag *fedayees* of czarist Russia and prewar Turkey. He did, however, want them to know about them and feel some connection to them, revolutionary executions and all, as evidenced over two decades later when he published an abridged English translation of revolutionary leader Rouben Der Minasian's memoirs (see Chapter 6).

      On the role of ethnic leaders encouraging Americanness alongside ethnic identity, see Victor R. Greene, *American Immigrant Leaders, 1800–1910: Marginality and Identity* (Baltimore: Johns Hopkins University Press, 1987), 1–16, esp. 13.

19   *Armenian Mirror-Spectator*, February 8, 1940, 2.

20   *Armenian Mirror-Spectator*, February 8, 1939, 5.

21   *Armenian Mirror-Spectator*, February 1, 1939, 2.

22   As at all other points in the chronology, Armenian Americans were asked to
     donate money to Armenian humanitarian causes overseas. In 1939, for example,
     AGBU and the ADL vehemently promoted the Dollar-a-Bushel campaign, to aid
     a growing number of Armenian refugees in Syria. The youth groups of both of
     these organizations were included in the solicitation. *Armenian Mirror-Spectator*,
     February 15, 1939, 1; March 8, 1939, 2.
23   Peter L. Benson and Dorothy Williams, *Religion on Capitol Hill: Myths and Realities*
     (San Francisco: Harper and Row, 1982), 117–19. That this book takes a heavily
     prescriptive tone in places may have played a part in the limited attention it received
     from sociologists of religion.
24   *Armenian Mirror*, June 19, 1935, 2; August 21, 1935, 1, 2.
25   *Armenian Mirror*, February 6, 1935, 1.
26   *Hairenik Weekly*, April 8, 1938, 2.
27   *Hairenik Weekly*, April 8, 1938, 2.
28   *Hairenik Weekly*, April 29, 1938, 2.
29   *Hairenik Weekly*, May 6, 1938, 2. In her memoir, Sonia Meghreblian recalls that,
     while in high school in the 1940s, she rarely received permission to attend evening
     social events. If a male escort was involved, permission was even rarer. Her strict
     father did, however, make an exception for her senior prom in 1948: he held
     back from making a big fuss over the lateness of her return home, a phenomenal
     concession given his predilections. Meghreblian, *An Armenian Odyssey* (London:
     Gomidas Institute, 2012), 57–8.
30   *Armenian Mirror*, July 10, 1935, 2.
31   *Armenian Mirror*, July 17, 1935, 2.
32   *Armenian Mirror*, July 24, 1935, 2.
33   *Armenian Mirror*, July 31, 1935, 2.
34   *Armenian Mirror*, January 8, 1935, 2. An even more explicit version of this language
     comes through in a 1942 editorial by M. Brenon in the merged *Armenian Mirror-
     Spectator*, the main thrust of which was an exhortation to Armenian Americans to
     arrive at events on time. "Is the custom of beginning our affairs almost at the very
     hour they should be over a matter of ancient tradition, or, more or less, a recently
     acquired habit? We believe both elements exist at the root of the evil. For despite
     our being rightfully characterized as the 'occidentals of the Orient,' we could not
     possibly escape the characteristic attitude of the East towards the element of time.
     Yet, after mature deliberation, we are inclined to think that, to a large extent, the
     evil is of comparatively recent origin. At least it is not as deep rooted as some think.
     For no one can say that our fellow Armenians have not been holding their own for
     punctuality in the factories and shops and offices of this land of the stop-watch and
     the time-clock. Mr. Garabedian, for instance, is as prompt in occupying his seat at
     the playhouse as is his neighbor, Mr. Jones; it is only in haigayan [Armenian-related]
     affairs that the former uses all his ingenuity to see or hear the last scene or last
     speaker first and last." *Armenian Mirror-Spectator*, March 4, 1942, 1.

Chapter 5

1   Armenian *Mirror-Spectator*, July 28, 1945, 3. Norehad claimed to have seen the letter
     in the April 6, 1945, edition of *Hairenik Weekly*, but the present author has found
     no such line in extant copies. There is a letter by a serviceman in that issue critical

of John Roy Carlson, but not with any overtly expressed fantasies of killing him.
Presumably, however, Norehad read this line somewhere in print, as he presented it
as a direct quotation.

2   Avedis Derounian papers, esp. Box 23 and Drawer D-3, NAASR, Belmont, MA; John
    Roy Carlson, *Under Cover* (New York: E. P. Dutton & Co., 1943); Barbara Dianne
    Savage, *Broadcasting Freedom: Radio, War, and the Politics of Race, 1938–1948*
    (Chapel Hill: University of North Carolina Press, 1999), 21–62; Diana Selig,
    Americans All: The Cultural Gifts Movement (Cambridge, MA: Harvard University
    Press, 2008), 243–9.

3   Peter Balakian, *Black Dog of Fate* (New York: Basic Books, 2009), 178; Gregory
    Aftandilian, "World War II as an Enhancer of Armenian-American Second
    Generation Identity," *Journal of the Society for Armenian Studies* 18, no. 2 (December
    2009): 37–8; *Hairenik Weekly*, March 29, 1944, 4.

4   *Armenian Mirror-Spectator*, January 6, 1943, 3, 8; January 20, 1943, 1.

5   *Armenian Mirror-Spectator*, June 3, 1942, 1, 5, 8; September 15, 1943, 1; *Hairenik
    Weekly*, March 1, 1944, 1; Sevan Nathaniel Yousefian, "The Postwar Repatriation
    Movement of Armenians to Soviet Armenia, 1945–1948" (PhD diss., University of
    California, Los Angeles, 2011), 120–1.
        The practice of soliciting support from ethnic groups for non-ethnic-specific
    American causes was also shown when the March of Dimes put together a committee
    of Armenian American physicians to help solicit Armenian American money for
    the fight against infantile paralysis. The *Mirror-Spectator* obliged with an editorial
    endorsing the campaign: January 27, 1943, 2.

6   *Armenian Mirror-Spectator*, January 6, 1943, 2; January 13, 1943, 2.

7   *Armenian Mirror-Spectator*, April 22, 1942, 8; May 20, 1942, 8; *Hairenik Weekly*,
    April 15, 1942, 2.

8   *Armenian Mirror Spectator*, January 27, 1943, 2; *Armenian Mirror Spectator*,
    August 4, 1943, 1; *Armenian Mirror Spectator*, September 8, 1943, 2; *Hairenik Weekly*,
    March 31, 1943, 2.

9   *Hairenik*, August 29, 1942, 4; October 4, 1942, 4; *Baikar*, November 1, 1942, 2;
    November 3, 1942, 2; *Armenian Mirror-Spectator*, May 20, 1942, 4.

10 Yves Ternon, *The Armenian Cause* (Delmar, NY: Caravan Books, 1985), 114; *Mirror-
    Spectator*, September 1, 1945, 1–3, quotation on 2; James G. Mandalian, "Dro:
    Drastamat Kanayan (1884–1956)," *Armenian Review* 10 (Summer 1957): 3–14,
    quotation on 12; Levon Thomassian, *Summer of '42: A Study of German-Armenian
    Relations during the Second World War* (Atglen, PA: Schiffer Military History, 2012),
    40, 152, 159–60; Department of State, Office of Research and Intelligence, "Notes on
    Armenian National Aspirations and on the Soviet Claims to the Eastern Provinces of
    Turkey," March 12, 1946, 10–1, quoted in Ronald Grigor Suny, *Looking toward Ararat:
    Armenia in Modern History* (Bloomington: Indiana University Press, 1993), 173.

11 *Armenian Mirror-Spectator*, August 18, 1943, 2; *Armenian Mirror-Spectator*, August
    25, 1943, 1; *Hairenik Weekly*, September 1, 1943, 2 (bold type appears in original).

12 *Hairenik Weekly*, June 21, 1945, 2; June 28, 1945, 1, 4, 5. The corresponding issues
    of the *Mirror-Spectator* were similarly vituperative to the Tashnags, recycling the
    standard memory of Tashnags' collaboration with the Young Turks after the Adana
    Massacres of 1909 and subsequent misdeeds from the First World War era. *Armenian
    Mirror Spectator*, June 23, 1945, 2, 3.

13 *Hairenik*, July 18, 1942, 2; July 19, 1942, 2; July 21, 1942, 2; Felix Corley, "The
    Armenian Church under the Soviet Regime, Part 1: The Leadership of Kevork,"
    Religion, State & Society 24, no. 1 (March 1996): 16.

14   *Hairenik Weekly*, August 30, 1944, 2.

15   Vahe Sahakyan, "Between Host Countries and Homeland: Institutions, Politics and
     Identities in the Post-Genocide Armenian Diaspora (1920s to 1980s)" (PhD diss.,
     University of Michigan, 2015), 272–3. Sahakyan notes that the ARF in the United
     States showed a toning-down of anti-Soviet rhetoric in the 1943 publication of Simon
     Vratsian's pamphlet *Armenia and the Armenian Question* and in the resolutions of its
     1944 deputational meeting in Boston.

16   Thomas G. Paterson, *On Every Front: The Making and Unmaking of the Cold War*
     (New York: W. W. Norton, 1992), 66–7, 152–3; Bruce R. Kuniholm, *The Origins
     of the Cold War in the Near East: Great Power Conflict in Iran, Turkey, and Greece*
     (Princeton, NJ: Princeton University Press, 1980), 53–5, 111–13, 255–70, 359–82;
     Robert O. Krikorian, "Kars-Ardahan and Soviet Armenian Irredentism, 1945–46," in
     Armenian Kars and Ardahan, ed. Richard G. Hovannisian (Costa Mesa, CA: Mazda,
     2011), 393–409; Ternon, *Armenian Cause*, 125–6.

17   *Armenian Mirror-Spectator*, April 21, 1945, 1. The word *genocide* came into existence
     in 1943. See Chapter 8.

18   *New York Times*, May 31, 1947, 2; Hovhannes Mugrditchian, *To Armenians with
     Love: The Memoirs of a Patriot* (Hobe Sound, FL: Paul Mart, 1996), 130–1; *Armenian
     Mirror-Spectator*, April 26, 1947, 1, 2. In later years the Hairenik press would dismiss
     that congress as Communist-dominated and would use Tiran Nersoyan's speech
     at this congress as evidence of his own questionable proclivities. *Hairenik Weekly*,
     September 6, 1956, 2.

19   *Armenian Mirror-Spectator*, June 14, 1947, 1; *New York Times*, June 6, 1947, 7;
     Hairenik Weekly, April 3, 1947, 2; April 10, 1947, 2. In the Cold War years, the
     United States treated Turkey as an important ally in the struggle against Soviet
     expansion. Michael Bobelian discusses the international Armenian irridentist
     campaign and its frustration by Cold War politics in *Children of Armenia: A
     Forgotten Genocide and the Century-Long Struggle for Justice* (New York: Simon &
     Schuster, 2009), 92–105.

20   Charles A. Vertanes, "The Case of the Cholakian Family: A New Phase in the History
     of the Struggle for Religious Freedom in America," *Armenian Affairs* 1 (Winter 1949–
     50), 35–51; Vertanes, "The Cholakian Case to Date," *Armenian Affairs* 1 (Summer
     and Fall 1950): 315–22; Vertanes to Dr. Walter W. Van Kirk, Executive Director of the
     Department of International Justice and Good Will, National Council of Churches,
     June 10, 1954, in Vertanes Papers, folder 87, NAASR; Bishop Tiran quotation in a
     letter addressed to the *New York Times* (but apparently not published) by John Roy
     Carlson, January 5, 1955, in Vertanes Papers, folder 87, NAASR; *New York Times*,
     November 24, 1949, 18; November 30, 1949, 2; *Hairenik Weekly*, January 8, 1948,
     2; April 6, 1950, 1, 8; Edward Minasian, *They Came from Ararat: The Exodus of the
     Armenian People to Armenia* (Lafayette, CA: Big Hat Press, 2018), 197.

21   George Mardikian, *The Song of America* (New York: McGraw-Hill, 1956), 248–75,
     quotation on 251; *Hairenik Weekly*, December 25, 1947, 1; January 8, 1948, 4;
     February 5, 1948, 1; Hratch Zadoian, *Our Brothers' Keepers: The Armenian National
     Committee to Aid Homeless Armenians (ANCHA)* (New York: SIS Publications, 2012),
     18–22.

22   John Roy Carlson, "The Armenian Displaced Persons: A First-Hand Report on
     Conditions in Europe," *Armenian Affairs* 1 (Winter 1949–50): 16–34; Araxie Le
     Vin to Derounian, Box 10, Folder "Council for Immigration and Resettlement of
     Armenians," NAASR.

23   Charles A. Vertanes to Bishop Tiran Nersoyan, November 26, 1949, Charles A.
      Vertanes Papers, Folder 55, NAASR.
24   George Mardikian to Commissioners Gibson, O'Connor, and Rosenfield, January 9,
      1951, Records of the Displaced Persons Commission, 1948–1952, Box 44, ANCHA
      folder, NARA, College Park, MD; Minasian, *They Came from Ararat*, 204.

Chapter 6

1   *Hairenik Weekly*, May 22, 1952, 1.
2   I previously discussed some of the information in this chapter in "The American
     Armenians' Cold War: The Divided Response to Soviet Armenia," in *Anti-Communist
     Minorities in the U.S.: Political Activism of Ethnic Refugees*, ed. Ieva Zake (New York:
     Palgrave-MacMillan, 2009), 67–86.
3   Richard M. Fried, *The Russians Are Coming! The Russians Are Coming! Pageantry and
     Patriotism in Cold-War America* (New York: Oxford University Press, 1998), 67–86;
     David S. Foglesong, *The American Mission and the "Evil Empire": The Crusade for a
     "Free Russia" since 1881* (New York: Cambridge University Press, 2007), 107.
4   Bennett Kovrig, *Of Walls and Bridges: The United States and Eastern Europe*
     (New York: New York University Press, 1991), 32; Scott Lucas, *Freedom's War: The
     American Crusade against the Soviet Union* (New York: New York University Press,
     1999), 66–7, 80–81.
5   Lucas, *Freedom's War*; Foglesong, *American Mission*, 109.
6   Edward Barrett, *Truth Is Our Weapon* (New York: Funk and Wagnalls, 1953), 79.
     A 1952 State Department memorandum observed, "Public controversy now centers
     around the question whether we should pursue the policy of 'roll-back' or the policy
     of 'containment.' Probably successful containment would in fact merge into a policy
     of roll-back by creating opportunities of one kind and another for moving back
     the Iron Curtain. It should be noted that the objectives are the same and that the
     controversy concerns, therefore, means, not ends." *Foreign Relations of the United
     States, 1952–54, National Security Affairs* (Washington, DC: Government Printing
     Office, 1984), 1: 67. By 1955, Eisenhower and others around him had explicitly
     (though mostly privately) disavowed the goal of inducing a regime change in the
     Soviet Union, and U.S.-Soviet relations actually showed more room for dialogue
     and cordiality, to which end the pressure for an aggressive "captive nations"
     stance on behalf of the non-Russian nationalities under Soviet control would be
     counterproductive. Foglesong, *American Mission*, 131.
7   Foglesong, *American Mission*, 127; *New York Times*, August 18, 1951, 1; October
     11, 1951, 30; Jonathan H. L'Homedieu, "Baltic Exiles and the U.S. Congress:
     Investigations and Legacies of the House Select Committee, 1953–1955," *Journal of
     American Ethnic History* 31, no. 2 (Winter 2012): 47; *Hairenik Weekly*, March 6, 1952,
     1. See also Kenneth Osgood, *Total Cold War: Eisenhower's Secret Propaganda Battle at
     Home and Abroad* (Lawrence: University Press of Kansas, 2002), 354.
8   *Hairenik Weekly*, March 6, 1952, 1; April 7, 1955, 1.
         One can find a highly noteworthy element of ethnic anti-Communism in the Cold
     War era by examining Lev Dobriansky's preface to Roman Smal-Stocki's 1960 book *The
     Captive Nations*. Dobriansky recited an exhaustive list of instances in which the U.S.
     government and the private sector had aided the Soviets. In this passage, Dobriansky

made highly significant use of the first person plural: "*our* record in relation to Russia looks almost absurd"; aspects of this absurdity include "*our* material contribution to the material salvation of the Russian Bolshevik regime" through humanitarian aid after the First World War; "the diplomatic negation of *our* atomic monopoly and overwhelming overwhelming air superiority"; "*our* participation in the Geneva Summit Conference"—all of which "almost suggests a bent toward national suicide." He thus let his readers know that, even though he was an émigré and an ethnic leader lobbying for the liberation of his homeland, he could also speak as a patriotic American and lecture his fellow Americans on their lack of resolve, addressing them not as "you" but as "we." Lev Dobriansky, preface to Roman Smal-Stocki, *The Captive Nations* (New Haven, CT: College and University Press, 1960), 10 (emphasis added). Rozmarek similarly linked American patriotism with Polish nationalism in a speech at a National Park Service ceremony naming a park in Washington, DC, for Casimir Pulaski, the Polish national who had fought in the American Revolution; Rozmarek used this occasion to criticize the United Nations for limiting its forces' bombing options in the Korean War and to call upon western nations to cut off aid to any nations that traded with Communist countries. "Trade with the Reds," he told the gathering, "is aid to the Reds." *Washington Post*, October 11, 1954, 8.

9   Reuben Darbinian, "America and the Russian Future," *Armenian Review* 4, no. 2 (Summer 1951): 19 (emphasis in original); Darbinian, "Toward the Policy of an Eye for an Eye," *Armenian Review* 5, no. 1 (Spring 1952): 21; *Hairenik Weekly*, July 30, 1959, 2; August 6, 1959, 2.

10   *Armenian Guardian*, esp. May 1948, 1; "First Annual Assembly of the Armenian Church Youth of America, May 30, May 31, and June 1, 1947, Philadelphia, PA"; Bishop Tiran Nersoyan to ACYOA Central Council Chairman Zaven Housepian; "First Annual Assembly," ACYOA archives, box 1-A, Armenian Apostolic Church of America Eastern Diocese, New York, NY.

11   *Hairenik Weekly*, March 27, 1952, 1; April 17, 1952, 4.

12   *Hairenik Weekly*, April 10, 1952, 2.

13   *Hairenik Weekly*, April 10, 1952, 5.

14   *N. W. Ayer & Son's Directory, Newspapers and Periodicals, 1949* (Philadelphia: N. W. Ayer & Son, 1949).

15   Antranig Chalabian, *Dro (Drastamat Kanayan): Armenia's First Defense Minister of the Modern Era*, trans. Jack Chelabian (Los Angeles: Indo-European Publishing, 2009), 253–4; see also Levon Thomassian, *Summer of '42: A Study of German-Armenian Relations during the Second World War* (Atglen, PA: Schiffer Military History, 2012), 151.

16   E. G. Fitch to D. M. Ladd, Office Memorandum, July 25, 1946, FBI HQ: Investigative Records: Classified Subject Files, Released under the Nazi & Japanese War Crimes Disclosure Acts, Classification 105: Foreign Counterintelligence, Record Group 65, A1 136AB, Box 156, folder "Kanayan, Drastmas," National Archives and Records Administration, College Park, MD (hereafter Dro FBI file, NARA-CP).
       General Sibert also recruited some far more significant figures, including Reinhard Gehlen, a general for the Nazi regime, who provided much intelligence service to the CIA. John Ranelagh, *The Agency: The Rise and Decline of the CIA* (New York: Simon and Schuster, 1986), 91–2.

17   "Second Release of Name Files under the Nazi War Crimes and Japanese Imperial Government Disclosure Acts, 1936–2000 (Security Set)," RG 263, Box 64, NARA, College Park, MD (hereafter Dro CIA file, NARA-CP). The record of the

December 1 interview is in a document written either by or to D. G. Huefner, Chief, Foreign Branch M, December 2, 1948. On US Middle East policy during this time, see H. W. Brands, *Into the Labyrinth: The United States and the Middle East, 1945–1994* (New York: McGraw-Hill, 1994), 17–30.

18 Dro CIA file, NARA-CP.

19 Dro CIA file, NARA-CP.

20 Dro CIA file, NARA-CP; Chalabian, *Dro*, 254.

21 J. Edgar Hoover to Dennis A. Flinn (at State Dept.), November 30, 1955, Dro FBI file, NARA-CP; letter to Hoover from Chief, Division of Near East and Africa (name blotted out), December 22, 1955, Dro CIA file, NARA-CP.

22 *Hairenik Weekly*, March 15, 1956, 1; March 29, 1956, 1; *Armenian Mirror-Spectator*, April 14, 1956, 2.

23 Raymond H. Kévorkian and Vahé Tachjian, eds., *The Armenian General Benevolent Union—One Hundred Years of History* (New York: AGBU, 2006), 2: 298.

24 Hovhannes Mugrditchian, *To Armenians with Love: The Memoirs of a Patriot* (Hobe Sound, FL: Paul Mart, 1996), 135–7; Sonia Meghreblian, *An Armenian Odyssey* (London: Gomidas Institute, 2012), 64. The Mugrditchians had their unpleasant surprises in Armenia, but their overall experience was not nearly as horrific as those of others, and their return to the United States in 1963 was not the kind of desperate rout that others went through.

25 Sevan Nathaniel Yousefian, "The Postwar Repatriation Movement of Armenians to Soviet Armenia, 1945–1948" (PhD diss., University of California, Los Angeles, 2011), 113–17; Yousefian, "Picnics for Patriots: The Transnational Activism of an Armenian Hometown Association," *Journal of American Ethnic History* 34, no. 1 (2014): 31–52; *Hairenik Weekly*, April 18, 1946, 2; July 25, 1946, 2; September 12, 1946, 2.

    Yousefian, unlike Felix Corley, emphasizes the efforts of diasporan groups and of Soviet Armenian officials in Yerevan in persuading Stalin to see the interests of the Soviet state as being well served by allowing Armenians to repatriate, which would fulfill Armenian dreams of returning to their homeland. Yousefian cites correspondence from Yerevan to Moscow making this pitch, with Stalin's acquiescence coming after. However, even if Stalin was influenced by these pleadings, the overall scenario was one, not of Armenians achieving a favorable policy by lobbying for it, but rather of their walking into a trap.

26 Meghreblian, *Armenian Odyssey*, 67–72.

27 Corley, "Armenian Church under the Soviet Regime, Part 1," 35–36; *New York Times*, March 14, 1948, 25; James G. Mandalian, "The 151 Repatriates from America," *Armenian Review* 4, no. 1 (Spring 1951): 93–4.

28 Mandalian, "151 Repatriates"; Jo Laycock, "Armenian Homelands and Homecomings, 1945–49: The Repatriation of Diaspora Armenians to the Soviet Union," *Cultural and Social History* 9, no. 1 (2012): 103–23; Meghreblian, *Armenian Odyssey*, 86.

29 Appeal to President Eisenhower, June 7, 1956, Bureau of European Affairs, Office of Soviet Union Affairs, Bilateral Political Relations Section, Bilateral Political Relations Subject Files, 1921–1973 Box 5, Folder "Armenians, 1415(e)—Armenians, 1947–1963," RG 59, NARA, College Park, MD.

30 Harry G. Barnes, Jr. to Harry Grossman, June 21, 1961, and June 27, 1961, Folder "Armenians, 1415(e)—Armenians, 1964–1968," RG 59, NARA, College Park, MD.

31 Virginia James to Dexter Anderson, August 26, 1965, Folder "Armenians, 1415(e)—Armenians, 1964–1968," RG 59, NARA, College Park, MD.

For further repatriate experiences, see Tom Mooradian, *The Repatriate: Love, Basketball, and the KGB* (Seattle: Moreradiant Publishing, 2008).

32 *Hairenik Weekly*, June 26, 1952, 1; July 10, 1952, 1; February 23, 1953, 1; February 24, 1955, 1.

33 *Armenian Mirror-Spectator*, December 25, 1948, 1, 3; December 6, 1952, 1. Dr. Johnson was, indeed, the author of an apologia for Communism. Hewlett Johnson, *The Soviet Power* (New York: Modern Age Books, 1940). Archbishop Nersoyan's controversial booklet *A Christian Approach to Communism*, published three years after Johnson's book, is discussed in Chapter 7.

34 *Armenian Mirror-Spectator*, December 13, 1952, 2. Non-Tashnag celebration of November 29 was by no means unanimous. In the same 1952 issue of the *Mirror Spectator* that reprinted the *Baikar* editorial, there appeared a letter expressing an alternate view, written by the brother of John Roy Carlson. Steven Derounian, who had just been elected to the House of Representatives by New York's second district, wrote, "For 32 years now, Armenia has been under the heel of Soviet tyranny .... It is inconceivable that any Armenian living in a free country today should rejoice that the people of Armenia are subjugated to the cruel and inhuman rule of the Communist tyrant." Shortly after, the *Mirror-Spectator* printed a letter from Iris Stephanie Noorian, concurring with Derounian. December 13, 1952, 2; January 10, 1953, 2.

35 "Church in People's Democracies" (typewritten manuscript), Vertanes Papers, Box 6, Folder 49, NAASR. Vertanes is something of an enigma. Large portions of his career appear to have been neither political nor particularly Armenian-centered. According to in-house historical records of the Presbyterian Church of Sweet Hollow on Long Island, New York, Vertanes, while living on Long Island, casually came upon this church, not Armenian in its membership, learned that it needed a pastor but could not afford to pay a salary, and did the job on a volunteer basis for several years. Email to author from William T. Walker, Elder, Presbyterian Church of Sweet Hollow, August 22, 2010.

36 *Armenian Mirror-Spectator*, March 10, 1951, 1; *Hairenik Weekly*, April 12, 1951, 2; Reuben Darbinian, "In Retrospect: A Glance at the Past Thirty Years," *Armenian Review* 6, no. 3 (Autumn 1953): 49–65.

Vertanes's papers at NAASR include some vigorous notes objecting to the British government's having blocked that conference from happening in Sheffield and Prime Minister Clement Attlee's dismissal of the event as Soviet-inspired. "But did Hitler and Goebbels start a peace movement in Germany?" he writes. "How can the leaders of a state afford to pound into the heads and hearts of their people a passion for peace when they are really preparing for aggressive war?"

37 As an example of this pattern, the Tashnag press applauded *Chicago Tribune* contributor John T. Flynn in his feud with Avedis Derounian (John Roy Carlson). Flynn was both a Cold War hawk and a virulent critic of the New Deal and of FDR personally. See *Hairenik Weekly*, March 15, 1945, 4; February 6, 1947, 5; January 8, 1948, 4. For Flynn's views on FDR, see John T. Flynn, *The Roosevelt Myth* (New York: Devon-Adair, 1956). See also Michele Flynn Stenehjem, *An American First: John T. Flynn and the America First Committee* (New Rochelle: Arlington House, 1976).

38 *Hairenik Weekly*, July 12, 1951, 4.

39 *New York Times*, June 25, 1955, 7; Reuben Darbinian, "The Ramgavars before the Tribunal of Public Opinion," *Armenian Review* 8, no. 3 (Autumn/September 1955): 5–6, 11, and passim.

40 Varoujan Samuelian (editor of *Mirror-Spectator*) to Avedis Derounian, July 13, 1955, August 9, 1955, and other dates, Derounian Papers, NAASR, Box 10, Folder "Correspondence Misc"; "Internal Security Subcommittee of the Senate Judiciary Committee, 1951-1975," Subject Files, Box 120, RG 46, NARA, Washington, DC.

41 Raymond Pearson, *The Rise and Fall of the Soviet Empire* (New York: St. Martin's Press, 1998), 33–8, 46–52. For American policy toward Tito's Yugoslavia, see Lorraine M. Lees, *Keeping Tito Afloat: The United States, Yugoslavia, and the Cold War* (University Park: Pennsylvania State University Press, 1998). Khrushchev's "Crimes of Stalin" speech had more to do with positioning himself on the winning side for the present and future than with any actual moral revulsion at the earlier actions. Khrushchev had actively participated in the party purges of the 1930s, and his speech was narrowly tailored so as not to raise exaggerated hopes of a new age of moderation. Robert Service, *A History of Modern Russia from Nicholas II to Vladimir Putin*, 3rd ed. (Cambridge, MA: Harvard University Press, 2009), 338–42.

42 Charles Gati, *Failed Illusions: Moscow, Washington, Budapest, and the 1956 Hungarian Revolt* (Washington, DC: Woodrow Wilson Center Press, 2006); Pearson, *Rise and Fall of the Soviet Empire*, 45–64; Johanna Granville, "'Caught with Jam on Our Fingers': Radio Free Europe and the Hungarian Revolution of 1956," *Diplomatic History* 29, no. 5 (November 2005): 811–40; *New York Times*, November 5, 1956, 1; November 14, 1956, 34.

43 *Hairenik Weekly*, November 1, 1956, 1, 2.

44 *New York Times*, January 5, 1959, 1, 8.

45 *Hairenik Weekly*, January 15, 1959, 1, 2, 4; *Hairenik Weekly*, January 22, 1959, 1, 6; January 29, 1959, 2, 3; February 5, 1959, 1, 4, 5; February 12, 1959, 2.

Chapter 7

1 Tiran Nersoyan, *A Christian Approach to Communism: Ideological Similarities between Dialectical Materialism and Christian Philosophy* (London: Frederick Muller, 1942), esp. 13–18, 22–6, 30–2.

2 Felix Corley, "The Armenian Church under the Soviet Regime, Part 1: The Leadership of Kevork," *Religion, State & Society* 24, no. 1 (March 1996): 10, 34, 48n7.

3 Nickolas Lupinin, "The Russian Orthodox Church," in *Eastern Christianity and the Cold War, 1945–91*, ed. Lucian N. Leustean (London: Routledge, 2010), 20–1; Corley, "Armenian Church under the Soviet Regime, Part 1," 10–15; Corley, "The Armenian Apostolic Church," in Leustean, *Eastern Christianity*, 190–1.

4 Corley, "Armenian Church under the Soviet Regime, Part 1," 32–4.

5 Corley, "Armenian Church under the Soviet Regime, Part 1," 10–16, 34.

6 Corley, "The Armenian Church under the Soviet Regime, Part 2: The Leadership of Vazgen," *Religion, State and Society* 24, no. 4 (December 1996): 289–94.

7 *Armenian Mirror-Spectator*, October 15, 1955, 1, 4; Dickran Boyajian, *A Light through the Iron Curtain* (New York: Vantage Press, 1958), esp. 29–30, 50–4, 58–64 (emphasis in original).
  After nearly two decades of relative religious toleration—within tightly drawn limits, to be sure—another harsh crackdown came in 1959 under the reputedly more moderate leader Nikita Khrushchev. Restrictions and persecutions lightened again

in 1964 when Khrushchev died and Leonid Brezhnev succeeded him, and then eased up further in 1975 when the Soviet Union became a signatory to the Helsinki Human Rights Accords. Nothing, of course, altered the fact that the Soviet state officially espoused and promoted atheism and always seriously limited the activities of churches. Lupinin, "Russian Orthodox Church." See also Lucian N. Leustean's introduction to that same edited volume, "Eastern Christianity and the Cold War: An Overview," in Leustean, *Eastern Christianity*, 1–15.

8   *Armenian Mirror-Spectator*, October 15, 1955, 4; *Hairenik Weekly*, October 20, 1955, 2.

9   Dickran Karnick Kouymjian, "The Recent Crisis in the Armenian Church" (MA thesis, American University of Beirut, 1961), 21–3. For the confessional structure of politics in twentieth-century Lebanon, see Nikola Bagrad Schahgaldian, "The Political Integration of an Immigrant Community into a Composite Society: The Armenians in Lebanon, 1920–1974" (PhD diss., Columbia University, 1979), esp. 116–51. For where Armenian party politics fit in, see Schahgaldian, and also Tsolin Nalbantian, "Fashioning Armenians in Lebanon, 1946–1958" (PhD diss., Columbia University, 2011); for effects of repatriation, see Nalbantian, 115–16.

10 Reuben Darbinian, "In Retrospect: A Glance at the Last Thirty Years," *Armenian Review* 6, no. 3 (Autumn 1953): 62.

11 Sarkis Atamian, *The Armenian Community: The Historical Development of a Social and Ideological Conflict* (New York: Philosophical Library,1955), 440–1; Kouymjian, "Recent Crisis," 27–9; *Hairenik Weekly*, October 24, 1955, 4; *Armenian Mirror-Spectator*, March 3, 1956, 1.

12 *Hairenik Weekly*, October 24, 1955, 4; Kouymjian, "Recent Crisis," 34–9.

13 Kouymjian, "Recent Crisis," 39–44.

14 Kouyjmian, "Recent Crisis," 44–8.

15 Kouymjian, "Recent Crisis," 48–53.

16 *Hairenik Weekly*, March 8, 1956, 3; *New York Times*, February 18, 1956, 11; February 21, 1956, 12; Kouymjian, "Recent Crisis," 53–60; Nicola Migliorino, *(Re)constructing Armenia in Lebanon and Syria: Ethno-Cultural Diversity and the State in the Aftermath of a Refugee Crisis* (New York: Berghahn Books, 2008), 101; Nalbantian, "Fashioning Armenians in Lebanon," 123–4.

17 Kouymjian, "Recent Crisis," 53, 61–79.

18 Kouymjian, "Recent Crisis," 79–89; *Armenian Mirror-Spectator*, April 14, 1956, 2; Ara Sanjian, "The British Foreign Office, the Church of England and the Crisis at the Armenian Church in Antelias, 1956–1963" (paper presented at Armenian Studies at a Threshold, Society for Armenian Studies 35th Anniversary Conference, University of California, Los Angeles, March 26–8, 2009), 3. I thank Prof. Sanjian for sharing that paper with me.

19 *Hairenik Weekly*, April 5, 1956, 1; July 18, 1957, 4; *Armenian Mirror Spectator*, April 14, 1956, 2; Nalbantian, "Fashioning Armenians in Lebanon," 134–41.

20 Sanjian, "British Foreign Office," 5–6; *New York Times*, February 15, 1956, 6; March 14, 1956, 32.

21 Reuben Darbinian, "The Armenian Church Break," *Armenian Review* 10, no. 4 (Winter 1957): 3–16; *Crisis in the Armenian Church: Text of a Memorandum to the National Council of the Churches of Christ in the United States of America on the Dissident Armenian Church in America* (Boston: Central Diocesan Board, Armenian National Apostolic Church of America, 1958), quotation from 10 (emphasis in original); Bedros Norehad, *The Armenian Church and Its "Defenders"*

(New York: Gotchnag Press, 1958); *Armenian Mirror-Spectator*, April 27, 1968, 2; May 25, 1968, 2; Darbinian, "Armenian Church Break."

22 For example, *Armenian Mirror-Spectator*, January 2, 1960, 3; June 27, 1964, 3; February 15, 1969, 2; *Hairenik Weekly*, May 19, 1960, 8; April 4, 1963, 2.

23 *New York Times*, January 5, 1960, 3; June 7, 1960, 35; *Hairenik Weekly*, January 21, 1960, 1. The case itself, as finally resolved, was *Kreshig et al v. Saint Nicholas Cathedral of the Russian Orthodox Church of North America*, 363 U.S. 190 (1960).

24 *New York Times*, September 3, 1989, 44 (obituary); *Hairenik Weekly*, January 7, 1960, 1, 4.

25 Ara Sanjian, "The Armenian Church and Community of Jerusalem," in *The Christian Communities of Jerusalem and the Holy Land: Studies in History, Religion and Politics*, ed. Anthony O'Mahoney (Cardiff: University of Wales Press, 2003), 71–84; *Hairenik Weekly*, January 7, 1960, 2; January 14, 1960, 1; January 28, 1960, 1; February 4, 1960, 1, 4, 5; February 11, 1960, 1, 2; February 18, 1960, 2.

26 Schahgaldian, "Political Integration of an Immigrant Community," 220–1.

27 Michael Bobelian, *Children of Armenia: A Forgotten Genocide and the Century-Long Struggle for Justice* (New York: Simon and Schuster, 2009), esp. 107–20.

Chapter 8

1 Leon Z. Surmelian, *I Ask You, Ladies and Gentlemen* (New York: E. P. Dutton, 1945), esp. 305–11.

2 Interviews conducted by the author with Dr. Martin Deranian, October 26, 2002; Noubar Dorian, October 19, 2002; and Fr. Krikor Maksoudian, October 21, 2002; Christopher Hagop Zakian, *The Torch Was Passed: The Centennial History of the Armenian Church of America* (New York: St. Vartan Press, 1998), 274–95; Program of the Diamond Jubilee Banquet Commemorating the Seventy-fifth Anniversary of the First Armenian Church, October 22, 1967, in folder "First Armenian Church—Belmont, MA, 1959–1975," NAASR archives, Belmont, MA. See also Anthony P. Mezoian, *The Armenian People of Portland, Maine* (Durham, NH: National Materials Development Center, 1985), 25; and Arshag Merguerian, "A Century of Church Buildings as Expressions of the Armenian Diaspora," in *The Armenians of New England*, ed. Marc A. Mamigonian (Belmont, MA: Armenian Heritage Press/NAASR, 2004), 160; Vahram Shemmassian, "The Experience of Musa Dagh Armenian Immigrants in the United States during the 1910s–1940s," *Haigazian Armenological Review* 31 (2011): 199.

3 *Armenian Mirror-Spectator*, January 25, 1939, 4.

4 Harold Nelson, "The Armenian Family: Changing Patterns of Family Life in a California Community" (PhD diss., University of California, Berkeley, 1953), 112–19; Nelson, "Armenian Family," 723; Mary Bosworth Treudley, "An Ethnic Group's View of the American Middle Class," *American Sociological Review* 11, no. 6 (February 1949): 717–23.

5 *Armenian Mirror-Spectator*, July 29, 1950, 2; *Armenian Mirror-Spectator*, April 30, 1949, 2 (*Nor Or* editorial reprint); *Hairenik Weekly*, March 17, 1949, 2.

6 *Armenian Mirror-Spectator*, July 7, 1951, 3; Diana Alexanian Jalelian, "To O'Hara House with Love," *Ararat* 43 (Summer 2003): 11–15; Anna Khederian Azizian, "Where Else but Asbury?," *Ararat* 43 (Summer 2003): 16–19.

7   Arnold Rosner, "An Analytical Survey of the Music of Alan Hovhaness" (PhD
     diss., State University of New York at Buffalo, 1972), 7–10. See also Şahan Arzruni,
     "Alan Hovhaness: The Wellspring of His Music," *Journal of Armenian Studies* 3
     (Winter 1986–87): 157–60. For a time, Hovhaness was the organist at St. James
     Armenian Church in Watertown. Khachadoor Pilibosian with Helene Pilibosian,
     They Called Me Mustafa (Watertown, MA: Ohan Press, 1992), 61.

8   *Armenian Mirror-Spectator*, February 16, 1946, 5; March 2, 1946, 2 (Balakian piece).
     Hairenik Weekly, March 14, 1946, 5. More detail, as well as praise, of Hovhannes can
     be found in *Armenian Mirror-Spectator*, March 24, 1951, 4.

9   *Armenian Mirror-Spectator*, March 2, 1946, 1; interview with Anahid Ajemian by the
     author, August 7, 2002.

10   Marjorie Housepian, *A Houseful of Love* (New York: Random House, 1954), esp.
     124, 125.

11   William Saroyan, *Here Comes, There Goes, You Know Who* (New York: Simon
     and Schuster, 1961); Margaret Bedrosian, *The Magical Pine Ring: Culture and the
     Imagination in Armenian-American Literature* (Detroit: Wayne State University Press,
     1991), 142–59; Dickran Kouymjian, "William Saroyan and the Armenian Ethnic
     Experience in America," *Journal of Armenian Studies* 3 (Winter 1986–87): 161–74;
     David Stephen Calonne, "William Saroyan and Massachusetts," in Mamigonian,
     Armenians of New England, 59–67; Robert Mirak, "Armenians," in *Harvard
     Encyclopedia of American Ethnic Groups* (Cambridge, MA: Harvard University Press,
     1980), 148.

12   *New York Times*, June 27, 1945, 17.

13   John Cooper, *Raphael Lemkin and the Struggle for the Genocide Convention*
     (Basingstoke, UK: Palgrave Macmillan, 2008), 56–75; Steven Leonard Jacobs, "'The
     Journey of Death': Lemkin and the Armenian Genocide," *Journal of the Society for
     Armenian Studies* 17 (2008): 7–18; *New York Times*, January 21, 1945, 102.

14   "Convention on the Prevention and Punishment of the Crime of Genocide" (1948),
     United Nations Office on Genocide Prevention and the Responsibility to Protect,
     https://www.un.org/en/genocideprevention/genocide.shtml.

15   *The Genocide Convention: Hearings before a Subcommittee of the Committee on
     Foreign Relations, United States Senate, Eighty-First Congress, Second Session, on
     Executive O, the International Convention on the Prevention and Punishment of the
     Crime of Genocide, January 23, 24, 25, and February 9, 1950* (Washington, DC:
     Government Printing Office, 1950, hereafter *Genocide Convention Hearings*), 106, 78,
     98. The reference to migratory birds is explained later in the chapter.

16   See, for example, the testimony of Jacob Blaustein, president of the American Jewish
     Committee, on Soviet aggressions against ethnic groups. *Genocide Convention
     Hearings*, 85–97. See also J. Otto Pohl, *Ethnic Cleansing in the USSR, 1937–1949*
     (Westport, CT: Greenwood Press, 1999), and Norman M. Naimark, *Stalin's Genocides*
     (Princeton, NJ: Princeton University Press, 2010).

17   *Genocide Convention Hearings*, 549.

18   *Genocide Convention Hearings*, 552.

19   *Genocide Convention Hearings*, 31–2, 46, 199–200.

20   *Genocide Convention Hearings*, 131, 262. Persons fearful of ratifying the Genocide
     Convention might not have found the statement of the Armenian National Council
     of America, of which Rev. Vertanes was probably the principal author, reassuring.
     "No death in a race riot would be an international crime (though perhaps it should
     be) unless it was part of a deliberate attempt to destroy the race." A later portion

reads, "Nowhere [in the arguments that ratification would put the United States in a vulnerable position internationally] is there an admission that the United States might ever be mistaken; nowhere any indication of a willingness to submit to any judicial procedures where we are not in complete command; nowhere, certainly, (and unfortunately), any glimmer of a realization that if we are ever to have world peace, we should without a doubt be prepared to submit to international legal procedures established and agreed to in advance without knowing what the outcome in specific instances will be; and nowhere any idea that we should be willing to change our laws, if necessary, to harmonize with the will of the international community." *Genocide Convention Hearings*, 553–4.

21 *New York Times*, April 13, 1950, 5; August 20, 1950, 17; June 11, 1953, 28.
22 Shemmassian, "Experience of Musa Dagh Armenian Immigrants," 212–13.
23 Gregory Doudoukjian, "Oral History: An Intergenerational Study of the Effects of the Assassination of Archbishop Leon Tourian in 1933 on Armenian-Americans" (Master of Divinity thesis, St. Vladimir's Orthodox Theological Seminary, Crestwood, NY, 1993), 39.

The catchphrase "naming and claiming" appears in the title of Winona LaDuke's *Recovering the Sacred: The Power of Naming and Claiming* (Cambridge, MA: South End Press, 2005), which deals with a Native American community in California and its campaigns for preservation of sacred sites. The term is also used in clinical contexts, in connection with survivors of every kind of trauma. While I honestly do not remember whether I had been exposed to the phrase before I thought of using it in the title of this chapter, I do believe that I am using it in a manner consistent with its usage in these other places.

24 *Hairenik Weekly*, November 7, 1963, 1; *Armenian Mirror-Spectator*, December 7, 1963, 2.
25 *Armenian Mirror-Spectator*, April 18, 1964, 1.
26 *Armenian Mirror-Spectator*, November 21, 1964, 2; January 16, 1965, 2; January 23, 1965, 3.
27 *Hairenik Weekly*, April 23, 1964, 2; *Armenian Mirror-Spectator*, April 11, 1964, 2.
28 Frederick G. Dutton to Adam C. Powell, May 11, 1964, U.S. State Department papers, Box 5, Folder "1415(e)—Armenians, 1964–1968," RG 59, National Archives and Records Administration, College Park, MD (NARA-CP); *Hairenik Weekly*, April 22, 1965, 5; *Armenian Mirror-Spectator*, January 30, 1965, 1 (bold type in original).
29 *Hairenik Weekly*, April 15, 1965, 2; April 22, 1965, 3; April 29, 1965, 3, 1; *Armenian Mirror-Spectator*, April 10, 1965, 1; April 17, 1965, 1; Michael Bobelian, *Children of Armenia: A Forgotten Genocide and the Century-Long Struggle for Justice* (New York: Simon and Schuster, 2009), 125–6.
30 Claudia Der-Martirosian, "Armenians in the 1980, 1990, and 2000 U.S. Census," *Journal of the Society for Armenian Studies* 17 (2008): 130–2.
31 *Armenian Reporter*, May 18, 1978, 2; Ingrid Poschmann O'Grady, "Ararat, Etchmiadzin, and Haig (Nation, Church, and Kin): A Study of the Symbol System of American Armenians" (PhD diss., Catholic University, 1979), 155–57; Vahe Sahakyan, "Between Host Countries and Homeland: Institutions, Politics and Identities in the Post-Genocide Armenian Diaspora (1920s to 1980s)" (PhD diss., University of Michigan, 2015), 398. Sahakyan also posts an important reminder about the dangers of overgeneralizing these patterns. "Certainly, not all the Middle Eastern Armenians were actively involved in the organizations marginalizing the American-born Armenians, and certainly, not all American-born Armenians felt

resentment in their encounters with the Middle Eastern Armenians. Yet these generalizations and stereotyping were further reinforced, as the Middle Eastern Armenians became more visible within Armenian political organizations, the Prelacy churches and schools, and became more pro-active in dictating a new 'standard' of Armenianness." Sahakyan, 407. See also Armen Gavakian, "Homeland, Diaspora and Nationalism: The Reimagination of Armenian-American Identity since Gorbachev" (PhD diss., University of Sidney, 1997), 170–1.

32 *Armenian Reporter*, May 18, 1978, 2, 4. Writing in the mid-1980s, scholar Harold Takooshian observed that the old-line Armenian Americans had a full spectrum of attitudes toward the new immigrants, encompassing both hostility and a welcoming of "new blood." Harold Takooshian, "Armenian Immigration to the United States from the Middle East," *Journal of Armenian Studies* 3, nos. 1–2 (1986–87): 146–7.

33 Gaïdz Minassian, *Guerre et terrorisme arméniens* (Paris: Presses Universitaires de France, 2002), 22–9; Ara Sanjian, "Limits of Conflict and Consensus among Lebanese-Armenian Political Factions in the Early 21st Century" (paper presented at International Conference on the Armenian Diaspora, Boston University, February 13–14, 2010), 5.

34 Suha Bolukbasi, *The Superpowers and the Third World: Turkish-American Relations and Cyprus* (Lanham, MD: University Press of America, 1988), 167–226; Ellen B. Laipson, "Cyprus: A Quarter Century of U.S. Policy," in *Cyprus in Transition, 1960–1985*, ed. John T. A. Koumoulides (London: Trigraph, 1986), 68–76.

35 *Armenian Weekly*, October 24, 1974, 2; *New York Times*, October 18, 1974, 1; *Armenian Mirror-Spectator*, March 16, 1974, 2.

36 For example, *Armenian Weekly*, February 6, 1975, 7.

37 *Armenian Reporter*, November 28, 1974, 3. See also *Armenian Mirror-Spectator*, May 29, 1976, 2.

38 *Armenian Weekly*, January 30, 1975, 2. Another such letter, as if part of a campaign, appeared the following week. *Armenian Weekly*, February 6, 1975, 2.

39 *Armenian Reporter*, May 4, 1972, 3; May 18, 1972, 3.

40 *Armenian Mirror-Spectator*, September 28, 1974, 1; *Armenian Weekly*, January 30, 1975, 2.

41 Sahakyan, "Between Host-Countries and Homeland," 355; Jenny Phillips, *Symbol, Myth and Rhetoric: The Politics of Culture in an Armenian-American Population* (New York: AMS Press, 1989), 174–75; *New York Times*, April 24, 1975, 37. Phillips notes that not all individuals in the marches abided by the no-flag rule.

42 Bobelian, *Children of Armenia*, 127–33; *Asbarez*, May 7, 1971, 3.

43 *Asbarez*, May 21, 1921, 3; Bobelian, *Children of Armenia*, 138, 139, 271n60; Gerard Libaridian, email to the author, September 2, 2022.

44 *Armenian Mirror-Spectator*, August 12, 1972, 1; *The Armenian Assembly Summary Report: First National Convocation, Airlie, Virginia, May 5–7, 1972, and Regional Assemblies, 1972–1973: Fresno, Los Angeles, Boston, Detroit, New York, Washington, D.C.* (Washington, DC: Armenian Assembly, 1973); *Armenian Mirror-Spectator*, May 20, 1972, 5; October 12, 1974, 1; interviews by the author with Gerard Libaridian, July 3, 2015, Rouben Adalian, December 1, 2015, Harold Takooshian, February 29, 2016, and Dennis Papazian, March 8, 2016.

45 *New York Times*, March 30, 1974, 30; August 13, 1974, 11; *Armenian Mirror-Spectator*, September 28, 1974, 1; Yves Ternon, *The Armenian Cause*, trans. Anahid Apelian Mangouni (Delmar, NY: Caravan Books, 1985), 178–79.

46 *New York Times*, February 7, 1974, 2; *Armenian Mirror-Spectator*, April 27, 1974, 1, 2.

47 Bobelian, *Children of Armenia*, 168; *Washington Post*, April 12, 1975, A2; Dennis R. Papazian, interview by the author, March 8, 2016.

48 *Armenian Mirror-Spectator*, May 22, 1976, 1, 3; *Investigation into Certain Past Instances of Genocide and Exploration of Public Options for the Future: Hearings before the Subcommittee on Future Foreign Policy Research and Development of the Committee on International Relations, House of Representatives, Ninety-Fourth Congress, Second Session* (Washington, DC: U.S. Government Printing Office, 1976), 4, 22–3, 41–4.

49 *Los Angeles Times*, January 28, 1973, 20; Bobelian, *Children of Armenia*, 144–63.

50 Sahakian, "Between Host-Countries and Homeland," 357–60; Laura Dugan, Julie Y. Huang, Gary LaFree, and Clark McCauley, "Sudden Desistance from Terrorism: The Armenian Secret Army for the Liberation of Armenia and the Justice Commandos of the Armenian Genocide," *Dynamics of Asymmetric Conflict* 1, no. 3 (November 2008): 233, 235. See also, with caution: Michael M. Gunter, "*Pursuing the Just Cause of Their People*": *A Study of Contemporary Armenian Terrorism* (New York: Greenwood Press, 1986); Francis P. Hyland, *Armenian Terrorism: The Past, the Present, the Prospects* (Boulder, CO: Westview Press, 1991); and Christopher Gunn, "Secret Armies and Revolutionary Federations: The Rise and Fall of Armenian Political Violence, 1973–1993" (PhD diss., Florida State University, 2014).

51 Markar Melkonian, with Seta Melkonian, *My Brother's Road: An American's Fateful Journey to Armenia* (London: I.B. Tauris, 2005), Athens incident on 84. Melkonian tells his own story in *A Self-Criticism*, trans. Seta Melkonian, ed. Gregory Topalian (London: Gomidas Institute, 2010, published posthumously).

52 Melkonian, *My Brother's Road*, 97–8; Bobelian, *Children of Armenia*, 159–62; *New York Times*, September 25, 1981, A1; July 31, 1983, 17.

53 *Armenian Weekly*, January 14, 1984, 1, 6, 7 (advertisement); February 11, 1984, 6, 7, 9.

54 *Armenian Mirror-Spectator*, August 13, 1983, 2.

55 *Armenian Mirror-Spectator*, April 13, 1985, 1, 3; Bobelian, *Children of Armenia*, 169–70.

56 Dugan et al., "Sudden Desistance from Terrorism"; Gerard Libaridian, email to the author, September 2, 2022.

57 Vartan Matiossian, *The Politics of Naming the Armenian Genocide: Language, History and "Medz Yeghern"* (London: I.B. Tauris, 2022), 113–16; *New York Times*, April 24, 2009, A10; *Armenian Weekly* (online), April 24, 2009, https://armenianweekly.com/2009/04/24/statement-of-president-barack-obama-on-armenian-remembrance-day/.

58 Matiossian, *Politics of Naming the Armenian Genocide*, esp. 117–18. *Asbarez* ran the headline "Obama Refuses to Recognize the Armenian Genocide," which elicited a letter to the editor with essentially the same suggestion as the present writer offers here.

59 "Statement by President Joe Biden on Armenian Remembrance Day," April 24, 2021, https://www.whitehouse.gov/briefing-room/statements-releases/2021/04/24/statement-by-president-joe-biden-on-armenian-remembrance-day/; Kevin Derby, "Gus Bilirakis Wants U.S. Schools to Teach about the Armenian Genocide," *Florida Daily* (online), April 25, 2022, https://www.floridadaily.com/gus-bilirakis-wants-u-s-schools-to-teach-about-the-armenian-genocide/.

60 Michael J. Bazyler and Rajika L. Shah, "The Unfinished Business of the Armenian Genocide: Armenian Property Restitution in American Courts," *Southwestern Journal of International Law* 23 (2017): 223–78.

Epilogue

1   Abraham Ascher, *Russia: A Short History*, revised ed. (London: Oneworld, 2017), 241–50.

2   Thomas de Waal, *Black Garden: Armenia and Azerbaijan through Peace and War*, revised ed. (New York: NYU Press, 2013), 23; Gerard J. Libaridian, *Modern Armenia: People, Nation, State* (New Brunswick, NJ: Transaction Publishers, 2004), 205.

3   de Waal, *Black Garden*, 8–12; Marina Kurkchiyan, "The Karabagh Conflict: From Soviet Past to Post-Soviet Uncertainty," in *The Armenians: Past and Present in the Making of National Identity*, ed. Edmund Herzig and Marina Kurkchiyan (London: RoutledgeCurzon, 2005), 147–8. See also Levon Chorbajian, ed., *The Making of Nagorno-Karabagh: From Secession to Republic* (New York: Palgrave, 2001).

4   *Armenian Reporter*, March 3, 1988, 1, 2, 20, 21; March 10, 1988, 2; March 1, 1988, 1, 18.

5   Ohannes Geukjian, *Ethnicity, Nationalism and Conflict in the South Caucasus: Nagorno-Karabakh and the Legacy of Soviet Nationalities Policy* (Farnham, Surrey: Ashgate, 2012), 134–51; Ronald Grigor Suny, "Soviet Armenia," in *Armenian People from Ancient to Modern Times* (New York: St. Martin's Press, 2004), 2:379–80; de Waal, *Black Garden*, 13–16; Nora Dudwick, "Armenia: Paradise Regained or Lost?," in *New States, New Politics: Building the Post-Soviet Nations*, ed. Ian Bremmer and Ray Taras (Cambridge: Cambridge University Press, 1997), 483–5; *Armenian Reporter*, December 8, 1988, 18.

6   Simon Payaslian, *The History of Armenia: From the Origins to the Present* (New York: Palgrave Macmillan, 2007), 192; Razmik Panossian, "Between Ambivalence and Intrusion: Politics and Identity in Armenia-Diaspora Relations," *Diaspora* 7, no. 2 (1998): 166; *Armenian Mirror-Spectator*, October 8, 1988, 1, 12.

7   de Waal, *Black Garden*, 64–5; Dudwick, "Armenia," 487; Geukjian, *Ethnicity, Nationalism and Conflict*, 163; Libaridian, *Modern Armenia*, 206–7; *Armenian Mirror-Spectator*, December 14, 1991, 2.

8   *Armenian Reporter*, December 15, 1988, 1, 4, 14, 20; December 22, 1988.

9   Ann Elizabeth Robertson, "Should We Stay or Should We Go? State-Building via Political Decree" (PhD diss., George Washington University, 2003), 71–2; Libaridian, *Modern Armenia*, 208–10; Rudwick, *Armenia*, 489.

10 de Waal, *Black Garden*, 65, 113–40; Geukjian, *Ethnicity, Nationalism and Conflict*, 185–7.

11 de Waal, *Black Garden*, 63.

12 Libaridian, *Modern Armenia*, 210.

13 Dudwick, *Armenia*, 489–91; Geukjian, *Ethnicity, Nationalism, and Conflict*, 188–90.

14 Carol Migdalovitz, "Armenia-Azerbaijan Conflict," Congressional Research Service Issue Brief for Congress, updated December 26, 2001, https://apps.dtic.mil/sti/citations/ADA476402.

15 Payaslian, *History of Armenia*, 201–3; Suzanne Goldenberg, *Pride of Small Nations: The Caucasus and Post-Soviet Disorder* (London: Zed Books, 1994), 132–3; *Armenian Mirror-Spectator*, 1, 11.

16 Payaslian, *History of Armenia*, 204; interview in *Armenian International Magazine*, March 1994, 32, quoted in Razmik Panossian, "The Diaspora and the Karabagh Movement: Oppositional Politics between the Armenian Revolutionary Federation and the Armenian National Movement," in *The Making of Nagorno-Karabagh: From Secession to Republic*, ed. Levon Chorbajian (New York: Palgrave, 2001), 165.

17   *Armenian Reporter*, August 13, 1994, 11; October 5, 1995, 1; Payaslian, *History of Armenia*, 204–5; Panossian, "Between Ambivalence and Intrusion," 172; Panossian, "Diaspora and the Karabagh Movement," 168–9; *Armenian Weekly*, June 18, 1994, 2, 16; August 6/13, 1994, 2, 10; August 20, 1994, 2; December 31, 1994, 1, 10; *Armenian Mirror-Spectator*, August 27, 1994, 7.

18   Panossian, "Between Ambivalence and Intrusion," 176–8; Panossian, "Diaspora and the Karabagh Movement," 166–71; *Armenian Weekly*, February 8, 1992, 2; January 1, 1992, 2; December 17, 1994, 3; *Armenian Reporter*, February 11, 1995, 10.

19   Heather S. Gregg, "Divided They Conquer: The Success of Armenian Ethnic Lobbies in the United States," Working paper #13, Inter-University Committee on International Migration, Center for International Studies, MIT, August 2002, 18–25; *Washington Post*, August 1, 1996, A22.

20   Payaslian, *History of Armenia*, 210–15; *Armenian Weekly*, January 20, 1996, 1, 5. Kocharian lifted the ban on the ARF's political activity in Armenia and attended the opening ceremony of the Third Congress of the ARF of Armenia in July of 1998. *Armenian Weekly*, July 18, 1998, 1. The election of Karekin is discussed at length in the *Armenian Reporter*, October 14, 1995, 3, 21.

      The calming of partisan hostilities in these later years should not be overstated. Early in 1993, two editors were physically assaulted in separate incidents in Los Angeles: Shahen Haroutunian of *Yergounk* and Hovhanness Balayan of a satirical paper called *Katch Nazar*. Both strongly believed their attackers were Tashnag Armenians. The *Mirror-Spectator* took no formal position on whether they were right but did not, in its editorial on the subject, seem to consider the theory outlandish. *Armenian Mirror-Spectator*, January 16, 1993, 1; January 30, 1993, 2.

21   Benedict Anderson, *Imagined Communities: Reflections on the Origin and Spread of Nationalism*, 2nd ed. (London: Verso, 1991); Panossian, "Between Ambivalence and Intrusion," 163. Panossian also writes of homeland-diaspora relations in "Diaspora and the Karabagh Movement"; "Homeland-Diaspora Relations and Identity Differences," in *The Armenians: Past and Present in the Making of National Identity*, ed. Edmund Herzig and Marina Kurkchiyan (London: RoutledgeCurzon, 2005), 229–43; "Armenia-Diaspora Relations in the Post-Independence Period," in *Arméniens et Grecs en diaspora: Approches comparatives*, ed. Michael Bruneau, Ioannis Hassiotis, Martine Hovanessian, and Claire Mouradian (Athens: École française d'Athènes, 2007), 235–56; and *The Armenians: From Kings and Priests to Merchants and Commissars* (New York: Columbia University Press, 2016).

22   Milton Gordon, *Assimilation in American Life: The Role of Race, Religion, and National Origins* (New York: Oxford University Press, 1964), 71, 80–1; Richard Alba and Victor Nee, "Rethinking Assimilation Theory for a New Era of Immigration," *International Migration Review* 31 (Winter 1997): 863; Matthew A. Jendian, *Becoming American, Remaining Ethnic: The Case of Armenian-Americans in Central California* (New York: LFB Scholarly Publishing, 2008), 75. For further insights into the theme of American ethnicity, see (among many other works) Elliot Robert Barkan, "Race, Religion, and Nationality in American Society: A Model of Ethnicity—from Contact to Assimilation," *Journal of American Ethnic History* 14, no. 2 (Winter 1995): 38–101; Werner Sollors, ed., *The Invention of Ethnicity* (New York: Oxford University Press, 1989); Kathleen Neils Conzen, David A. Gerber, Ewa Morawska, George E. Pozzetta, and Rudolph J. Vecoli, "The Invention of Ethnicity: A View from the U.S.A.," *Journal of American Ethnic History* 12, no. 1 (Fall 1992): 3–41.

Bibliography

Primary Sources—Archived Papers:

American Philosophical Society, Philadelphia, PA:
    Franz Boaz Papers on *Cartozian v. United States*
Armenian Apostolic Church of America Eastern Diocese, New York, NY:
    Files of the Armenian Church Youth of America (ACYOA)
Armenian Democratic Liberal Party, Watertown, MA:
    Files of the Ramgavar Party, especially minutes from annual deputational meetings, 1923–55
National Association for Armenian Studies and Research, Inc. (NAASR), Belmont, MA:
    Avedis Derounian (John Roy Carlson) Papers
    Charles Vertanes Papers
United States Government, National Archives, College Park, MD:
    Justice Department Records on *Cartozian v. United States*
    State Department Records
University of Montana, Missoula, MT:
    James W. Gerard Papers

Primary Sources—Newspapers:

Armenian Guardian
Armenian Herald
Armenian Mirror
Armenian Mirror-Spectator
Armenian Reporter
Armenian Weekly
Asbarez
Azk
Azk-Bahag
Bahag
Baikar
Gotchnag
Hairenik
Hairenik Weekly
Interpreter
New Armenia
New York Times

Interviews Cited

This list is limited to those whom I have formally cited in endnotes for formal interviews. It does not even begin to include the many people whose conversations have given me insight.
Rouben Adalian, December 1, 2015
Anahid Ajemian, August 7, 2002
Martin Deranian, October 26, 2002
Noubar Dorian, October 19, 2002
Diana Keleshian, June 5, 2002
Gerard Libaridian, July 3, 2015
Fr. Krikor Maksoudian, October 21, 2002
Dennis Papazian, March 8, 2016
Harold Takooshian, February 29, 2016

Emails Cited

Gerard Libaridian, September 2, 2022
Edward D. Simsarian, January 14, 2016
William T. Walker, August 22, 2010

Books, Articles, and Dissertations

Adamic, Louis. *From Many Lands*. New York: Harper & Brothers, 1939.
Adamic, Louis. *A Nation of Nations*. New York: Harper & Brothers, 1944.
Aftandilian, Gregory. *Armenia, Vision of a Republic: The Independence Lobby in America, 1918–1927*. Charlestown, MA: Charles River Books, 1981.
Aftandilian, Gregory. "The Cold War Writings of Reuben Darbinian in The Armenian Review." *Armenian Review* 56, no. 3–4 (2019): 1–25.
Aftandilian, Gregory. "World War II as an Enhancer of Armenian-American Second Generation Identity." *Journal of the Society for Armenian Studies* 18, no. 2 (December 2009): 33–54.
Alba, Richard, and Victor Nee. "Rethinking Assimilation Theory for a New Era of Immigration." *International Migration Review* 31 (Winter 1997): 826–74.
Alexander, Ben. "Contested Memories, Divided Diaspora: Armenian Americans, the Thousand-day Republic, and the Polarized Response to an Archbishop's Murder." *Journal of American Ethnic History* 27, no. 1 (2007): 32–59.
Alexander, Benjamin F. "The American Armenians' Cold War: The Divided Response to Soviet Armenia." In *Anti-Communist Minorities in the U.S.: Political Activism of Ethnic Refugees*, edited by Ieva Zake, 67–86. New York: Palgrave-MacMillan, 2009.
Alexander, Benjamin F. "Divided Diaspora: Armenian-American Responses to the Republic." *Armenian Review* 56, no. 3–4 (2019): 25–42.
Alexander, Benjamin F. "'To Supply Armenia with Architects': The Press, the Parties, and the Second Generation in the 1930s." *Journal of the Society for Armenian Studies* 17 (2008): 189–206.

Alexander, Edward. *A Crime of Vengeance: An Armenian Struggle for Justice.* New York: Free Press, 1991.

Alexander, June Granatir. *Ethnic Pride, American Patriotism: Slovaks and Other New Immigrants in the Interwar Era.* Philadelphia: Temple University Press, 2004.

Anderson, Benedict. *Imagined Communities: Reflections on the Origin and Spread of Nationalism,* 2nd ed. London: Verso, 1991.

Arkun, Aram. "Into the Modern Age, 1800–1913." In *The Armenians: Past and Present in the Making of National Identity,* edited by Edmund Herzig and Marina Kurkchiyan, 65–88. London: RoutledgeCurzon, 2005.

Arzruni, Şahan. "Alan Hovhaness: The Wellspring of His Music." *Journal of Armenian Studies* 3 (Winter 1986–87): 157–60.

Ascher, Abraham. *Russia: A Short History.* London: Oneworld, 2017.

Atamian, Sarkis. *The Armenian Community: The Historical Development of a Social and Ideological Conflict.* New York: Philosophical Library, 1955.

Avakian, Knarik. "The Early History of Armenian Emigration to the USA: Evidence from the Archives of the Armenian Patriarchate of Constantinople." *Journal of the Society for Armenian Studies* 17 (2008): 112–13.

Avakian, Knarik. *The History of the Armenian Community of the United States of America (From the Beginning to 1924).* Yerevan, Armenia: Gitutiun, 2000.

The AYF Legacy: Portrait of a Movement in Historical Review, 1933–1993. Watertown, MA: Armenian Youth Federation, 1994.

Azizian, Anna Khederian. "Where Else but Asbury?" *Ararat* 43 (Summer 2003): 16–19.

Bakalian, Anny. *Armenian-Americans: From Being to Feeling Armenian.* New Brunswick, NJ: Transaction Publishers, 1996.

Balakian, Peter. *Black Dog of Fate.* New York: Basic Books, 2009.

Balakian, Peter. *The Burning Tigris: The Armenian Genocide and America's Response.* New York: HarperCollins Publishers Inc., 2003.

Balayan, Schnorhig (or Beatrice). "The Armenians in the United States of America." MA thesis, University of Chicago, 1927.

Bamberger, Joan. "Family and Kinship in an Armenian-American Community." *Journal of Armenian Studies* 3 (Winter 1986–87): 77–86.

Barkan, Elliott Robert. *And Still They Come: Immigrants and American Society, 1920 to the 1990s.* Wheeling, IL: Harlan Davidson, 1996.

Barkan, Elliott Robert. "Race, Religion, and Nationality in American Society: A Model of Ethnicity—from Contact to Assimilation." *Journal of American Ethnic History* 14, no. 2 (Winter 1995): 38–101.

Barrett, Edward. *Truth Is Our Weapon.* New York: Funk and Wagnalls, 1953.

Barsoumian, Hagop Levon. *The Armenian Amira Class of Istanbul.* Yerevan: American University of Armenia, 2007.

Barsoumian, Hagop Levon. "The Dual Role of the Armenian *Amira* Class within the Ottoman Government and the Armenian *Millet* (1750–1850)." In *Christians and Jews in the Ottoman Empire,* edited by Benjamin Braude and Bernard Lewis, 171–84. New York: Holmer & Meyer, 1982.

Barsoumian, Hagop Levon. "The Eastern Question and the Tanzimat Era." In *Armenian People from Ancient to Modern Times,* vol. 2, *Foreign Dominion to Statehood: The Fifteenth Century to the Twentieth Century,* edited by Richard G. Hovannisian, 2nd ed., 175–201. New York: St. Martin's Press, 2004.

Baynton, Douglas C. *Defectives in the Land: Disability and Immigration in the Age of Eugenics.* Chicago: University of Chicago Press, 2016.

Bazyler, Michael J., and Rajika L. Shah. "The Unfinished Business of the Armenian Genocide: Armenian Property Restitution in American Courts." *Southwestern Journal of International Law* 23 (2017): 223–78.

Bedoukian, Kerop. *Some of Us Survived: The Story of an Armenian Boy*. New York: Firrar Straus Giroux, 1978.

Bedrosian, Margaret. *The Magical Pine Ring: Culture and the Imagination in Armenian-American Literature*. Detroit: Wayne State University Press, 1991.

Benson, Peter L., and Dorothy Williams. *Religion on Capitol Hill: Myths and Realities*. San Francisco: Harper and Row, 1982.

Bobelian, Michael. *Children of Armenia: A Forgotten Genocide and the Century-Long Struggle for Justice*. New York: Simon and Schuster, 2009.

Bodnar, John. *The Transplanted: A History of Immigrants in Urban America*. Bloomington: Indiana University Press, 1985.

Bogigian, Hagop. *In Quest of the Soul of Civilization*. Washington, DC: self-published, 1925.

Bogosian, Eric. *Operation Nemesis: The Assassination Plot That Avenged the Armenian Genocide*. New York: Little, Brown, 2015.

Bolukbasi, Suha. *The Superpowers and the Third World: Turkish-American Relations and Cyprus*. Lanham, MD: University Press of America, 1988.

Bonsal, Stephen. *Suitors and Suppliants: The Little Nations at Versailles*. New York: Prentice-Hall, Inc., 1946.

Bournoutian, George A. *A History of the Armenian People*, 2 vols. Costa Mesa, CA: Mazda Publishers, 1993, 1994.

Boyajian, Dickran. *A Light through the Iron Curtain*. New York: Vantage Press, 1958.

Boyajian, Levon, and Haigaz Grigorian. "Psychosocial Sequelae of the Armenian Genocide." In *The Armenian Genocide in Perspective*, edited by Richard G. Hovannisian, 177–85. New Brunswick, NJ: Transaction Publishers, 1986.

Boyajian, Levon Z. *Hayots Badeevah: Reminiscences of Armenian Life in New York City*. Reading, UK: Taderon Press, 2004.

Brands, H. W. *Into the Labyrinth: The United States and the Middle East, 1945–1994*. New York: McGraw-Hill, 1994.

Braude, Benjamin, and Bernard Lewis, eds. *Christians and Jews in the Ottoman Empire: The Functioning of a Plural Society*, 2 vols. New York: Holmer & Meyer, 1982.

Brophy, Anne Miriam. "'What of Youth Today?': Social Politics, Cultural Pluralism, and the Construction of Second-Generation Ethnicity in Detroit, 1914–41." PhD diss., Cornell University, 1999.

Bryson, Thomas A. "The Armenian American *[sic]* Society: A Factor in American-Turkish Relations, 1919–1924." *Armenian Review* 29, no. 1 (Spring 1976): 53–76.

Bryson, Thomas A., III. "Woodrow Wilson, the Senate, Public Opinion and the Armenian Mandate Question, 1919–1920." PhD diss., University of Georgia, 1965.

Bulbulian, Berge. *The Fresno Armenians: History of a Diaspora Community*. Fresno: The Press at California State University, Fresno, 2000.

Burnham, Irene H. *Not by Accident: The Story of Moses H. Gulesian's Career*. Boston: Christopher Publishing House, 1938.

Burton, Orville Vernon, and Armand Derfner. *Justice Deferred: Race and the Supreme Court*. Cambridge, MA: Belknap Press of Harvard University Press, 2021.

Caprielian, Ara. "The Armenian Revolutionary Federation: The Politics of a Party in Exile." PhD diss., New York University, 1975.

Carlson, John Roy (pseudonym for Avedis Derounian). "The Armenian Displaced Persons: A First-Hand Report on Conditions in Europe." *Armenian Affairs* 1 (Winter 1949–50): 17–34.

Carlson, John Roy. *Under Cover: My Four Years in the Nazi Underworld of America.* New York: E. P. Dutton & Company, 1943.

Chalabian, Antranig. *Dro (Drastamat Kanayan): Armenia's First Defense Minister of the Modern Era.* Translated by Jack Chelabian. Los Angeles: Indo-European Publishing, 2009.

Chalabian, Antranig. *General Antranik and the Armenian Revolutionary Movement.* Self-published, 1988.

Chorbajian, Levon, ed. *The Making of Nagorno-Karabagh: From Secession to Republic.* New York: Palgrave, 2001.

Clifford, J. Garry. *The Citizen Soldiers: The Plattsburg Training Camp Movement, 1913–1920.* Lexington: University Press of Kentucky, 1972.

"Convention on the Prevention and Punishment of the Crime of Genocide" (1948). United Nations Office on Genocide Prevention and the Responsibility to Protect. https://www.un.org/en/genocideprevention/genocide.shtml.

Conzen, Kathleen Niels, David A. Gerber, Ewa Morawska, George E. Pozzetta, and Rudolph J. Vecoli. "The Invention of Ethnicity: A View from the U.S.A." *Journal of American Ethnic History* 12, no. 1 (Fall 1992): 3–41.

Cook, Ralph Elliott. "The United States and the Armenian Question, 1894–1924." PhD diss., The Fletcher School of Law and Diplomacy, Tufts University, 1957.

Cooper, John. *Raphael Lemkin and the Struggle for the Genocide Convention.* Basingstoke, UK: Palgrave Macmillan, 2008.

Cooper, John Milton. *Breaking the Heart of the World: Woodrow Wilson and the Fight for the League of Nations.* Cambridge, UK: Cambridge University Press, 2001.

Cooper, John Milton. "A Friend in Power? Woodrow Wilson and Armenia." In *America and the Armenian Genocide of 1915*, edited by Jay Winter, 103–12. Cambridge, UK: Cambridge University Press, 2003.

Corley, Felix. "The Armenian Apostolic Church." In *Eastern Christianity and the Cold War, 1945–91*, edited by Lucian N. Leustean, 189–203. London: Routledge, 2010.

Corley, Felix. "The Armenian Church under the Soviet Regime, Part 1: The Leadership of Kevork." *Religion, State & Society* 24, no. 1 (March 1996): 9–53.

Corley, Felix. "The Armenian Church under the Soviet Regime, Part 2: The Leadership of Vazgen." *Religion, State and Society* 24, no. 4 (December 1996): 289–343.

Crisis in the Armenian Church: Text of a Memorandum to the National Council of the Churches of Christ in the United States of America on the Dissident Armenian Church in America. Boston: Central Diocesan Board, Armenian National Apostolic Church of America, 1958.

Dadourian, Astrid, and Harry Keyishian, eds. "The Summers That Were." Special issue, *Ararat* 44 (Summer 2002).

Dadrian, Vahakn N. *The History of the Armenian Genocide: Ethnic Conflict from the Balkans to Anatolia to the Caucasus.* New York: Berghahn Books, 2004.

Dadrian, Vahakn N., and Taner Akçam. *Judgment at Istanbul: The Armenian Genocide Trials.* New York: Berghahn Books, 2011.

Daniel, Robert L. "The Armenian Question and American-Turkish Relations, 1914–1927." *Mississippi Valley Historical Review* 46, no. 2 (September 1959): 252–75.

Daniels, Roger. *Guarding the Golden Door: American Immigration Policy and Immigrants since 1882.* New York: Hill and Wang, 2004.

Darbinian, Reuben. "America and the Russian Future." *Armenian Review* 4, no. 2 (Summer 1951): 12–24.

Darbinian, Reuben. "The Armenian Church Break." *Armenian Review* 10, no. 4 (Winter 1957): 3–16.

Darbinian, Reuben. "In Retrospect: A Glance at the Past Thirty Years." *Armenian Review* 6, no. 3 (Autumn 1953): 49–65.

Darbinian, Reuben. "The Ramgavars before the Tribunal of Public Opinion." *Armenian Review* 8, no. 3 (Autumn/September 1955): 3–19.

Darbinian, Reuben. "Toward the Policy of an Eye for an Eye." *Armenian Review* 5, no. 1 (Spring 1952): 21–33.

Deranian, Hagop Martin. *Worcester Is America: The Story of Worcester's Armenians: The Early Years*. Worcester, MA: Bennate Publishing, 1998.

Deranian, Marderos. *The Village of Hussenig: Memories from the Heart and Hearth*. Translated by Hagop Martin Deranian with the assistance of Rev. Dr. Herald A. G. Hassessian. Boston: Baikar Press, 1981.

Derby, Kevin. "Gus Bilirakis Wants U.S. Schools to Teach about the Armenian Genocide." *Florida Daily* (online), April 25, 2022. https://www.floridadaily.com/gus-bilirakis-wants-u-s-schools-to-teach-about-the-armenian-genocide/.

Der-Martirosian, Claudia. "Armenians in the 1980, 1990, and 2000 U.S. Census." *Journal of the Society for Armenian Studies* 17 (2008): 127–41.

Der Matossian, Bedross. *The Horrors of Adana: Revolution and Violence in the Early Twentieth Century*. Stanford, CA: Stanford University Press, 2022.

Derogy, Jacques. *Resistance and Revenge: The Armenian Assassination of the Turkish Leaders Responsible for the 1915 Massacres and Deportations*. New Brunswick, NJ: Transaction Publishers, 1990.

de Waal, Thomas. *Black Garden: Armenia and Azerbaijan through Peace and War*, revised ed. New York: NYU Press, 2013.

Dobkin, Marjorie Housepian. *Smyrna 1922: The Destruction of a City*. Kent, OH: Kent State University Press, 1988.

Dobrianski, Lev. Preface to Roman Smal-Stocki, *The Captive Nations*, 7–12. New Haven, CT: College and University Press, 1960.

Doudoukjian, Gregory. "Oral History: An Intergenerational Study of the Effects of the Assassination of Archbishop Leon Tourian in 1933 on Armenian-Americans." Master of Divinity thesis, St. Vladimir's Orthodox Theological Seminary, Crestwood, NY, 1993.

Dudwick, Nora. "Armenia: Paradise Regained or Lost?" In *New States, New Politics: Building the Post-Soviet Nations*, edited by Ian Bremmer and Ray Taras, 471–504. Cambridge: Cambridge University Press, 1997.

Evans, Laurence. *United States Policy and the Partition of Turkey*. Baltimore: Johns Hopkins University Press, 1965.

Ewen, Elizabeth. *Immigrant Women in the Land of Dollars: Life and Culture on the Lower East Side, 1890–1925*. New York: Monthly Review Press, 1985.

Fass, Paula. *The Damned and the Beautiful: American Youth in the 1920s*. New York: Oxford University Press, 1977.

Flynn, John T. *The Roosevelt Myth*. New York: Devon-Adair, 1956.

Foglesong, David S. *The American Mission and the "Evil Empire": The Crusade for a Free Russia" since 1881*. New York: Cambridge University Press, 2007.

Foner, Nancy. *From Ellis Island to JFK: New York's Two Great Waves of Immigration*. New Haven, CT: Yale University Press / New York: Russell Sage Foundation, 2000.

Foreign Relations of the United States, 1952–54, National Security Affairs, vol. 1. Washington, DC: Government Printing Office, 1984.

Fried, Richard M. *The Russians Are Coming! The Russians Are Coming! Pageantry and Patriotism in Cold-War America*. New York: Oxford University Press, 1998.

Gans, Herbert J. "Symbolic Ethnicity: The Future of Ethnic Groups and Cultures in America." *Ethnic and Racial Studies* 2, no. 1 (1979): 1–20.

Gati, Charles. *Failed Illusions: Moscow, Washington, Budapest, and the 1956 Hungarian Revolt*. Washington, DC: Woodrow Wilson Center Press, 2006.

Gavakian, Armen. "Homeland, Diaspora and Nationalism: The Reimagination of Armenian-American Identity since Gorbachev." PhD diss., University of Sidney, 1997.

Gelfand, Lawrence E. *The Inquiry: American Preparations for Peace*. New Haven, CT: Yale University Press, 1963.

The Genocide Convention: Hearings before a Subcommittee of the Committee on Foreign Relations, United States Senate, Eighty-First Congress, Second Session, on Executive O, the International Convention on the Prevention and Punishment of the Crime of Genocide, January 23, 24, 25, and February 9, 1950. Washington, DC: Government Printing Office, 1950.

Gerson, Louis L. *Woodrow Wilson and the Rebirth of Poland, 1914–1920: A Study in the Influence on American Policy of Minority Groups of Foreign Origin*. New Haven, CT: Yale University Press, 1953.

Ghazarian, Vatche. *A Village Remembered: The Armenians of Habousi*. Waltham, MA: Mayreni Publishing, 1997 (a publication of the Compatriotic Union of Habousi).

Gidney, James B. *A Mandate for Armenia*. Kent, OH: Kent State University Press, 1967.

Gleason, Philip. *Speaking of Diversity: Language and Ethnicity in Twentieth-Century America*. Baltimore: Johns Hopkins University Press, 1992.

Goldenberg, Suzanne. *Pride of Small Nations: The Caucasus and Post-Soviet Disorder*. London: Zed Books, 1994.

Goldstein, Erik. *The First World War Peace Settlements, 1919–1925*. London: Pearson, 2002.

Goode, William J. *World Revolution and Family Patterns*. New York: Free Press of Glencoe, 1963.

Gordon, Milton. *Assimilation in American Life: The Role of Race, Religion, and National Origins*. New York: Oxford University Press, 1964.

Grant, Madison. *The Passing of the Great Race*. New York: Charles Scribner's Sons, 1916 (successive revisions through 1923).

Granville, Johanna. "Caught with Jam on Our Fingers: Radio Free Europe and the Hungarian Revolution of 1956." *Diplomatic History* 29, no. 5 (November 2005): 811–40.

Gregg, Heather S. "Divided They Conquer: The Success of Armenian Ethnic Lobbies in the United States." Working paper #13, Inter-University Committee on International Migration, Center for International Studies, MIT, August 2002.

Gregorian, Arthur, and Phebe Gregorian. *Armenag's Story*. Newton, MA: Lower Falls Publishing Company, 1989.

Greene, Victor R. *American Immigrant Leaders, 1800–1910: Marginality and Identity*. Baltimore: Johns Hopkins University Press, 1987.

Grew, Joseph C. *Turbulent Era: A Diplomatic Record of Forty Years*, edited by Walter Johnson. Boston: Houghton Mifflin, 1952.

Gunn, Christopher. "Secret Armies and Revolutionary Federations: The Rise and Fall of Armenian Political Violence, 1973–1993." PhD diss., Florida State University, 2014.

Gunter, Michael M. *"Pursuing the Just Cause of Their People": A Study of Contemporary Armenian Terrorism*. New York: Greenwood Press, 1986.

Gzoyan, Edita. "The Plan to Solve the Armenian Mandate Question through a Non-State Organization." *Armenian Review* 56, no. 3–4 (2019): 55–79.

Hambartsumian, Vahan. *Village World: An Historical and Cultural Study of Govdoon*. Translated by Murad A. Meneshian. Providence, RI: Govdoon Youth of America, 2001 (original printing, Paris: Daron Publishing House, 1927).

Haney-López, Ian F. *White by Law: The Legal Construction of Race*. New York: NYU Press, 1996.

Hapak, Joseph T. "Recruiting a Polish Army in the United States, 1917–1919." PhD diss., University of Kansas, 1985.

Hapak, Joseph T. "Selective Service and Polish Army Recruitment during World War I." *Journal of American Ethnic History* 10, no. 4 (Summer 1991): 38–60.

Harb, Aliza, with Florence Gilmore. *Aliza: An Armenian Survivor Torn between Two Cultures*. Belmont, MA: NAASR, 2003.

Hartunian, Abraham H. *Neither to Laugh nor to Weep*. Boston: Beacon Press, 1968.

Herzig, Edmund, and Marina Kurkchiyan, eds. *The Armenians: Past and Present in the Making of National Identity*. London: RoutledgeCurzon, 2005.

Higham, John. "The Ethnic Historical Society in Changing Times." *Journal of American Ethnic History* 13, no. 2 (Winter 1994): 30–44.

Higham, John. *Strangers in the Land: Patterns of American Nativism, 1860–1925*. New Brunswick, NJ: Rutgers University Press, 1955.

Hoogasian-Villa, Susie, and Mary Kilbourne Matossian. *Armenian Village Life before 1914*. Detroit: Wayne State University Press, 1982.

Housepian, Marjorie. *A Houseful of Love*. New York: Random House, 1957.

Hovannisian, Richard G. *Armenia on the Road to Independence, 1918*. Berkeley: University of California Press, 1967.

Hovannisian, Richard G., ed. *The Armenian Genocide in Perspective*. New Brunswick, NJ: Transaction Books, 1986.

Hovannisian, Richard G., ed. *The Armenian People from Ancient to Modern Times*, 2 vols. Houndmills, Basingstoke, Hampshire: Macmillan, 1997.

Hovannisian, Richard G. "The Armenian Question in the Ottoman Empire, 1876–1914." In *Armenian People from Ancient to Modern Times*, vol. 2, *Foreign Dominion to Statehood: The Fifteenth Century to the Twentieth Century*, edited by Richard G. Hovannisian, 2nd ed., 203–38. New York: St. Martin's Press, 2004.

Hovannisian, Richard G. *The Republic of Armenia*, 4 vols. Berkeley, CA: University of California Press, 1971–96.

Howard, Harry N. *The Partition of Turkey: A Diplomatic History*. 1931; repr. New York: H. Fertig, 1966.

Hutchinson, E. P. *Immigrants and Their Children, 1850–1950*. New York: John Wiley and Sons, 1956.

Hyland, Francis P. *Armenian Terrorism: The Past, the Present, the Prospects*. Boulder, CO: Westview Press, 1991.

Israel, Fred L. *Major Peace Treaties of Modern History, 1648–1967*. New York: Chelsea House, 1967.

Jacobs, Steven Leonard. "'The Journey of Death': Lemkin and the Armenian Genocide." *Journal of the Society for Armenian Studies* 17 (2008): 7–18.

Jacobson, Matthew Frye. *Special Sorrows: The Diasporic Imagination of Irish, Polish, and Jewish Immigrants in the United States*. New York: Cambridge University Press, 1995.

Jacobson, Matthew Frye. *Whiteness of a Different Color: European Immigrants and the Alchemy of Race*. Cambridge, MA: Harvard University Press, 1998.

Jafarian, Boghos. *Farewell Kharpert: The Autobiography of Boghos Jafarian*. Madison, WI: Claire Mangasarian, 1989.

Jafferian, Serpoohi Christine. *Winds of Destiny: An Immigrant Girl's Odyssey*. Belmont: Armenian Heritage Press, 1993.

Jalelian, Diana Alexanian. "To O'Hara House with Love." *Ararat* 43 (Summer 2003): 11–15.

Jaroszyńska–Kirchmann, Anna D. *The Polish Hearst: Ameryka-Echo and the Public Role of the Immigrant Press*. Champaign: University of Illinois Press, 2015.

Jendian, Matthew Ari. *Becoming American, Remaining Ethnic: The Case of Armenian-Americans in Central California*. New York: LFB Scholarly Publishing, 2008.

Jernazian, Ephraim K. *Judgment unto Truth: Witnessing the Armenian Genocide*. New Brunswick, NJ: Transaction Publishers, 1990.

Johnson, Hewlett. *The Soviet Power*. New York: Modern Age Books, 1940.

Kaligian, Dikran Mesrob. *Armenian Organization and Ideology under Ottoman Rule*. New Brunswick, NJ: Transaction Publishers, 2010.

Kalajian, Hannah, as told to Bernadine Sullivan. *Hannah's Story: Escape from Genocide in Turkey to Success in America*. Belmont, MA: NAASR, 1990.

Kallen, Horace. *Culture and Democracy in the United States*. New York: Boni and Liveright, 1924.

Kallen, Horace. "Democracy versus the Melting Pot." *The Nation*, February 18, 1915, 190–4; February 25, 1915, 217–20.

Kaprielian-Churchill, Isabel. "Armenian Refugee Women: The Picture Brides, 1920–1930." *Journal of American Ethnic History* 12 (Spring 1993): 3–29.

Kaprielian-Churchill, Isabel. "Changing Patterns of Armenian Neighborhoods." In *Armenians of New England*, edited by Marc A. Mamigonian, 17–23. Belmont, MA: National Association for Armenian Studies and Research, 2004.

Kaprielian-Churchill, Isabel. *Like Our Mountains: A History of Armenians in Canada*. Montreal: McGill-Queen's University Press, 2005.

Karentz, Varoujan. *Mitchnapert (The Citadel): A History of Armenians in Rhode Island*. Lincoln, NE: iUniverse, 2004.

Kennedy, David. *Over Here: The First World War and American Society*. New York: Oxford University Press, 1980.

Kerr, Stanley E. *The Lions of Marash: Personal Experiences with American Near East Relief, 1919–1922*. Albany, NY: SUNY Press, 1973.

Kévorkian, Raymond. *The Armenian Genocide: A Comprehensive History*. London: I.B. Tauris, 2011.

Kévorkian, Raymond H., and Vahé Tachjian, eds. *The Armenian General Benevolent Union—One Hundred Years of History*. New York: AGBU, 2006.

Kherdian, David. *Finding Home*. New York: Greenwillow Books, 1981.

Kherdian, David. *The Road from Home: The Story of an Armenian Girl*. New York: Greenwillow Books, 1979.

King, Desmond. *Making Americans: Immigration, Race, and the Origins of the Diverse Democracy*. Cambridge, MA: Harvard University Press, 2000.

Kivisto, Peter. "What Is the Canonical Theory of Assimilation? Robert E. Park and His Predecessors." *Journal of the History of the Behavioral Sciences* 40 (Spring 2004): 149–63.

Kivisto, Peter, and Dag Blanck, eds. *American Immigrants and Their Generations: Studies and Commentaries on the Hansen Thesis after Fifty Years*. Urbana: University of Illinois Press, 1990.

Kooshian, George Byron, Jr. "The Armenian Immigrant Community of California: 1880–1935." PhD diss., University of California, Los Angeles, 2002.

Kouymjian, Dickran. "William Saroyan and the Armenian Ethnic Experience in America." *Journal of Armenian Studies* 3 (Winter 1986–87): 161–74.

Kouymjian, Dickran Karnick. "The Recent Crisis in the Armenian Church." MA thesis, American University of Beirut, 1961.

Kovrig, Bennett. *Of Walls and Bridges: The United States and Eastern Europe*. New York: NYU Press, 1991.

Kraut, Alan M. *The Huddled Masses: The Immigrant in American* Society, *1880–1921*, 2nd ed. Wheeling, IL: Harlan Davidson, 2001.

Krikorian, Robert O. "Kars-Ardahan and Soviet Armenian Irredentism, 1945–46." In *Armenian Kars and Ardahan*, edited by Richard G. Hovannisian, 393–409. Costa Mesa, CA: Mazda, 2011.

Kulhanjian, Gary A. "From Ararat to America: The Armenian Settlements of New Jersey." *Journal of Armenian Studies* 3 (Winter 1986–87): 35–46.

Kulhanjian, Gary A. *The Historical and Sociological Aspects of Armenian Immigration to the United States, 1890 to 1930*. San Francisco: R and E Research Associates, 1975.

Kuniholm, Bruce R. *The Origins of the Cold War in the Near East: Great Power Conflict in Iran, Turkey, and Greece*. Princeton, NJ: Princeton University Press, 1980.

Kurkchiyan, Marina. "The Karabagh Conflict: From Soviet Past to Post-Soviet Uncertainty." In *The Armenians: Past and Present in the Making of National Identity*, edited by Edmund Herzig and Marina Kurkchiyan, 147–65. London: RoutledgeCurzon, 2005.

LaDuke, Winona. *Recovering the Sacred: The Power of Naming and Claiming*. Cambridge, MA: South End Press, 2005.

Laipson, Ellen B. "Cyprus: A Quarter Century of U.S. Policy." In *Cyprus in Transition, 1960–1985*, edited by John T. A. Koumoulides, 68–76. London: Trigraph, 1986.

LaPiere, Richard Tracy. "The Armenian Colony in Fresno County, California: A Study in Social Psychology." PhD diss., Stanford University, 1930.

Laycock, Jo. "Armenian Homelands and Homecomings, 1945–49: The Repatriation of Diaspora Armenians to the Soviet Union." *Cultural and Social History* 9, no. 1 (2012): 103–23.

Lees, Lorraine M. *Keeping Tito Afloat: The United States, Yugoslavia, and the Cold War*. University Park: Pennsylvania State University Press, 1998.

Lewis, Bernard. *The Emergence of Modern Turkey*, 3rd ed. New York: Oxford University Press, 2002.

L'Homedieu, Jonathan H. "Baltic Exiles and the U.S. Congress: Investigations and Legacies of the House Select Committee, 1953–1955." *Journal of American Ethnic History* 31, no. 2 (Winter 2012): 41–67.

Libaridian, Gerard J. *Modern Armenia: People, Nation, State*. New Brunswick, NJ: Transaction Publishers, 2004.

Light, Ivan, and Steven J. Gold. *Ethnic Economies*. San Diego: Academic Press, 2000.

Lucas, Scott. *Freedom's War: The American Crusade against the Soviet Union*. New York: NYU Press, 1999.

Lupinin, Nickolas. "The Russian Orthodox Church." In *Eastern Christianity and the Cold War, 1945–91*, edited by Lucian N. Leustean, 19–39. London: Routledge, 2010.

MacCurdy, Marian Mesrobian. *Sacred Justice: The Voices and Legacy of the Armenian Operation Nemesis*. New Brunswick, NJ: Transaction Publishers, 2015.

MacMillan, Margaret. *Paris 1919: Six Months That Changed the World*. New York: Random House, 2003.

Maintenance of Peace in Armenia: Hearings before a Subcommittee of the Committee on Foreign Relations, United States Senate, Sixty-Sixth Congress, First Session, on S.J.R. 106: A Joint Resolution for the Maintenance of Peace in Armenia. Washington, DC: Government Printing Office, 1919.

Malcom, M. Vartan. *Armenians in America*. Boston: Pilgrim Press, 1919.

Malkasian, Mark. "The Disintegration of the Armenian Cause in the United States, 1918–1927." *International Journal of Middle East Studies* 16, no. 3 (August 1984): 349–65.

Mamigonian, Marc A. "'Armenia Will Call upon Us in Vain': U.S. Relations with the First Republic of Armenia." *Armenian Review* 56, no. 3–4 (2019): 81–97.

Mamigonian, Marc A., ed. *The Armenians of New England*. Belmont, MA: Armenian Heritage Press/NAASR, 2004.

Mandalian, James G. "The 151 Repatriates from America." *Armenian Review* 4, no. 1 (Spring 1951): 89–100.

Mandalian, James G. "Dro: Drastamat Kanayan (1884–1956)." *Armenian Review* 10 (Summer 1957): 3–14.

Marashlian, Levon. "The Armenian Question from Sèvres to Lausanne: Economics and Morality in American and British Policies, 1920–1923." PhD diss., University of California, Los Angeles, 1992.

Mardikian, George M. *The Song of America*. New York: McGraw-Hill, 1956.

Marrus, Michael R. *The Unwanted: European Refugees from the First World War through the Cold War*. Philadelphia, PA: Temple University Press, 2002.

Matiossian, Vartan. *The Politics of Naming the Armenian Genocide: Language, History and "Medz Yeghern."* London: I.B. Tauris, 2022.

Matossian, Mary Kilbourne. *The Impact of Soviet Policies in Armenia*. Leiden, Netherlands: E. J. Brill, 1962.

Matossian, Nouritza. *Black Angel: The Life of Arshile Gorky*. Woodstock, NY: Overlook Press, 2000.

Meghreblian, Sonia. *An Armenian Odyssey*. London: Gomidas Institute, 2012.

Melkonian, Markar, with Seta Melkonian. *My Brother's Road: An American's Fateful Journey to Armenia*. London: I.B. Tauris, 2005.

Melkonian, Monte. *A Self-Criticism*. Translated with a preface by Seta Melkonian; edited by Gregory Topalian. London: Gomidas Institute, 2010.

Mesrobian, Arpena S. *"Like One Family": The Armenians of Syracuse*. Ann Arbor, MI: Gomidas Institute, 2000.

Merguerian, Arshag. "A Century of Church Buildings as Expressions of the Armenian Diaspora." In *The Armenians of New England*, edited by Marc A. Mamigonian, 159–71. Belmont, MA: Armenian Heritage Press/NAASR, 2004.

Mezoian, Anthony P. *The Armenian People of Portland, Maine*. Durham, NH: National Materials Development Center, Department of Media Services, University of New Hampshire, 1985.

Migdalovitz, Carol. "Armenia-Azerbaijan Conflict." Congressional Research Service Issue Brief for Congress, updated December 26, 2001. https://apps.dtic.mil/sti/citations/ADA476402.

Migliorino, Nicola. *(Re)constructing Armenia in Lebanon and Syria: Ethno-cultural Diversity and the State in the Aftermath of a Refugee Crisis*. New York: Berghahn Books, 2008.

Minasian, Edward. "The Armenian Immigrant Tide: From the Great War to the Great Depression." In *Recent Studies in Modern Armenian History*, edited by National Association for Armenian Studies and Research (NAASR), 105–17. Cambridge, MA: Armenian Heritage Press, 1972.

Minasian, Edward. "The Forty Years of Musa Dagh: The Film That Was Denied." *Journal of Armenian Studies* 3 (Winter 1986–87): 121–31.

Minasian, Edward. *Musa Dagh: A Chronicle of the Armenian Genocide Factor in the Subsequent Suppression, by the Intervention of the United States Government, of the*

Movie Based on Franz Werfel's "The Forty Days of Musa Dagh." Nashville: Cold Tree Press, 2007.

Minasian, Edward. *They Came from Ararat: The Exodus of the Armenian People to the United States.* Lafayette, CA: Big Hat Press, 2018.

Minassian, Gaïdz. *Guerre et terrorisme arméniens.* Paris: Presses Universitaires de France, 2002.

Minassian, John. *Many Hills Yet to Climb: Memoirs of an Armenian Deportee.* Santa Barbara, CA: Jim Cook, 1986.

Minassian, Oshagan. *A History of the Armenian Holy Apostolic Orthodox Church in the United States (1888–1944).* Monterey, CA: Mayreni, 2010.

Mintz, Steven, and Susan Kellogg. *Domestic Revolutions: A Social History of American Family Life.* New York: The Free Press, 1988.

Mirak, Robert. "Armenians." *Harvard Encyclopedia of American Ethnic Groups.* Cambridge, MA: Harvard University Press, 1980, 136–49.

Mirak, Robert. *Genocide Survivors, Community Builders: The Family of John and Artemis Mirak.* Arlington, MA: Armenian Cultural Foundation, 2014.

Mirak, Robert. *Torn between Two Lands: Armenians in America, 1890 to World War I.* Cambridge, MA: Harvard University Press, 1983.

Mohl, Raymond A. "The International Institute Movement and Ethnic Pluralism." *Social Science* 56 (Winter 1981): 14–21.

Mooradian, Tom. *The Repatriate: Love, Basketball, and the KGB.* Seattle: Moreradiant Publishing, 2008.

Morawska, Ewa. "In Defense of the Assimilation Model." *Journal of American Ethnic History* 13 (Winter 1994): 76–87.

Morgenthau, Henry. *Ambassador Morgenthau's Story.* 1918; repr., Detroit: Wayne State University Press, 2003.

Moya, Jose C. "Immigrants and Associations: A Global and Historical Perspective." *Journal of Ethnic and Migration Studies* 31, no. 5 (2005): 833–64.

Mugrditchian, Hovhannes. *To Armenians with Love: The Memoirs of a Patriot.* Hobe Sound, FL: Paul Mart, 1996.

Mukhitarian, Onnig. *The Defense of Van: An Account of the Glorious Struggle of Van-Vasbouragan* (first published in Armenian in 1930, translated by Samuels S. Tarpinian in 1967). Michigan: General Society of Vasbouragah, 1980.

Naimark, Norman M. *Stalin's Genocides.* Princeton, NJ: Princeton University Press, 2010.

Nakasian, Samuel. *America's Adopted Son: The Remarkable Story of an Orphaned Immigrant Boy.* Charlottesville, VA: Bookwrights Press, 1997.

Nalbandian, Louise. *The Armenian Revolutionary Movement: The Development of Armenian Political Parties through the Nineteenth Century.* Berkeley: University of California Press, 1967.

Nalbantian, Tsolin. "Fashioning Armenians in Lebanon, 1946–1958." PhD diss., Columbia University, 2011.

Nassibian, Akaby. *Britain and the Armenian Question, 1915–1923.* New York: St. Martin's Press, 1984.

National Association for Armenian Studies and Research, Inc. (NAASR). *Recent Studies in Modern Armenian History.* Cambridge, MA: Armenian Heritage Press, 1972.

Nelson, Harold. "The Armenian Family: Changing Patterns of Family Life in a California Community." PhD diss., University of California, Berkeley, 1953.

Nersoyan, Tiran. *A Christian Approach to Communism: Ideological Similarities between Dialectical Materialism and Christian Philosophy.* London: Frederick Muller, 1942.

Norehad, Bedros. *The Armenian Church and Its "Defenders."* New York: Gotchnag Press, 1958.

Nubar Pasha, Boghos. *Boghos Nubar's Papers and the Armenian Question, 1915–1918.* Edited/translated by Vatche Ghazarian. Waltham, MA: Mayreni Publishing, 1996.

N. W. Ayer & Son's Directory, Newspapers and Periodicals, 1949. Philadelphia: N. W. Ayer & Son, 1949.

O'Grady, Ingrid Poschmann. "Ararat, Etchmiadzin, and Haig (Nation, Church, and Kin): A Study of the Symbol System of American Armenians." PhD diss., Catholic University, 1979.

Osgood, Kenneth. *Total Cold War: Eisenhower's Secret Propaganda Battle at Home and Abroad.* Lawrence: University Press of Kansas, 2002.

Øverland, Orm. *Immigrant Minds, American Identities: Making the United States Home, 1870–1930.* Urbana: University of Illinois Press, 2000.

Panossian, Rasmik. "Armenia-Diaspora Relations in the Post-Independence Period." In *Arméniens et Grecs en diaspora: Approches comparatives*, edited by Michael Bruneau, Ioannis Hassiotis, Martine Hovanessian, and Claire Mouradian, 235–56. Athens: École française d'Athènes, 2007.

Panossian, Rasmik. *The Armenians: From Kings and Priests to Merchants and Commissars.* New York: Columbia University Press, 2016.

Panossian, Rasmik. "Between Ambivalence and Intrusion: Politics and Identity in Armenia-Diaspora Relations." *Diaspora* 7, no. 2 (1998): 149–96.

Panossian, Rasmik. "The Diaspora and the Karabagh Movement: Oppositional Politics between the Armenian Revolutionary Federation and the Armenian National Movement." In *The Making of Nagorno-Karabagh: From Secession to Republic*, edited by Levon Chorbajian, 155–77. New York: Palgrave, 2001.

Panossian, Rasmik. "Homeland-Diaspora Relations and Identity Differences." In *The Armenians: Past and Present in the Making of National Identity*, edited by Edmund Herzig and Marina Kurkchiyan, 229–43. London: RoutledgeCurzon, 2005.

Papazian, K. S. *Patriotism Perverted.* Boston: Baikar Press, 1934.

Papazian, Souren A. *Odyssey of a Survivor.* Self-published, 2002.

Papers Relating to the Foreign Relations of the United States, 1917, Supplement 2, the World War. Washington, DC: Government Printing Office, 1932.

Papers Relating to the Foreign Relations of the United States, The Paris Peace Conference, 1919. Washington, DC: Government Printing Office, 1943.

Partizian, A. *Hay Ekeghets'voy tagnapě ev anor pataskhanatunerě.* Boston: Hairenik Press, 1936.

Paterson, Thomas G. *On Every Front: The Making and Unmaking of the Cold War.* New York: W. W. Norton, 1992.

Payaslian, Simon. *The History of Armenia: From the Origins to the Present.* New York: Palgrave Macmillan, 2007.

Payaslian, Simon. *United States Policy toward the Armenian Question and the Armenian Genocide.* New York: Palgrave Macmillan, 2005.

Pearson, Raymond. *The Rise and Fall of the Soviet Empire.* New York: St. Martin's Press, 1998.

Peiss, Kathy. *Hope in a Jar: The Making of America's Beauty Culture.* New York: Metropolitan Books, 1998.

Phillips, Jenny K. *Symbol, Myth, and Rhetoric: The Politics of Culture in an Armenian-American Community.* New York: AMS Press, 1989.

Phillips, Terry. *Murder at the Altar.* Bakersfield, CA: Hye Books, 2008.

Pilibosian, Helene. *My Literary Profile: A Memoir*. Watertown, MA: Ohan Press, 2010.

Pilibosian, Khachadoor, with Helene Pilibosian. *They Called Me Mustafa: Memoir of an Immigrant*. Watertown, MA: Ohan Press, 1992.

Pohl, J. Otto. *Ethnic Cleansing in the USSR, 1937–1949*. Westport, CT: Greenwood Press, 1999.

Portes, Alejandro. *Immigrant America: A Portrait*. Berkeley: University of California Press, 1996.

Ranelagh, John. *The Agency: The Rise and Decline of the CIA*. New York: Simon and Schuster, 1986.

Redgate, A. E. *The Armenians*. Oxford: Blackwell, 1997.

Reimers, David M. *Still the Golden Door: The Third World Comes to America*. New York: Columbia University Press, 1985.

Robertson, Ann Elizabeth. "Should We Stay or Should We Go? State-Building via Political Decree." PhD diss., George Washington University, 2003.

Rosner, Arnold. "An Analytical Survey of the Music of Alan Hovhaness." PhD diss., State University of New York at Buffalo, 1972.

Roster of the First Training Regiment (Plattsburg), August 10th to September 6th, September 8th to October 6th, 1915. New York: Committee on Regimental Affairs, 1915.

Ruskoski, David T. "The Polish Army in France: Immigrants in America, World War I Volunteers in France, Defenders of the Recreated State in Poland." PhD diss., Georgia State University, 2006.

Sahakyan, Vahe. "Between Host Countries and Homeland: Institutions, Politics and Identities in the Post-Genocide Armenian Diaspora (1920s to 1980s)." PhD diss., University of Michigan, 2015.

Sanjian, Ara. "The Armenian Church and Community of Jerusalem." In *The Christian Communities of Jerusalem and the Holy Land: Studies in History, Religion and Politics*, edited by Anthony O'Mahoney, 71–84. Cardiff: University of Wales Press, 2003.

Sanjian, Ara. "The British Foreign Office, the Church of England and the Crisis at the Armenian Church in Antelias, 1956–1963." Paper presented at Armenian Studies at a Threshold, Society for Armenian Studies 35th Anniversary Conference, University of California, Los Angeles, March 26–28, 2009.

Sanjian, Ara. "Limits of Conflict and Consensus among Lebanese-Armenian Political Factions in the Early 21st Century." Paper presented at International Conference on the Armenian Diaspora, Boston University, February 13–14, 2010.

Sapsezian, Aharon. *Armenian Christianity*. Paramus, NJ: Armenian Missionary Association of America, 1996.

Sarkissian, Hagop. *From Kessab to Watertown: A Modern Saga*. Watertown, MA: Ohan Press, 1996.

Saroyan, William. *Here Comes, There Goes, You Know Who*. New York: Simon and Schuster, 1961.

Savage, Barbara Dianne. *Broadcasting Freedom: Radio, War, and the Politics of Race, 1938–1948*. Chapel Hill: University of North Carolina Press, 1999.

Schahgaldian, Nikola Bagrad. "The Political Integration of an Immigrant Community into a Composite Society: The Armenians in Lebanon, 1920–1974." PhD diss., Columbia University, 1979.

Selig, Diane. *Americans All: The Cultural Gifts Movement*. Cambridge, MA: Harvard University Press, 2008.

Service, Robert. *A History of Modern Russia from Nicholas II to Vladimir Putin*, 3rd ed. Cambridge, MA: Harvard University Press, 2009.

Shemmassian, Vahram L. *The Armenians of Musa Dagh: From Obscurity to Genocide Resistance and Fame, 1840–1915*. Fresno: The Press, California State University, Fresno, 2020.

Shemmassian, Vahram L. "The Experience of Musa Dagh Armenian Immigrants in the United States during the 1910s–1940s." *Haigazian Armenological Review* 31 (2011): 195–26.

Shemmassian, Vahram L. *The Musa Dagh Armenians: A Socioeconomic and Cultural History, 1919–1939*. Beirut: Haigazian University Press, 2015.

Shipley, Alice Muggerditchian. *We Walked, Then Ran*. Self-published, 1983.

Soghoian, Florence. *Portrait of a Survivor*. Hanover, MA: Christopher Publishing House, 1997.

Sollors, Werner, ed. *The Invention of Ethnicity*. New York: Oxford University Press, 1989.

Somakian, Manoug. *Empires in Conflict: Armenia and the Great Powers*. London: Tauris Academic Studies, 1995.

Stenehjem, Michele Flynn. *An American First: John T. Flynn and the America First Committee*. New Rochelle, NY: Arlington House, 1976.

Suny, Ronald Grigor. *Armenia in the Twentieth Century*. Chico, CA: Scholars Press, 1983.

Suny, Ronald Grigor. *Looking toward Ararat: Armenia in Modern History*. Bloomington: Indiana University Press, 1993.

Surmelian, Leon. *I Ask You, Ladies and Gentlemen*. New York: E. P. Dutton, 1945.

Tachjian, Vahé. "Reconstructing Armenian Village Life: Manoog Dzeron and Alevor, Unique Authors of the 'Houshamadyan' Genre." In *Ottoman Armenians: Life, Culture, Society*, edited by Vahé Tachjian, 1: 203–33. Berlin, Houshamadyan, 2015.

Taft, Elise Hagopian. *Rebirth*. Plaindome, NY: New Age Publishers, 1981.

Takooshian, Harold. "Armenian Immigration to the United States from the Middle East." *Journal of Armenian Studies* 3 (Winter 1986–87): 133–56.

Tashjian, James H. *The Armenian American in World War II*. Watertown, MA: Hairenik Associates, 1952.

Tashjian, James H. *Armenians of the United States and Canada: A Brief Study*. Boston: Armenian Youth Federation, 1947.

Tashjian, James H. "Life and Papers of Vahan Cardashian." *Armenian Review* 10, no. 1 (Spring 1957): 3–15.

Ternon, Yves. *The Armenian Cause*. Translated by Anahid Apelian Mangouni. Delmar, NY: Caravan Books, 1985.

Thomassian, Levon. *Summer of '42: A Study of German-Armenian Relations during the Second World War*. Atglen, PA: Schiffer Military History, 2012.

Topalian, Naomi Getsoyan. *Breaking the Rock of Tradition: An Autobiography*. Watertown, MA: Baikar, 2000.

Topalian, Naomi Getsoyan. *Dust to Destiny*. Watertown, MA: Baikar, 1986.

Treudley, Mary Bosworth. "An Ethnic Group's View of the American Middle Class." *American Sociological Review* 11, no. 6 (February 1949): 715–24.

Vertanes, Charles A. *Armenia Reborn*. New York: Armenian National Council of America, 1947.

Vertanes, Charles A. "The Case of the Cholakian Family: A New Phase in the History of the Struggle for Religious Freedom in America." *Armenian Affairs* 1 (Winter 1949–50): 35–51.

Vertanes, Charles A. "The Cholakian Case to Date." *Armenian Affairs* 1 (Summer–Fall 1950): 315–22.

Warner, W. Lloyd, and Leo Srole. *The Social Systems of American Ethnic Groups.* New Haven, CT: Yale University Press, 1945.

Weiss, Richard. "Ethnicity and Reform: Minorities and the Ambience of the Depression Years." *Journal of American History* 66, no. 3 (1979): 566–85.

Werfel, Franz. *The Forty Days of Musa Dagh.* New York: Viking Press, 1934.

Wilson, Woodrow. *Boundary between Turkey and Armenia: As Determined by Woodrow Wilson, President of the United States of America.* Washington, DC: Department of State, 1920.

Wilson, Woodrow. *Papers of Woodrow Wilson* (PWW). 69 vols. Edited by Arthur S. Link. Princeton, NJ: Woodrow Wilson Foundation, Princeton University, 1966–94.

Winter, Jay, ed. *America and the Armenian Genocide of 1915.* Cambridge, UK: Cambridge University Press, 2003.

Yeghiayan, Vartkes. *Vahan Cardashian: Advocate Extraordinaire for the Armenian Cause.* Glendale, CA: Center for Armenian Remembrance, 2008.

Yousefian, Sevan N. "Picnics for Patriots: The Transnational Activism of an Armenian Hometown Association." *Journal of American Ethnic History* 34, no. 1 (2014): 31–52.

Yousefian, Sevan N. "The Postwar Repatriation Movement of Armenians to Soviet Armenia, 1945–1948." PhD diss., University of California, Los Angeles, 2011.

Zadoian, Hratch. *Our Brother's Keepers: The American National Committee to Aid Homeless Armenians (ANCHA).* New York: SIS Publications, 2012.

Zakian, Christopher Hagop, ed. *The Torch Was Passed: The Centennial History of the Armenian Church of America.* New York: St. Vartan Press, 1998.

Zieger, Robert H. *America's Great War: World War I and the American Experience.* Lanham, MD: Rowan and Littlefield, 2000.

Index

Printed in the USA
CPSIA information can be obtained
at www.ICGtesting.com
LVHW021645161123
764105LV00005B/237